LONDON, NEW YORK, MUNICH, MELBOURNE, DELHI

Managing editor Anna Kruger
Managing art editor Alison Donovan
Production editor Jonathan Ward
Production controller Wendy Penn
US Editor Christine Heilman
Jacket concept Sophia Tampakopoulos, Bryn Walls

Editorial consultant Pauline Pears

Produced for Dorling Kindersley by

cobaltid

The Stables, Wood Farm, Deopham Road,
Attleborough, Norfolk NR17 1AJ
www.cobaltid.co.uk

ART EDITORS Paul Reid, Alison Gardner
EDITOR Louise Abbott

First American Edition, 2008

Published in the United States by
DK Publishing
375 Hudson Street
New York, New York 10014

08 09 10 11   10 9 8 7 6 5 4 3 2

GD113—6/08

Published in Great Britain
by Dorling Kindersley Limited.

A CIP catalog record for this book is available from the
Library of Congress

ISBN 978-0-7566-3677-7

DK books are available at special discounts when purchased
in bulk for sales promotions, premiums, fund-raising, or
educational use. For details, contact:
DK Publishing Special Markets, 375 Hudson Street, New York,
New York 10014 or SpecialSales@dk.com.

Printed and bound by Mohn, Germany

Mixed Sources
Product group from well-managed
forests and other controlled sources
www.fsc.org Cert no. SA-COC-1592
© 1996 Forest Stewardship Council

Discover more at
www.dk.com

Grow Organic

CONTENTS

1

10 Introduction
12 The organic way: an introduction
18 So what is organic gardening?
22 "Going organic"

2

24 The Soil
26 Getting to know your soil
32 Managing soil organically
34 Bulky organic soil improvers
36 Making garden compost 44 Making
leaf mold 46 Worm composting
50 Green manures 52 Animal manures
54 Organic fertilizers

3

56 Water and Watering
58 How to use less water
60 Using water well
62 Which water to use?

4

68 Weeds and Weeding
70 Know your weeds
72 Using mulches to control weeds
76 Weeding

5

82 Plant Health
84 A natural balance
86 Growing problems 88 Plant diseases
90 Plant pests 92 Keeping the garden
healthy 96 The gardener's friends
100 Organic pest control

6

104 Gardening for Wildlife
106 Safe havens 108 Homes for wildlife
114 Food for all 118 Water for wildlife
124 Meadows and wild flowers

7

126 Garden Planning
128 Planning power 130 Landscaping
and materials 132 Lumber 134 Hard
surfaces 138 Walls, fences, and screens
142 Hedges 146 Lawns and lawn care

8

152 Woody Plants
154 The importance of trees
158 Pollarding and coppicing
162 Shrubs 166 Climbers 168 Roses
170 Caring for woody plants

9 · 174 **Herbaceous Plants**
176 What is an herbaceous plant?
178 Planting styles **184** Herbaceous plants in containers **190** Caring for herbaceous plants **196** Raising your own plants

10 · 204 **Growing Vegetables**
206 Why grow organic vegetables?
210 Where to grow vegetables
212 Vegetable beds **216** "No-dig" vegetable growing **218** Edible landscaping **222** Vegetables in containers **224** Crops under cover
228 Planning the produce year
230 Crop rotation **234** The cabbage family **238** The onion family
240 The cucumber family
242 The pea and bean family
244 The beet family **246** The lettuce family **248** The potato family
252 The carrot family **254** Sowing vegetables **260** Planting vegetables

264 Caring for vegetables
268 Harvesting and storing

11 · 272 **Growing Herbs**
274 Why grow herbs?
276 Where to grow herbs
282 Caring for herb plants
284 Harvesting herbs for drying

12 · 286 **Growing Fruit**
288 Why grow fruit?
294 Apples **300** Pears
302 Plums **304** Cherries
306 Peaches and nectarines
308 Strawberries **310** Raspberries
312 Blackberries and hybrid berries
314 Black currants **316** Red and white currants **318** Gooseberries
319 Blueberries

320 **A–Z of Plant Problems**
342 Index
352 Acknowledgments

Foreword

Garden Organic is a UK-based nonprofit organization that has been at the forefront of organic horticulture for 50 years and is dedicated to researching and promoting organic gardening, farming, and food. Garden Organic actively campaigns on issues vital to both people and the environment, including health, sustainability, and climate change.

Garden Organic is a membership organization, and everyone is welcome to join. Members can access basic and expert advice for all levels of gardeners through its quarterly magazine, members-only website, and information sheets, as well as Garden Organic's dedicated team of advisors, who answer more than 5,000 organic gardening queries every year.

Garden Organic runs major research and international development programs that help growers around the world adopt organic methods. Its free educational program helps students learn about food and organic growing, while adults trained by Garden Organic spread the home composting message through the organization's sustainable waste program.

The organization also manages demonstration gardens showing all aspects of organic growing, including Garden Organic's walled kitchen garden at Audley End, Essex, England, and Garden Organic Ryton, the nonprofit's headquarters. Audley End is a glorious Jacobean stately home owned by English Heritage. Garden Organic painstakingly restored its walled kitchen garden from an overgrown, semiderelict state in 1999. Garden Organic Ryton has over 30 individual gardens in ten acres of beautifully landscaped grounds.

It boasts the world's first public biodynamic garden, an award-winning organic shop, and the Vegetable Kingdom. The site is also home to the organization's Heritage Seed Library, which protects over 800 varieties of rare vegetable seeds from the threat of extinction.

Garden Organic's "Organic Gardening Guidelines" have been used as the reference source as to what is, and is not, regarded as organic for all the gardening advice in this book. Based on recognized standards for commercial organic growers, these gardening guidelines cover almost every aspect of gardens and gardening.

For further information on Garden Organic, see www.gardenorganic.org.uk

1. Introduction

Put simply, organic gardening is an environmentally friendly, people-friendly style of gardening. Its methods can be used by everyone, to create and maintain almost any shape, size, and style of garden, in any location, from an urban backyard to a rural idyll. Organic gardening gives you the chance to create the garden you want, knowing that you are also doing your part to protect the wider environment.

Digging in Organic methods allow us to return to the roots of cultivation: respect for the land we live on and what it can provide for us.

The organic way: an introduction

Organic methods allow you to create any garden you want. In times of growing concern about environmental damage and climate change, they provide practical and effective solutions for managing any planted space.

From food to flowers

The organic movement really started in the middle of the 20th century, when forward-thinking, visionary individuals such as Lawrence D. Hills (founder of the UK-based Garden Organic organization) began to question the direction that farming and food production, and in their wake, gardening, were taking. Their concern was, in particular, for healthy food production, and it is in the area of food production that organic growing is most advanced. But organic methods are not just for the fruit and vegetable patch. They can be applied to all areas of the yard, from lawns to shrubs to windowsills.

The future is organic

The last decade has seen a phenomenal rise in interest in all things organic. The organic movement—for a long time an energetic, committed, active, but relatively small group of enthusiasts—has really come of age. Organic food is widely available both in supermarkets and in specialty stores; many governments are supporting organic farming and research; and more and more people are turning to organic methods of gardening. Every time there is another food scare, or the dangers of another pesticide come to light, more people turn to eating, and growing, organically. As the effects of climate change become more obvious, and we are encouraged to reduce our "carbon footprint," organic gardening offers practical ways in which we can do this in the garden.

(Left) **Food for thought** Healthy, safe food production prompted Lawrence D. Hills to found Garden Organic, originally under the name of the Henry Doubleday Research Association, in tribute to a pioneering Victorian horticulturist.

(Right) **New ways to garden** Organic methods address global concerns such as water conservation—promoting, for example, new ornamental plant choices and moisture-conserving mulches to make best use of the soil's resources.

What can organics offer you?

The organic way of gardening has a great number of healthy benefits to offer you, your family, and your wider environment.

Healthy eating

Organically grown produce can never be guaranteed pesticide-free—our world is too polluted to claim that—but it is grown without recourse to the arsenal of pesticides that may be used in conventional growing. Deaths from pesticide poisoning in the developed world are few, but we have no idea of the cumulative, chronic effects of the cocktail of low levels of pesticides that we all consume in and on conventionally grown food. Babies and young children, with their low body weight, are particularly at risk. Pesticides are even found in breast milk. By growing your own organic fruit, herbs, and vegetables, you can be sure your food is as healthy—and as fresh—as it can be. You can enjoy a much wider range of varieties than you could find at the store, too. What's more, analysis shows that fresh, organically grown food tends to be nutritionally superior in terms of vital ingredients such as vitamin C.

And it's not just food that can contain pesticide residues. Cut flowers, often imported from countries where pesticide use is less strictly controlled, may have been sprayed with substances that are banned in other nations—so growing your own makes sense.

Healthy gardening

By gardening organically, you can avoid using any pesticides at all. You, your children, your family pets, and visiting wildlife can enjoy the garden environment in safety.

Healthy wildlife

Wildlife has inevitably suffered, in both numbers and species range, as the environment has become progressively degraded. It is alarming to find that once-common species of birds such as evening grosbeaks, northern bobwhites, and eastern meadowlarks are now harder to find. Countless lesser-known species maintain only a precarious existence.

Not surprisingly, wildlife flourishes on organic farms and in organic gardens, and it is to be hoped that as more farmers and gardeners abandon chemicals, the steady decline of wildlife will be reversed. Scientific studies have shown that organic farms support a greater number, and diversity, of wild creatures than most conventionally managed farmland. In spite of the relatively small area of land devoted to gardens in comparison with farmland, it is still significant. Even a modestly sized organic garden can attract a diverse and plentiful wildlife community. In fact, one of the great pleasures of gardening organically is enjoying the birds, butterflies, and other small creatures that inhabit your yard with you. With diversity comes balance, so pests are less of a problem in gardens where wildlife flourishes.

(Below, left to right) **Reaping the rewards** Organic gardening creates a healthy environment and food for your family. Growing your own fresh, healthy crops will allow you to rediscover the seasonal pleasures of harvesting, and also to grow lesser-known, even traditionally local varieties of fruits and vegetables. Not only beautiful border plants but also good-looking cut flowers for the house can be managed entirely using organic methods.

Healthy environment

Environmental pollution is an increasingly common factor in modern life. Waste disposal sites and incinerators, designed to dispose of the ever-increasing mountains of garbage, do not make pleasant neighbors. Organic gardening encourages reuse and recycling of items often thrown away or burned, helping to reduce the waste mountain.

It's hard to overestimate the damage to the environment that has been wrought by agricultural intensification during the last half-century. Precious landscape features, such as prairies, wetlands, and old fencerows, have been destroyed on a massive scale. Overuse of fertilizers has polluted lakes and rivers, in many cases choking them almost to death through the proliferation of algal blooms and aquatic weeds. Pesticides are everywhere in the environment—on land, in the sea and even at the North and South poles, where they accumulate in the body fat of creatures at the top of the food chain, such as seals, penguins, and polar bears.

Organic farming and gardening, which do not rely on artificial inputs, cause little pollution. They preserve and enhance landscape features that provide habitats for the wildlife that is vital for pest control. It is little wonder that scientific comparisons consistently rate organic growing as the most sustainable there is.

Healthy budget

The hidden costs of conventional agriculture are huge. The annual costs of cleaning up drinking water to reduce the pesticide content to an "acceptable" level are staggering. Removing nitrates costs yet more money.

These costs are paid, of course, by the consumer. It's not surprising that many water companies support organic growing.

Organic gardening methods can cut your costs. Making compost and leaf mold, for example, can eliminate the need to purchase soil improvers and fertilizers, and you can save considerable amounts of money on organic produce by growing your own.

Healthy future

The idea that we do not inherit the earth from our ancestors, but borrow it from our children, is a compelling one. Organic methods help us to fulfill this philosophy.

Worldwide, there is pressure to intensify food production, resulting in an increasing reliance on chemical inputs and a rapid decline in the range of crops and cultivars bred to respond to those inputs. Genetic modification (GM) is the latest and most worrisome embodiment of this trend, which is the antithesis of organic growing. These developments deny local knowledge, traditional expertise, sustainability, diversity, and devolution of power and control. Industrial agriculturists may protest that theirs is the only way to feed the world, but many would take issue with this. The organic movement offers a healthy, sustainable alternative view of the future.

(Below, left to right) **Best of both worlds** Growing plants to attract wildlife may bring an appreciation of the gentle beauty of wild and native plants, but organic gardening is not all nostalgia. It uses the best of traditional methods (especially those that save on labor, like "no-dig" potatoes, below left) but also searches for ways to use and recycle today's materials.

So what is organic gardening?

Organic gardening is not just a matter of replacing chemicals such as artificial fertilizers and pesticides with more natural products, as it is often simplistically described. There is a great deal more to it than that, in both theory and practice.

Basic principles
The organic approach recognizes the marvelous complexity of our living world; the detailed and intricate ways in which all living organisms are interconnected. It aims to work within this delicate framework, in harmony with nature.

Feeding the soil
Conventional fertilizers are generally soluble, their ingredients directly available to plants. The organic way, on the other hand, relies on soil-dwelling creatures to make food available to plants.

Unbelievable as it may sound, a single teaspoonful of fertile soil can contain more bacteria and fungi than the number of humans living on the planet. These microorganisms, which are invisible to the naked eye, break down compost, manure, and other organic materials that are added to the soil, to provide a steady supply of nutrients for plants to take up. Their activities also help to

(Clockwise from top left) **Incentives and benefits** Not only nostalgic cottage gardens but also formal, modern, even "designer" gardens can be managed using organic principles. The trick is to arrange for nature to do some of the work for you—by encouraging beneficial insects such as ladybugs to patrol for pests, for example, or utilizing natural cycles of decay and renewal to enrich your soil.

ORGANIC GARDENING "DO'S"

▓ Manage the whole yard organically—edible crops, ornamentals, lawns, and paths.

▓ Make the garden wildlife-friendly, encouraging birds, insects, and small animals to control pests.

▓ Learn to distinguish pests from their predators.

▓ Play to your garden's strengths, capitalizing on its particular characteristics.

▓ Make soil care a priority.

▓ Make compost and leaf mold to feed the soil.

▓ Reuse and recycle, to cut down on the use of finite resources and reduce pressure on landfills.

▓ Use organically grown seeds where possible.

▓ Consider the environmental implications when choosing materials for hard landscaping, soil improving, and so forth.

▓ Collect rainwater, and reduce the need for watering by improving soil and growing appropriate plants.

▓ Make local sources your first choice.

▓ Use traditional methods where appropriate.

▓ Make use of the latest scientific findings where acceptable organically.

▓ Stop using artificial fertilizers.

▓ Give up smoke-producing bonfires.

▓ Control weeds without the use of herbicides.

▓ Avoid the use of pesticides and preservative-treated wood.

▓ Say no to genetically modified cultivars.

▓ Recognize the value of genetic diversity and preservation of threatened cultivars.

improve soil structure. Soil fed in this way tends to produce healthier plants that are better able to withstand attack from pests and diseases, or have a much better chance of recovery.

Natural pest control

All creatures, whatever their size, risk attack by pests and diseases. They are part of a great food chain. Ladybugs prey on aphids, robins eat Japanese beetles, and toads devour slugs. As an organic gardener, you can capitalize on the situation by creating the right conditions to attract these unpaid pest controllers—the gardener's friends. There are other strategies in the organic cupboard, too—barriers and traps, pest- and disease-resistant plant varieties, companion planting, and crop rotation all provide realistic alternatives to the use of pesticides.

Recycling weeds Hand-weeding may seem like a chore compared to the application of sprays, but when those weeds are composted, all the energy and nutrients they have taken from the soil can be returned to the garden without any taint of chemicals.

Managing weeds

Weeds can be a valuable resource as a compost ingredient or food for wildlife, but they can also smother plants, compete for food and water, and spoil the look of a path or border. Organic gardeners don't use weedkilling sprays, but there are plenty of effective alternatives, both for clearing ground and for keeping weeds under control: hoeing, mulching, cultivation, hand-weeding, and the use of heat in the form of flame or infrared burners.

Conservation and the environment

By taking a holistic approach to the use of finite resources and by minimizing impact on the environment, organic growing makes a positive contribution toward creating a sustainable future for all life on Earth. This means recycling and reusing, instead of dumping or burning or buying new; providing habitats where wildlife can flourish; and avoiding the use of nonreusable resources. It also involves choosing locally available materials, rather than those transported over long distances.

Welfare considerations

Animal welfare is an important element of organic farming. There is no place in the organic philosophy for factory farming, such as battery and broiler hen houses or intensive feedlots. As a logical extension, organic gardeners do not use by-products—such as manure—from intensive agriculture. There is concern for people, too—standards governing the trade in organic food are gradually converging with those concerned with "fair trade," to provide better livelihoods for those employed in farming, particularly in developing countries.

The use of animal manures is an integral part of most organic farming systems, but it is quite possible to garden without using any products of animal origin if you prefer. Garden compost, leguminous green manures, leaf mold, and plant-based fertilizers are all "animal-free" organic gardening ingredients.

(Right, from top) **Materials and methods**
High-tech materials such as spun fleece are just as acceptable within the organic ethos as traditional equipment such as glass cloches, provided that sustainability is always kept in mind. Why buy bird-scarers when shiny CDs are frequently delivered with our mail? Or use imported lumber, when a local company may be able to supply sustainably produced wood?

"Going organic"

As this book will show, "going organic" is not simply a question of changing your brand of pesticide or fertilizer (though you may well do this). It involves a change of approach, treating the garden as a complete entity where natural systems are promoted and encouraged to thrive. You will start developing long-term strategies for maintaining soil fertility and managing pests and diseases.

HOW GREEN IS YOUR GARDEN?

You may already use many organic methods—check out the list of organic "do's" on page 18. And your garden may also already contain features that are a vital part of organic gardening:

- Compost pile
- Leaf-mold store
- Plants for wildlife
- Mulch
- Rainwater collection
- Pond or water feature
- Habitats for wildlife

(Left to right) **Organic features**
Nesting box; bark mulch; rain barrel to collect and recycle rainwater.

Getting started

The best way to go organic is to take the plunge—to start using organic methods, and give up chemical methods, in every area of your yard at once. This book is full of practical advice to help in the conversion process, whether you're starting with bare ground, clearing a weed patch, or converting an existing garden.

All the information in this book conforms to Garden Organic's Guidelines for Organic Gardeners. These practical guidelines let you know just what is, and isn't, appropriate to do or use in an organic garden. They concentrate on practices that aim to make a garden as self-sufficient as possible—but, recognizing that there may be a need to buy organic fertilizers, for example, or to use a pest-killing spray, particularly when you are converting a garden, the Guidelines also advise on what products are acceptable.

How long does it take?

Commercial growers converting to organic methods are required to go through a transition period, usually three years. During this period the land is managed organically, but produce cannot yet be sold as organic. Depending on past management, you may find

that your garden takes time to adapt—
or everything may flourish from the start!

Change the way you shop

Organic gardening products are available in
some garden centers. Specialty mail order
catalogs usually supply a greater range. In
an ideal world, anything you use in an organic
garden would itself have been grown or
produced organically. Unfortunately, this is not
yet possible; although the range is growing, at
times you will have to use conventionally grown
seed, for example, or manure from animals not
raised organically.

To conform to the organic principles of
sustainability, always try to reuse and recycle
waste materials from your own garden and
locality. One exception to this rule is to dispose
of any unsuitable pesticides and herbicides as
soon as possible. However, you must not add

Weighing up your choices A compost bin is an organic
essential—but what is yours made from? Use scrap or recycled
lumber if possible, such as old wooden pallets, and avoid the use
of wood preservatives.

these to household trash or pour them down
sinks or sewers. Call your university extension
for advice on disposing of them safely.

Outside help

If you are new to organics, or simply need
advice or new ideas, there are organizations
that can help. Organic gardening groups can
be found all over the country, and these are
especially helpful for advice on local subjects
such as tackling problem soil. Your university
extension service may be able to suggest organic
solutions to pest problems. And many of the
large gardening websites have organic forums
where you can find advice or encouragement.

2. The Soil

To an organic gardener, the soil is the most important aspect of the garden. Building and maintaining fertile, healthy soil must be the first priority. Much can be done to improve poor soil, but before work begins, it is important to find out more about your soil type, its "texture," and its "structure." Soil texture or type depends on the physical location and the geology of the area. Soil structure is determined by previous cultivation—how the soil has been managed, if at all, in the past. Both texture and structure have an effect on soil chemistry—whether it is more acidic or alkaline. This in turn will determine which plants are likely to grow well, and the amount of life in the soil.

A world below ground The soil is a living environment, exerting as much influence on the plants that grow in it as do the conditions above ground.

Getting to know your soil

As you garden, you will gradually get to know your soil as you cultivate, sow, plant, and weed, and notice which plants thrive and which are less successful. If you are getting acquainted with a new garden or yard, however, take a close look at the soil right at the start. Pick up a handful and feel it to check its type (*see p.28*); watch closely to discover which creatures have made it their home; and use a simple kit to determine whether your soil is acidic, alkaline, or neutral.

Soil structure

The fertility of soil is not simply a question of the quantity of plant foods that it contains—it is the sum of all the features that are necessary for plant growth. The structure of the soil—the way it is put together—is just as important. Heavy clay soil, for example, can be rich in plant foods, but grow poor plants, because it is too heavy and waterlogged for adequate root growth. Air spaces

Reaping the rewards The more you improve your soil's structure by replenishing organic matter and managing it with care, the healthier your plants will become.

SOIL STRUCTURE INDICATORS

Good structure

- Plant roots penetrate deeply.
- Sweet, earthy smell.
- Water does not sit long in the bottom of a hole after rain.
- The soil is relatively easy to dig.
- No hardpan (compacted layer) in the topsoil.
- Lots of worms and worm channels.
- Top layers of soil are crumbly and friable both when wet and when dry.

Poor structure

- Plants are shallow-rooting.
- Unpleasant smell.
- Water sits in holes or on the surface (*below*), or drains through immediately.
- Soil is sticky or in hard lumps, or very dry.
- Compacted layer in topsoil.
- Few worms.
- Surface layer slumps when wet, and dries out to a crust.

between the soil particles—also known as crumbs—are as vital for plants as they are for soil-dwelling creatures. When water displaces all the air in the soil and it remains sodden for days, the plants "drown"—and when such soil dries out, it can become rock-hard, as anyone who has tried to dig clayey soil after a period of drought will testify. Simply improving such soil's structure, allowing more air into the soil by adding bulky, spongy organic matter, can make a dramatic difference.

Conversely, in light, sandy soil, the air spaces between the soil particles are simply so big that water drains straight through, down to levels that plant roots—especially those of young plants—cannot reach. In addition, as the water runs through the soil it washes away, or leaches out, the few nutrients that such soil possesses. The simple addition of a low-fertility soil improver such as leaf mold, which increases the soil's ability to hold on to food and water, can again make a dramatic improvement.

Happily, then, unlike soil type, soil structure is something that the gardener can alter. This chapter describes how to understand and improve soil structure, and, just as importantly, how to avoid destroying it.

What's in soil?

Around half the volume of soil is made up of mineral particles from weathered rocks, organic matter, and living organisms; the other half is water and air. Plant foods, or nutrients, are supplied by the mineral particles and the breakdown of organic matter.

Rock particles and soil type

Over millions of years, rocks are weathered down into small particles, which form the basic ingredient of almost all soil. The size and chemical composition of the particles depends on the rock they came from—that is, the physical location and geological profile of your area—and determines the type of soil you have. There are three types of weathered rock particles that make up soil: sand, silt, and clay. The proportion of the different particles found in a soil determines its type—what name it is given—and how it behaves and should be managed. Most soil contains a mixture of all

Get a feel for it Soil that contains sand will feel gritty and crumble through your fingers (*left*); clay soil, when moist, clumps and sticks together (*right*) as you mold it.

three particle types. If they are in roughly equal proportions, the soil is called loam. If one type begins to predominate, then it will be called sandy, silty, or clay loam—and the soil will begin to take on the characteristics of that particular particle type. It is not always easy to work out exactly what type of soil you have, particularly in a yard where additional soil may have been brought in. However, handling moist soil, rubbing it between your fingers and trying to roll it into a ball, can give you some indication of the predominating particles.

■ **Clay soil** Soil in which clay particles predominate will stick together in a ball or sausage shape; it tends to be dense, sticky, and heavy to work because the tiny clay particles settle together, with little room for air. But it is usually rich in plant nutrients.

■ **Sandy soil** At the other extreme, soil with a high sand content tends to be dry and gritty. The relatively large spaces between sandy soil particles are too big to hold water, so it drains through quickly, taking plant nutrients with it. Sandy soil is, however, easy to work and does warm up quickly in spring.

■ **Silty soil** This falls somewhere between clay and sand. It feels silky—almost soapy—and leaves your fingers dirty. It is fertile, but compacts easily and may be heavy to work.

■ **Peaty soil** This forms where wet, acidic conditions prevent full decomposition of organic matter. Peaty soil is black and feels spongy, and cannot be rolled into a ball. It is rich in organic matter and very easy to work, but can get very dry in summer and may be very acidic (*see* Soil chemistry, *p.30*).

■ **Saline soil** Found in arid regions, saline soil has a high salt content that can harm plants.

Soil life

Soil teems with many different kinds of life—from microscopic bacteria and fungi to more noticeable creatures such as earthworms, beetles, slugs, and insect larvae. Many of these creatures are responsible for recycling organic matter (*see below*), breaking it down so that the nutrients it contains are once again available to plants. Their activities also build soil structure.

Some soil-living organisms can be plant pests, and others may cause disease—but most do no harm, or are positively beneficial. As in the environment above ground, the more diverse and active the community, the less likely it is that one particular organism will get out of hand. Ensuring that soil is rich in organic matter encourages a diverse and active micro flora and fauna.

Organic matter

The term "organic matter" is used to describe the dead and decomposing remains of living things, such as plant debris, animal remains, and manures. It is a crucial part of the soil, providing food for soil-living creatures; for plants in particular, it is a major source of nitrogen. Without it, soil would be just sterile

Some visible ground-dwellers

Worms (*right, top*) are the most obvious and well-known creatures found in soil. They help process organic matter by dragging it down into the soil before eating it. Their tunnels serve to aerate the soil and help it drain; their casts provide a source of nutrients, and they help to form soil crumbs. Other creatures you may see in your soil include woodlice (*center*), centipedes, and ground beetles (*bottom*), the latter being valuable pest predators. Less welcome visitors for the gardener—although still indicative that your soil supports a healthy diversity of life—include millipedes, slugs, and leatherjackets (the larvae of the cranefly).

rock dust. Organic matter is continually being broken down by soil creatures and by natural oxidation. In nature it is replenished in the natural cycles of life and death. Humus is the final product in the breakdown of organic matter. It acts as a valuable reservoir of water and plant nutrients, and helps soil structure. In short, organic matter:

■ Feeds soil-living creatures;

■ Encourages diversity in soil life;

■ Improves the physical structure of the soil;

■ Absorbs water;

■ Both supplies plant foods and helps the soil retain them.

Plant nutrients

Plant foods are supplied by the breakdown of mineral particles and organic matter. Soil contains a wide range of nutrients that are required, in larger amounts (macronutrients) or smaller amounts (micronutrients or trace elements), for healthy plant growth. Most nutrients required for plant growth come from the basic mineral particles that make up the soil skeleton. They are also found in organic matter. Nitrogen is only found in living (or decaying) tissue, so bulky organic matter is a major source.

The complete range of plant foods can be found in most soil. Depending on what you are growing, you may need to augment the levels of nitrogen, phosphorus, potassium, and possibly magnesium—the nutrients that plants use in greatest amounts. Deficiencies of these and other trace elements may result in a variety of symptoms. However, deficiency symptoms are not always due to a shortage of a particular nutrient in the soil. An excess of one nutrient—

caused by adding too much fertilizer, for example—can make other nutrients unavailable to plants. Poor structure, water shortage, or unsuitable pH (*see* Soil chemistry, *below*) can also prevent plants from obtaining the nutrients they need. Some nutrients, including nitrogen, are easily washed out of the soil.

There is generally no need to be concerned about the precise levels of plant foods in your soil. Using organic methods of soil management, you should be able to provide plants with a good balanced diet. In a new garden, however, or where plants are failing for no obvious reason, a soil analysis may be useful to highlight any particular deficiency or imbalance. Ideally, use a soil analysis service designed for organic growers; this will indicate the potential of the soil, not simply the nutrients currently available.

Soil chemistry

An important characteristic of soil is its level of alkalinity or acidity, known as pH. The pH scale runs from 1, extremely acidic, to 14, extremely alkaline. Most soils range from 4 to 8, with the majority of plants growing in the range of 5.5–7.5. Ornamentals tend to tolerate

What nutrients do While the difference between a healthy plant and one lacking in nutrients is clear, it can often be hard to determine which nutrient is in short supply. Feeding the soil is often a more practical solution than trying to treat the plant.

The effects of soil chemistry One of the most striking yet familiar demonstrations of how soil pH affects plants is provided by these mophead hydrangeas. In areas where the soil is acidic, the flowers are blue; in alkaline conditions, they are pink.

quite a wide pH range, although some, such as many rhododendrons and heathers, will only grow in more acidic soil. Vegetables tend to prefer a pH in the range of 6.5–7, while fruit thrives in a pH of 6–6.5, except blueberries and cranberries, which need acidic conditions. The calcium level in the soil controls pH. Calcium can be washed out of soil, especially if it is free-draining, making the soil more acidic.

What effects does pH have?

The pH of a soil governs the availability of nutrients to plants. In very acidic soil, plant foods may be washed out, or dissolve in the soil water at toxic levels. At the alkaline end of the scale, plant foods may be locked up in the soil, unavailable to plants. Plants that can grow in more extreme pHs have adapted to deal with these problems. Soil pH also has an effect on the diversity, and activity, of soil life. The pests leatherjackets and wireworms are

more common in acidic conditions; earthworms, which are beneficial creatures, dislike acidic soil. Certain diseases, such as potato scab, are more troublesome in alkaline soil, while clubroot is much less so; this is why liming the soil is often recommended before growing brassicas.

Why test the pH? These simple kits are readily available, easy to use, and tell you your soil's pH in seconds. An initial pH test when you take over a new garden can help you choose the appropriate plants for the site. Always test the pH in a new vegetable patch.

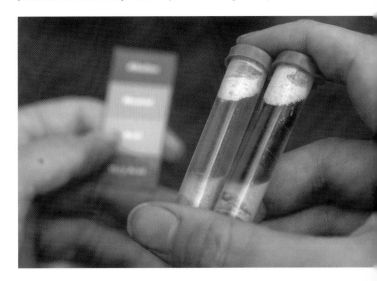

Managing soil organically

How you treat your soil depends on the soil type, how it has been managed in the past, and what is growing, or will be growing, in it. If drought-loving plants are chosen for poor, sandy soil, for example, they will need little attention, while a wildflower meadow, which needs low-nutrient soil, will soon be taken over by other species if you start to fertilize it. Remember that, in the natural environment, plants are never artificially fed, mulched, or watered. The plants that thrive are those suited to the local conditions. Choosing the right ornamental plants for the growing environment in your garden will make for easier gardening; in the vegetable plot, you may need to manage the soil more actively to grow the crops you enjoy.

The organic approach

The organic approach to soil care is a combination of good horticultural practice and the use, as needed, of bulky organic materials such as composts, animal manures, and green manures, supplemented only when necessary with organic fertilizers (natural products of animal, plant, or mineral origin). Organic inputs are often recycled waste products. As well as benefiting the soil, their use helps to avoid the pollution that their disposal—in landfill sites or a bonfire—would cause. Organic gardeners, following nature's example, recycle plant and animal wastes, feeding the soil, rather than feeding plants directly. Soil-living creatures break down bulky organic materials in the soil. In the process, structure is improved, and foods are made available to plants. Biologically active soil is a healthy place to grow.

Distributing your weight When ground is wet, working from a board will spread your weight evenly and protect the soil structure, especially in clay or silty soil.

Avoiding soil compaction

Compaction occurs when soils are regularly walked on or cultivated in wet conditions. It is a particular problem in heavy soil. Avoid it by creating paths that follow the routes you want to take around the garden, and planting beds that are narrow enough to be worked on from paths. Regular use of a mechanical cultivator can also create compacted hardpan below the soil surface that plant roots cannot penetrate.

Digging and mulching

Dig only when necessary. Digging is essential to break up hard and compacted ground, but regular digging increases the rate at which essential organic matter breaks down. Digging can encourage weeds too, bringing a new batch of weed seeds to the surface to germinate every time you turn over the soil. It is possible to garden without regular digging, even in the kitchen garden (*see p.216*). Once good soil structure is established, mulches of organic matter spread over the soil will be incorporated naturally by soil-dwelling creatures.

Dig only when soil conditions are right, especially if your soil is heavy. It should not be so wet that it sticks to your spade, nor so dry that you have to break up huge clods.

PRINCIPLES OF ORGANIC SOIL CARE

■ **Feed the soil** Bulky organic soil improvers (*see overleaf*) feed the soil-living creatures that build soil structure and fertility.

■ **Walk with care** Trampled, compacted soil is airless, difficult for roots to penetrate, and a poor environment for soil-living creatures.

■ **Dig only when necessary** Digging has its uses, but it can destroy soil structure.

■ **Keep it covered** Persistent heavy rain can erode soil and leach out its nutrients. A covering of plants, or in winter, a mulch over bare ground, protects the soil structure.

■ **Take care with plant nutrients** More problems are caused by overfertilizing than underfertilizing. The performance of your plants should be your guide.

Working from paths These narrow beds are an ideal solution for heavy soil; raising and edging the beds allows plenty of organic matter to be added, and working from paths avoids compacting the ground by stepping on it.

Bulky organic soil improvers

Bulky materials of living origin maintain and improve soil structure—helping light soils to hold on to food and water, and heavy soils to drain more effectively. They may also supply plant foods, released as they are broken down by soil-living creatures.

The panel on the opposite page lists a range of bulky organic soil improvers. Each has a fertility rating as a guide to its nutrient value, especially its nitrogen content. These can only be a broad indication, as the exact nutrient content of this type of material can vary quite widely, depending on the basic ingredients, and the method and length of storage. Remember that there is often no need to use a nutrient-rich material. Low-fertility soil improvers can be extremely effective in maintaining soil fertility, despite their low nutrient value.

Many materials, such as kitchen and garden waste and animal manures, are composted before use to stabilize the plant foods they contain, and to make them easier to apply.

Sources of organic soil improvers

Recycling, one of the basic tenets of organic growing, reduces the need to bring in outside inputs, and also cuts down on the volume of waste to be disposed of from your kitchen and garden. It is rarely possible to be totally self-sufficient in a garden situation, but all bulky organic materials from the house and garden should be recycled and used. These can be augmented with supplies brought in from other appropriate sources in the locality.

Commercial soil improvers, such as composted manures and plant wastes, can be purchased if you are unable to make enough

Bulky organic soil improvers
1. Leaf mold—decomposed fallen leaves; **2.** Spent mushroom compost; **3.** Garden compost; **4.** Manure and other waste from a chicken run; **5.** "Green waste" compost from a municipal composting plant; **6.** Coarse bark chips.

of your own. Where possible, choose a product that has some form of accreditation from an organic certifying body. When in doubt, check with the supplier for the source of the ingredients. The word "organic" is not sufficient on its own; it may simply mean that the ingredients are "of living origin," not that they are appropriate for an organic garden.

Applying organic matter to the soil

All soil improvers can be applied as a mulch. Most can also be dug into the soil (see the panel below for exceptions). Keep them in the top 6–8 in (15–20 cm) or so of the soil, where the main feeding roots of plants are at work and where good structure is most critical. Apply medium- and high-fertility materials in the spring and summer only; their goodness will be wasted if applied over winter when plant growth is minimal. As for application rates, the maxim "if some is good, more must be better" does not apply when adding nutrient-rich materials to the soil. Too much nitrogen, for example, encourages leafy growth rather than fruits and flowers. Any excess may just be wasted, washed out of the soil and into our water supplies. Let the performance of your plants be your guide.

SOME ORGANIC SOIL IMPROVERS

■ **Garden compost** (*see also pp.36–43*) Medium fertility. Dig in or mulch.

■ **Green waste compost** Low fertility. Dig in or mulch. Available from large-scale municipal recycling centers; may be low in nitrogen but high in potassium.

■ **Commercial bagged compost** Variable fertility; check labels. Dig in or mulch.

■ **Worm compost** (*see also pp.46–49*) High fertility. Usually only available in small quantities.

■ **Strawy animal manures** (*see also pp.52–53*) Medium to high fertility. Must be well-rotted before being dug into the soil. Source from nonintensive farms and stables. You are unlikely to be able to get manure from an organic farm.

■ **Spent mushroom compost** Medium fertility. Tends to be alkaline, so not suitable for acid-loving plants. Source from organic mushroom-growers.

■ **Leaf mold** (*see also p.44–45*) Low fertility. Mulch or dig in, depending on age.

■ **Straw** Low fertility. Source from an organic farm if possible. Best as a mulch.

■ **Bark chips and shredded prunings** Low fertility. Best used as a mulch only, in the ornamental garden. If dug in, they can rob the soil of nitrogen as they decay. This also applies to horse manure with wood shavings.

Making garden compost

A compost pile is both a recycling facility for kitchen and garden waste, and a small processing plant, producing a first-class, medium-to-low fertility soil improver: garden compost. No garden should be without one—or two, or three... Making compost is often seen as a complex art, but in fact it is not that difficult. Anyone can learn to do it. The actual process of converting waste to compost is carried out by naturally occurring creatures, from worms to microbes, that appear as if by magic. All you have to do is to supply a suitable mixture of ingredients, and let them get on with it.

Where to make compost

You can make compost in a simple covered pile in a corner of your yard, but a compost box or bin (*see pp.40–43*) looks neater and can be easier to manage. Your compost pile or bin is best sited on bare soil or grass, not on a hard surface such as paving slabs. It can be in sun or shade; what is important is that it is accessible, with plenty of room around it for adding, removing, and turning material. The size of the pile or bin will depend on how much material you generate. Larger piles (within reason) are better, but choose a size that suits you. If you have a large garden, you will need more than one bin. If you do not generate very much garden waste, but still want to compost kitchen scraps, consider a high-fiber pile (*see opposite*) or a neat worm-composting bin (*see pp.46–49*).

The composting miracle If you get the mix of ingredients right, then time, and the activity of helpful organisms, is all you need to transform your kitchen and garden waste (*below left*) into finished compost (*below right*): a rich, crumbly soil-like material with a pleasant earthy smell.

What goes on a compost pile?

The main ingredients in a garden pile are likely to be weeds, mowings and other green waste, plus fruit and vegetable scraps, and low-grade paper and cardboard from the house. Other items, such as strawy manure, can be brought in to augment supplies. Anything once alive will compost, but some items (*see p.39*) are best avoided for health or practical reasons.

"Greens" and "browns"

The key to making good compost is to use a mixture of types of ingredients. Young, sappy materials, such as grass mowings, rot quickly to a smelly sludge; these are known as "greens." They need to be mixed with tougher, dry items like old bedding plants—"browns," which are slow to rot on their own. "Browns" add the fiber that gives the compost a good structure.

Many compostable items themselves contain a good balance of "green" and "brown." When you have been making compost for a while, you will get a feel for the right mixture. If the contents of your compost pile tend to be wet and smelly, mix in more "browns"; if they are dry, bring in the "greens."

The only other ingredients needed are air and water. Mix materials that tend to slump and clump, such as grass mowings, with more open items to ensure a supply of air. Water dry items, or mix them with the moister "greens."

High-fiber composting

One of the main problems in composting, especially in smaller gardens, is a lack of "brown" materials to balance the "greens," which tend to be predominantly kitchen waste. To address this problem, try the "high-fiber" composting technique, which uses waste paper and packaging—such as paper towels, paper bags, and cardboard cartons and tubes—to provide the balance of ingredients required.

High-fiber composting If you have only a small garden, particularly a low-maintenance one, you may find that the proportions of composting materials you can gather together are imbalanced, with not enough coarse garden waste and too much kitchen material that turns sloppy and smelly. Adding crumpled and shredded paper and items such as cardboard tubes can open up the pile, and help shrink your paper recycling load.

These are crumpled up before being added to the pile. Roughly equal volumes of kitchen waste and paper products are added as they become available. The composting process is slow, but requires no further attention.

Compost activators

"Greens," which are quick to rot, will activate a pile; in other words, get it started. There are various types of "activators" on the market said to speed up composting, but a mixed pile should compost perfectly well without these.

Composting weeds and diseased material

To avoid the risk of spreading troublesome weeds, compost them before they seed. Put

Ready to be composted
1. Spent summer bedding plants;
2. Dying cut flowers; **3.** Grass
clippings, opened up with the
addition of some crumpled sheets
of newspaper; **4.** Old straw;
5. Garden weeds; **6.** Kitchen waste;
7. Soft hedge clippings; **8.** Bedding
from rabbit and hamster cages.

perennial roots in a black plastic sack, mixed with some grass mowings, and leave to rot for a year. When dead, add to the compost pile.

The biological activity and heat in a compost pile is so great that it can break down many plant diseases. Even so, it is probably wise not to add plants infected with very persistent diseases of vegetables such as clubroot and white rot. Potato and tomato foliage infected with potato blight can be safely composted.

Hedge clippings and woody prunings
Add soft young clippings—from a regularly pruned hedge, for example—to the compost pile. Tougher prunings in any quantity, including evergreen hedge clippings, are best composted separately, preferably after shredding. Pile them up or put them in a compost bin, and water well. Mix with a "green" material to speed up the process. Use after six months or more as a mulch on established shrubs and trees.

Recycling woody waste
Tough and chunky material will compost much more quickly if chopped up into smaller pieces. Hire a shredder for occasional use, or if buying one, try out a range—some are much quieter and easier to use than others. It is essential to wear adequate safety protection when using a shredder. Never use it in a confined space; be very careful when shredding plants such as laurel and hellebore, which contain toxins.

If you have space, woody items can just be stacked in an out-of-the-way corner and left to decay over a period of years. They will make a valuable wildlife habitat (*see also pp.108–111*). Some may be suitable for use around the garden, as plant supports, for example. Your local waste disposal site may recycle woody items if you cannot. Avoid bonfires, which cause pollution and nuisance, unless you need to dispose of diseased woody plant material.

WHAT TO COMPOST
Most organic waste can be recycled on to the compost pile. Large quantities of items marked * are best dealt with in piles of their own. Other miscellaneous compostable items include wood ash and eggshells.

"Greens"—quick to rot
- Grass mowings
- Poultry manure (without bedding)
- Young weeds and plants, nettles of any age

Intermediate
- Fruit and vegetable scraps
- Rhubarb leaves
- Tea bags, tea leaves, and coffee grounds
- Remains of vegetable plants
- Strawy animal manures
- Cut flowers
- Soft hedge clippings
- Bedding from herbivorous pets—rabbits, hamsters, etc.
- Perennial weeds*

"Browns"—slow to rot
- Old straw
- Tough plant and vegetable stems
- Old bedding plants
- Fall leaves*
- Woody prunings, evergreen hedge clippings *
- Cardboard tubes, egg cartons
- Crumpled paper and newspaper

Do not compost
- Meat and fish scraps
- Dog feces, used cat litter
- Disposable diapers
- Coal ashes
- Plastic, polystyrene, glass, metal

Compost bins

Compost bins can be purchased or homemade, and are preferably made from recycled or reused materials. As long as it fulfills the basic criteria (*right*), the design choice is yours. Choose one that suits your needs and garden. Place it in an accessible spot, directly on bare ground. It can have a fixed site or, depending on the model, it can be moved to different parts of the garden between batches.

Once you have started making compost, you may find that you need two or more containers, although it is possible to get by with just one. Once it is maturing, compost can be turned out in a pile and covered with a plastic sheet, freeing up the bin that it was in.

Filling the bin

■ Collect a mixed batch of "greens" and "browns" (*see p.39*) suitable for composting.
■ Add it to the compost bin, spreading it out to the edges. Firm down gently and water if dry.
■ Continue to add to the bin as and when material becomes available. If you add kitchen waste on its own, mix it in with what is already in the bin.
■ You may never fill the bin completely, as everything decreases in volume as it decays.
■ After 6–12 months, or sooner if the bin is almost full, stop adding any more.
■ Leave it to finish composting, and start filling another bin.

(Clockwise from top left) **A variety of compost bins**
1. A sectional or "beehive" wooden box (*see also overleaf*) makes filling and removing the compost simple.
2. Recycled plastic containers are compact; they may have a door at ground level to access the finished compost, but usually have no base; you simply lift them off the ground.
3. A traditional wooden New Zealand box. Using two of these side by side is ideal. One bay is filled while the other is maturing. Removable slats are taken out to access the compost.
4. Four posts, some wire netting, and a slatted wooden front make a simple, inexpensive bin.

WHAT MAKES A GOOD COMPOST BIN?

■ Solid sides.
■ Open base.
■ Wide top opening for easy filling.
■ Rainproof lid or cover that does not blow away.
■ A minimum volume of 55 gallons (220 liters), or 30 x 30 x 40 in (75 x 75 x 100 cm).
■ Removable side, or lift-off container, to access compost.

■ Alternatively, check progress by lifting off the bin or removing the front. Remove any compost that has formed in the lower layers. Replace the uncomposted material in the bin, adjusting the mixture if it is too wet or dry. Continue to add to this pile.

Hot tips for quicker compost

■ If you fill the compost bin all at once with a good mixture of materials, the pile should get hot, speeding the process and killing weed seeds.
■ Chop up tough and bulky items with a spade or shredder.
■ Keep it warm. The bottom layers of a pile are usually the first to decompose, generating heat that will rise through the pile and be lost from an unlidded bin or uncovered pile. The heat is valuable to the composting process, so use the lid, or cover the heap to keep it in. A cover will also conserve moisture, while keeping out the rain. You can add extra insulation by making a compost "comforter"—a thick plastic sack filled with fallen leaves.
■ Turn the pile. Remove everything from the bin, mix it all up, and replace it in the container. Turning a "hot" pile that has cooled will reactivate it; this can usually be repeated once or twice. Turning a slow pile now and again gives you an opportunity to see how it is working, and to adjust the mixture if necessary.

FILLING A BEEHIVE BOX

One of the easiest wooden bins
to construct, the beehive type of
compost bin has the advantage of
looking neat in a garden setting.
It can be painted and stained;
some people make wooden lids to
complete the effect. The wooden
"squares" used to build the bin up
in horizontal layers are all built the
same way, with the corner battens
that hold them together slightly
raised (*see above*), so each will fit
securely on top of the one below.

1 The bin can be built up at the
same rate as you add the
compost; every time the contents
reach the top, add another square.

2 Keep filling the box until you
have used all your squares—
a bin of four or five layers is
manageable. Spread the material
out evenly. Water if it is dry and
firm down gently.

3 Turning the compost is easy
with this type of bin, provided
that the piece of ground next to it is
left clear. Simply take off the layers
and restack them next to the heap,
turning the compost into the "new"
bin as you go.

How long does it take?

Compost is ready to use when it looks like dark soil (*as shown on p.36*), and none of the original ingredients is recognizable—apart from the odd twig, eggshell, or corn cob. It can be ready to use in as little as 12 weeks in summer, if you follow the "hot tips" on p.41, but it can also take up to a year or more. Both quick and slow compost can be equally valuable.

Using compost

Garden compost can be classified as a medium-fertility soil improver (*see pp.34–35*). Apply it where required at an average rate of around 25 gal/50 sq ft (100 liters/5 sq m). This is a layer of approximately ½ in (1 cm) thick spread out evenly over the ground. Apply compost in spring or summer as a mulch, or dig it into the top 8 in (20 cm) of the soil.

TRENCH COMPOSTING

Another way to recycle kitchen and vegetable waste is to bury it in a trench or pit, and then grow either peas or beans, or "cucurbits"—zucchini, squash, pumpkins, or cucumbers—on top of it. It provides nutrients and moisture exactly where they are required. In fall, dig a trench or pit, one spade deep. For peas and beans, dig it one spade wide, and as long as the row. Make a pit around 3 x 3 ft (1 x 1 m) for each plant. Gradually fill with kitchen waste, covering each addition with soil. When full, cover with the rest of the soil and leave it for a couple of months. Sow or plant into the trench at the appropriate time for the crop, after the soil has settled.

Composting in the larger garden
If you have a fair-sized garden, and especially if you grow vegetables, two compost bins side by side is a much better option than one large pile. Once you have filled one of the bins, use a fork to transfer the contents into the adjacent bin, mixing it up as you go. By the time you have filled the first bin again, the compost in the other bin should be ready to use, so you can empty it and repeat the process, or you can add another bin.

Making leaf mold

When leaves drop from trees in the fall, they decay on the ground to form a rich, dark material called leaf mold, which is an excellent soil conditioner. Making leaf mold in your yard is easy to do. All you need is a supply of fallen leaves, and a simple container to stop them from blowing away. Throwing leaves out with the trash, or burning them, is a waste of a valuable resource.

Which leaves to use?

Any leaves from deciduous trees and shrubs can be gathered up in fall to make leaf mold. Do not use evergreens, such as laurel and holly. Leaves of some species take longer than others to decay, but all rot down eventually. An easy way to collect leaves from a lawn is to run the mower over them. The grass and chopped leaf mixture in the mower bag will rot down easily. (Alternatively, mow without the bag on the mower; worms will soon take the chopped leaves down into the lawn.) To supplement supplies, collect leaves from quiet streets or, with permission, from parks and cemeteries. Leaves from busy roadsides can be polluted with oil and vehicle emissions. Some communities collect leaves and produce leaf mold to sell or give to the public. Never collect leaves or leaf mold from woodlands.

Making the leaf mold

Collect fallen leaves in the fall, preferably after rain so they are wet. If the leaves are dry, soak well with water. Stuff them into a container or stack them in a corner, and leave to decay.

Simple leaf mold containers can be made with netting and posts, or bought. There is no need for a lid or solid sides, nor is size critical—just big enough to hold your supply of leaves. Smaller quantities can be stuffed into plastic bags. Make a few air holes with a garden fork when the bags are full, and tie the top loosely. An even simpler method is to just pile the leaves in a sheltered corner and wait.

A leaf mold heap may heat up very slightly, but the process is generally slow and cold. It can take anything from nine months to

LEAF MOLD AGING

1 Freshly collected leaves can be stored whole or run over with a mower to chop them.

2 The following fall—rough, year-old leaf mold makes an excellent mulch.

3 Two-year-old leaf mold is much finer and can be used as soil improver, in a topdressing mixture for lawns, or as an ingredient in potting mix for container plants.

two or more years to make a usable batch of fine leaf mold, depending on the tree species and how you are going to use it.

Using leaves and leaf mold

Leaf mold can generally be used as a low-fertility soil improver (*see pp.34–35*) and a moisture-retaining mulch after one year. It should be darker and more crumbly than the newly fallen leaves, but does not have to be fully rotted. For a finer product, for use in seed and potting mixes or as a topdressing for

Leaf mold containers The simplest cages are made from four wooden stakes driven into the ground, then wrapped with chicken wire or rabbit fencing, which is then stapled to the posts. The leaves decrease dramatically in volume as they decay.

lawns, leave it to decay for another year, or even two if the leaves are very slow to rot.

Apply leaf mold in a layer up to 4 in (10 cm) thick, leaving it as a surface mulch or lightly forking it in if required. It can be applied to any plants at any time of year. It makes a good moisture-retentive mulch if applied in spring once the soil has warmed up. It is also valuable as a winter cover for bare soil, especially where small seeds, such as carrot, are to be sown in spring. It can also be used to protect the crown of tender perennials such as penstemons: a blanket of leaf mold or of fallen leaves, held down with conifer prunings, will keep off the frost. Leaf mold can also be mixed with loam and sand to make a topdressing mix for lawns.

Worm composting

Certain types of earthworms, found naturally in piles of leaves and in manure and compost piles, specialize in decomposing plant wastes. Colonies of these worms can be housed in a container and fed kitchen and garden waste, which they will convert into a rich manure known as worm compost—a high-fertility soil improver. A worm compost system can be kept working all year. It is a good choice when the main material available for composting is kitchen scraps and vegetable waste, which are usually available every few days in relatively small amounts. Composting worms cannot cope with large volumes of material added all at once.

Small is beautiful A worm bin is compact and self-contained, ideal for small and even courtyard gardens. Keep it out of full sun. A shed or garage is also suitable, particularly in winter.

Working worms

The common earthworms seen in soil are not suitable for use in worm composting bins. Red wigglers, also called brandling worms or manure worms, are the type most commonly used. They are very efficient recyclers of organic waste and will reproduce quickly in the confines of the bin. It is a good idea to start a worm bin with at least 1,000 worms—about 18 oz (500 g) in weight. They can be extracted from a maturing compost pile, a manure stack, or another worm bin, or they can be purchased by mail order or over the Internet. The dark, moist conditions that worms need to live in can be provided by keeping them in a plastic bin or a wooden box of some form.

Worm bins

Worm bins can be purchased, or you can make your own—or adapt existing containers such as wooden crates or boxes, or a plastic storage bin. As worms like to feed near the surface, the most effective bins have a relatively large surface area. There is no need for the container to be "wormproof"; the worms will stay put if the conditions are right for them. Good drainage is vital, as kitchen waste can produce

Worms for a worm bin Red wigglers, have a characteristic red-and-yellow banding; they are also known as tiger worms. Their eggs are borne in tiny, lemon-shaped cocoons.

Additional visitors Small white, thread-like enchytraid worms may appear in large numbers in a worm bin. They are harmless, but can be a sign that the contents of the bin are rather acidic.

a lot of moisture (see Worm liquid, *p.49*), and the worms will drown if conditions are too wet. If there is no reason to move your worm bin, you can make one without a base; two or three "squares" from a beehive compost bin (see *p.42*), set directly on the ground and covered, makes a practical worm bin.

Where to keep a worm bin

Worms work best at temperatures between 50 and 77°F (12–25°C). They will survive considerably lower temperatures, but their rate of producing compost will slow down. Keep a worm bin where temperatures do not fluctuate widely—out of direct sunlight in summer. Bring the bin into a garage or warm greenhouse in winter, or insulate it well before the cold weather starts. A worm bin with an integral drainage sump can be kept indoors, in a shed or porch, for example, and moved out in the summer. Other bins may need to be set on bare soil to absorb any excess liquid produced.

Feeding the worms

A worm compost bin is, typically, used to process kitchen and vegetable scraps, which are usually available "little and often." This suits the worms, which cannot process large quantities at once. Remember that they are, in effect, livestock, with limited appetites! Excess food will spoil before they can process it, resulting in an unpleasant smell. The worms will not process

WHAT CAN I PUT IN MY WORM BIN?

YES

- Vegetable peelings
- Vegetable crop waste
- Eggshells
- Fruit peelings
- Cooked leftovers
- Shredded paper, paper bags
- Paper towels
- Coffee grounds
- Tea leaves
- Onion skins
- Egg cartons

NO

- Large amounts of citrus peel
- Dairy products
- Meat and fish
- Cat/dog feces
- Purchased flowers

Extracting the worms When the finished worm compost is spread out, the worms will move to gather in the cooler, damper conditions under a sheet of wetted newspaper. They can then be gathered up and returned to the bin.

Cool customers Red wigglers seek out cool, dark, moist environments, but their activity slows when temperatures drop. Some people like to bring their bins under cover in a shed or garage for winter and insulate it with bubble wrap or straw.

WAYS TO USE WORM COMPOST

■ Apply as a topdressing to greedy feeders such as squash and other fruiting vegetables during the growing season.

■ Apply as a topdressing for patio pots or house plants—if necessary, remove the top 1 in (2 cm) of the potting mix, and replace with worm compost. Water as usual.

■ Add to commercial potting mix to enrich it and improve its water-holding capacity—for hanging baskets, for example.

■ Use as an ingredient in homemade potting mixes and other growing media.

putrefying food, and may well die. A worm bin can also be used to process garden waste if it is added in small quantities. A sprinkling of ground limestone (*see p.55*) every month will help to keep conditions in the bin sweet.

How much your worm bin can process in a week depends on the temperature and the number of worms. Add no more than 3–4 quarts (liters) of suitable food at a time. Start slowly, and build up the feeding gradually; judge what is happening before adding any more. Chop up larger items to speed up the process. A worm bin will survive many weeks without food being added. Do not be tempted to add lots of extra food before you go away on vacation, as it may putrefy before the worms can process it.

Common problems

A worm compost system that is working well does not smell. If a worm bin begins to smell unpleasant, and the food you add is not being processed, this is a sure sign that something is wrong. The two main causes are overfeeding, and excess moisture, which may be the result of poor drainage or overfeeding. If there are still some live worms in the compost, stop feeding for a while.

Mix in moisture-absorbing materials, such as newspaper, egg cartons, paper towels, and cardboard tubes. Add a sprinkling of limestone and clear any drainage holes. If on investigation you cannot see any active worms at all, you will have to assume that they are dead. Clear out the bin and start again.

Tiny black fruit flies may appear in a worm bin, especially in summer. They are not a health hazard, but can be annoying. Burying waste as you add it may cut down their numbers. Alternatively, they can be caught in a trap; an open jar of orange juice, wine, or vinegar works well, or you can buy lobster-pot-style flytraps. Never use pesticides on a worm compost bin.

Removing the compost

After a few months of regular feeding, the worms will have begun to produce a rich, dark compost in the bottom of the bin. To remove a small amount, scrape back the top layer of uneaten material and worms and take what you need.

If you want to remove larger quantities of compost, first scoop off the top layer of partly decomposed food and worms and set this aside, and then replace this material when you have emptied out the compost.

Extracting the worms

If the compost you dump out of the bin is full of worms, you may want to extract them, or some of them at least, to put back into your worm bin. On a dry, sunny day, spread the compost out on a hard surface, in a layer no more than 2 in (5 cm) deep. Place a layer of wet newspaper, several sheets thick, over one-third to one-half of the compost. Go away and do something else for several hours. The worms will hide under the newspaper and can be shoveled up in the damp compost below. By repeating the process, you can collect nearly all of the worms.

Using worm compost

Worm compost made from vegetable waste is a high-fertility soil improver (*see pp.34–35*), with a fine crumbly texture. It tends to be richer than garden compost, and the plant foods it contains are more readily available. It is rich in humus, and has good water-holding capacity. These qualities, and the fact that it tends to be available in relatively small quantities, mean that it is usually used more like a concentrated fertilizer than a bulky organic compost (see panel, facing page, for some suggestions).

Collecting liquid This worm bin has a spigot at the base to drain off liquid rich in nutrients. Set the bin up on bricks so that you can get a collecting vessel under it.

WORM LIQUID

Vegetable waste has a very high moisture content. Liquid will tend to accumulate in plastic worm bins, and the worms may drown unless adequate drainage is provided. If there is a reservoir at the bottom of the bin, the liquid can be drained off through a spigot. This liquid contains some plant foods, which can be recycled by watering it onto the compost pile. It may also be used to feed container-grown plants (diluted in at least 10 parts by volume of water) but the results are likely to be variable.

Green manures

Green manures are plants that are grown and then dug in to improve the soil, rather than grown for food or ornament. Their beneficial characteristics include nitrogen-fixing, dense foliage for weed suppression, and extensive or penetrative roots, ideal for opening up heavy soil and improving light soil.

Why grow green manures?

■ **To add plant foods** Clovers and related green manures absorb nitrogen, a major plant nutrient, from the air and store it in nodules on their roots. It becomes available to plants when the green manure is dug in and decomposes. Other green manures root down to extract minerals from deep in the soil, bringing them up for subsequent shallow-rooted plants.

■ **To protect soil** Green manures protect soil from compaction by heavy rain, particularly relevant to heavy clay. Green manures also mop up plant foods from the soil, so they are not washed out by rain, but are returned to the soil when the plants' remains decay.

■ **To improve structure** Winter rye, for example, with its very extensive fine root system, improves heavy soil by opening up the structure; in lighter soil, the roots bind with soil particles, helping them hold water.

■ **To smother weeds** Green manures germinate quickly and grow rapidly, smothering weed seedlings on bare ground (*see also* Weeds and Weeding, *p.74*).

■ **To control pests** Frogs, beetles, and other pest predators appreciate the cool, damp cover provided by green manure. Some pests can be confused by the presence of green manure planted between food crops.

■ **To "rest" your soil** To give your soil a break, sow a longer-term green manure and leave it to grow for a whole season. This will help soil recover from constant cultivation and improve fertility and structure with little effort. A green manure cover can look very pleasing.

Choosing a green manure

The specific green manure you choose will depend on what you want to achieve, how long the ground needs to be covered, what was

there before, what you will be planting next, the time of year, and the type of soil you have. At first, the list of possibilities seems long and confusing, but if you apply some simple rules, you can choose the best plant for your situation. These are the questions you need to ask when choosing which green manure to use:

■ How does the green manure fit into my crop rotation? (*See Vegetables, pp.230–233.*)

■ When do I want to sow? Choose hardy varieties to overwinter.

■ How long do I want the green manure to grow? Some mature quicker than others.

■ What am I going to plant next? Winter rye can inhibit seed germination for several weeks after it has been incorporated, so it is best not to grow it before sowing small seeds. On the other hand, a leguminous manure such as clover or winter vetch will fix nitrogen in the soil that will benefit nitrogen-hungry crops such as brassicas, if they are to follow.

■ What variety suits the garden soil best?

Armed with this information, you can choose a suitable green manure. Whichever one you use, the principle is the same—the seeds are sown, the plant grows, and at a certain point it is incorporated back into the soil. Dig the plants into the top 6–8 in (10–15 cm) of soil, chopping them up with a sharp spade as you go.

Digging in green manure Green manure plants need to decompose quickly once incorporated into the soil. Younger plants will rot down more rapidly, so dig them in before growth begins to toughen up, ideally before flower buds appear. If you leave the plants to flower, seed may form and ripen, and drop into the soil to reseed, which may or may not be useful. Tougher green plants can be cut down and left on the surface as a mulch, or added to your compost pile.

When to dig in

Digging in is best done some weeks before you want to use the ground for sowing or planting. Early spring is usually a good time when green manures have been used over winter. Allow anything from a week to a month or more for the foliage to decompose and the soil to settle before using the ground again. The younger the plants and the warmer the soil, the quicker the turnaround can be.

No-dig green manures

If you are using the "no-dig" technique (*see p.216*), you can still grow green manures. Instead of digging in the plants, simply cut them down and leave the foliage on the surface to decompose; you can plant through this layer, treating it exactly as a mulch, or move it to one side to sow seeds. Alternatively, cut, remove, and compost the crop.

(Left to right) **Green manures** Alfalfa; winter rye; clover; phacelia, which if allowed to flower is a magnet for beneficial insects.

Soil improver While there are plenty of alternatives for those who wish to avoid animal products, manures are valuable fertility boosters for the soil.

Animal manures

Animal manures are a traditional source of soil fertility in an organic garden. They are most valuable when they come with some form of bedding material. Once well-rotted or composted, the resulting medium- to high-fertility soil improver provides both bulk, to build soil structure, and nutrients, which are released into the soil as the manure decomposes.

Finding manure

Most organic farmers recycle their manures on the farm. Any other manure is likely to be polluted with residues of veterinary products used to treat the animals. If manure from an organic farm is not available, try to source it from pasture-raised herds or less intensive livestock units. You may find local stables that are eager to give away their manure, but do ask when their horses were last wormed.

Storing manure

Animal manures should be composted or well-rotted before use. This is to stabilize their nutrients, which might otherwise be washed out by the rain, and to avoid any risk of damage to plants. Manures can be added to a compost pile, or if mixed with bedding they can be stacked up as a separate manure pile. If poultry manure, which is very rich, has no bedding material with it, mix it into a compost pile or stack it with lots of straw.

MAKING A MANURE PILE

- Stack the manure where it can remain undisturbed for several months.
- If the bedding is dry, soak it well.
- Step down the material.
- Cover with a waterproof sheet.
- Leave for three months if from an organic source, otherwise six months to allow for any unwanted pollutants to break down. If based on a bedding material of wood shavings rather than straw, at least a year will be needed, and even then the end product is best used only as a mulch.

Buying composted manure

Commercial brands of composted manures are also available. Where possible, choose a product that has a symbol or logo from an organic certifying body. When in doubt, check with the supplier for the source of the raw ingredients. The word "organic" is not sufficient recommendation on its own; this may simply mean that the ingredients are "of living origin," not that they are appropriate for use in an organic garden.

Other manure-based products

Chicken manure pellets, available as a retail product, are a highly concentrated source of nutrients and should be regarded as a fertilizer rather than a manure (see Organic fertilizers, overleaf). Again, check labeling carefully to be sure that the product is suitable for an organically managed garden. Farmyard manure is also used as the basis of some liquid fertilizers, usually with the addition of trace elements.

Using animal manures

Well-rotted manures improve soil structure and water-holding capacity, and supply nitrogen, potassium, and other plant foods. Their nutrient content will vary with the proportion of manure and urine to straw or other bedding, and on whether they have been stored under cover or outdoors in the rain. However, they should be medium- to high-fertility soil improvers. Apply at a rate of one or two wheelbarrow loads (12–24 gal) per 50 sq ft (50–100 liters/5 sq m). When handling any animal-based product, keep cuts covered, wash your hands under running water before handling food, and be sure your tetanus vaccination is up to date.

USING MANURE

Well-rotted manure can be dug into the soil or spread over it as a mulch, especially if it contains plenty of straw. Don't let it touch living plant stems. The main use for manures is in the vegetable garden, on hungry crops such as potatoes, zucchini, pumpkins, squashes, tomatoes, and brassicas. They also make a good topdressing for roses that are pruned hard every year, and for herbaceous plants, applied every two or three years.

Chicken run Manure from the pens of these free-range chickens will be rich in nitrogen, so use it sparingly in the garden.

Organic fertilizers

Organic fertilizers are products of plant, animal, or mineral origin. The nutrients they contain are generally released slowly over a period of time, as the fertilizer is broken down by microorganisms. This slow-release feeding is generally much better for plants than the "quick fix" of chemical fertilizers, avoiding the fast, sappy growth that can cause plants to be more susceptible to insect attack and late spring frost. Some organic fertilizers, such as soybean meal, alfalfa meal, seaweed meal, and compound mixtures, supply a range of plant foods. Others, such as rock phosphate, are more specific. As these products are all of natural origin, they will also tend to contain a range of minor and trace elements as well.

Natural source Seaweed is a rich source of plant nutrients, and is used to make both dry fertilizer products and liquid fertilizers. However abundant it seems, however, you should not gather seaweed from beaches or estuaries for garden use.

It is sensible to follow basic hygiene rules when applying any fertilizer, especially the animal-based products. Always follow the instructions, and do not be tempted to add extra "just for luck." Where specific mineral deficiency symptoms occur in plants, the cause may not be a simple shortage of that mineral. There may be factors preventing the plant from taking up the mineral from the soil (*see also* Plant Health, *pp.86–87*). The solution should be to deal with the cause rather than symptoms, but for short-term relief, more soluble mineral sources can be used. The major ones are Epsom salts (which supplies magnesium), borax (boron), and seaweed with iron. Wood ash is a good natural source of potash (potassium), but as it is very soluble, it is generally best recycled through the compost pile.

Some organic fertilizers

■ **Bonemeal** Promotes strong root growth; use as a base dressing before planting shrubs, fruit, and other perennials.

■ **Plant-based fertilizers** These include comfrey, alfalfa, and soy to feed vegetables.

■ **Soybean meal** High-nitrogen source. Use on annual vegetable beds or as a base dressing in poor soil.

■ **Seaweed meal** Helps build up humus levels in soil. Apply to annual beds, fruit trees and bushes, and lawns.

■ **Rock phosphate** Use to correct a phosphate deficiency: this is a good non-animal alternative to bonemeal.

■ **Organic garden potash (plant source)** Supplies potash, released over one season. Use it to feed fruit and vegetables.

■ **Gypsum** Supplies calcium without altering pH. A gypsum/dolomitic limestone mix (80:20) can be used to help lighten heavy clay soils.

Altering the pH of soil

If you need to raise the pH of your soil—that is, make it more alkaline—use ground limestone (calcium carbonate) or dolomitic limestone (calcium magnesium carbonate). These slow-acting limestones are gentler on the soil than slaked or hydrated lime. They are usually applied in fall, to allow them to act on the soil before the next growing season, but it can take a year for the full effect to develop. The rate used will depend on the pH change required. As a general rule, add 7 oz/sq yd (200 g/sq m) annually until you reach the desired pH. Dolomitic limestone is the preferred choice where magnesium levels tend to be low.

(Right, above) **Applying fertilizers** When applying fertilizers around individual plants, wear gloves and wash your hands after application, especially when handling products of animal origin.

(Right, below) **Adding limestone** If adding limestone to a vegetable garden to raise the pH—for example, to suit brassicas—wear gloves and also a face mask to avoid inhaling it; never scatter limestone on a windy day when it might be blown around.

3. Water and Watering

Every living thing needs water—without it, life cannot exist. Plants need water so that the vital processes of photosynthesis, respiration, and absorption of nutrients can occur. In other words, they need water to grow, flower, and fruit. Being an organic gardener means being aware of the resources used in the garden, and the wider implications of their use—and this includes water. Rainwater can be collected from house, garage, and greenhouse roofs to use in place of tap water, which may have been through intensive purification processes. Organic methods of soil care and management, careful plant choice, and correct timing and appropriate delivery of water all help minimize use of this valuable resource.

Building up reserves Good management helps soil absorb precious moisture when rainfall is plentiful, and retain it for use by plants.

How to use less water

There is a whole range of techniques that can be employed in every area of the garden to reduce the need for watering, and a wide choice of drought-loving plants that will positively thrive in sunny spots in well-drained soil.

■ Choose plants that suit the soil and climate. Where water is scarce, attractive ornamental plantings can be made using succulents and drought-resistant perennials, grasses, and shrubs (*see also overleaf*). Plants that cope well with water shortages often have gray leaves, which may also be covered in hairs, or felted, like stachys. Plants adapted to coastal conditions often have tiny or needlelike leaves, to cope with strong drying winds. Alternatively, leaves may be fleshy and succulent, with tough skins, allowing them to store water.

■ Increase the soil's water-holding capacity or, in the case of heavy clay, increase the availability of the water to your plants by incorporating bulky organic soil improvers (*see pp.34–35*).

■ Dig, where appropriate, to break up compacted ground, to encourage extensive plant rooting.

■ Do not dig soil in dry weather, as this increases the rate at which it dries out.

The arid approach Desert gardens demand good water conservation and careful plant choice—strategies useful to all organic gardeners.

■ Mulch the soil surface (*see pp.72–73*) with low-fertility soil improvers such as leaf mold, bark chips, or other bulky material to help cut moisture loss and reduce weed growth. Applied as a mulch, these materials will improve the structure of the soil at the surface, allowing rain to be absorbed more effectively and reducing runoff and puddle formation. Make sure the soil is moist before applying a mulch. You want the mulch to keep moisture in, rather than out. If the ground is dry, water thoroughly before laying down the mulch.

■ In dry climates, a mulch of rocks and gravel will often trap and condense moisture and direct it to the soil surface.

■ Remove weeds; they will compete with your plants for scarce water supplies.

■ When planting a tree or shrub in grass, keep a 3-ft (1-m) square around it grass-free (preferably mulched) for at least two years.

■ Shelter plants from drying winds by building, or growing, windbreaks to protect them.

■ When making new lawns, sow drought-tolerant grass types. Allow grass to grow longer—up to 3 in (8 cm)—in dry weather. Grass that is not mown too frequently develops deeper roots and is more drought-resistant.

■ Use drip- and soaker-hose irrigation systems (*see pp.64–65*) rather than overhead sprinklers.

■ Shade seedlings and very young plants in hot weather.

Lateral thinking Let the grass grow in summer—it will look better for longer in dry weather. Think of lawn weeds as wildflowers: you might be tempted to develop the meadow look (*see p.124*).

FACTORS THAT INCREASE WATER LOSS FROM PLANTS

■ Sunshine: bright sun causes more water loss than cloudy days.

■ Temperature: the hotter plants are, the more water they lose.

■ Humidity (lack of): plants lose water more quickly when the air is dry.

■ Wind: this increases the rate of water loss from leaves.

Drought-resistant trees and shrubs

1 Broom (*Cytisus*)
Small to medium-sized, floriferous shrubs with wiry stems and tiny leaves. Pineapple broom (*Cytisus battandieri*) is much larger, with a distinctive scent.

2 Sweet chestnut
Castanea sativa prefers sandy, slightly acidic soil and makes a handsome tree. May not bear nuts in cold areas.

3 Tamarisk
Trees and shrubs that are very resistant to strong winds in mild coastal regions. Different species flower in spring and in late summer/early fall.

4 Rock rose (*Cistus*)
Mediterranean evergreen shrubs that flower all summer long. Some are low-growing and spreading, ideal for raised beds; others are more upright.

5 Caryopteris
Small, late-flowering, mound-forming shrub with blue flowers; responds well to being cut back hard each year.

6 Lavender
A classic choice for the edge of paths and beds. Intensely fragrant, with narrow gray leaves. These crested types are known as French lavender.

7 Eucalyptus
Can be grown as trees but in most yards are best pruned hard to make larger-leaved, more manageable shrubs.

8 Cotton lavender (*Santolina*)
Low-growing shrub; another good edging choice. Flowers vary from primrose yellow to bright gold.

Drought-resistant perennials

1 Red-hot pokers (*Kniphofia*)
Robust, clump-forming plants with narrow, straplike leaves, some evergreen. All are attractive to bees.

2 Spurges (*Euphorbia*)
A huge choice of heights and sizes, all with striking flowerheads in green to lime, yellow, and orange.

3 Eryngiums
Spiky, sturdy plants that, because of their finely cut silvery leaves, have a graceful, elegant look. The steely flowerheads are very long-lasting.

4 Sedums
The taller perennials, like 'Ruby Glow', 'Herbstfreude' and 'Brilliant', bring attractive warm pink tones to a fall border, the flowerheads fading to brown but persisting into winter.

5 Mulleins (*Verbascum*)
Tall spikes of flowers above rosettes of usually grayish, hairy or woolly leaves. In the wild, most grow on dry, stony hillsides or in open grassland.

6 Lambs' ears (*Stachys*)
Most species form spreading carpets of gray or silver woolly leaves. They thrive in a gravel garden.

7 Pinks (*Dianthus*)
Lovely, cottagey flowers, good for cutting, often with a spicy fragrance. If deadheaded regularly they should keep flowering all summer.

8 Agapanthus
Vigorous plants hailing from Africa that look especially good grown in large containers against a plain background.

Using water well

A plant's requirement for water varies with the stage it is at in its life cycle. Seedlings, which have a small root system, are very susceptible to water shortage, and may never recover if they dry out. Newly planted trees and shrubs will need additional watering in dry conditions for a year or two, but once they are established, most will survive unaided.

When to water

Some plants have a critical period when water is essential if they are to perform to your requirements. Peas and beans, for example, need a good water supply to encourage flowering and seed set, but not until the flowers start to form. A camellia may drop all its flower buds in the spring if it was short of water in the previous early fall. Critical times for watering various crops are given in the panel on the opposite page. The least thirsty vegetable crops to grow, once established, are: beets, sprouting broccoli, Brussels sprouts, winter cabbage, spring cabbage, carrots, leeks, winter cauliflower, onions, parsnips, radishes, rutabagas, and turnips.

Plant type can determine water requirements. Drought-resistant plants, adapted to surviving extremely dry conditions, positively thrive where water is short, and may fail if the soil is too wet. The location of the plant also has a bearing on its watering requirements. Plants in containers, for example, rely on you, the gardener, for their supply. Plants in "rain-shadow" locations—such as next to a house, wall or fence, where the soil is sheltered and thus receives less rain—are more likely to be short of water.

PLANTS IN CONTAINERS

Plants in pots, tubs, seed trays, baskets, and other containers need careful watering. They should never dry out completely, but neither should the growing medium be waterlogged. Supply water as it is needed rather than sticking to a routine. In hot dry weather, when plants are growing vigorously, a hanging basket or a tomato plant in a large pot, for example, may need to be watered twice a day. Always make sure that you are directing the water onto the soil (as left), not on the leafy top growth, or it will run off.

If a pot has dried out, water may simply run through the potting mix without wetting it. Where possible, set the pot in a container of water, leaving it until the surface of the soil is moist. Remove and allow to drain well. A very dry pot may need total immersion (see also p.194).

CRITICAL TIMES FOR WATERING CROPS

When the weather is dry, all seedlings and young plants of vegetable crops need regular watering. Thereafter, once they are established, the really important times to water certain crops—only, of course, in dry conditions—are:

While flowering

- Peas and all types of beans
- Potatoes
- Sweet corn

While fruiting

- Peas and beans
- Sweet corn, as cobs swell
- Tomatoes
- Zucchini

All the time

- Leafy vegetables, such as lettuce and spinach
- Summer cabbage

What time of day?

The most effective times to water are early morning and evening, when the air and soil are cool, and less water will be lost by evaporation. You also avoid scorching the foliage—when strong sun is magnified through water droplets on the leaves. Avoid watering slug-susceptible plants in the evening, though; watering leaves a film of moisture on plants and soil, creating ideal conditions for slugs and snails.

How much water?

It is not easy to advise on how much water you should apply, and how often, as this depends on the plants you are growing, the temperature, and a host of other factors. The golden rule is to give plants an occasional thorough soaking rather than watering little and often. During dry weather 2 gallons/sq yd (10 liters/sq m) on row crops should be sufficient to moisten the root zone successfully. Once you have watered a plant or a bed, check the soil to make sure that the water has penetrated down to the roots. A wet soil surface may hide dry soil beneath. Water again if necessary.

Watering vegetables

Vegetables respond to watering in different ways, depending on the crop, and its growth stage. Water encourages vegetative (leaf and shoot) growth, which is useful for leafy crops, but can delay cropping of peas, beans, and tomatoes, and may reduce flavor. More leafy growth does not necessarily mean higher yields of root crops. Where time, and water, is short, water only those plants that will benefit, at the key stages that will give maximum response (see p.63).

Methods of applying water

You can deliver water to plants in many ways, ranging from the most basic to very high-tech. It depends on your budget, the time you have available, and how much water you have. Water is best directed to the plant's roots, avoiding soaking the leaves, flowers, and stems, where it may encourage disease. Sprinklers are one of the least efficient ways of watering and should be avoided where possible, as much of the water is blown away or evaporates before it reaches the soil. In dry climates, where watering may be an essential and often daily task, it makes good sense to avoid surface evaporation by directing the water below ground level to the plant roots using seep irrigation (see Irrigation systems, opposite).

Watering by hand

Water can simply be applied with a watering-can or hose. This has the advantage of allowing you to give individual plants water when they need it, and in the correct quantity. The disadvantage is that it can take up a lot of time, and you also need to arrange cover if you are to be away. Hoses with a trigger-operated mechanism reduce the water wasted as you move between plants. Water delicate seedlings with a fine spray to avoid damaging them. If they are in a seed tray or pot, stand it in a tray of water until the soil is moist, rather than watering from above.

You can increase the efficiency of watering by hand by directing the water below ground to where the roots are. This reduces evaporation and keeps the surface dry, which helps to prevent weed growth. Traditionally, an unglazed pot is buried next to a plant, into which water is poured. This seeps out gradually. Other possibilities include a large funnel, or an inverted plastic soda bottle with the base cut off, and the cap loosely secured so that water can escape. For trees and shrubs, a piece of perforated drainage pipe with one end at root level and the other at the surface works well.

Irrigation systems

Gravity-fed irrigation channels are found in many parts of the world. The same principles can be adapted to garden-scale operations if you have a suitable water source and sloping site. However, drip- or soaker-hose irrigation is usually more practical. Water passes along porous pipes, soaking into the surrounding soil through small holes. If the pipes are buried below the surface, or under a loose mulch or weedproof

MAKING BEST USE OF WATER

- Give priority to seedlings, transplants and newly planted specimens.
- Water in the early morning.
- Apply water directly to soil, not plants.
- Soak ground well; do not just wet the surface.
- Water at critical growth stages.
- Do not water plants that do not need it.
- Use a soaker hose rather than a sprinkler.
- Use a timer to control supply.
- Do not water lawns.

membrane (*see* Weeds and Weeding, *pp.74–75*), evaporation is reduced to almost nothing, ensuring that the plants get all the water. The water supply is turned on only for as long as is necessary to water the plants, then switched off—or an automatic timer can be installed.

For more widely spaced plants, trickle irrigation, where individual drippers are fitted at specified locations along a pipe, is more appropriate. This sort of system can also be used for a series of hanging baskets or planters.

A basic system that can be used in a greenhouse—or for houseplants, when you go on vacation—is to sit the pots on capillary matting, which is then draped into a reservoir of water at one end. Water is drawn along the mat by capillary action to the soil in the pots; in effect, the plants take what they need.

Methods of watering Porous drip hose or soaker hose, laid between plants (*far left*) or just below the soil, is one of the most valuable modern contributions to water conservation. Clay pots sunk between lettuces (*center left*) have been given lids to reduce evaporation; this is a traditional method known as "pitcher irrigation." Always direct water at the soil around the plant, either with a hose or spray (*near left*), or by filling reservoirs sunk into the soil, such as porous clay pots, open lengths of pipe, or plastic bottles upended with the lids loosened.

Which water to use?

Rain is a free source of clean water, but even if collected and stored, it may be inadequate in our changing climate. If supplementary irrigation is required, remember that there is little need to use drinking-quality water on the garden.

City water or well water

Tap water is undoubtedly convenient: it is clean, usually available whenever you want it, and supplied at high pressure. The provision of this service, however, may come at an unnecessary cost—both financial and environmental. The chlorine in tap water may harm your soil's microbe population and damage sensitive plants. Tap water may also have a high pH (see pp.30–31), making it unsuitable for use on lime-hating plants.

Rainwater

Rainwater is generally of good quality, free from contaminants, and relatively low-pH, making it suitable for use on all types of plants. Surprisingly large volumes can easily be harvested from roofs via gutter downspouts and stored in rain barrels, tanks, and ponds. To work out how much water you are likely to be able to collect, you need to know your roof's surface area and the average rainfall in your region. By multiplying these, you can calculate the likely volume of water your roof will yield. Bear in mind that there will be some inefficiencies; a figure of about 75 percent of the total is realistic.

   Store as great a volume as you can. The supply from a single rain barrel will not last long in dry weather, so set up as many as

Water storage Plastic rain barrels are relatively cheap and come in many sizes; some are made from recycled plastic, which is a bonus. Wooden barrels are undoubtedly more attractive, but they do tend to leak if not kept completely full.

possible. They can be linked so several barrels can be filled from one downspout. Containers with tight-fitting, light-excluding covers are preferable, to reduce evaporation, discourage mosquitoes, stop leaves and other detritus from accumulating, prevent algae from growing, and keep children and wildlife out. If your tank or barrel is sited uphill from the garden, you may be able to let gravity do the work of moving the water, using a hose attached to the spigot. If not, use a watering can or small pump.

Gray water

"Gray water" is the term used for domestic waste water, excluding sewage. As the volumes produced are quite large, gray water can be valuable as long as it is handled correctly, and it is not too contaminated with soaps, detergents, and grease. Waste water from dishwashers is unsuitable; the detergents they use can harm plants. Water from the tub or shower (avoid bubble bath, oils, and perfumed gels and soaps

if you can), or that used for washing vegetables is most suitable. It can simply be transported in a dishpan or siphoned from the bathtub, or—if permitted in your state—you can have a gray water recycling system installed in your house.

Gray water, with the exception of that which has simply been used to wash vegetables, should not be used on plants for eating. Nor is it suitable for use on acid-loving plants. Rotate gray water applications around the garden to avoid a potential buildup of harmful substances in the soil in any one spot.

Bath or shower water is likely to contain bacteria, some of which could be potentially harmful to health, so this gray water should be used immediately. Gray water filtering systems, which overcome this difficulty, are already available for domestic installation in some countries, and are currently the focus of much research and development: it is hoped that, in the not-too-distant future, every new home will incorporate such technology.

The gray way Waste water can be diverted from a sink or bathtub before it disappears into the sewer or septic tank. It should not be stored like rainwater because harmful bacteria could grow in it. Most states restrict the use of gray water, so seek advice before altering your plumbing.

Using gray water Every day we all send gallons of water down the drain instead of reusing it. Clean gray water that does not contain oils, soaps, or detergents can even be used to water crop plants. Pour it onto the soil rather than splashing it over the leaves, or much will be lost through evaporation.

4. Weeds and Weeding

Whether a plant is a weed or not depends on the identity of the particular plant, where it is growing, and the effect it may have on the plants around it. Simply put, a weed is an invasive plant, growing where you do not want it. The aim in an organic garden is not to eradicate every weed, but to keep them at an acceptable level appropriate to the situation. Plants we call weeds can also make a positive contribution to a garden—in which case they are no longer weeds!

Heave hoe A hoe is a useful tool, cutting through the weeds at or just below soil level.

Know your weeds

A weed can be an annual, a biennial, an herbaceous or shrubby perennial, or even a tree species. This chapter introduces you to the way weeds work—how and why they are so efficient—and the range of organic methods you can employ to clear weeds and keep them under control. It is useful to be able to identify common garden weeds, especially perennials (*see pp.80–81*). Knowing how they reproduce, spread, and survive adverse conditions can help you to develop an effective control strategy.

WEEDS—THE GOOD SIDE

Weeds do have some positive attributes. They may:

- Look attractive;

- Be edible;

- Attract insects that in turn are food for birds and bats;

- Provide food for seed-eating birds and other creatures;

- Offer vital habitats for caterpillars of certain species of butterflies and moths;

- Support beneficial insects that will also eat garden pests;

- Feed honey bees, bumble bees, and butterflies and other endangered wildlife;

- Enrich your compost pile by bringing up minerals from deep in the soil.

How weeds work

Weeds use a variety of techniques to achieve their aim: survival and invasion.

- **Annuals and biennials** Annual weeds grow, set seed, and die in the space of a year. Some may produce several generations in one year—some, like chickweed, even reproducing through mild winters. Seed is their mechanism for spread and survival. Some weeds can even produce seed after they have been hoed off while in flower. Annual weeds are most common in regularly disturbed ground such as vegetable gardens and annual borders.

Biennials flower in their second year and spread by seed. They are more common in perennial and shrub beds and plantings, where ground is not disturbed every year.

- **Perennial survival** Perennial weeds make use of a range of mechanisms for their long-term survival and spread. This can include both seed and vegetative means such as runners, stolons, rhizomes and long, deep taproots.

Effective organic weed control

- Know your weeds. Recognizing a weed, and knowing how it survives and reproduces, helps in choosing the most effective method of dealing with it.
- Design out problem areas; design in effective weed prevention.

HOW WEEDS SPREAD

1 **Seeds** Often produced in huge quantities, seeds are spread by wind, water, animals, and mechanical propulsion, when the pods pop open.

2 **Runners and stolons** Runners are creeping stems that grow along the ground. Buds along them produce plantlets, which root quickly. Stolons are stems that arch over and produce roots at the tip, even before touching the soil.

3 **Roots and rhizomes** Tough, fleshy taproots can regrow after cutting or dying back. Even chopped-up pieces of taproot may regrow, as can small chopped or broken-up sections of the rootlike, underground creeping stems known as rhizomes.

4 **Bulbs and bulbils** Fleshy storage organs that break off easily when the plant is dug up or pulled out. Each will readily produce a new plant. Cultivation simply spreads them.

■ Take time to clear perennial weeds effectively before any permanent planting—even if this could take a year or more.

■ Choose methods to suit the time and energy you have available.

■ When clearing ground, be realistic. Do not clear more than you are able to keep weed-free.

■ Never leave soil bare: plant it, cover it, or sow a green manure (*see pp.50–51*).

■ Mulches (*see overleaf*) can both prevent and eradicate weeds—for little effort.

Invasive ornamental plants

Some of our current most problematic weeds were originally introduced into gardens for their appearance and abundant growth.

Japanese knotweed, for example, was introduced into British gardens in 1825, as "a plant of sterling merit." It is now Britain's most troublesome weed, and a serious problem in parts of North America, too.

We can still, unwittingly, plant potential weeds today, because they are widely offered for sale as garden plants. Russian vine (*Fallopia baldschuanica*), for example, is a useful fast-growing creeper that can cover an ugly fence or garden shed in a few months; but in a few years it can overwhelm a full-sized tree. Yellow archangel (*Lamium galeobdelon*) and periwinkle (*Vinca major*) give quick ground cover, but can soon take over the whole border.

Using mulches to control weeds

Mulching is a key technique in organic soil management, but it is also an incredibly useful way of suppressing weeds. A thick covering of a loose mulch will prevent weed seeds in the soil from germinating. A mulch membrane—such as cardboard or permeable plastic—laid over the soil will prevent weed growth.

Loose mulches

On weed-free ground, a loose mulch, 4 in (10 cm) deep, will provide effective weed control. Any weeds that may appear are easily removed. An organic, biodegradable material is the preferred organic option: as a bonus, this sort of mulch will attract beetles, centipedes, and other pest-eating creatures that enjoy the dark, moist conditions.

Biodegradable mulch materials

■ Composted bark products make an attractive, dark-colored mulch. Use on perennial beds only.

■ Wood chips: forest waste, or chipped scrap wood, composted before sale. Lower cost than bark. Best not used on young plants. For perennial beds only.

■ Coarse-grade municipal compost (recycled green waste), which is quicker to degrade than bark or wood chips. For perennial beds only.

■ Shredded prunings, either home-produced or from a tree care company. Compost for a few months before use, on perennial beds only, or use fresh on paths.

■ Straw and hay give an informal appearance, and should last for a season. Use a layer 6 in (15 cm) thick. Hay will feed plants as it decays, but may produce its own crop of seedling weeds. May be used on annual or perennial beds.

■ Leaf mold (see pp.44–45) is a homemade, short-term mulch. Best used over a membrane. For annual or perennial beds.

Other loose mulches

■ Gravel and slate waste are good around plants that like dry, hot conditions. A mulch membrane beneath the gravel will stop them from working down into the soil and hence make these decorative mulches last longer.

■ For something different, glass chips, made from recycled glass, are available in a range of colors. They have no sharp edges. Only for use over a mulch membrane.

■ Cocoa shells are a waste product of the chocolate industry. Apply in a layer at least 2 in (5 cm) deep.

Applying a loose mulch

Wait until the soil has warmed up, and is well soaked. Clear the ground of weeds, and add any soil improvers or fertilizers required. Level the ground. Apply the mulch within a few days of clearing weeds. Apply a thick layer of mulch that will settle to the required depth; to be effective, at least 4 in (10 cm) deep. Do not mulch right up to plants; leave a small circle around the stems or trunk. A retaining edge may be needed to keep mulch from migrating to surrounding areas. Keep the mulch topped off as necessary.

(Clockwise from top left) **Biodegradable mulches**
An ornamental bark mulch, good around shrubs and at the base of hedges; lawn clippings used as a mulch in the vegetable plot, here spread over layers of newspaper (see also overleaf); one-year-old leaf mold; well-rotted straw.

CHOICES FOR LIVING MULCHES

Effective ground-cover plants are tough, rapidly spreading ornamentals (for example, thyme, *top*) that will compete successfully with weeds for food, water, and light. Low-maintenance, ground-cover shrubs (*see also p.163*) are particularly useful in areas where access is difficult. Green manures (*see pp.50–51*), such as buckwheat, winter rye, and phacelia, make good weed-preventing living mulches. Grow them where ground is to be left bare for a few months or more—over the winter months, for example, or when you have prepared a plot but are not yet ready to plant it. They can also be sown between widely spaced shrubs. Vigorous, fast-growing annual flowers such as *Limnanthes douglasii* and candytuft can be used in the same way. Trefoil, a low-growing green manure that tolerates some shade, can be grown between rows of corn (*above*). Broadcast-sow the trefoil when the corn is around 6 in (15 cm) high. When the corn is cut down at the end of the season, the trefoil can be left to protect the ground over winter.

Living mulches

A dense covering of low-growing plants can effectively smother weed growth—becoming, in effect, a "living mulch." A permanent planting of ground-cover shrubs, for example, will keep an area weed-free, once they have covered the ground. A dense sowing of hardy annuals, or green manures (also known as smother crops), gives a quicker, shorter-term effect.

Mulch membranes

A mulch membrane, weed barrier, or weed control fabric is simply a sheet of synthetic or biodegradable material that forms a physical and light-excluding barrier to weed growth. Membranes can be used to clear annual and perennial weeds from open ground and beds. They are also used to prevent weeds from growing on ground that has been cleared. Holes can be cut to allow planting through the membrane as appropriate. Membranes may be covered with a loose mulch, to hold them in place, extend their life span, and improve their appearance. A mulch membrane must be permeable, to allow air and water into the soil, unless it is only to be kept in place for a few months. However, to suppress the more vigorous perennial weeds (*see also pp.80–81*), the membrane may need to be in place for several years; while there are several biodegradable choices of membrane material, a nonbiodegradable material is the more practical option in such situations.

Biodegradable membrane materials

■ Newspaper is a no-cost option for a single season: for example, for vegetable beds and new plantings of perennials. Lay overlapping opened-out newspapers, at least 8 sheets thick, around and between existing plants. Top with grass mowings or leaf mold to keep in place.

■ Cardboard is another free option for a single

season. Lay on soil, overlapping well to prevent weeds from growing through. Keep in place with straw or hay. Vigorous plants such as pumpkins can be planted through the cardboard.
■ Paper mulch is a sturdy paper sold in a roll, for use on annual vegetable beds.
■ Starch-based biodegradable mulching "films."

Nonbiodegradable materials
■ Synthetic spun fabrics: these materials may also be sold as "landscape fabrics" or occasionally "geotextiles," for long-term weed control. They allow water to permeate through them into the soil, but can degrade where exposed to the sun, so cover with a loose mulch to protect them from the light.
■ Woven plastic provides medium-term weed control and allows water to penetrate. Cover with loose mulch to extend life.
■ Black polythene sheeting (400–600 gauge) is suitable only as a ground-clearing mulch (*see also p.79*). Do not cover ground for more than a few months without removing the polythene to allow air and water into the soil. Hold in place by burying the edges in the ground or weighting with heavy items such as wooden planks, bricks, or car tires.

Planting through a mulch membrane
Clear the ground, or cut down existing vegetation. Add any soil improvers required, bearing in mind the life span of the mulch, and if necessary, level the ground. Spread the membrane over the soil. Depending on the material chosen, spade the edges 10–12 in (25–30 cm) into the soil, pin it down with wire staples, or hold the edges down with heavy planks or bricks. Set the plants out in their proposed positions. With a sharp knife, cut crosses in the membrane where each plant is to go. Plant your plants, and water them in. Top the membrane, if necessary or desired, with 2 in (5 cm) of loose mulch. Perennial weeds may grow up around the planting cut. Cut them off with a knife or scissors to weaken their growth.

Mulch membranes Cardboard (*below, left*) used as a mulch membrane around nonornamental plants; synthetic landscape fabric (*right*) controlling weeds in a strawberry patch.

Weeding

Preventive measures can never be rigorous enough to eliminate the need for some weeding. Hoeing and hand-weeding can be a relaxing and satisfying occupation. The key is to do the weeding when the weeds are small, which means weeding regularly. Only when you put it off does it become a chore. Hand-clearing neglected ground can be a long job, but here again, knowing your weeds will help: overleaf and on pp.80–81 are some tried and tested strategies that can be used to beat some of the most persistent perennial weeds.

(Above) **Easing out grass** Clumps of grass develop a dense, fibrous root mass that resists the hoe, and the width of the clump can make it difficult to get hold of it and pull it out, especially when the roots have crept under slabs. Loosen the entire rootball with a fork, then ease it out and shake.

(Left) **Hand-weeding** If you hand-weed regularly, and the soil is moist, you can develop a quick "nipping" action that makes weeding almost pleasurable. Weeds that have only gained a superficial foothold in a loose mulch are particularly satisfying to remove.

Hand-weeding

Hand-weeding is the only really selective organic method of weed control, allowing you to remove nuisance weeds and retain self-sown ornamentals and other "weeds" that you would like to keep. Use a hand fork or weeding hoe to loosen weeds when necessary; even annual weeds can regrow if the top breaks off as you are trying to pull the whole plant out. Hand-weeding is easiest after a good rainstorm, and on uncompacted soil, in beds that are never walked on and those that are well mulched.

Paths and patios can also be hand-weeded. There are tools specially designed to help pry weeds from cracks between paving slabs.

Hoeing

Hoes come in many shapes and sizes, suitable for large or restricted areas, and for use standing up or kneeling. Once you have learned the art, hoeing can be a quick and effective method of keeping ground, and gravel paths, weed-free. Hoeing works best against seedling weeds (annual and perennial), but it can also be quite effective in removing the tops of perennial weeds, though regular hoeing over a period of years will be needed to kill them completely.

Thermal weeding

Thermal weeders kill weeds with a short blast of heat—no more than a few seconds. The plants do not burn, they simply wilt and die. The heat may be applied as a flame, hot air, steam, infrared radiation from a heated grid, or a combination of these. Their main use in the organic garden is on hard surfaces—paths, driveways, and patios. Seedling weeds are easily killed with a single pass. More established annuals and biennials may need anything from three to six treatments. Perennial weeds will be gradually weakened, and may eventually die. Thermal weeding should also kill weed seeds on the ground.

TIPS FOR EFFECTIVE HOEING

■ Choose a hoe that you find easy to use, with a handle of the correct length. The type you push away from you is a Dutch hoe (*below*); a draw hoe is the kind you pull toward you. There are also hoes that work in both directions.

■ Invest in a sharpening stone to keep the blade sharp; it makes a remarkable difference.

■ Hoe regularly, when weeds are small.

■ Hoe on a dry day. Gather up the weeds if rain is forecast.

■ When sowing and planting vegetables, remember to leave sufficient space between rows to allow for easy hoeing, unless you are growing in beds using close spacing to smother weeds.

Clearing weed-infested ground

Weeds rapidly colonize bare, neglected ground. At first there will probably be a mixture of annual and perennial weeds, but if the neglect continues, perennials will soon dominate. However daunting the task may look, an overgrown garden or lawn can be cleared without using herbicides, using one, or a combination, of the methods below.

Cutting down

Simply cutting down the topgrowth of weeds can be a quick short-term solution to a weed problem, preventing seeding and spreading. Repeated cutting over years can, eventually, clear even persistent perennial weeds.

The most effective time to cut, to weaken the roots of perennials and avoid seeding, is when flower buds are just beginning to show. Scything is a quiet, pollution-free option, though it does require practice and the scythe blade must be kept sharp. The alternative is an electric- or gas-powered line trimmer; or, on level ground, a lawnmower.

Digging or forking over

Forking the ground over, removing weeds and roots, is a relatively quick, but physically challenging, way to clear ground of many perennials. Breaking up the ground first with a spade or a digging hoe will ease the work, as will covering the ground with a mulch membrane for a few weeks or more before starting. This method is good for weeds with tap roots such as dandelions and docks, and can be effective against couch grass and ground elder if you are diligent.

Never strip off the top layer of soil together with the weed roots. You will be removing the most fertile soil from the area.

Mechanical cultivation

A mechanical cultivator (rototiller) can be useful when clearing a large area of ground, but it does have its drawbacks. Using a cultivator can be hard work if the ground is thick with perennial weeds and grasses. If perennial weeds are present, they will be chopped up into many pieces; each portion of root or rhizome may regrow, potentially multiplying the problem. Rototillers are best used in late spring or early summer when the soil is dry and weeds are growing well. Leave the ground until it is "greening up" with weed

Forking out For weeds such as Canada thistle, loosen the soil all around the root area in order to pull out the entire root run.

KNOW YOUR ROOTS

1 Some weeds, particularly annuals such as groundsel, bittercress, and chickweed, have shallow, fibrous roots that are easily removed.

2 Weeds with a network of spreading, creeping roots such as creeping thistle, bindweed, and quackgrass need to have the soil around their roots well loosened so that every piece of root can be removed.

3 The long taproots of weeds such as dandelion and dock must be dug out to prevent regrowth. Dandelion in particular can regrow from even the deepest portion of its root. Fortunately, weeds like these with a single main taproot tend not to spread by underground means, but by seed, so provided that you are vigilant in not allowing them to go to seed, then digging them out in their entirety should prevent any offspring from appearing.

regrowth, then cultivate again. Repeat as necessary. If you can only cultivate once, it may be possible to hoe off the regrowth, otherwise choose another method. It is much more difficult and time-consuming to dig out hundreds of chopped-up pieces of root than it is whole plants. Lightweight mechanical cultivators can be used for weed control between row crops.

Clearing ground without digging

A light-excluding mulch membrane will stop weeds from growing, and will, in time, kill them. If you want to convert an area of lawn into a vegetable or flower bed, mulch it in the spring and it will be clear by the fall, if not before. Persistent perennials may take a couple of years or more to die. Vigorous annual plants, such as squashes and sunflowers, can be planted through the mulch, though perennial weeds may grow up through the holes cut for the plants; pulling out as much as you can of these opportunists should eventually weaken them to the point of dying. Mulching is most effective during the season when weeds are actively growing.

Grassing down

Where there is a severe perennial weed problem such as ground elder or horsetail, put the ground in grass, by either sowing seed or laying sod. Regular mowing for two or three years should solve the problem. A rather extreme measure, perhaps, but worth it in the long run.

Strategies for perennial weeds

1 Broadleaf plantain
Do not allow to go to seed. Dig out carefully: leaf rosettes have deep taproots. Alternatively, cover with a mulch membrane for several years.

2 Bishop's weed
Small patches: dig out, removing every piece of white root. Larger areas: try persistent, regular hoeing, or a mulch membrane for 2–3 years. Alternatively, grass down and mow for a few years.

3 Dock
Hoe off seedlings; dig out big docks, removing at least the first 6 in (15 cm) of the root. Do not allow to go to seed.

4 Field bindweed
Small patches: dig out, removing every piece of stem and root. Larger areas: try persistent, regular hoeing, or a mulch membrane for 2–3 years.

5 Common yellow wood sorrel
Grows from a taproot and seeds prolifically. Pull, hoe, mow, or cut before plants go to seed. Or cover plants with a mulch membrane for a full growing season.

6 Blackberry
Dig out young plants as soon as seen. Cut established plants to the ground regularly; dig out if practical.

7 Hedge bindweed
Small patches: dig out, removing every piece of stem and root. Larger areas: try persistent, regular hoeing, or a mulch membrane for 2–3 years.

8 Horsetail
Hoe persistently, or cover with a mulch membrane for several years. Vigorous ground-cover plants may succeed in smothering it. Or, grass down and mow for several years.

9 Creeping buttercup
Hoe off when small: established plants are hard to remove by hand. Dig them out, or use a mulch membrane for 1–2 years.

10 Ground ivy
Dig or pull out, being careful to remove as much of the plant as possible. For larger areas, cover with a mulch membrane.

11 Poison ivy
Be extremely cautious when tackling poison ivy. Always wear rubber gloves (goggles are also recommended) when pulling, cutting, or hoeing seedlings, and never burn cuttings—they can release irritating fumes. For larger patches, cover for two years with a mulch membrane.

12 Canada thistle
Hoe off young plants. Use a mulch membrane; alternatively, let the plants grow large, but cut them down before they flower. Repeat. Dig the ground, and sow a vigorous green manure such as vetch or crimson clover: it may succeed in smothering out the thistle.

13 Couch grass
Cultivate the soil, removing every piece of the tough white rhizomes. Hoeing in late summer can weaken it. Or use a mulch membrane for 2–3 years.

14 Dandelion
Pull off flowers as soon as seen: never let them go to seed. Dig out the whole taproot of individual plants; use a mulch membrane on large patches.

15 Perennial sow-thistle
Pull off flowers as soon as seen: never let them go to seed. Try persistent hoeing or a mulch membrane, or the "smothering" technique described above for Canada thistle (12).

16 Stinging nettle
Fork out, or undercut with a spade—or cover with a mulch membrane for several years. Do not allow to flower and go to seed.

5. Plant Health

It is only recent generations that have come to rely on artificial chemical inputs for pest and disease control, and in doing so many gardeners have forgotten that it is possible to produce good food and maintain beautiful gardens without their use. In this chapter the nature of plant pests and diseases will be described, along with the range of methods, ancient and modern, that organic gardeners use to maintain a healthy garden and keep problems at acceptable levels.

Striking sight Wildlife brings a beauty of its own into the garden, and gardeners should think twice before automatically seeking to banish creatures like this striking monarch butterfly caterpillar. Diversity is crucial to achieving a natural balance between pests and predators.

A natural balance

Natural environments, or ecosystems, are made up of a huge diversity of plant and animal species—often too small to be seen by the naked eye—and this is the key to success. It is the activities and the interrelationships of all these living things that keep our planet going. Organic methods aim to make the garden environment, both above and below ground, as diverse as possible, so that nature can get on with its work. Ladybugs and other natural predators will keep most pests under control if conditions are right for them. Soil managed organically is more able to maintain its own health and promote healthy plant growth. Although a garden can never be a totally natural ecosystem, sensitive design, planting, and management can encourage diversity, and with it, a lush, healthy garden.

WHAT CAN GO WRONG?

Most plants in a well-kept garden, or in any natural ecosystem, are healthy for most of the time. Like animals, they have well-ordered defense mechanisms against invaders and only occasionally submit to ill health. When plant health problems arise, they can be caused by:

■ Environmental factors, such as water shortage.

■ Mineral deficiencies, such as magnesium deficiency.

■ Pests, which are animals that may eat any part of a plant.

■ Disease, caused by fungi, bacteria, or viruses.

(Clockwise from top left) **Plant problems** Pea plants stressed by drought and heat; leaf yellowing between the veins, a common symptom of mineral deficiency; red currant bush with most of its leaves stripped to skeletons by the pest gooseberry sawfly; the fungal disease potato blight.

Working with the system

Organic gardeners seek to work with nature to limit damage from pests and plant disease, rather than to control nature using artificial inputs. The dream of the organic gardener is sustainable gardening. It is a different dream from the utopia of a pest- and disease-free garden promoted by the conventional garden industry. It is a more realistic approach, accepting that plants occasionally show spots and blemishes just as our bodies from time to time show imperfections. Instead of quick fixes with their environmental side effects, organic gardeners aim for prevention and sustainable management of pests and disease.

Strategies old and new

Going organic is not, as newcomers may assume, simply a question of replacing artificial or chemical inputs with some sort of more "natural" spray. Traditional good gardening—improving the soil, crop rotation, encouraging natural predators, picking off pests and diseased growth by hand, good hygiene and timing of sowing and planting—is combined with more modern techniques, including biological controls, resistant cultivars, pheromone traps, and lightweight crop covers. Those few so-called "organic" sprays that are available are to be used as a last, not a first, resort.

Resisting attack

Healthy plants have a great tolerance of pests and diseases and, rather like healthy young people, can readily shake off minor infections. However, if environmental conditions are not as good as they might be and the plant becomes stressed, or if it is very young or old, the same infections could be life-threatening. As a general principle, the bigger the plant, the more disease or pest damage it can tolerate. So while a small lettuce seedling, for example, is totally vulnerable, even to the very weak biting mouths of sowbugs, a large oak tree supports many thousands of insects and mites on its leaves, not to mention fungi feeding on the leaves, stems, and roots, without showing any ill effects.

Liquid seaweed extract (*see also p.195*) is a well-known plant tonic that can be used as a root drip, drench, or foliar spray, to help boost a plant's defenses against pests and diseases. There are a range of other plant-based tonics and stimulants available that are said to have similar effects. They may be worth trying while your garden is adjusting to an organic regimen.

Contemporary bird scarer There is nothing new about protecting crops from birds, but organic gardeners are always ready to explore the potential usefulness of new materials—especially when they provide an opportunity to recycle, as with these discarded CDs.

PLANT PROTECTION THE ORGANIC WAY

- Manage the soil organically.
- Choose plants that are suited to the site and soil.
- Start with healthy seed and plants.
- Grow resistant cultivars.
- Grow flowers and provide habitats to encourage natural predators.
- Introduce biological control agents.
- Keep out pests with barriers, traps, and crop covers.
- Avoid the use of pesticide sprays.

Growing problems

The environment that plants experience includes the conditions in the soil as well as the "weather," or climate above ground. So mineral imbalances in the soil can be classified as environmental problems, just like drought or exposure to too much wind. Environmental problems can have direct effects, and also indirect effects: they leave plants more vulnerable to attack from pathogens or pests.

Water

Shortage of water makes plants wilt, which even for short periods weakens them, leaving them more vulnerable to attack. Prolonged water shortage can result in stunted growth and tissue death in all or parts of the leaves. Water shortages can have delayed effects on plants: flower drop in camellias in spring is caused by dry conditions the previous fall.

Plants can also wilt as a result of too much water in the soil, caused by either poor drainage or overwatering. Waterlogged soil prevents the roots from breathing. The initial response is wilting, as the roots cease to function. This is followed by tissue death, allowing fungal and bacterial pathogens and rots to enter.

Frost

Even frost-hardy plants occasionally have parts that are subject to frost damage, notably spring buds, young shoots, and blossoms on fruit trees. As water in the plant cells freezes, it expands, causing the cells to burst; the cells die off, leaving black/brown areas of dead tissue, usually on the growing tips. Avoid frost damage by choosing later-flowering or frost-hardy cultivars of some plants, delaying sowing dates for vegetables in a cold spring, or using protective covers such as cloches or fleece.

Mechanical damage

Mechanical damage can be caused by hail or heavy rain and wind, and over- or under-exposure to sun. Scorch, caused by excessive sun, is aggravated by water droplets on the surface of the leaf, which act like a magnifying glass. The leaf surface turns brown and dries up. In tomatoes, scorch causes a condition known as green shoulders: the tops of the fruits fail to redden. Scorch can be minimized by watering early in the morning or in the evening, or by shading. Mechanical damage can also be caused to plants by trampling or misuse of equipment, especially nylon string trimmers.

Indirect effects Blossom end rot (*left*) is a disorder of tomatoes and peppers resulting from calcium deficiency, but usually caused by lack of water. The calcium may be present in the soil but the plant cannot take it up because of dryness around the roots; this is common in plants in pots that are watered irregularly, or only when the gardener notices they are wilting.

MINERAL DEFICIENCIES

Mineral deficiencies can cause plants to fail and show symptoms of "disease" (technically disorder), but in a well-ordered organic garden they are seldom a problem. When managed organically, most garden soils will provide all the nutrients plants require.

Occasionally, especially in alkaline soil, trace elements, although present, may not be soluble due to the high pH, and are therefore unavailable to the plant. On these occasions, additional supplies might be needed (*see pp.54–55*). Mineral deficiencies can also be caused by too much of another element; overdo potassium-rich fertilizers, for example, and you may "lock up" magnesium so that plants develop symptoms of magnesium deficiency.

Mottling, marking, and even crisping of leaves can all be the result of mineral deficiencies. Fruits may also spoil and wither. However, mineral deficiencies are often difficult to confirm from symptoms alone and can easily be confused with diseases, especially viruses. If a problem persists, it may be necessary to have the soil analyzed professionally (*see also* The Soil, *p.30*).

1 Iron deficiency is one of the most common plant disorders and almost always presents as a yellowing of leaves, especially between the veins. It is particularly common in alkaline soil, when it is known as lime-induced chlorosis.

2 Manganese deficiency (on potato leaves), common in poorly drained soil.

3 Phosphorus deficiency (on tomato leaves), often seen in acidic soil.

4 Potassium deficiency (on string beans), often seen in light or sandy soil.

5 Bitter pit in apples, caused by calcium deficiency, also common in light, sandy soil.

6 Boron deficiency on sweet corn; overliming can disrupt the uptake by plants of this trace element.

Plant diseases

All plant diseases result from the invasion of plant tissue by microscopic organisms. These can be fungi, bacteria, or viruses. Taking their nourishment from the plant tissue as parasites, they cause cell damage and death, and sometimes distortions of growth rather like tumors or cancers.

Fungal diseases

Fungi are plantlike organisms without chlorophyll: they cannot make energy by photosynthesis. Most feed on dead and decaying tissue, but some have developed the ability to overcome plant defenses and feed on living plant tissue.

Fungal diseases are grouped according to the type of disease (or symptoms) that they cause, such as mildews, molds, or rots. Most spread from plant to plant in the form of spores. Some, like clubroot, have dormant spores that can remain viable in the soil for 40 years or more. The fungus that causes apple scab overwinters on infected debris such as leaves on the ground. Fungal diseases are more common in warm, damp conditions, which allow the spores to move freely in moist air and on a film of water on the surface of leaves.

Fruiting bodies Most fungi that cause disease are so small that they go unnoticed, apart from their symptoms. Honey fungus, with its distinctive honey-colored toadstools, is an exception.

PERMITTED ORGANIC FUNGICIDES

Use these remedies only as a last resort, and always follow the rules on spraying safely (*see p.320*). Always check the label to be sure that the product is suitable for use on the disease and plant that you have in mind.

■ **Sulfur** Naturally occurring mineral used to control powdery mildew and rose black spot. It can harm predatory mites, so it should not be applied where biological controls are in use.

■ **Potassium bicarbonate** can be used against powdery mildew, black spot, and downy mildew on a range of plants including roses, fruits, and cucurbits.

Control of fungal diseases is limited to trying to avoid or prevent the conditions in which they thrive. Good garden hygiene, ensuring adequate ventilation around plants, avoidance of over-watering, the use of resistant cultivars, and the judicious use of permitted fungicides (*see panel above*) all help avoid or limit damage.

Bacterial infections

Bacteria are single-celled organisms; they reproduce rapidly simply by dividing into two. Plant-pathogenic bacteria cause numerous soft rots, wilts, cankers, blights, and galls on plants. Examples of bacterial infections include scab on potatoes, fireblight, and many cankers on fruit trees. Unlike fungi, bacteria usually only enter plants through wounds, caused by pruning or pests, for example. Treatment is limited to

Plant diseases Top row, symptoms of fungal diseases:
1. gray mold, or botrytis, on grapes; **2.** fungal leaf spot;
3. peach leaf curl. Bottom row, symptoms of: **4.** the bacterial
disease potato scab; **5.** bacterial canker on the trunk of an
apple tree; **6.** cucumber mosaic virus affecting a wisteria.

removing the affected material and prevention
is usually a matter of simple cleanliness.

Viruses

Viruses—simply, genetic material in a protein
coating—invade the cells of higher organisms,
including plants, and hijack the cells' genetic
codes for replicating themselves, diverting the
cells' energy into the production of masses of
viral material that spreads to adjacent cells,
often severely restricting the host's growth
or causing malformations and malfunctions.
Viruses cannot exist independently and usually
rely on insects or other animals to act as
vectors to carry them from infected to
uninfected plants. Bugs such as aphids,
whiteflies, and leafhoppers, with their sap-
sucking habits, are major virus vectors. Viral
infections can also be passed on by vegetative
propagation from infected plants. Certification
programs exist in many countries to ensure
that only virus-free plant stock is sold, most
particularly of very susceptible fruits such as
raspberries.

Viruses are too small to be seen with
conventional microscopy, so they are usually
named after the plant in which they were
first discovered and the symptoms they cause.
Control is restricted to planting virus-free
material, the use of resistant varieties, and
controlling the insect vectors of the virus.

HOW PESTS FEED

1 Sapsuckers
Pests such as aphids, whitefly, and red spider mite use needlelike mouth-parts to pierce plant stems and suck sap, resulting in reduced vigor and growth distortions (as in aphid damage, shown here). Bacterial infections can also enter the plant via the wounds. Sapsuckers can transmit viruses, and their waste (honeydew) provides a food source on which molds thrive.

2 Root-feeders
Many insect larvae, including some moth caterpillars, beetle grubs such as wireworms (shown here in a potato), vine weevil, cabbage root fly, and parasitic nematodes known as eelworms, graze on roots. Damage restricts nutrient and water uptake, restricting growth and causing wilting; root crops may be rendered inedible.

3 Leaf-feeders
Many caterpillars (here of a sawfly), adult beetles and their grubs, and of course slugs and snails, graze on leaves and sometimes stems. Other larvae mine or tunnel leaves. Leaf damage reduces the area where photosynthesis operates, sapping the plant's strength and reducing fruit set.

4 Flower-feeders
Earwigs, psylla, thrips, and Japanese beetles (shown) feed on flowerheads and buds. Damage may be significant, but is often only cosmetic. Many bird species strip fruit trees and bushes of flower buds in late winter and early spring, when food is scarce.

5 Gall-formers
The presence of some fly and wasp larvae, as well as mites, causes distortions of growth known as galls; this is an "oak apple" caused by a tiny wasp. Galls are usually harmless, but some gall-formers transmit viruses.

6 Fruit-feeders
Some caterpillars, beetle grubs, and fly larvae feed on developing fruits; birds and wasps (shown) feed on ripening fruit. Damage is usually limited, but the soiled fruit can be unpalatable, and other infections may enter the wounds.

Plant pests

Most garden creatures are not pests. Many are beneficial, acting as pollinators, helping to recycle nutrients for plants, or acting as nature's own pest-controllers. There are those, too, that have no direct effect on the activities of the gardener, but are part of the rich biodiversity of the garden ecosystem. The beauty of many of these animals and their interesting behavior enhances the enjoyment of any garden, and as such they should be encouraged by organic gardeners.

What are pests?

Pests are those animals, large, small, and microscopic, that cause unacceptable damage to plants in the garden, or reduce our enjoyment of the space that is the garden. Pests are often classified according to where and how they feed on the plant (*see facing page*). Although this is convenient, these categories are not mutually exclusive. Many leaf-feeders also feed on stems; some sap-sucking aphids also feed on roots and flowers.

Hard to classify

Some animals do not fit comfortably into either the pest or beneficial group, as their habits change with the seasons or their life cycle, or as the vulnerability of certain plants to pest attack changes. Earwigs notoriously destroy dahlia blooms, but in other circumstances and at other times of year they are significant predators of pests such as aphids and moth and vine weevil eggs. Even the most infamous garden pests, such as slugs and snails, have their part to play in breaking down rotting vegetation. It is only when plants are young and tender, or when particularly vulnerable plants such as hostas and delphiniums are left unguarded, that they cause so much damage.

Many animals feed on plants without causing significant damage and therefore in an organic garden do not deserve pest status. A good example would be the froghopper or spittle bug, often found on roses in late spring and summer. These sapsuckers are usually present only in ones and twos on each plant (one bug per mass of froth or "cuckoo spit"), whereas aphids can often appear in colonies of several thousands. Other animals are only pests when the plant is young and tender, moving on to feed on other material as it matures.

Pet or pest?

Most pests achieve pest status by feeding directly on plants, but some creatures might be considered pests because they incidentally damage plants, or because they foul the soil with their droppings. The domestic cat is one such example; some gardeners tolerate cats, but others dislike them.

Friend or foe? Earwig populations (this a female with eggs) should be tolerated in gardens, as they do a great deal of good. Although they are often found in holes in fruits, they are almost invariably only taking advantage of damage initially caused by other creatures.

Keeping the garden healthy

A number of techniques can be used by organic gardeners to ensure that pests and diseases stay below an acceptable threshold. Most are not new, and could be described simply as "good husbandry." These techniques are essentially preventive. Many are common-sense and have other advantages as well as reducing losses to pests and diseases.

Start with the soil
Soil can have a dramatic effect on plant health. Get to know your garden soil (*see pp.26–31*) and, where necessary, improve its structure and fertility. Composted organic materials can help to reduce pest and disease levels in the soil, and to grow plants less prone to attack.

Garden cleanliness
The spread of problems and the carryover of pests and diseases between seasons can be prevented with good housekeeping practices.

■ Compost garden waste, and ensure that anything that might be infected with fungal or bacterial pathogens or insect pests is well mixed into the middle of the pile. Any material infested with persistent diseases, such as clubroot-infected brassica roots, and material resistant to composting, such as woody prunings from canker-infected trees, should be burned or taken to a green waste recycling center.

■ Plants carrying a viral infection should be removed and composted as soon as symptoms are identified. Most viruses cannot survive without a living host; they will die with their hosts on compost piles.

(Above) **Seed potatoes** Virus-free certification programs exist for seed potatoes and some fruits; look for these, and for disease-resistant varieties.

(Left) **Compost pile hygiene** The heat generated by the process of decay will kill many pathogens, but material infected with certain very persistent diseases, such as clubroot, should be taken to a green waste recycling center.

■ Remove self-set (volunteer) potato and tomato plants, which often spring up on compost piles; they could be infected with blight.

■ Lift and remove any pest-infested crop rather than leaving it in situ for the pests to complete their development.

■ Ensure that pest colonies in overwintering plants, particularly on Brussels sprouts and other brassicas, are removed where possible. Any plant remains from these crops must be composted or buried in a trench once cropping has finished, or before planting out new crops that the pests could colonize.

■ Winter digging can expose overwintering pests for predation by birds and ground beetles. However, don't go too far when tidying up the garden; spare a thought for the beetles, centipedes, and toads that play a vital role in pest control. They need safe, undisturbed locations to thrive.

Plant choice

Choose plants that are suited to the climatic conditions and soil type in your garden. They will grow well and will be less susceptible to pests and diseases. When buying plants, make sure that they are healthy—not carrying infections or harboring pests—and only use certified seed from a reputable source. Be wary of gifts of plants. This may sound harsh, but the primary means of dispersal for many pests and diseases is on plants transported between gardens.

Resistance

Certain cultivars, or varieties, of plants have been bred for their resistance to some pests and diseases. None is completely immune, but nonetheless, some resistance can be invaluable, especially where the threat from a particular pest, disease, or virus is high.

Resistant roses Roses are often thought to be terribly prone to diseases, such as black spot and powdery mildew. The trick is not to grow roses all together in a "rose bed," where disease can spread; choose resistant roses (*see also p.169*) such as 'Buff Beauty', above, and mingle them in with other garden plants.

Crop rotation

Keeping to a strict rotation for vegetable crops (*see also p.230*) not only allows better use of nutrients, but also prevents the buildup of pests and pathogens in the soil. With perennial crops, such as roses, strawberries, apples, and pears, do not replant with the same species in the same place. New plants may fail to thrive due to high levels of host-specific pests or pathogens in the soil. The old established plants may have built up tolerance to these.

Companion planting

"Companion planting" is a term used to describe growing two different species of plant together to the benefit of one or both. The technique is often, perhaps misguidedly, thought of as a mainstay of organic pest and disease control. While there is certainly evidence to show that some plants can help to keep others healthy, it would be unwise to rely solely on companion planting to keep pests and diseases at bay. Much is written on the subject, and definitive lists of "good" and "bad" companions provided, but there is little hard evidence to show that these companionships work, or advice on what proportion of each plant is required to be effective.

Plants that simply attract beneficial predators and parasites (*see opposite, and also pages 98–99*) are of course "good companions" in the vegetable patch, and around fruit trees and bushes, to encourage natural pest control.

Mixed planting

Any monoculture creates a pest and disease paradise, so it is worth growing a diversity of plants where possible—in all parts of the garden, not just the vegetable patch. Mixed planting can be effective and attractive, and if particular combinations work in your garden, stick with them. What works in one situation may not be effective in another.

There is some evidence to show that the strong scent of French marigolds (*Tagetes patula*) may keep aphids out of a greenhouse,

Mixed and companion planting Pests that find their host plant by responding to its characteristic odor are often confused by strong-smelling companion plants. Traditional gardening tips like interplanting carrots with onions (*top*) and growing French marigolds with tomatoes (*center*) may have a basis in science. But planting or sowing any small annual flowers, especially open-centered ones, around vegetables (*bottom*) will encourage pollinating and predatory insects, as well as looking attractive.

but only when the marigolds are in flower. On a field scale, it has been shown that carrots grown with onions are less damaged by carrot fly as long as there are four times as many onions as carrots, but that the effect only lasts while the onions are actively growing, and stops once they start to produce bulbs. This may not be as effective on a garden scale.

Stacking the odds

Research is beginning to show that mixed planting can cut down on pest damage simply by reducing a pest's chance of landing on a suitable host. Cabbages interplanted with an unrelated crop such as string beans, or undersown with clover, show much lower infestations of cabbage aphid and cabbage root fly. When a cabbage root fly lands on a plant, it "tastes" it with its feet. If it lands on several suitable plants in a row, it stops to lay eggs. If the next plant is not suitable, it may fly off elsewhere.

Protector plants

Intercropping (*see p.259*) a disease-susceptible variety with a resistant one in the vegetable plot is a technique that is also looking promising, on a field scale at least. Research trials have shown that lettuces susceptible to downy mildew can be protected if, in the row, each plant alternates with one of a resistant lettuce variety.

PLANTS TO ATTRACT BENEFICIAL INSECTS

Insects are attracted to flowers by their color (including light of wavelengths—or colors—that we cannot see) and sometimes by their scent. Typical examples of flowers that will attract beneficial insects are:

1 Big, bold, open-centered flowers such as gaillardias, with "target" markings that guide insects to the center.

2 Plants with tubular flowers, even tiny ones bunched into heads, as on this phacelia; nectar-feeders with long tongues will seek them out.

3 The broad heads of umbellifers such as Queen Anne's lace; this is a carrot left to flower in its second year.

4 Open-centered annuals with a long flowering period, such as *Limnanthes*, the poached-egg flower.

See also Gardening for Wildlife, *pp.114–7*.

The gardener's friends

A major component of working with nature for organic pest management is allowing populations of pest predators and parasites to thrive and thus naturally keep pest populations in check. The use of pesticides upsets this balance. Often pesticides are more harmful to predator populations than they are to the target pest species. In the past, pesticides have actually given new species pest status as the pesticide wiped out the predator populations. The European red mite is a perfect example, emerging as a pest of fruit trees only after the introduction of tar-oil winter sprays in the 1930s.

Natural predators

Many animals in the garden feed on pests. Some, like lady beetles, are more obvious than others, and get most of the thanks. Some we like for aesthetic or sentimental reasons and readily inflate their importance in the pest control stakes, such as toads. But many insignificant creatures work unnoticed, keeping pest populations below threshold levels. The animals pictured and described overleaf are effective pest control agents in the garden. It is important to recognize these creatures so they can be encouraged and left alone to go about their helpful business.

To build up the numbers of natural predators and parasites in your garden, aim to avoid the use of pesticides (even those mentioned at the end of this chapter). Pesticides not only have a direct effect on predators and parasites (killing them) but also an indirect effect, by removing their food supply. Mixing flowering plants with vegetables and fruit encourages many useful pest predators such as parasitic wasps, hoverflies, and lacewings, the adults of which feed on the nectar from flowers.

Habitats and shelters

A pond (*see pp.118–123*) attracts predators that have an aquatic phase in their life cycle. Provide artificial nesting sites, such as piles of wood for solitary wasps, or overwintering boxes for lacewings (*see p.108–113*). A good mulch and minimal cultivation creates ideal conditions for ground beetles (the most effective slug predator), and dense, matted grass at the base of hedges provides winter homes for these and for lady beetles.

Robin feeding young Like most songbirds, robins capture countless insects and invertebrates to feed to their hungry offspring during the nesting season.

Ladybug on the march Adult lady beetles will eat aphids, but their wingless larvae inflict the most damage on aphid populations. The same is true of lacewings. You can augment garden populations by buying both lady beetles and lacewings from suppliers of biological controls (*see panel, right*).

TINY HELPERS

Many predators and parasites of pests can be purchased, usually by mail order. These are known as biological control agents. Some, such as lacewings and lady beetles, boost natural populations; more often they are exotic species that are introduced to control a specific pest, like the parasitic wasp *Encarsia formosa*, a parasite of greenhouse aphids. Many biological control introductions work best indoors (in greenhouses and conservatories), where movement is restricted and climatic conditions can be controlled to suit the predator, but some can be used outside provided that conditions are favorable and the nighttime temperature stays above the minimum required. The A–Z of Plant Problems (*pp.320–341*) contains recommendations for currently available biological controls. Remember that as these are living creatures, you need to plan ahead when you order so that you will be able to release them as soon as they arrive.

Useful pest predators

1 Predatory bugs
Bugs from several families (notably capsids and anthocorids) eat other plant-feeding bugs. Here an anthocorid bug nymph attacks a small aphid.

2 Tachinid flies
Adult females, resembling bristly houseflies, lay eggs on or near other insect hosts, especially butterfly and moth larvae, and the larvae, or maggots, develop as parasites within the host.

3 Lady beetles.
Both adults and larvae (shown) prey on aphids and other bugs. Available as biological control agents (*see p.97*).

4 Frogs and toads
Adults feed on many pest species; the young are aquatic, so a pond is required. This is an adult frog.

5 Nematodes
Parasitic, microscopic roundworms, available as biological control agents (*see p.97*) for slugs and vine weevil: these are multiplying within the body cavity of a vine weevil. Completely harmless to non-target organisms.

6 Hoverflies
Larvae of many common species are predatory mainly on aphids. Their color varies and they are sometimes almost transparent. They resemble flattened bait maggots. Here, bright green larvae are feeding on aphids on a rose shoot.

7 Parasitic wasps
Adult females lay eggs in other insects and the larvae develop as parasites, killing the host. A number of them can be purchased as biological control agents (*see p.97*).

8 Daddy longlegs
These are roving, spindly-legged ground-based predators related to spiders, but unlike spiders they have only one body part.

9 Lacewings
Each larva (shown here) is a ferocious predator of aphids and similar insects, consuming upwards of 300 during development; encourage over-wintering of populations by erecting lacewing boxes (*see p.112*). Also available as biological control agents (*see p.97*).

10 Wasps
Adult females of solitary species like this mason wasp collect pests as food for grubs. Social wasps are similarly useful predators in spring/early summer; however, they become pests of ripening fruit by late summer.

11 Mites
Many predatory mites feed mainly on plant-feeding mites; here one is feeding on red spider mite eggs. Certain types can be purchased as biological control agents (*see p.97*).

12 Lizards
Many species feed exclusively on insects and other invertebrate pests, including slugs and snails. This legless glass lizard is a major slug predator.

13 Centipedes
Ground-based predators, distinguished from millipedes, which eat plants, by having only one pair of legs per segment. They move much faster than millipedes. Centipedes feed on slugs, slug eggs, and soil-dwelling insects.

14 Predatory midges
A number of tiny midges have wandering, predatory larvae that feed exclusively on aphids. Some are available as biological control agents (*see p.97*).

15 Beetles
Many species of ground beetle and rove beetle (shown) are predatory both as adults and larvae, feeding on juvenile and egg stages of slugs and snails, as well as ground-based insects. Encourage beetles by minimizing soil disturbance and using mulches.

16 Spiders
All spiders are predatory on insects and other arthropods, although catching systems vary and not all spiders use webs as traps.

Organic pest control

In the organic garden, as elsewhere, prevention is always better than cure. There are plenty of ways to stop pests from getting at your plants—or persuade them to go elsewhere. Only use an organically approved pesticide as a last choice. And while you are spraying, think about how you might prevent the problem in the future!

Barring the way

Barriers such as walls or fences around gardens to keep rabbits out have been used since medieval times; fruit cages, too, are a traditional way of protecting soft fruit crops from birds. By contrast, barriers against insect pests are a relatively recent advance. They usually consist of a net with a mesh size through which insects cannot pass—usually less than 1.5 mm. This lets maximum light, water, and air through, while keeping insect pests out. Insect mesh is not to be confused with horticultural fleece, an unwoven fabric. Fleece is used to protect young plants from climatic damage; obviously, it keeps out some

pests, but its continued use prevents ventilation and provides ideal conditions for slugs and fungal diseases.

Sometimes, as with carrot rust fly, a simple fence 18–20 in (45–50 cm) high will act as a barrier. The host-seeking females of this pest keep low to the ground, as they are weak fliers and subject to being blown off-course by wind. The fence prevents the low-flying carrot rust flies from getting into the carrot patch, but it also acts like a chimney, taking the carrot odor

Preventing access Cages made with thin, twiggy prunings (*left*) can protect brassicas from bird damage. For younger plants, individual cloches made from old plastic soda bottles (*right*) keep off birds and, if pressed into the soil, protect against slugs.

Mix it up Birds soon learn that scaring devices represent no real danger, so it is worth improvising a variety of devices and replacing or moving them around from time to time. The hovering "bird of prey" (*above left*) made from feathers and a potato is a traditional twist on the scarecrow. Effective scarers usually create deterrent sounds, such as humming tape, or sights, like the reflective mirror ball (*above, center*). This windmill (*above right*), made from a detergent bottle, does both.

upward and away from the host-seeking females. Stronger fliers, like cabbage white butterflies, need complete crop cover to keep them out. This also protects brassicas from cabbage root flies, which lay their eggs adjacent to cabbage stems after a response is triggered by alighting on appropriate leaves. Special "brassica collars" (*see p.236*) or overturned yogurt cartons with the base removed prevent access to the base of brassica plants by egg-laying female cabbage root flies.

Insect barrier glue is a sticky non-setting glue that prevents crawling insects from passing. It is especially effective at controlling winter moths in orchards. The female winter moth has no wings, but climbs the tree in fall or winter to lay eggs. On trees less than four years old, the glue, or fruit tree grease, should be applied on a paper band, not directly to the trunk itself. If the tree is staked, remember to put a sticky band around the stake, too.

Trapping and hand-picking

In small gardens, the value of hand-picking pests should not be underestimated. Removing or squashing a few invaders at the start of an infestation can prevent colonies from becoming established, and continued action can control numbers of persistent pests such as slugs. Removing badly affected plants, pruning out damaged sections, or sometimes removing the

SLUG BARRIERS

Surrounding vulnerable plants with a dry or sharp-edged material—grit, eggshells, bran, even commercial products, usually a porous mined rock—will form a barrier that slugs and snails find unpleasant to cross. However, these barriers tend to be less effective in wet weather and seldom stay in place for long; also, slugs move under them through the soil. Copper, which gives slugs trying to cross it a shock, is more effective. You can use copper rings or a copper-coated fabric that can be cut to size around plants, and copper tape around pots.

PHEROMONE TRAPS

Pheromone traps for moth pests usually consist of a protected sticky board and a sachet of the female sex pheromone. Male moths home in on this pheromone's scent and are easily fooled into entering a trap and alighting on the sticky board. The removal of males has little effect on the population's viability, since surviving males will readily cover for their deceased colleagues, but in small gardens a few such traps can often either take out enough males to have an effect, or disrupt the mate-seeking process sufficiently to reduce the viability of the next generation.

sensitive part of an uninfested plant (as when pinching out the tender shoot tips of fava beans, which attract blackfly) can prevent pests spreading or becoming established.

Traps for garden pests can be used in conjunction with hand-picking. This is especially effective for slugs. Nighttime forays into the garden with a flashlight are usually the most productive sessions for slug collection from plants. But you can also set traps, or simply lay down items that provide daytime refuge (such as plastic plant trays or old pieces of wood or carpet) where slugs will congregate, then collect the slugs during the day. A simple slug trap is a plastic carton filled with beer (*see below, right*). Keep the rim just above soil level to stop beetles from falling in.

Sticky traps, working on the same principle as fly paper, and also pheromone traps (*see panel, left*) are primarily intended to be used to monitor pest populations, but in small areas they can help prevent pests from becoming established.

Introducing ducks or chickens into a garden can also control slug numbers. Ducks and bantams are particularly useful in this respect, as they tend not to cause significant damage to plants. On vegetable plots, chickens can be introduced for a short period between crops as part of a rotation.

Picking off and trapping pests Larger, more visible pests such as this sawfly caterpillar (*below left*) can be picked off plants and disposed of, as can entire leaves badly infested by smaller pests. Sometimes the pests need to be lured out of their hiding places; slugs are a prime example. Slugs will readily clamber over the rim of this cut-off plastic bottle base (*below right*) and drop into the beer that has attracted them, but the protruding lip will prevent helpful ground beetles from meeting the same fate.

Feeding pests!

When young vegetable and bedding plants are transplanted into a newly prepared bed, they become an attractive source of food for hungry slugs. Distract them with young lettuce plants, or old lettuce leaves tucked under bricks and tiles, put out several days in advance. Replace the leaves every few days, taking the slugs away with the old leaves. A heap of cut comfrey leaves can help to clear a bed of slugs before it is planted. The leaves, and the slugs feeding on them, should be left in place for a few days and removed at night. Surrounding new plants with a protective ring of cut comfrey leaves can distract slugs until the plants become established.

Pesticides in the organic garden

As a final resort organic gardeners may use a small range of insecticides (*see panel, right*). Although often less harmful or persistent than many synthetic pesticides, these organic pesticides are still poisons, and like synthetic pesticides can adversely affect non-target organisms. Their use is constantly under review by the bodies that set organic standards.

Legal issues surrounding pesticide use

The use of all pesticides is strictly controlled by law, and it is illegal to use any that have not been officially approved. The list of approved products varies from country to country. Depending on local regulations, organic gardeners may use *Bacillus thuringiensis* (Bt), insecticidal soap, pyrethrum, rapeseed oil, and derris as insecticides, and also potassium bicarbonate and sulfur as fungicides (*see p.88*). Quassia, neem, garlic oil, and granulosis virus may also be acceptable organically. Check with your university extension to find out what is permitted locally.

It is often thought that any pesticide of natural origin— usually this means plant extracts—is acceptable in an organic garden. Although some such products might be fairly harmless environmentally, their use cannot be recommended unless they have been officially approved for use. As the cost of testing and approval is very high, this is unlikely to happen. Some homemade products, such as nettle tea or boiled rhubarb leaves, may be relatively innocuous, but other homemade plant concoctions can be extremely poisonous, and none can be recommended.

Protecting garden friends Even organically approved pesticides are nonselective and will kill both harmless and helpful insects as well as the target pest. Always spray in the evening, when bees are not active, and never spray on a windy day when the pesticide might drift.

PERMITTED PESTICIDES

Use these remedies only as a last resort and always follow the rules on spraying safely (*see p.320*). Always check the label to be sure that the product is suitable for use on the pest and plant that you have in mind.

■ Plant oils and other plant-based products having a physical effect.

■ Starch-based products with a physical effect.

■ Natural pyrethrum products (pyrethrins extracted from *Chrysanthemum cinerariifolium*).

6. Gardening for Wildlife

A garden teeming with wildlife is a pleasing and relaxing place to be—good for our well-being and for the feelings it brings of continuity and interaction with the wider world. Bees, butterflies, and birds are as much of a delight as flowers and fruits, but lesser creatures can be equally stunning and are a vital part of the natural food chain. Organic gardens are miles ahead of conventionally managed yards when it comes to attracting and valuing wildlife.

Teeming with life A flowering meadow is a rich habitat for wildlife: many grasses are food plants for caterpillars, without which we would have no butterflies.

Safe havens

With the continuing increase in urban sprawl and the intensification of modern farming, which places great reliance on the use of pesticides, the private garden has become vitally important as a safe habitat for wildlife. It is estimated that the collective area of domestic gardens in the UK, for example, now covers twice the area of existing nature reserves. More and more wild creatures are finding in gardens not just a refuge but their only chance of long-term survival.

Organic gardens have a head start when it comes to attracting wildlife, as pesticides are rarely, if ever, used. Natural predators and parasites, which keep pests and diseases under control, in turn provide food for larger creatures. The use of bulky organic manures encourages a thriving microflora and fauna in the soil—and these in turn are the first vital link in the food chain. There is no need to be concerned that more wildlife will result in more pests: studies have shown that organic farms support a greater abundance and diversity of wildlife species than conventionally managed farms, and there is, if anything, a decrease rather than an increase in the number of pests.

Creating the right conditions

With a little extra planning, you can easily increase the range of creatures visiting and inhabiting your own backyard. If you are really eager to promote the right conditions for wildlife, you can create a mini-nature reserve, with every plant carefully selected for its wildlife value. The basic requirements of all the creatures that visit your garden are the same:

Winter pantry In this Continental-style planting, flowers and seedheads provide food for butterflies and seed-eating birds; leaving the seedheads over winter gives the birds a long-lasting store cupboard, and ladybugs a safe place to spend the winter.

food, somewhere to live and breed in safety, and water for drinking and bathing. This chapter describes how you can provide these necessities of life in your garden.

Don't expect too much too soon; you can only create the most suitable conditions for visits by wild birds, beasts, and insects, not drag them into your garden by force. Despite your best efforts, you may find that totally different species are drawn to your garden than those you originally intended to attract.

Neat versus natural

One of the harder aspects of wildlife gardening is to strike a balance between super-neat and messy designs. But you can incorporate plenty of wildlife-friendly ideas into an existing garden without having to make it look untidy or wild. A wildlife-friendly garden can look just as good as, or even better than, any other garden plot. The nostalgic country or cottage garden style is one way to achieve the happy medium of "benign neglect," while retaining some control over the planting. However, this is not the only option with wildlife appeal. More modern styles of "matrix" planting, with drifts of herbaceous perennials threading through grasses (*see pp.180–181*) are not only visually spectacular but benefit wildlife as well. We may not understand all the intricacies of the natural world, but by keeping your yard free of chemicals and providing a rich diversity of plants that offer both food and shelter, you will both attract and support a range of creatures.

CREATURES GREAT AND SMALL

Birds and small mammals are obvious delights for the wildlife gardener, but smaller creatures can be just as beautiful and fascinating to observe. The larger flying insects such as butterflies and dragonflies are easy to spot, but close inspection of your plants may reveal a host of smaller but no less interesting invertebrates.

■ **Dragonflies** (*below left*) and damselflies will fly some distance from water. Watch some of the males defend their territory against any other insect—even butterflies.

■ **Crab spiders** (*below center*) have as many distinctly different colors as birds. Females are often paler, but both sexes can change color to blend in with the background.

■ **Shield bugs** (*below right*) feed on grasses, wild legumes, and shrubs. They are often devoted parents. Shield bugs are also called stink bugs for their ability to deter attackers by excreting a bad-smelling liquid.

■ **Velvet mites** Velvet mites are tiny red creatures that swarm on hot, dry paving and usefully eat pests such as red spider mites.

Homes for wildlife

Every creature needs somewhere safe to rest, sleep, and breed, so it makes sense to provide some shelter for the wildlife in your garden. This may be in the form of a custom-built home, such as a nest box (*see pp.112–113*), or more everyday organic garden features such as compost piles, mulches, and log piles. Many creatures will make their home in or under a hedge.

The welcome mat Providing food as well as shelter will entice wildlife in and persuade them to stay. This lovely informal hedging combination includes bright-hipped wild roses and the fluffy seedheads of *Clematis vitalba*. More plants offering both living room and pantry are featured opposite.

Before you rush to dig a pond or put up a bat box, first take a look around your garden and identify the areas that are already attractive to wildlife. Then earmark any other areas that, with a little change in management, could be improved upon.

Hedges and edges

A hedge (*see also pp.142–145*) is an excellent place for creatures to take shelter from predators or the weather, court, mate, and feed, as well as build a nest. In windy winter conditions, a hedge is warmer and stays dry at the base. A hedge base full of leaf litter is also a rich food source for insect eaters—not only birds but also toads, voles, and shrews.

To avoid disturbing any nesting birds, hedge cutting should be delayed until mid- to late summer. Fruiting hedges can be left uncut until the birds have eaten the berries. The base of the hedge should remain undisturbed; there is no need to rake out fallen leaves. If your garden is too small to accommodate the width of a hedge, try creating a "living wall" along your boundary by growing ivy, honeysuckle, and clematis through a chain-link fence, or clothe your walls and fences with climbing plants. Train the plants so that the base of the support is well covered, and do not trim growth back too closely. Dense evergreen climbers make the most effective wildlife refuges.

Climbers and creepers

Leaving climbers unpruned provides welcome refuge. Many small birds, such as wrens, will hide in thick ivy on cold winter nights. Some owls appreciate tall, ivy-clad trees, and if a few of the branches are decaying, woodpeckers will welcome both the source of food and potential nest sites. Leave dead branches in place if they are not in immediate danger of falling so that they, too, can provide food for insects and shelter for birds.

TEMPTING SHELTERS

Hedge plants
Beech (*Fagus sylvatica*)
Briar rose (*Rosa rubiginosa*)
Crab apple (*Malus*)
Cranberrybush viburnum
 (*Viburnum trilobum*)
Elderberry (*Sambucus nigra*)
Hawthorn (*Crataegus crus-galli*)
Hazel (*Corylus avellana*)
Highbush blueberry (*Vaccinium
 corymbosum*)
Holly (*Ilex aquifolium*)
Hornbeam (*Carpinus betulus*)

Shrubs
Cotoneaster
Ilex verticillata
Privet (*Ligustrum*)
Prunus laurocerasus 'Otto Luyken'
Pyracantha
Japanese wineberry (*Rubus
 phoenicolasius*)

Climbers
Blackberry and related
 hybrid berries
Dog rose (*Rosa canina*) and other
 related species roses
Grapes
Honeysuckle (*Lonicera periclymenum*)
Ivy (*Hedera helix*)
Virgin's bower (*Clematis virginiana*)
Virginia creeper (*Parthenocissus*)

Creature comforts
1. Dog rose
2. Elderberry
3. *Crataegus laevigata* 'Paul's Scarlet'
4. Guelder rose
5. *Cotoneaster salicifolius*
6. *Prunus laurocerasus* 'Otto Luyken'
7. *Hedera helix* f. *poetarum*
8. Honeysuckle

Wildlife refuge Overzealous garden "tidying" removes the dead and decaying wood that is essential to the life cycle of the stag beetle. This female, lacking the spectacular "antlers" of the male, is selecting a spot in which to lay her eggs; the larvae that hatch can spend up to five years living in and feeding on the rotting wood.

Wildlife corridors

Small mammals prefer not to venture across bare ground, if possible, and closely mown lawns and wide areas of hard surfacing present them with a challenge. Try to ensure that all of your planted areas link to create wildlife corridors through your yard, enabling smaller creatures to come and go while remaining hidden from their predators. Thick shrubs and hedge bases provide excellent protection, but ground-cover plants linked to areas of longer grass and herbaceous beds will also provide good cover for creatures on the move. If you erect a fence, try to raise it off the ground a little—or cut holes in the baseboards at regular intervals—so that small animals such as toads can squeeze underneath.

Lawns

To create the best variety of habitat, alternate areas of mown grass with patches of longer grass. Birds such as robins and starlings need open areas of short grass to feed on, while amphibians require longer grass. Try to leave uncut grass wherever you can without making things look too unkempt— along the base of an informal hedge, for example, or under trees. A neat path of short-mown grass running through slightly taller grass that grows next to uncut areas of vegetation can add structure to a part of the garden that might otherwise look wild and neglected.

Do not cut or mow all areas of long grass on the same day. If you have to cut a large area of rough grass, start at one end and work inward from one side to allow creatures an escape route. Never cut grass in a circle—mice and frogs become trapped like rabbits in a hayfield.

Sheds and compost piles

Garden sheds can provide useful hiding places for different species. Butterflies may creep inside to hibernate, so leave the shed door open on sunny fall afternoons and shut it late in the evening. Remember that garden birds will sometimes nest in the most unlikely places; they might appreciate your shed as much as you do!

If you regularly make a leaf mold pile (*see pp.44–45*), you may well have an opossum sleeping in it for at least part of the year. Leave a gap in the chicken wire, or whatever supports your leaf heap, so that small animals can get in and out easily.

Grass snakes—which are completely harmless to us—occasionally lay their eggs, and hibernate, in compost piles. If you are privileged enough to have snakes visiting your garden, and want them to stay, make a large compost pile in a sunny position. Snakes, like swallows, often return to the same nest site year after year, but they need the heat of decaying vegetation to hatch their eggs, so you will need to rebuild the pile every year. The safest times to disturb the pile are during early October, or from mid-April to mid-May when the snakes have emerged.

Under cover

Small creatures love to lurk under mulches. A woodchip or bark mulch will shelter beetles, centipedes, and the like, while thicker mulches of hay and straw may be frequented by frogs, toads, shrews, and spiders. In winter, try to leave some areas of mulch undisturbed for creatures to hibernate in.

Cool and damp Frogs, toads, salamanders, beetles, and hoverflies may all make use of a cool, dark, probably damp site: make a leaf mold pile (*see pp.44–45*) or leave a pile of logs in a sheltered spot for them to nest in.

Reflected heat

Make mounds or banks in a sunny part of the garden by piling up rubble and packing it loosely with topsoil, leaving small gaps between stones. Not only is this a good site for growing a host of attractive plants that need good drainage, such as thymes, sea campion (*Silene maritima*), and rock roses (*Helianthemum*), but it is also the best habitat for hibernating amphibians or, in summer, basking lizards. Weasels also love to hide in between stones, though they may also take a shine to short lengths of drainpipe left hidden in dry, undisturbed garden areas.

Warm and dry Shrews, mice, toads, spiders, and even pupating butterflies and moths will be attracted to the crevices and gaps in sunny stone walls (*below*) and stony banks.

Buying and building shelters

You can buy a variety of custom-built boxes for a whole range of creatures to shelter and raise a family in. The design can be simple or intricate, as long as it fulfills the needs of whatever it is you aim to attract. The residents are unlikely to be fussy.

Toad and frog houses

Toad houses can be particularly important in urban areas where shelter is scarce. Finding a suitable shelter for winter is hard in neat gardens, so keep toads happy by siting a house under a hedge or thick shrub where they will be undisturbed. Frog boxes can also be of benefit; place these in a north-facing, shady spot out of the wind.

Bird boxes

Even if there are already many suitable nest sites, a bird box may encourage a normally shy species of bird to stay in your yard. Bird boxes can be made of untreated wood or "woodcrete" (a concrete/sawdust composition). The latter version is useful if your garden has predatory squirrels or even woodpeckers with a taste for young birds. All bird boxes should be positioned so that you can access them easily to clean them out in fall, which is important. Put your bird box on a sheltered wall or tree trunk, well away from predators, rain, and direct sunlight. Cats can climb up and reach into boxes from all sorts of unlikely angles, as can gray squirrels, so position the box carefully.

Insect hotels

Insects also appreciate having somewhere to live in winter. Lady beetles, earwigs, and other insects hibernate naturally in tufts of rough grass, dead leaves, and hollow plant stems, so delay cutting down flower stems and clearing your borders until the spring. You can also buy neat wooden boxes for lacewings to hibernate

What box for which bird? The size of the entrance hole determines which species will use a bird box. Entrances just over 1 in (2.5 cm) in diameter are suitable for chickadees; 1¼-in (3-cm) holes are needed for downy woodpeckers, titmice, nuthatches, and house wrens; and openings of 1½ in (4 cm) attract bluebirds, tree swallows, violet-green swallows, prothonotary warblers, and hairy woodpeckers.

Five-star rooms These sophisticated ready-made boxes are designed to house (*from left to right*) lacewings, mason bees, and bats. Though birds may use a bee box as a "feeder," don't worry—they will be unable to reach the deeper layers of eggs in their self-contained cells. Bat boxes should be positioned high above the ground. Consult a bat conservation group to find out which size and color of bat box is right for your climate, and where to place the box.

in, or make a simple insect "hotel" from a plastic bottle and some corrugated cardboard (*see right*). Plastic food containers can also be pressed into service for housing lady beetles and other predators. Make a series of small holes in the lid of a square tub with a knitting needle and stuff the inside with straw, then place the tub on its side under a bush or large herbaceous plant to keep it dry over winter.

Bees, especially orchard mason bees, which are useful fruit tree pollinators, will colonize holes drilled in blocks of wood or paper drinking-straws stacked in a waterproof box, or you can buy special bee boxes. Mason bees emerge early, so the boxes need to be erected in early spring before the apple buds burst. An open, sunny—preferably southwest-facing—site is essential.

Bat boxes

Bats are quite common in built-up areas, even in large cities. They need temporary and permanent roosts. A busy bat can eat up to 2,000 small insects, such as gnats, per hour, so they are good to have around!

A bat box should be made of untreated lumber and have rough wood inside so the bats can happily hang upside down. It should be sited as high as possible—at least 10 ft (3 m) above ground level, away from bright lights and prevailing winds. There should also be plenty of air space in front of it. Planting night-flowering annuals nearby will encourage moths and other insects to feed, which will in turn attract the bats. Try night-scented stock (*Matthiola bicornis*) or tobacco plants (*Nicotiana*). As with bird boxes, the bats may take a while to settle in.

Making your own lacewing hotel Cut the bottom off an empty 2-liter soft drink bottle. Cut a piece of corrugated cardboard about 32–36 in (80–100 cm) long, roll it up, and slide it inside the bottle. Push some thin wire through both sides of the bottle base to stop the cardboard from falling out. Tie a string around the bottle neck, leaving the top on, and hang the "hotel" up in a sheltered position in late summer or early fall.

Food for all

Birds are not the only creatures that come to a garden to feed. An organic garden is likely to provide rich pickings for both vegetarian and carnivorous wildlife visitors of all shapes and sizes. With a little extra thought, you can provide them with even better fare. Natural foods that can easily be included on the menu for wildlife include nectar, pollen, aphids, caterpillars, slugs, berries, and seeds.

Best for birds

Many gardeners gain enormous pleasure from putting out nuts, suet, and seeds for wild birds. But once you have started feeding the birds, you must keep it up, because supplementary feeding encourages a larger population than the habitat can naturally support. Rather than develop birds' overdependence on humans, it is better, wherever possible, to grow plants that will supply birds and other creatures with their own food sources. Berried shrubs attract a number of species, as do seedheads and grasses; leave some herbaceous plants to go to seed. Sunflowers, rudbeckias, and echinaceas make excellent garden plants as well as good food for many garden birds—hang up an old seedhead for cardinals. Once birds find a regular food supply, they return regularly, which is to the gardener's advantage. It has been estimated that one insectivorous bird will eat over 10,000 caterpillars, flies, snails, and other pests during a single breeding season. Note, however, that many cultivated fruits are as attractive to birds as they are to humans.

SHRUBS THAT FEED BIRDS

■ **Cherry** (*Prunus*): robins, bluebirds, woodpeckers, catbirds, thrushes, cardinals, blackbirds, orioles, waxwings.

■ **Dogwood** (*Cornus*): catbirds, mockingbirds, robins, thrushes, woodpeckers, song sparrows, bluebirds, cardinals, waxwings.

■ **Elderberry** (*Sambucus*): bluebirds, grosbeaks, sparrows, thrashers, catbirds, vireos, finches, woodpeckers, flickers, waxwings.

■ **Juniper** (*Juniperus*): bluebirds, catbirds, purple finches, mockingbirds, thrushes, waxwings.

■ **Viburnum** (*Viburnum*): robins, catbirds, thrushes, thrashers, cardinals, bluebirds, waxwings.

Flower food

Flowers grown to feed wildlife do not have to be native wildflowers; cultivated blooms (except those with double flowers) can be even more nectar-rich and will extend the season. Many of the best-suited flowers for insects are smaller, old-fashioned cottage garden varieties. Different flowers suit different feeding methods, so grow a range of flowers to suit all tastes (*see also p.95*). Grow deep-throated flowers for bees and butterflies (*see overleaf*), which reach the nectar with long, probing tongues. Bumble bees have much shorter tongues than, for example, Red Admiral butterflies, but longer ones than honeybees, so you need a good mix of plants. Simple, flat-opening flowers, or flat flowerheads like those of cow parsley and fennel, are best for hoverflies, parasitic wasps, and other small fliers.

Moving up the food chain

The insects attracted by flowers, and especially their eggs, grubs, and caterpillars, will in turn become food for birds, predatory beetles, parasitic wasps, voles, and amphibians. Many creatures regarded as garden pests are actually a valuable food source for other creatures.

Butterfly and moth nurseries A great many butterfly and moth caterpillars feed on grasses, so leaving an area where the grass can grow tall is important. Some caterpillars hibernate, and many pupate, on grass stems over winter, so wait until late spring before cutting back patches of long grass.

A pair of meadowlarks, for example, may feed their nestlings up to 10,000 grasshoppers, plus many other kinds of bugs. Aphids and codling moth pupae are favorite winter foods for several bird species. Clusters of aphids left on strong, established plants that can tolerate them will make a "nursery" for parasitic wasps and predators to feed and breed on. So give nature a chance before you take action against a pest attack; you may find that the job has been done for you.

Frogs and toads will take up permanent residence in your yard if they can find a food supply, and their taste for small invertebrates—especially slugs—makes them the gardener's friends. Mealworms and bait maggots make good supplementary amphibian fodder. Toads in particular can be taught to take food from your finger and will quickly learn to reappear at the same place at their regular feeding time.

Flowers for bees

1 *Rosa canina*
Dog rose
Honeybees enjoy the "wilder" type of single-flowered rose, with its central boss of golden stamens.

2 *Lonicera periclymenum*
European honeysuckle
A vigorous climber, worth planting where you can enjoy the heady fragrance as well as the buzzing of bumblebees.

3 *Perovskia* 'Blue Spire'
Russian sage
Somewhere between a shrub and a herbaceous perennial; ideal for the foreground of a sunny planting on not-too-fertile, free-draining soil.

4 *Monarda* 'Mahogany'
Bergamot, beebalm
A prairie flower of North America, this perennial's common name reveals its attraction for bees.

5 *Echium vulgare* 'Blue Bedder'
Viper's bugloss
Biennials grown for their vivid blue flowerspikes; those of 'Blue Bedder' are about 18 in (45 cm) tall, but some less hardy echiums grow to 12 ft (4 m).

6 *Iberis umbellata* Fair Series
Candytuft
Flowers of perennial iberis tend to be white; this is an annual mix of pastel shades grown as summer bedding.

7 *Verbena* Tapien Violet
Verbena
All verbenas are popular with bees. Many are perennial, but this is one of several popular series used as half-hardy bedding.

8 *Achillea filipendula* 'Parker's Variety'
Yarrow
Cultivated versions of the wild yarrow all have these flat "landing stages" composed of myriad tiny flowers.

Flowers for butterflies

1 *Aster amellus* cultivars
Asters
Cultivars of this species are among those asters that are more resistant to mildew.

2 *Sedum spectabile*
Sedum, iceplant
Very long-lasting, late summer- to fall-flowering perennials.

3 *Buddleja* x *weyeriana*
Buddleja
More unusual in color, but just as popular with butterflies as the more traditional "butterfly bush," purple-flowered *Buddleja davidii*.

4 *Lunaria annua* 'Variegata'
Honesty
The plant shown here is a variegated version, with white-splashed green leaves. Like all the annual honesties, it self-seeds profusely.

5 *Coriandrum sativum*
Cilantro
A lovely annual plant for the wild garden, or dotted informally in a kitchen garden. Both the leaves and seeds (coriander) can be used in cooking.

6 *Origanum* 'Kent Beauty'
Oregano, marjoram
This marjoram cultivar is so named because its pinky-green flowers resemble the hops traditionally grown in Kent, England. Low-growing and sweet-smelling, ideal for a low sunny wall.

7 *Scabiosa caucasica* 'Clive Greaves'
Pincushion flower, scabious
Both these and the closely related *Knautia*, sometimes called field scabious, are perfect for cottage gardens.

8 *Hebe* 'Great Orme'
Hebe
Butterflies like all of these useful shrubs, but this cultivar and 'Midsummer Beauty' are especially popular.

Water for wildlife

A pond, even a tiny one, can be the heart of your wildlife oasis. Your pond will be used by a wide range of creatures for many and various purposes. Some will drink from it, or hunt for food over it. Others will use it for cover, and feed and breed in it. Some will spend their whole lives in the pond, while others will use it for only part of their life cycle.

A pond is not the only worthwhile water supply in a garden. Even the smallest water container will be attractive to birds and amphibians. Birds need water for daily bathing as well as drinking and will visit fresh clean water in any shallow type of container; even an upturned trash can lid can be pressed into service. Sink the container into the ground, or build a ramp of bricks up to one edge to make it accessible to toads.

Garden oasis This pond is not large, yet it forms a wildlife feature of enormous value. Water plants can be vigorous, and you may need to "edit" them from time to time to keep a small pond from becoming choked—but any creatures you disturb will soon return.

If you have young children and an open pool is inappropriate, consider a bubble-fountain or a wall-mounted basin, or cover your pond with a safety grating of rigid mesh until they are older.

Choosing a site

A pond is best sited in a sunny position, away from overhanging trees. A pond in shade will support some life, but there will be a greater diversity of species in full sun. Provide an area of rough grass or planting along at least one edge to act as a refuge and feeding ground for amphibians, which actually spend more time on land than they do in the water. Undisturbed areas, such as long grass, thick mulches, and heaps of stones or logs, provide safe havens and hibernating sites for frogs and toads.

If your pond is visible from the house, create an area of short grass on the side nearest the window so you can watch what is going on. To avoid harming emerging frogs, mow this grass regularly, starting in mid-spring before young creatures start to leave the pond. Always check for froglets before mowing after rain.

Creating a wildlife pond

The size of a pond depends, obviously, on the site available—but it should be at least a yard (meter) square. At least one side should gently slope, to allow small creatures safe access. Most wildlife will inhabit areas of shallow water around the margins. There should also be a deeper area, at least 24 in (60 cm), in the center, which will remain frost-free during winter and cool in summer. There are various materials available to line a pond— you can choose from concrete, bentonite clay, ready-made plastic molds, or a butyl sheet liner. A butyl liner is the most flexible, and probably the easiest to deal with when creating an irregularly shaped pond (*see overleaf*). Natural clay in mat form will last the longest. You need to allow plenty of overlap to anchor the liner securely around the edges—your supplier will be able to help with the size needed if given the intended dimensions of the pond.

The pond can be filled with rain or tap water. If using city water, wait at least 48 hours for the chlorine to dissipate before introducing floating or oxygenating plants. Wildlife will move in rapidly of its own accord, and within a year your pond should have a full complement of creatures. It is not uncommon for new ponds to suddenly turn a vivid green. Do not be alarmed: this algal bloom will clear by itself, although you can help it to disperse (*see p.123*).

NEW FRIENDS

Creatures that may visit or live in garden ponds include:

Frogs (*below, top*)
Salamanders
Bats
Whirligig beetles
Pond skaters (*center*)
Water measurers
Water boatmen
Water snails
Diving beetles
Damselflies and dragonflies
Swallows (*bottom*)

Making a pond for wildlife

Early spring is the best time to create a new pond. This gives plants and wildlife time to settle in before the following winter. This pond is lined with a flexible butyl sheet liner. PVC is not recommended for use in the organic garden: it contains potentially carcinogenic plasticizers and also poses a threat of chlorine pollution on disposal.

When buying lining material, allow for an overlap of at least 12 in (30 cm) around the pond; the supplier should be able to give advice if needed on dimensions.

1 Dig the hole slightly larger than you want the pond to be to allow for a protective underlay. At least one side should slope gently (by 15–30°), and there should be an area 24 in (60 cm) deep or more, depending on the severity of your winters, which will remain frost-free. Incorporate a shelf for marginal plants in pots.

2 Remove all sharp stones, roots, and anything else that might puncture the lining. Firm the sides and edges and make sure that the edges are all level. For additional protection, gently smooth a 4-in (10-cm) layer of sand all around the inside of the hole. Lay a protective underlay, such as old carpet, cardboard, or custom-made pond underlay.

3 With assistance (a butyl liner is heavy), lay the liner over the hole. Let it dip down into the hole, and weight down the edges with heavy stones. Put soil in the middle if you are going to plant directly in the pond.

4 Fill the pond. The weight of water will mold the liner to the shape of the hole. Do not stand in the same place for too long, or you will prevent the liner from being drawn down evenly. Once the pond is full, trim the liner to leave 12–18 in (30–45 cm) of excess all around.

5 Bury the exposed edges of the liner under soil, sod, or stones to protect it from the light, which degrades the butyl fabric, reducing its life span (normally about 20 years). You can mortar stones in place for stability, but do not let any mortar fall into the water.

6 If you have filled the pond with city water, wait 24 hours for the chlorine it contains to dissipate before adding your plants; this will also allow the water temperature to come into equilibrium with the garden surroundings.

1

4

PLANT SPECIES FOR PONDS

Oxygenating/submerged plants
Anacharis (*Egeria densa*)
Water starwort (*Callitriche*)
Wild celery (*Vallisneria americana*)

Floating plants
Duckweed (*Lemna*)
Waterlilies for a small pond need to
  be carefully selected, as native
  species are too vigorous. Try the
  fragrant *Nymphaea odorata* cultivars,
  such as 'W.B. Shaw', or look for
  N. pygmaea and *N. tetragona*

Plants for shallow water
Aquatic canna (*Canna*)
Arrowhead (*Sagittaria sagittifolia*)
Brooklime (*Veronica beccabunga*)
Dwarf papyrus (*Cyperus prolifer*)
Flowering rush (*Butomus umbellatus*)
Irises (*Iris*)
Southern blue flag (*Iris virginica*)
Sweet flag (*Acorus calamus*)
Taro (*Colocasia*)
Water plantain (*Alisma*)

Planting the pond

A good assortment of plants will provide food and shelter for an extensive range of creatures. Plant a mixture of floating, oxygenating, and shallow-water species. Floating leaf cover helps to prevent a pond from clogging up with algal growth. Aim for a 50–60% cover of the surface of the pond. Plants with submerged and semi-submerged stems and leaves provide food and shelter for water-dwelling creatures, and make egg-laying sites. Use as many species native to your area as possible. Avoid planting some of the more invasive alien species—often sold in garden centers. Particular pond thugs to resist include hydrilla (*Hydrilla verticillata*), water hyacinth (*Eichornia crassipes*), water lettuce (*Pistia stratiotes*), and Eurasian milfoil (*Myriophyllum spicatum*). When planting in baskets, use a special, low-nutrient aquatic planting mix or garden subsoil.

Encouraging frogs

Migrating frogs will tend to colonize a suitable pond within a year or two. If none appear, the pond is either unsuitable or cut off from their migration. If you suspect the latter, introduce some frog spawn taken from a healthy garden pond within, if possible, half a mile of your garden. Do not take frog spawn from the wild.

Don't introduce fish into a wildlife pond—they will upset the natural ecosystem.

Pond maintenance

Once a pond is established, it may not need much maintenance from the wildlife's point of view. Some insects prefer overgrown, muddy ponds, and frogs certainly don't mind weedy water. You may prefer a slightly more "managed" pond, but try not to disturb it unless really necessary.

During the summer, remove excess blanket weed; twist it around a stick or rake it out. Free-floating plants such as duckweed can be lifted out with a sieve. Leave any debris or plant matter on the pond side overnight, to allow creatures to escape back into the pond, then add it to your compost pile.

Vigorous and invasive pond plants can be cut back or removed gradually; reduce the volume of submerged plant foliage, such as pond weed, by about one-third. Late summer is the best time, before creatures hibernate. Avoid disturbing a pond early in the year, or in very cold weather. Other pond plants can be divided every two or three years if necessary.

Cover the pond with netting for a few weeks in fall if it collects large quantities of falling leaves, or remove the leaves by hand. Also remove dead and decaying foliage, or this will add nutrients to the water, encouraging algal growth. Always leave some debris at the bottom of the pond, however.

Algal blooms

One of the most common pond problems is an algal bloom—the water turns the color of pea soup, or silts up with swaths of blanket weed. This is usually a symptom of warm, nutrient-rich water. The "pea soup" is generally a short-lived phenomenon, appearing in spring as the weather warms up, then vanishing once the oxygenating plants start growing. Blanket weed can be more persistent; it can be physically removed by winding it around a stick, or raking it out. Barley straw or lavender clippings in a mesh bag can also be used (*see right*). To prevent blooms:

■ Have submerged oxygenating plants occupying around 25–33% of the volume of water.

■ Let floating plant foliage cover at least half and no more than two-thirds of the surface to shade the water.

■ If you need to top off the pond in prolonged dry spells, use rainwater, not mineral-rich tap water.

■ Use aquatic potting mix rather than the usual garden growing media when planting aquatics in pots.

■ Clear the pond annually, if necessary.

SAFE PASSAGE

When dragging or netting water weeds from your pond, do not carry them off to the compost pile immediately. Leave them at the pond edge for a day so that any creatures they contain can escape back into the water.

Clearing algae These barley straw pads, available in garden and aquatic centers, are rapidly colonized by beneficial bacteria that naturally eliminate algae.

Meadows and wild flowers

For the organic gardener eager to encourage wildlife into the garden, an area of rough grass and meadow flowers is highly desirable. This rich habitat will be enjoyed by butterflies, bees, and other insects, spiders, invertebrates, and small mammals. Compare a meadow to a clean-cut lawn and you will see how one is teeming with life while the other is bereft of visible activity.

Converting a lawn

You can simply leave an area of grass uncut and see what grows. Grasses and flowers (plants otherwise regarded as weeds in this situation) will develop, flower, and go to seed. The grass must be cut at some point, or else shrubby plants will start to move in. Cutting at the correct time ensures that seeds are released and scattered to grow another year. To encourage spring-flowering species, cut from midsummer; to encourage summer-flowering species, delay mowing until early fall.

Leave the mown grass on the surface for two or three days to release any ripe seeds, then rake away all the debris, which can be composted. Removing the cut grass helps to keep the fertility

SOWING A MEADOW

1 Mix the meadow seed mixture with sand to make it easier to broadcast and see which areas have been sown and which have not.

2 Using canes, mark out a grid to help you distribute the seed at the recommended rate, and scatter the seed evenly over the ground.

3 Once the area is sown, press down gently to ensure that the seeds are in contact with the soil. Do not cover them: the seeds of many meadow species need light to germinate successfully.

4 If the weather is dry, keep the area well watered until the seeds have germinated and the seedlings have become established. Annual mixes may flower within 6 weeks; perennial mixes may take 2 years to establish.

Country casual The tranquillity of a traditional flowering meadow can be recreated in all but the smallest gardens. Most gardeners today cut meadows with a nylon line trimmer, which tends to shatter the peaceful atmosphere, although hand-scything can be learned.

Meadow mowings Leave mowings on the surface to dry, then shake well to release their seed as you collect them up.

down, allowing wildflowers to flourish. The floral content of these rough weedy lawns can be enriched by clearing small areas and sowing or planting specific wildflowers. From field scabious to primrose, yarrow to clover, a wide range of flowers is available to suit different soils and situations, and to flower in different seasons. You can add small spring bulbs, too.

Sowing a wildflower meadow

Numerous seed mixes are available that contain different selections of wildflowers and grasses, suited to different soil types and situations. They are best sown in spring. Ideally, choose species that are native to your locality. Do not collect seed from the wild, although you could perhaps do so from a friend's meadow planting.

Wild flowers grow best in poorer soil, not in cultivated and enriched garden soil. Start by digging over the area, turning over the richer topsoil and burying it beneath poorer subsoil.

If your topsoil is deep, remove it and replace it with poorer soil. Firm the soil down and rake it level; do not add any compost or fertilizer. Leave the area for a few weeks after preparation, then hoe off any germinating weeds so that you have completely clear ground to sow into (*see facing page*).

Alternatives to a traditional meadow

If your soil is very fertile, a wildflower meadow is unlikely to do well. For a similar visual effect, consider instead sowing a mixture of annual meadow flowers such as cornflowers, field poppies, and corn marigolds, combined with oat or barley seed. This gives a magnificent spring and summer annual display, but the downside is that the ground will be bare over winter. As long as the plants are allowed to seed, and the ground is gently dug over each year in early spring, one sowing should last for many years.

7. Garden Planning

As increasingly large tracts of the planet are suffocated below asphalt or concrete, or diminished by industrial agriculture, the living landscape of our gardens becomes ever more important. The potential of our yards as thriving ecosystems is affected by the design and composition of the garden framework. This includes all aspects of landscape construction—patios, paths, driveways, fences, walls, hedges, lawns, garden buildings, and special features.

The garden framework Lumber and stone usually make up the "hard landscaping" of the garden, while plants could be termed the "soft furnishings." There are design choices to be made: hedges and lawns, for example, are "soft" alternatives to fences and paving.

Planning power

There is a greater choice of design options and building materials for the garden today than ever before. Gardening television programs and magazines inspire us to make full use of these materials for everything from basic paths and fences to expressing a creative talent. How does this affect the organic gardener?

If the philosophy of organic gardening is to be applied to hard landscaping, we need to take a detailed and critical look at materials, including extraction of the raw materials, processing, transportation, their use in the garden, how they affect garden ecology, and, finally, recycling. Organic gardeners should be searching for sustainable ways of providing and maintaining the garden framework from the planning stage onward, while also being mindful of how those decisions will support the green living world. We need to consider not only the design of the garden and the selection of the materials, but also maintenance requirements.

Forming the guidelines

Assessing the environmental costs of garden building materials and practices is a comparatively new area, and the situation is constantly changing as companies set about improving their environmental policies.

As yet, there are no organic standards for hard landscaping, so the basic principles of organic gardening—sustainability and low environmental impact—must be applied. Some materials, such as locally sourced and well-managed lumber, will always score highly in terms of being sustainable and environmentally friendly. Other materials should be avoided, due to toxicity, perhaps, or the fact that extraction of the raw materials may damage natural habitats, or their manufacture may cause pollution. Sometimes compromises have to be made; some materials, such as glass, fall between these two extremes. This chapter raises the issues, and aims to help you to make sustainable, organic choices.

Garden choices A plastic-coated obelisk will consume energy in its production and cause pollution when eventually discarded. In contrast, this homemade twig tepee will decompose naturally at the end of its life.

New technology Always consider solar power as a source of sustainable energy for small features such as garden lights and water pumps.

Landscaping and materials

Building materials and products carry environmental costs that you may not have considered. The information in the panels on the facing page will help you start to make more environmentally sound choices. Unfortunately, products rarely fulfill all the criteria that we would wish them to, so there will have to be compromise somewhere along the line. For example, although natural stone is a nonrenewable resource, it is very durable, and should last for many generations. Bamboo canes are a sustainable product, but may have traveled far. Aim to strike a balance.

CHOOSING PLASTICS

Whether offered as flexible sheeting or as a rigid material, such as in shed construction, always seek an alternative to PVC for use in the garden. PVC contains dioxin, a persistent organic pollutant (POP) that accumulates in the food chain and can be released during manufacture and disposal. PVC can also contain phthalates, plasticizers that make materials flexible. Phthalates have been linked to cancer, kidney damage, and problems with the reproductive system.

Making your choices

The information needed to make informed decisions may not always be available, or easily accessible, but it is always worth asking. Where do the raw materials come from? Does the manufacturer have an environmental policy? What steps do they take to repair environmental damage?

How you can help

If your questions cannot be answered satisfactorily, let producers know that you will be making an alternative choice. Over the last decade, it is public demand that has fueled the enormous increase in the availability of organic food and "fair trade" products. Ecological awareness has led to huge developments in products to replace peat (see pp.186–187), in composting green waste, and in the avoidance of garden furniture and related products made from tropical hardwoods. Public interest and pressure can improve things.

The problems with plastics

There are many different types of plastic. Some of them are implicated in serious environmental pollution, and some governments are restricting their use. It is hard for the consumer to distinguish between the most and least harmful types. New and recycled PVC have been particularly highlighted by environmental organizations (see left), but there are alternatives. Furthermore, most types of plastic will not rot. At the end of their lives, they will end up in a landfill site or in an incinerator where they may produce toxic fumes and residues. Until manufacturers, or other bodies, guarantee a safe disposal or recycling service for these plastic items, they will remain an environmental problem.

THE SOLUTIONS

■ **Avoid damage** Be aware of products and practices that cause harm to people or the environment.

■ **Use sustainable resources** Look for wood from well-managed forests, coppice products, and home-grown bamboo.

■ **Use nonrenewable resources efficiently** For example, use metal only where its strength and lightness are essential.

■ **Reuse and recycle** Can existing materials in the yard be put to new uses? Are reclaimed building products available locally? Can store-bought materials be recycled or composted at the end of their life?

■ **Use local resources** Locally available materials, such as the reused poles below, reduce pollution caused by transportation.

■ **Use handmade products** Labor and craftsmanship are a renewable source of energy, unlike industrial processing.

■ **Conserve soil** Use excavated soil on site. Do not mix good soil with nonorganic waste.

■ **Consider maintenance** Hard landscaping can be designed to minimize maintenance such as string trimming and the use of fossil fuels, engine noise, pollution, and work time this entails.

THE COSTS

■ **Extracting the raw material** Quarrying and other extraction processes can damage and pollute habitats, water tables, and wildlife. Processes may be hazardous to workers' health, and products may not be fairly traded.

■ **Transportation** Long-distance transport consumes energy and causes pollution. Heavy imported terra-cotta pots like the ones above may seem like a bargain, but the environmental costs are high.

■ **Processing** Industrial processes may use fossil fuels and could cause pollution of air, land, or water.

■ **Sustainability** Materials may be from finite, rather than renewable, sources and may be used inefficiently. The techniques used to install them may be energy-intensive.

■ **Disposal** If the product cannot be composted or reused in another form, an environmental and financial cost will be attached to its disposal.

■ **Durability** The material may not serve its purpose well, and may require frequent maintenance.

■ **Toxicity** Treated wood and masonry may leach harmful substances into the environment.

Lumber

Lumber is potentially the most environmentally friendly of all building materials, and can be used for surfaces, fences, screens, and supports. In an organic garden it is important to use lumber from sustainably managed forests, whatever the type of wood and the country it comes from. Look for the Forest Stewardship Council (FSC) label, which guarantees that the wood comes from a well-managed, sustainable forest. Coppice wood (*see p.158*) is also a sustainable resource, cut from mixed woodlands that in themselves are a valuable wildlife habitat.

AN ALTERNATIVE TO CONVENTIONAL PRESERVATIVES

Boron rods provide an alternative wood preservative, which is considered safe for people and the environment. They are made of boron compounds that have been subjected to high temperatures to form water-soluble, glasslike rods. These rods are inserted into drilled holes in the wood, strategically positioned where decay is most likely; the holes are then plugged to keep the rods in place. When the wood becomes wet, boric acid is released, which prevents fungal decay. Boron pastes have a similar effect. Manufacturers of boron rods are seeking to make these rods available for home use.

Wood preservatives

The key problem with buying lumber for use in the yard is that so much of it—posts for outdoor use, fence panels, and compost bins, for example—is routinely treated with some sort of preservative before sale. Organic gardeners should, if possible, avoid treated lumber and products, unless a relatively environmentally friendly product has been used.

Items in contact with the soil, such as posts, gravel boards, and compost bins, are at most risk from decay, so they are often made from lumber that has been pressure-treated with toxic chemicals. Chromated copper arsenate (CCA), which is a very effective long-term wood preservative, is being phased out for residential use in the United States, but old stocks of CCA-treated or "green-treated" lumber may still be for sale and are a source of highly toxic arsenic. Such chemicals have no place in the organic garden. Nor should this type of lumber ever be burned, as it releases highly toxic fumes.

Wood that is not in direct contact with the ground, and so is less prone to rot, is usually treated with less toxic preservatives; but even so, there is currently no legislation that requires that any form of treatment need be mentioned on any labeling.

Change the way you shop

Until the use of more environmentally friendly methods of preservation are used as standard throughout the lumber industry, you may prefer to ask a sawmill or fencing supplier to supply untreated wood. You can treat this yourself using eco-friendly products based on natural plant oils, resins, and other less toxic materials.

Think about the use to which the wood is to be put before deciding that you really need to have wood treated with preservatives. Consider how long the lumber needs to last. Tree stakes generally need only be in place for a couple of years, so using a treated stake that will survive for 25 years is totally unnecessary. Nonstructural lumber, such as bed edging and wood for a compost bin, could simply be left untreated. It will of course rot eventually, but you can then simply replace it.

Railroad ties are not generally appropriate in an organic garden because of the tar that permeates them, which may be exuded in some conditions; landscape timbers made of similar-sized blocks of hardwood that have not been treated are available as an alternative.

Natural resistance

One way to avoid the use of any preservative is to use wood that is naturally resistant to decay. The heartwood of more naturally rot-resistant species, such as oak, can be used untreated. Other woods that last well without treatment are larch, which will last about 10 years in contact with the soil, or up to 20 years if not in contact with soil; Western red cedar, which will give service for about 20 years; and sweet chestnut, traditionally used for fence palings and posts. Untreated pine lasts for about five years. Well-seasoned wood that has been allowed to dry out evenly is more expensive than greenwood (freshly cut undried wood), but in its favor, it tends to last longer and can be less prone to distortion as it weathers.

(Right, from top) **Wood in the garden** A compost bin cobbled together from scrap lumber is perfectly serviceable; your own garden may well be able to provide a useful harvest of material for making plant supports and screens (*see also pp.158–161*); garden furniture made from well-weathered, naturally resistant lumber acquires a fascinating patina with age.

Hard surfaces

Hard surfaces, such as patios, pathways, driveways, and pads for utility areas, account for most of the building materials used in gardens. They often require a substantial depth of foundation material, which involves excavating topsoil. Sustainability and conservation of resources should govern your choices.

Planning and design

Keep areas of continuous, unbroken paving to a minimum. They cannot support the same biodiversity as a border with soil, and they do not act as a soakaway for rainfall—an increasingly necessary feature as flooding becomes more prevalent. However, broken paving, with herbs or alpines planted between gaps, can provide a valuable wildlife habitat. The stones absorb heat in summer, and provide a basking spot for snakes and other small animals, while the nearby plants give cover. If laid on only a minimal foundation of sharp sand, the stones will also provide cover for invertebrates such as beetles.

Minimizing weeds in paving

If you want a very neat garden, there are ways to reduce weeds. First, provide an impenetrable foundation layer: a geotextile membrane (*see p.75*) under gravel, or a substantial construction below slabs or bricks. If the paving includes joints—filled-in gaps of about ½ in (1 cm) between each unit—they should be grouted with mortar, rather than filled with sand, which gives weeds an ideal rooting medium. Cement and concrete products are not the most environmentally sustainable materials and you may wish to consider more sustainable options. Lime mortars can be used in place of cement in many areas, including paving foundations and grouting.

Excavations

Establishing an area of paving will often necessitate the excavation of topsoil. Consider, at the planning stage, how the soil is to be removed and what is to be done with it. Can it be used

ROCK FEATURES IN THE ORGANIC GARDEN

Garden rock features raise considerable anxiety and opposition from environmentalists. This is because the rock that makes the most convincing, attractive garden features is taken from valuable habitats. Waterworn limestone, for example, is taken from a very specialized habitat that has evolved over thousands of years, supporting plants that will not grow anywhere else. UK horticulturist Geoff Hamilton recognized this, and developed a homemade "rock" that weathers well and supports rock plants very effectively. Natural stone is a limited resource that is best reserved for building purposes. If you do not want to make your own "rocks" you could consider using reconstituted stone made from stone dust, or reclaimed stone.

Lime mortars The use of cement has been heavily criticized by environmentalists for the energy and emissions involved in its manufacture and for its inappropriate use. Mortars for laying and grouting paving materials can be made using less environmentally costly lime in place of cement.

elsewhere in the yard—for example, for a raised bed—or somewhere nearby? If machines are used, ensure that they are the lightest and smallest possible. The fuel they consume and the noise and pollution they create while working are all part of the equation. Do not forget that energy and materials are used to create any machine, although the environmental cost of this will be spread over its working life.

Using stone
Natural stone, such as granite, sandstone, limestone, and slate, is a very limited resource but provides a very durable building material. Reconstituted stone products are made using stone dust from quarrying operations, bonded with cement or synthetic resins. Synthetic stone is made from minerals such as sand and ash bonded with synthetic resins. More energy is required to produce a reconstituted or synthetic product than to use stone in its natural state, and the production of the resins used can cause pollution.

Local stone may be a good choice for paving. It forms the character of the varied regions in which we take such a pride. All stone extraction involves quarrying, and potentially, it is environmentally destructive, depending on how the company manages and restores the site. This cost is offset to some extent because natural stone should last for many generations. If it is used in its natural form, the requirement for energy-intensive processing is minimal and local craft skills are kept alive.

Secure footing Bricks and paving can become slippery if colonized by algae. Path-clearing algicides are not suitable for use in an organic garden; a pressure-washer is just as effective.

Reclaimed materials

Reclaimed building materials such as brick, stone, concrete slabs, wood, and quarry tiles can all be used to create new paving. Ensure that secondhand bricks for outdoor use are weather-resistant. Heavier, more dense bricks, such as reclaimed engineering bricks, generally last longer as paving than facing bricks, although some types of fired-clay facing brick can be extremely hard-wearing. Ask a reputable dealer if you are uncertain.

Pleasing designs can be achieved by combining different materials, such as quarry tiles, bricks, and bottle ends. If the area is to appear in harmony with its surroundings, some aspect of it, such as a color or matching brick, should relate to the nearby buildings. If a combination of materials is being used, a repeated sequence of materials will make the area look well-planned. This can also be achieved by including random materials within a uniform edging material. Selecting materials of similar depth and preparing foundations carefully will make a uniform finished level easier to achieve. Again, using lime mortars for bedding and grouting these materials is environmentally preferable to the use of cement.

Gravel and stone chips

Gravel and crushed rock—stone chips—are obtained by quarrying. Some gravels are collected by sea dredging, which destroys marine environments. However, secondary aggregates, such as crushed rubble from demolition works, offer an alternative to newly quarried materials, and make an attractive, durable surface.

For general garden use, a 1–2-in (2.5–5-cm) layer of chips over a weedproof geotextile membrane (*see p.75*) will suffice. For areas of heavy pedestrian or vehicular use, lay a foundation of crushed stone, 4 in (10 cm) deep for paths, and double that for driveways. Regular traffic can help prevent seedling weeds from establishing. To keep the gravel in place, use an

Wooden surfaces Decking is increasingly popular as a garden surface; a raised deck (*below left*) needs substantial lumber foundations. Log rounds surrounded by a bark mulch (*below right*) make a pretty woodland-style path, but shade can aggravate problems with slippery algae on the wood.

edging of wooden planks, or reclaimed bricks or tiles. Driveways need a heavier edging material; thicker lumber, for example, or mortared bricks laid on a suitable foundation.

Hoggin

Hoggin is a naturally occurring mixture of clay, sand, and gravel, which can be rolled to give a durable surface to patios, pathways, and drives. The clay content acts as a binder. The surface is hardest in dry conditions and requires excellent drainage facilities if waterlogging and surface erosion are to be avoided. When hoggin is well-laid and compacted, weeds are slow to colonize.

Certain types of subsoil with a high percentage of gravel or grit can be reemployed as a hardwearing surface material. A proportion of new crushed stone may be necessary to give a stable surface, but this will be a much smaller quantity than if the whole area was paved.

Wood as a paving material

Wood is potentially the most environmentally friendly of all building materials, and it makes attractive and durable garden surfaces. However, it can be treacherous when wet, and surfaces should be grooved to create a nonslip surface.

Wooden paving may take the form of decking, log rounds, heavy timbers (reclaimed or new timber beams), pavers, or bark and woodchip mulches. (For general advice on choosing wood and wood preservatives, *see pages 132–133*). Wooden decking may be constructed from new or reclaimed wood, preferably a durable hardwood like oak, which does not require a preservative. Where the deck has a structural purpose, always consult a structural engineer to check both the design and suitability of the wood.

Precut heavy timber paving can be used for patios, pathways, and drives. It combines well with other materials such as decorative aggregates or reclaimed slate to create attractive patterns. Log rounds make good stepping stones, or an informal paving material, held in place with a retaining edge. A base layer may be needed on damp clay soils. Use the spaces between as planting pockets, or fill with grit or with fine silver sand, soft enough to be walked on barefoot.

For the ultimate soft surface, choose a bark or woodchip mulch, spread in a thick layer over a weedproof membrane—both economical and easy to lay.

Loose stone Crushed stone chips (*top*) in a variety of colors and textures—byproducts of the quarrying industry—make an acceptable alternative to quarried gravel or dredged gravel (*bottom*). A "scree garden" made with such chips or crushed brick waste is an effective way to display alpine plants, avoiding the environmental concerns caused by garden rock features (*see p.134*).

Walls, fences, and screens

Boundary and screening walls perform the same function as fences, but a wall is normally of a more solid and bulky construction, requiring substantial foundations, and if well-built will afford greater strength and durability. Walls absorb more heat than fences; this is slowly released during the night, giving a slightly warmer microclimate for adjacent plants. But solid walls do not make good windbreaks; they can create more turbulence than permeable barriers that filter the wind. Consider what purpose you need the barrier to serve before making your choice.

A hedge (*see pp.142–145*) is without doubt the most environmentally beneficial garden barrier. But hedges take time to mature, require trimming, and occupy space. Solid walls and fences provide a practical alternative where space is limited and a secure definition of boundaries is an immediate priority.

Design considerations

■ **Decide on priorities** Is the barrier for security, privacy, screening, defining boundaries, decorative or architectural value, or plant support?

■ **Consider the requirements of the site** Windy areas need fences with some permeability. Wood-rail fences, with gaps between the rails as wide as the rails themselves, are less easily blown down than solid fences. A heavy-duty trellis with a close mesh allows wind permeability at the same time as affording more privacy.

■ **Incorporate wildlife-friendly features** Allow small animals to come and go by building access holes into the base of walls, cutting gaps in gravel boards, or placing a drainpipe "underpass" at ground level. An average yard is too small a territory on its own, and if the walls and fences are impenetrable, it will remain free of toads and other beneficial creatures. Consider adding extra planking as bat roosts across the top section of fences.

Garden wall Low walls need only simple building skills and can increase the planting opportunities in your garden. This small retaining wall creates a raised bed with good drainage for sun-loving plants. Leave gaps in the mortar, or poke holes in it with a pencil when it is wet, to about 6 in (15 cm) deep; you may encourage the nesting of mason bees, a beneficial insect.

Garden walls

Walls in gardens account for the use of many tons of quarried materials—a finite resource—so recycled materials should be used wherever possible. Stone walls should ideally only be built where their strength and durability are actually needed. Substantial walls can also be built from reclaimed heavy-duty timbers, and they do not require large quantities of quarried foundation materials.

Walls can be a wildlife habitat in the garden. The dense evergreen growth and protection of an ivy-covered wall will shelter nesting or roosting birds and many insects. Unmortared stone walls are an ideal habitat for small mammals, reptiles, and scree plants.

Fences

Wood is the most commonly used fencing material, and is also, potentially, the most environmentally friendly choice. Unfortunately, most fencing is made from nondurable softwoods, and strong chemicals may have been used to preserve it (*see pp.132–133*). In fact, as fence panels are rarely in contact with the ground— which is where wood is most at risk from decay— a simple water-repellent stain should protect them. Fence posts are most at risk from decay at ground level, where wood, air, and soil meet. Posts made from oak or cedar are recommended for their natural durability (*see also p.133*). Concrete post bases extend the life of wooden posts and make them easier to replace.

PREFERRED FENCING CHOICES

▨ Homemade or locally made panels from coppice products or garden prunings.

▨ Untreated woods from sustainable forests.

▨ Panels made of natural vegetative materials such as heather, reed, or bamboo.

▨ Sustainable woods treated only with eco-friendly products.

▨ Recycled or scrap wood.

Do not use

▨ CCA pressure-treated lumber.

▨ Creosote-treated lumber.

▨ Tropical woods or any wood from poorly managed forests.

▨ Plastics or recycled PVC.

Conventional wooden fencing includes the familiar post-and-rail, solid board, and picket. However, fencing panels can also be made from compressed woody prunings, and other natural materials such as reed and heather. Such panels can be homemade or bought. They are particularly suitable for lightweight screening within the garden, as are trellises and screens made from bamboo.

Store-bought bamboo canes may have traveled halfway around the world, so growing your own, for plant supports, light structures, and screens, is an environmentally friendly alternative. The canes must be dried slowly, for three to six months. Lash them together with cord. They can also be drilled, but do not nail them or they will split.

(Below, from left) **Natural choices** A simple low fence of untreated wood will last until the hedging plants at its base have grown; a trellis painted green with eco-friendly paint focuses attention on the climbing plants; a lightweight woven rush screen can be recycled as a sheet mulch at the end of its life; a "living" screen of willow wands plunged into the ground (*see also pp.160–161*), just coming into growth in spring.

Other materials

Fences, barriers, and posts made from "synthetic wood" can be useful; they have a long life span and never rot. There is, however, the question of how they are to be ultimately disposed of. Other fencing products made of plastics or a combination of plastic and wire can be difficult to separate and recycle, and at present only add to the problems caused by landfill and incineration.

Metals, which are also nonrenewable and use energy-intensive production processes, are best reserved for special applications; for example, around balconies and roof gardens where their strength and lightness is essential. Decorative ironwork may also be required to preserve the architectural style of a building; it can often be found in salvage yards.

Alternatives to brick and stone

In areas where lumber and natural stone were scarce or too expensive, walls were traditionally made of cob—local mud mixed with straw. Well-built cob walls can last for years. They are

usually less weatherproof than stone, and to last need damp-proof foundations and a coping—like a tiny roof overhanging the sides, traditionally made from thatch or slate. A stucco of lime mortar will protect the sides. Mud can also be made into unfired bricks for "lump-wall" construction, but unless you have a suitable clay-containing soil, lime or cement must be added to make the bricks durable.

Rammed earth or "pisé" walls consist of clay-containing earth built up in layers between removable shuttering. "Wattle and daub," a hazel lattice covered in mud and straw, is another variation on the theme. If you have space, straw bales make cheap building units, but need a good coat of stucco.

An effective and environmentally friendly acoustic barrier consists of a framework of woven, freshly cut willow, filled with soil, into which the willow stems root. Variations include a soil-filled framework of dried willow, in which ground-cover plants are established. Dense, compressed reed walls designed to reduce noise are also available.

Bamboos for canes Many hardy species can be grown for canes. Canes 6–10 ft (2–3 m) long take around three years to grow. Cut them above a joint, where they are solid, to stop rain from getting into the base of the cane, leading to rot. Look for: *Phyllostachys aureosulcata* var. *aureocaulis* (*above left*), *P. nigra* (*above right*), *P. violascens*, *P. viridiglaucescens*, and *P. vivax*; *Pleioblastus simonii*; *Pseudosasa japonica*; *Semiarundinaria fastuosa*; and *Yushania anceps*, *Y. maculata*, and *Y. maling*.

Hedges

When low-level screening or a windbreak is required in a garden, a hedge is ideal. It will create an attractive background, while also offering food and shelter to wildlife. In a very exposed location, if space is available, it is worth planting a real shelter belt, consisting of several rows of mixed trees and shrubs that will catch the wind and disperse it, to protect the rest of the garden.

Which plants to use

Both trees and shrubs can be used for hedging (see overleaf for some popular choices). Your choice will depend not only on appearance, and how you want to maintain the hedge—neatly clipped or billowing with blossoms—but also whether the plants are suited to your soil and climate, and whether the hedge is in a very windswept site or not. Among the best choices for cold exposed sites are beech, privet, and *Cornus mas*. Plants for coastal sites must in addition tolerate salt-laden winds. And if the hedge is intended to keep out browsing animals such as deer, you must obviously choose species that do not appeal to the marauders but are not toxic, as yew is, for example.

Formal hedges

Evergreens are the classic choice for clipped hedges, giving a solid backdrop of color and structure year-round. Yew (*Taxus baccata*) and boxwood (*Buxus*) make traditional hedges with a smooth finish; boxwood is ideal for low hedges as it grows more slowly than yew. An interesting alternative to boxwood is *Ilex crenata*, an evergreen holly with small rounded leaves that also lends itself to crisp clipping. Privet (*Ligustrum*) is tough but only partially evergreen, and can look somewhat dull in winter. Beech (*Fagus sylvatica*) and hornbeam (*Carpinus betulus*) are deciduous, but will retain their dried leaves, rustling in the wind as they glow coppery orange in winter sunlight. A fast

HEDGE-PLANTING TIPS

■ Bareroot plants, available in winter, are the cheapest option. You can buy mixed bundles of native species.

■ Plant evergreens in fall and deciduous species from fall to early spring.

■ Don't just dig individual holes: prepare a trench 2–3 ft (60–90 cm) wide (*as shown right*).

■ Use tree guards to protect young plants from grazing animals.

■ Provide shelter for the young plants initially in windy areas.

■ Mulch for weed control and water retention. Water in dry weather during the first year.

Firethorn feast An informal hedge of mixed pyracantha forms a tapestry of color: there are red-, orange-, and yellow-berried cultivars. You will probably find that the birds leave the yellow ones until last. Pyracantha's thorns make it a good deterrent to intruders.

effect is often obtained with leylandii conifers (x *Cupressocyparis leylandii*) but this, being a tall forest tree, will keep growing rapidly to a huge height unless you are very strict with the pruning from an early age. Let it grow to within 12 in (30 cm) of the desired height and then start pruning the top. The hedge will require pruning at least twice a year to keep it under control.

Informal hedges

Not all hedges need to be crisply trimmed, and flowering and fruiting hedges are among the richest food sources for wildlife (*see also pp.108–109*). For a more relaxed effect, try *Viburnum tinus*, which can be loosely clipped into cloudlike shapes. In warmer climates, griselinia makes an attractive hedge, as do fuchsias. Several flowering shrubs lend themselves to being grown as a hedge, either crisply or loosely cut. For a late winter show, the soft yellow flowers of *Cornus mas*, followed in late summer by shiny red edible berries, are unusual. The spring-flowering forsythias can also make a good hedge. Barberry, with its prickles, will discourage intruders; it makes a good flowering boundary.

Another way of creating an informal screen is to plant a living willow screen (*see p.141, and also pp.160–161*). Fresh willow branches are inserted into the ground during the winter months and are woven into a screen. By spring they will root, and start growing. Their sideshoots can then be woven into the existing structure.

CLIPPING HEDGES

With the exception of fast-growing hedges such as leylandii and *Lonicera nitida* that need to be pruned twice or even three times a year to keep them neat, most established hedges can be pruned once a year. If you prune twice, give the first trim after the last frost, as sensitive shoots of boxwood, for example, can be damaged. Otherwise, it is best to prune in late summer, after the main growth season is over. This way you can enjoy a crisp, neat hedge until the following spring. Prune hard, getting as close to the last cut as possible, or your hedge will soon get too fat or too tall. Only the looser-growing flowering hedges such as *Viburnum tinus* should be pruned with a light hand, following the natural contours formed by the shrubs.

Deciduous hedging plants

1 *Berberis thunbergii* 'Rose Glow'
Barberry
Covered with flowers and berries, but armed with sharp spines too, making a secure barrier.

2 *Carpinus betulus*
Hornbeam
Will retain some of its coppery dead leaves well into winter, as beech does.

3 *Cornus mas*
Cornelian cherry
Rather ungainly in its growth habit, but very hardy indeed, with welcome winter blossoms on its bare branches.

4 *Fagus sylvatica*
Beech
With hornbeam, one of the very best choices for a clipped deciduous hedge.

5 *Fuchsia magellanica* var. *molinae*
Fuchsia
Not all "hardy" fuchsias are immune to frost, so choose one to match the conditions in your region.

6 *Rosa rugosa*
Species roses
Most species roses have single flowers, but *R. rugosa* has gorgeous, blowsy cerise blooms, followed by red hips.

7 *Forsythia* 'Northern Gold'
Forsythia
Needs to be pruned correctly both to flower well and to keep it in shape; cut back the flowered stems after flowering.

8 *Crataegus laevigata* 'Rosea'
Hawthorn
One of the few hedges that will still flower even if regularly trimmed.

Evergreen hedging plants

1 *Griselinia littoralis*
Griselinia
The glossy leaves are very tolerant of salty winds, so this is a good choice to shelter an exposed coastal garden.

2 *Taxus baccata*
Yew
The red fleshy part of the fruit is not toxic, and is popular with birds, but all other parts are poisonous.

3 *Ilex aquifolium* 'Argentea Marginata'
Hollies
Clipping will reduce berrying, but there are lots of cultivars with attractive leaf variegation in white, cream, and yellow.

4 *Aucuba japonica* 'Crotonifolia'
Spotted laurel
One of the toughest, most pollution-tolerant and shade-tolerant of shrubs, ideal for city gardens.

5 *Ligustrum ovalifolium*
Privet
Clipped privet is neat, if dull; as a more informal hedge it will bear distinctively scented white flowers.

6 *Viburnum tinus* 'Eve Price'
Laurustinus
Best allowed to grow quite naturally; makes quite a wide, billowing hedge.

7 *Potentilla fruticosa* 'Red Ace'
Potentilla
Shrubby potentillas grow to about 3 ft (1 m) tall; they make excellent low hedges along garden paths, for example.

8 *Buxus sempervirens*
Boxwood
With yew, makes the finest evergreen formal hedges. Boxwood can grow to 15 ft (5 m) if unpruned, but there are many smaller and even dwarf cultivars.

Lawns and lawn care

Despite new trends for decking and patios, a lawn remains a garden essential for many of us. Wildlife certainly gains more benefit from a lawn than from any hard surface, and it acts as a good soakaway for heavy rainfall. From perfect turf to hard-wearing play area, all types of lawn can be managed organically.

PRINCIPLES OF ORGANIC LAWN CARE

■ Choose grass seed to create the type of lawn you require, and to suit the location.

■ Maintain good soil structure to promote grass growth.

■ Increase frequency of mowing as growth increases, but never mow too short.

■ Leave mowings on the lawn surface during summer to feed the grass.

■ Rake out moss (*see p.151*) before it accumulates and smothers the grass.

Lawns provide different things for different people, forming an important part of a landscape design, a foil for more colorful planting, access through the yard, or simply an area for play and relaxation. A lawn creates a sense of space, to be used or viewed as an open area that lets in light and provides views to the garden beyond. Managed organically, this green carpet can also contribute richly to the biological diversity of the garden.

For the organic gardener, the lawn is as much an ecosystem as the pond or fencerow. You may want a formal, relatively weed-free lawn, or you may prefer a more relaxed green swath made up of a diversity of plant species. Both can be created organically, though the former will require a lot more care and attention than the latter.

Informal organic lawns are exciting habitats in their own right, full of variety, and with great value to insects, birds, and other wildlife. By accepting that a variety of different plants can exist together in a lawn in addition to grass, organic gardeners can create rich habitats that support a range of insects and other creatures. Adjusting mowing and cultural regimens can create wilder areas, allowing flowers to self-seed, insects to feed and breed, and birds to forage for food and collect nesting materials.

Grassroots level An organically managed lawn containing a variety of grasses and flowers can become a useful habitat for insects and a feeding ground for birds.

Organic lawn care

Lawns are one of the few areas of the yard permanently covered with growth, preventing bulky organic soil improvers from being dug in. However, they can be applied as a topdressing (*see below*), to build and maintain soil structure and health. Supplementary fertilizers may also be necessary, but feeding is not an annual necessity. If grass growth and color is good, do not feed; you will only encourage more grass growth, which means more mowing! If growth is poor, apply a general organic fertilizer (*see p.54*) or a complete organic lawn feed over the whole lawn in early spring. An application of seaweed meal or extract (*see p.195*) in spring and summer improves grass growth and color. If growth continues to be slow, fertilize again in summer, and topdress in fall to improve soil structure.

Scarifying and aerating

Thatch is the name given to the fibrous material and organic debris that can accumulate in the depths of a lawn. It can prevent water from reaching the soil, encourage diseases, and stop grass from thickening up. Where necessary, remove thatch by vigorous raking, using considerable downward pressure. This process is known as scarification. Scarifying is best done in early fall, when it will encourage the grass to thicken up. If large bare patches appear after scarifying, sow with grass seed.

Aerating creates holes in the soil, allowing air and water to penetrate. It can be very beneficial on compacted areas of lawn. It can also be very hard work; only attempt it where compaction is a real problem. The best time to aerate is early fall, when the soil is moist. If you use a hollow-tined aerator, which takes out a core of soil about 4 in (10 cm) deep, then once every three years should be enough. The alternative is to simply spike the grass, using a fork on small areas, or a powered machine on larger lawns. However, spiking does compress the surrounding soil, so a hollow-tined aerator is better, particularly in heavy soil.

Topdressing

Good soil structure in the lawn encourages worm activity, which in turn improves drainage. The sprinkling of various soil-improving materials onto the lawn surface is a process known as topdressing. These materials are applied in layers thin enough for the grass to grow up through. For greater effect, particularly on compacted areas of the lawn, use a hollow-tined aerator before applying the

Clean sweep Fallen leaves need to be swept from the lawn to keep it healthy, but should never be burned: pile or bag them up to make leaf mold (*see pp.44–45*). You can fashion a besom, or lawn broom, yourself by binding a bundle of twiggy prunings to a wooden shaft. An alternative if leaf-fall is not too heavy is to mow over the leaves and leave them, shredded, in situ; worms will soon take them down into the soil.

Trimmed to shape Shears will be needed to keep this novel play furniture made from sod-covered mounds looking neat.

Lawn rake This useful tool, known as a spring-tine rake, will not snag on the grass as frequently as an ordinary rake will, yet combs out debris from the lawn most effectively.

top-dressing, which can then be brushed down into the channels.

Fall and spring are both good times to apply a topdressing. Start by scarifying, if necessary, then mow the grass to a length of about 1 in (2.5 cm). Do not cut lower or the dressing may smother the grass. For the topdressing, on light to normal soil, use a mixture of 2 parts loam to 3 parts low-fertility bulky organic material, such as leaf mold or municipal green waste compost (*see also pp.34–35*). If your soil is heavy and tends to be wet, use a mix of 3 parts sharp sand to 1 part loam and 1 part bulky organic material.

Sprinkle the topdressing mix evenly over the whole area to a depth of up to ½ in (1 cm). Hollows can be filled slightly more, and by adding a topdressing regularly through the year

these can be firmed and filled to gradually level the lawn surface. Brush or rake the topdressing through the grass onto the soil surface below using a stiff broom or besom brush. Heavy rain will help to do this if you time the treatments to coincide with wet weather.

Cutting the lawn
Grass can grow year-round provided conditions are warm and moist enough, but you will only need to mow regularly between spring and fall. Frequency of mowing depends on the speed of grass growth. During spring, a weekly trim may be sufficient, but for neater lawns and play areas this can be increased to twice a week from late spring onward. Summer mowing is a regular task, and for some a time-consuming chore, so simply mowing paths or formal areas keeps these looking good while leaving some areas undisturbed for wildlife. Grass growth decreases again in fall, requiring less frequent

mowing. In winter, grass may still grow slowly, but conditions are usually too wet to mow; it is best not to try, except during prolonged warm and dry periods.

The length of cut depends very much on the quality of grass in your lawn and how the lawn is being used. Long grass withstands drought better than shorter grass, and also provides stronger competition for weeds. Take care not to scalp the surface if the area is slightly bumpy.

What to do with lawn clippings

Grass mowings are a good source of nitrogen, which is released as they decompose. Where possible, leave them on the lawn to feed the grass; otherwise, recycle them in other ways. During the main mowing season—late spring and summer—mow regularly so that short clippings can be left on the lawn to rot down naturally. Consider investing in a mulching mower (*see panel, right*). In early spring and fall, and when the grass is long, clippings are best collected in the grass box on your mower. Left on the lawn, they can smother growth and encourage disease. They are a useful material for recycling elsewhere in the garden and should never be burned or discarded. Use them as "greens" on the compost pile (*see p.37*); mix with autumn leaves in a leaf mold pile, or use as a mulch around trees, shrubs, fruit bushes, and vegetables.

Clear contrast These grass paths may not be immaculately maintained, but look well-groomed in this context, forming neat strips of green carpet between "beds" of rough grasses and wild flowers. The effect looks intentional, rather than the result of neglect.

MOWERS AND MOWING

For small, level lawns, hand-powered cylinder mowers are a good choice for organic gardeners who do not wish to use electricity or gasoline. They are cheap, efficient, and economical to use, providing extra exercise too. For larger areas of grass, you will need a power mower. The mulching mower is an excellent choice for organic gardeners with large lawns. Grass cuttings are chopped finely, then blown down into the sod. Deposited close to the soil surface, they quickly decompose, or are taken down by worms, to feed the soil. Mulching mowers have been shown to improve grass growth, recycling nutrients back into the lawn, and so decreasing the need for fertilizer.

■ Lawn mowers are one of the most dangerous tools used regularly in the yard, so follow the safety advice provided by the manufacturer.

■ Check cords on electric models before mowing, and use a ground-fault circuit interrupter (GFCI) outlet.

■ Noise pollution is a growing problem in urban areas; choose a hand-powered mower or a quieter power model. Mow with consideration for neighbors.

■ Have blades sharpened regularly, and replace them if damaged by stones.

■ Check that frogs or small animals are not hiding around the edges of lawns or in longer areas of grass before cutting.

■ Do not strain the mower by tackling very long, wet, or rough grass. Cut long grass in stages, starting with the mower blades set high and lowering in stages until the grass is the desired height.

■ To avoid damaging trees or other features in the lawn, replace an area of sod around them with a mulch.

Lawn problems

A single-species lawn is a virtual monoculture—a very unnatural state of affairs. Left to its own devices, a lawn soon becomes a more varied community of plants, including coarser grasses and wildflowers, and much more attractive to a wider range of wildlife. Some gardeners spend a great deal of time preventing anything other than grass from growing in their lawns.

Others take a more balanced approach, and are quite happy to tolerate "weeds" such as clover and daisies.

Some weeds can be positively beneficial. The roots of clover (*see panel, left*) fix nitrogen from the air in the soil, providing the plant with a ready source of this essential nutrient and so cutting down the need to add fertilizer. Grasses growing in close association with clover can take up small amounts of nitrogen released into the soil. Small-leaf clover resists drought well, remaining green in dry conditions. And how do you make a daisy chain without daisies?

Weed control

By following the advice on lawn care on these pages, your lawn should reward you by growing strongly and resisting weed infestations. If weeds do become a problem, various methods can be used.

■ **Remove individual weeds** like daisies, plantains, and dandelions by hand, using an old kitchen knife or special tool, such as an asparagus fork.

■ **Fill in holes** left after removing weeds with soil or all-purpose potting mix, and sow grass seed into this.

■ **Avoid mowing too low** Short grass offers less competition for weeds, and cutting too short can weaken grass, making it easier for weeds to invade.

■ **Scarify** (*see p.147*) to remove debris and improve conditions for grass growth.

■ **Improve drainage** with a hollow-tined aerator (*see p.147*) to prevent waterlogged conditions, which harm grass and encourage moisture-loving weeds and moss.

Common lawn weeds

Different soils and situations encourage their own types of weeds. Identifying problem weeds can tell you something about them and help

THE VALUE OF CLOVER

Far from treating lawn clover as a problem, organic gardeners should consider actively encouraging it. Clover flowers are a rich source of nectar for bees, and the ability of clover to take nitrogen from the air and convert it into useful nitrogen fertilizer for itself in its roots means the clover will grow well even in poor soil without the need for additional feeding. During periods of drought, the greenest part of a lawn is often an area covered with clover, which stays green when surrounding grasses have browned off.

Rather than wait for wild clovers to find a way into your lawn, you can overseed with white Dutch clover seed. Scarify the lawn first to remove debris and expose the soil surface. Then sow clover seed sparingly over the required area at a rate of about ¼–½ oz per sq yard (7.5–15 g per square meter). This produces an even carpet of small-leafed clover that should grow in the company of grasses to create an attractive lawn.

(Right, from top) **Lawn problems** Moss can be raked out, but it is better to identify the cause and remedy it; standing water after heavy rain can be a sign of surface compaction or poor drainage, and can be alleviated by aerating; low-growing, rosette-forming weeds such as plantain escape the mower and must be dug out.

point you in the right direction to control them. Ground ivy, for example, quickly spreads in moist, shaded areas. Chickweed is a good indication of somewhat alkaline soil. Dandelions are more numerous in compacted soil and in lawns mown very short. Clover grows well in poor soil. Fertilizing the lawn will tend to deter it (*but see also* The value of clover, *opposite*). Sheep's sorrel can be a problem in acidic soil conditions. Liming soil (*see below*) can help. Plantain and thistles grow where grass is thin or patchy. Lawn pests include ants, leatherjackets, and moles; see the A–Z of Plant Problems (*pp.320–341*) for advice on these.

How to control moss

Moss can develop for a variety of reasons. It relishes moist areas where drainage is poor, and will also thrive on drier soil where soil fertility is poor and acidity high (*see also* Liming lawns, *below*). Moss colonizes areas in shade, and spreads over soil where grass is mown too short. Rake out moss regularly with a lawn rake, each spring and fall if the problem is serious. Bare patches should be reseeded. Fertilize an ailing lawn to strengthen grass growth, and set mower blades to about 2 in (5 cm) to avoid mowing too short. Improving drainage will also discourage moss.

Remember that moss is valued by birds for nest-building, so consider leaving a mossy patch for them to obtain nesting material, or leave piles of raked-out moss in an open position for them to collect.

Liming lawns

Soil chemistry (*see pp.30–31*) can affect the overall health of a lawn. If you garden in acidic soil, you may find that liming your lawn to raise the pH value will encourage stronger growth. Acidic soil conditions encourage a buildup of thatch and cause poor grass growth. Acidic soil also favors moss (*see above*) and certain other weeds, like sheep's sorrel. If the pH is below 5.5–6.0, lime the area to bring it up to around 7. Ground limestone or dolomitic lime (*see p.55*), evenly sprinkled over the lawn and gently raked in, is the appropriate organic treatment. Repeat annually until the required pH level is reached.

8. Woody Plants

Trees, shrubs, and woody climbers supply the permanent backdrop for a garden. Shrubs and trees provide structure and height, and add depth and character to the garden scene. Climbers clothe bare walls and fences; trained on arbors, arches, and even up into trees, they make striking garden features. All of these plants provide cover for birds, mammals, and insects, and are an important source of food and nesting material; in exchange for room and board, these creatures will play a vital part in maintaining a garden organically. And woody prunings can be put to a number of uses, both practical and inventive, in the garden.

Color and shape The red stems of *Cornus alba* add brilliant color to the winter garden. Many other shrubs can be coppiced, as this one is, for bolder leaves and striking stems.

The importance of trees

The old saying "Weed as if you will die tomorrow, plant trees as if you will live forever" should be put into practice more often. Many people are reluctant to plant trees, thinking they will never see them reach maturity. If the word "maturity" conjures up visions of old, gnarled oaks, then you're right. If, on the other hand, you would be satisfied with a trunk sufficiently large to comfortably wrap your arms around and a canopy sufficient to provide shade for an afternoon nap, then you should be outside digging a hole for it now. Planting a tree is always special, making it the perfect way of commemorating a landmark occasion such as a move into a new house, a birth, a wedding, or a special anniversary.

Spring beauty Apple, pear, and plum trees and their ornamental relatives in the genera *Malus*, *Pyrus*, and *Prunus* are some of the first trees to blossom in spring, usually flowering in profusion. This provides a welcome treat not only for the gardener, but also for hungry flying insects such as bees that have ventured out early in the year.

Welcome shade Increasingly warm summers mean that shade in the garden is becoming as important in more northerly latitudes as it has always been in, for example, Mediterranean countries. A small deciduous tree will provide a shaded play area in summer, its leaves dropping in fall to let in more light during the darker days.

Trees play a vital role in our environment. They clean up the air we breathe, absorb dust and noise, provide food and shelter for wildlife, and play an important role as a climatic thermostat. During summer they create welcome shade that is several degrees cooler than that cast by a building. During cold winter weather their network of branches creates air pockets, trapping air and creating a sheltered microclimate.

Choosing the right tree

The main criteria to consider when planting a tree are its suitability for the soil conditions and climate, and its ultimate size. In a small yard in particular, it is also important that the tree rewards you with the maximum interest all year. Attractive bark, unusual leaf coloration or markings, fall color, flowers, and fruits (*see overleaf*) are all options. The proposed location of the tree will also have a bearing on your choice.

Siting trees

Horror stories often blame trees for damage to houses— foundations ruined by tree roots, septic systems clogged, and so on. Tree roots themselves, however, rarely cause damage to buildings. Most problems only occur in clay soil where the clay either shrinks, following severe dry weather, or heaves (expands), usually after a tree has been removed. A healthy tree takes up large quantities of water from the soil, and during exceptionally dry spells, clay soil can dry out and shrink. When a tree is removed, it is no longer drawing water out of the soil; this can cause clay soil to heave.

Tree roots sometimes do find their way into broken water pipes, where over time they expand, causing the pipes to crack. In heavy soil in particular, birch, cherry, apple, pear, and plum should be planted no less than 12 ft (4 m) from the house. Ash, false acacia, chestnut, linden, sycamore, maple, and willow trees should be planted no less than 22 ft (7 m) away, while oak and poplar are safest kept at a minimum distance of 40 ft (12 m) from the house or garage.

Use common sense when planting trees. Look at the sun's position during the day, and imagine where the shadows will be. Make sure your favorite breakfast corner will not be thrown into deep shade in the morning. Remember that tree roots will spread beyond the crown of the tree, affecting moisture and nutrient levels in the soil in the surrounding area.

TREES FOR SMALL YARDS

Acer griseum, *A. campestre*,
  A. palmatum and cultivars (the
  "Japanese" maples)
Amelanchier lamarckii
Cornus kousa var. *chinensis*
Crataegus monogyna
Enkianthus campanulatus
Euonymus europaeus
Laburnum anagyroides
Liquidambar styraciflua (*above*)
Malus 'Golden Hornet',
  M. 'John Downie' and many
  other crab apples
Prunus (many)
Sorbus (many)

Trees for fall color

1 *Acer campestre*
Field maple
Leaves are tinged purple when young,
then dark green in summer, turning to
a clear yellow. Fast-growing and robust.

2 *Quercus coccinea*
Scarlet oak
Large, strikingly divided leaves which
in their fall tints are popular with flower
arrangers. Best in acidic soil.

3 *Nyssa sinensis*
Chinese tupelo
Forms a broadly conical tree with
graceful, sweeping branches. Needs
shelter from cold, dry winds; colors
best after a hot summer.

4 *Parrotia persica*
Persian ironwood
Mature trees have the added attraction
of beautiful, peeling gray-fawn bark.
Tiny, spidery red flowers are borne on
the bare branches in late winter.

5 *Acer palmatum*
Japanese maple
A wide choice of cultivars with fall tints
of red, purple, orange or, like 'Sango-
kaku' (*pictured*), a soft yellow,
contrasting with its coral red stems.

6 *Acer japonicum*
Full-moon maple
This is the cultivar 'Aconitifolium', with
especially large, coarsely toothed leaves
in burgundy red.

7 *Cornus kousa*
Cornel, dogwood
Perfect for a small garden, with showy
flowers followed by fleshy red fruits,
flaking bark, and glowing fall color.

8 *Stewartia monadelpha*
Stewartia
A pretty tree from East Asia, related
to camellias; when mature, it bears
cup-shaped white flowers in summer.

Trees for flowers and fruits

1 *Malus* 'Red Sentinel'
Crab apple
There are myriad crab apple cultivars, all with beautiful blossoms in spring and conspicuous fruits in a variety of shades.

2 *Prunus* x *subhirtella*
Higan cherry, rosebud cherry
'Pendula Rosea Plena' (*pictured*) has weeping branches covered with big blowsy flowers very early in the year.

3 *Ilex aquifolium*
Holly
This is 'Amber', an unusual yellow-berried cultivar, but most have the more familiar red berries and prickly leaves.

4 *Sorbus vilmorinii*
Vilmorin's rowan
From one of the most popular genera of berrying trees, most with white flowers but fruiting in a variety of colors.

5 *Prunus padus*
Bird cherry
These plumes of white flowers are followed by black fruits, very bitter to our taste but loved by birds.

6 *Euonymus europaeus*
Spindle tree
'Red Cascade' (*pictured*) forms a small tree or large shrub, with spreading branches covered with fuchsia-pink fruits that split to reveal orange inside.

7 *Aesculus pavia*
Red buckeye
Much smaller than but closely related to the European horse chestnut, with the same "candle"-type flower clusters, but daintier, in a rich red.

8 *Cornus nuttallii*
Pacific dogwood
All of the flowering dogwoods have these showy bracts surrounding the flowerheads, in shades of cream, pale yellow or pink. This is 'Colrigo Giant'.

Pollarding and coppicing

With regular pruning and training, it is possible to grow potentially large trees in confined spaces. Many tall trees, such as chestnuts, lindens, and willows, can be pollarded, meaning that they are cut back to the main stem at about head height. Coppicing, a similar practice, involves cutting the wood down to ground level. Coppiced hazel is popular as it provides pliable stakes, useful in the garden. Both coppicing and pollarding are also used to ornamental effect. Renewable and sustainable, coppice products and garden prunings can provide the organic gardener with natural and versatile building materials.

An ancient craft

Traditionally, trees were pollarded to provide wood for domestic use while keeping the young shoots out of reach of grazing animals. Coppicing is another ancient woodcraft that is still very much alive today, being used to restore and maintain ancient and valuable woodlands in Europe. When carefully managed, an area of coppice can support a great diversity of flora and fauna and is one of the richest habitats of a temperate climate.

Charcoal is a valuable byproduct of some woodland management initiatives, and a local supply of this sustainable resource should always be sought out by the organic barbecue chef, rather than buying charcoal that may have traveled long distances and been sourced from unsustainable, poorly managed woods and tropical forests.

Coppicing and pollarding usually extend the natural life of a tree. An ash tree lives for about 200 years, whereas if it is coppiced regularly, it will continue to grow from the same root plate for centuries longer. Coppiced ash trees growing on waterlogged soil in Bradfield Woods, near Bury St. Edmunds, England, have been dated at 1,000 years old.

(Below, from left) **Valuable harvest** Using a billhook to harvest hazel poles from a regularly coppiced stool; the cut poles, stacked for drying before being used to make screens and fences; the garden shrub *Cornus stolonifera* 'Flaviramea', pruned in exactly the same way each year for its colorful winter stems.

Traditionally coppiced trees include hazel, ash, sweet chestnut, oak, alder, sycamore, willow, hornbeam, maple, and linden. However, most deciduous trees are suitable for coppicing, and they can be harvested on a cycle, ranging from annually for willow, to every 20 years for larger ash or chestnut poles. Hazel for fencing spars is generally harvested on a six- to eight-year cycle. Chestnut is used for traditional hop poles and ash for woven fencing. They are harvested on a 15-year cycle.

Coppice products

Coppice wood is the term given to the poles and branches produced by the "stool" of a coppiced tree—a tree stump or root plate that is cut at ground level every few years. The stool continues to live, sending up slender young branches after each harvest. A pollarded tree is managed in a similar way, except that the branches are cut at a greater height, from a permanent trunk called a "bolling."

Adopting these techniques in the garden allows you to grow tree and shrub species that would, if left to grow unchecked, become unmanageably large for a small space. Willows (*Salix*) and dogwoods (*Cornus*) are the most popular choices, since many of them have brilliantly colored bark on their young stems that brings welcome color to the winter garden.

Eucalyptus, cotinus, and catalpa are also often grown as coppiced or pollarded shrubs in shrub or mixed borders since their leaves become strikingly larger when grown in this way, forming an attractive backdrop to other plants. Plants may be cut back annually or, to make a more substantial presence in the garden, every two or three years.

Using the pruned stems

Woody material from garden pruning can be used in the same way as coppice wood. Garden trees and shrubs can provide small-diameter wood with a huge range of durability, flexibility,

Maintaining a pollarded tree
1. Enjoy pollarded and coppiced trees and shrubs (this is a willow) through the winter, before pruning in spring. **2.** First remove all the weak stems with pruners, to make it easier to cut through the thicker branches. **3.** Leave a short stump as you cut; the new shoots will spring from buds on this stub. Switch from pruners to loppers for the thicker stems. **4.** The finished plant may look very "naked," but will soon grow back with renewed vigor.

(Below, top) **Edging for beds** Nail sturdy poles between pegs, as shown here, or weave more flexible rods between closely spaced pegs.

(Below, bottom) **Supports for climbers** This is one of the simplest structures to make, from trimmed poles lashed together with twine. Pushed securely into the ground, it will be used to support runner beans.

strength, and color. It is well worth experimenting with the species in your own garden. *Cornus alba* cultivars, willows, and ash trees (*Fraxinus*) provide some of the richest bark colors for decorative panels in woven screens. For a paler, cleaner look, branches can be stripped of their bark.

Many species that are normally brittle can be used if they are cut in spring when the rising sap makes the branches more flexible for bending and weaving, especially if very young shoots are used. Otherwise, the normal time to cut coppice wood is during winter, when the trees are dormant.

Making plant supports

Supports for climbing plants can be made from coppiced wood, or even shrub and hedge prunings of a suitable length. They will last for a year or two if in contact with soil, longer if not. Twiggy materials are best for plants such as sweet peas that cling with tendrils; straight rods work well for twining climbers.

Create tepees with flexible rods. To provide greater stability for heavier climbers such as roses, weave fine willow rods in spiral fashion around the tepee frame to create a continuous woven band around the base.

To make an arch-shaped bentwood trellis, use a large bench or area of firm ground and lay out the framework pieces: two uprights and three or four main crosspieces. Wire together the tops of the two uprights to form an arch. Either nail or bind the crosspieces between the uprights to strengthen the arch. Then use finer stems to crisscross the framework in the pattern of your choice.

When using willow, strip the bark from the lower part of the rod (or whole stem if you like). This is easily done when newly cut. If the bark is not stripped, the stems will root into the ground. This is a growth habit that can be put to good use, however, in creating "living" willow structures.

Living willow screens and structures

Freshly cut green willow rods can be made into an elegant lattice fence (one is shown on p.141) that subsequently takes root and grows to produce a leafy, living screen known as a "fedge"—a cross between a fence and a hedge. Screens made from living willow are strong, and make effective windbreaks where other materials fail. Vigorous species such as *Salix daphnoides*, *Salix alba*, and *Salix purpurea* hybrids are most commonly used, although any species with flexible branches of sufficient length

Willow wonderland Living willow can be used to create an amazing range of screens, tunnels, domes, and arches. If neglected for any time, the willow stems will start to grow into full-sized trees, so be prepared to prune them annually.

and strength will do. The flexibility of willow rods allows them to be made into all kinds of structures, including arbors, tunnels, domes, and sculptures. The rods are cut and used fresh during winter to ensure that they will root. As the willows become established, vigorous new growth is produced each season. This must be pruned back in winter to maintain the shape of the structure. When siting a willow screen, remember that the summer growth can be wide-spreading—up to 3 ft (1 m) on each side.

Making a simple willow wall

Willow-weaving classes are increasingly available, and can be both useful and fun, but you could make a start on your own with a simple screen. For this you need a selection of freshly cut willow rods, sorted into bundles of similar length, and a roll of weed-suppressing landscape fabric (*see pp.74–75*) about 3 ft (1 m) wide to run the length of the screen, plus a metal rod and sledgehammer to make holes, and pruning shears and twine.

■ First, roll out the fabric and secure it, either by digging it into the ground or by tacking it down with large landscaping staples.

■ Using the metal rod, make planting holes in a straight line down the center of the fabric, 6– 8 in (15–20 cm) apart and 12 in (30 cm) deep.

■ Select fairly thick, strong rods and push these into the holes to form the uprights.

■ Now use lighter rods to establish diagonals. Make an angled planting hole at 45° to one side of each upright. Push rods in and weave them diagonally across four uprights. Mirror this on the other side with planting holes angled in the opposite direction on the other side of each upright.

■ Using long, fine rods, create a firm band of strong weaving across the top. Tie down the loose ends in decorative arcs across the top.

Shrubs

Interesting leaf shapes and colors, attractive stems, seasonal flowers and fruits, and appeal to wild birds are some of the features brought into the garden by shrubs. They can act as backdrop, ground cover, or feature plant, depending on how and where they are used. Even so-called foliage shrubs may have pretty leaf variegation or good fall color. There are tiny shrubs, such as rock roses, that are suited to the front of a border, while some rhododendrons can attain the size of a house.

There is a huge selection of shrubs to choose from, suiting most conditions and tastes. A little homework will help you find the right plants for your garden, and thus save you many hours of tending shrubs in the years to come. The acidic-soil-loving, stately rhododendrons, in all colors and sizes, flower between late winter and early summer; hydrangeas announce the coming of fall with their dainty lacecaps or spherical snowballs; viburnums with gorgeous scents flower at virtually every time of year, and ground-covering euonymus is tough and reliable. The ornamental dogwoods, such as *Cornus alba* 'Sibirica' and *C. stolonifera* 'Flaviramea', offer little in the way of flowers, but start performing in fall when their leaves turn pink and red, followed by stems that glow deep red and shine lime green, respectively. This effect can be enjoyed until late winter, when they should be cut back again (*see* Coppicing and pollarding, *pp.158–161*).

The effect becomes much more intense when they are planted in groups of five or more.

Versatile viburnums Red-berried guelder rose, *Viburnum opulus* (*left*, with snowberries), can be planted as a fruiting hedge or back-of-the-border shrub, while *V. plicatum* 'Mariesii', with its tiered habit and white lacecap flowers (*facing page, left*), makes a feature in its own right, deserving a prominent position. Powerfully fragrant *V.* x *bodnantense* 'Dawn' (*facing page, right*) is one of several that scent the air in midwinter to early spring.

Establishing a shrub border

Once established, shrubs, especially those that are evergreen, are effective weed suppressants, but until they have reached that stage there are several ways of dealing with the bare soil. Shrubs can be planted more densely than needed, then thinned out as they mature. If carefully dug up during the dormant season, the thinned-out shrubs can be moved to a new site. Alternatively, the space surrounding the shrubs can be filled with ground-covering herbaceous perennials such as pulmonaria, which will gradually disappear as competition from the growing shrubs increases. Another option is to plant through a permeable weedproof membrane (*see pp.74–75*), hidden by a gravel or bark mulch.

Ground-cover shrubs

Plants for ground cover have become very popular since the mid-20th century, as they cut down on garden chores considerably. A successful scheme should require little or no care once it is well established, making it the most labor-saving type of planting possible. Starting with a weed-free area, even young plants require little maintenance during the establishment years. The best plants to use as ground cover are evergreen or densely twigged ones with a low, spreading habit. This prevents light from penetrating through to the soil, discouraging weed growth. Prostrate conifers are effective, but do not offer much seasonal variety. Hebes, on the other hand, produce flowers over prolonged periods, but can be short-lived, particularly in colder areas. Certain ground-cover roses, such as 'Max Graf', grow into a colorful animal- and intruder-repellent cover, though as they lose their leaves in winter they are not the most effective weed-suppressors, and their thorns can make weeding unpleasant.

GROUND-COVER SHRUBS

Calluna vulgaris
Cotoneaster horizontalis (above),
    C. microphyllus
Erica
Euonymus fortunei and cultivars *
Gaultheria *
Hebe albicans, H. pinguifolia, H. 'Youngii'
Hypericum calycinum *
Leucothoe walteri and cultivars *
Mahonia aquifolium *, *M. repens* *
Pachysandra terminalis *
Rosmarinus officinalis Prostratus Group
Rubus pentalobus
Sarcococca hookeriana var. *humilis* *
Stephanandra incisa 'Crispa'

* Shade-tolerant

Shrubs you can prune hard annually

1 *Salix alba* var. *vitellina* 'Britzensis'
White willow cultivar
One of several willows that can be cut back hard each year (*see pp.158–161*) for colorful winter stems.

2 *Cotinus coggygria* 'Royal Purple'
Smokebush
Hard pruning each year results in few flowers, but greatly enhances the leaf size and rich color.

3 *Fuchsia* 'Mrs. Popple'
Hardy fuchsia
Will survive winter in mild climates, but makes a better-shaped, more freely flowering shrub if cut back hard in early spring.

4 *Hydrangea paniculata*
Panicle hydrangea
If cut back hard to a stubby framework each year, this less familiar hydrangea bears the biggest flower clusters.

5 *Philadelphus coronarius* 'Aureus'
Mock orange
A mock orange that is grown not for its flowers, but for its bright yellow-green leaves. Hard pruning enhances the leaf size and color.

6 *Rubus cockburnianus*
Rubus
Enjoy the brilliant white bloom on the stems through the winter, then cut them all back in the spring.

7 *Buddleja davidii* 'Fascinating'
Buddleja, butterfly bush
These vigorous shrubs need pruning back to a stubby framework each spring to keep them shapely and manageable.

8 *Hypericum* 'Hidcote'
St. John's wort, rose of Sharon
Tough hypericums like this one can be left to their own devices, but are reinvigorated by hard pruning.

Shrubs that need minimal pruning

1 *Daphne bholua*
Daphne
All of the daphnes hate to be pruned; do it only if necessary to remove dead, diseased or damaged stems.

2 *Berberis* x *carminea* 'Buccaneer'
Barberry
Although they tolerate pruning if a branch is awkwardly placed, and can be trimmed into a hedge if desired, none of the barberries need special pruning.

3 *Cotoneaster salicifolius*
Cotoneaster
Most cotoneasters need no special pruning; in the case of this species, it can spoil its naturally graceful habit.

4 *Hamamelis* x *intermedia* 'Jelena'
Witch hazel
Hamamelis do not make particularly elegant shrubs, but are best left unpruned unless dead, diseased, or damaged wood needs to be removed.

5 *Potentilla fruticosa* 'Princess'
Potentilla, cinquefoil
If grown as a low hedge, can be trimmed over lightly with shears after flowering to make them bushier.

6 *Choisya* 'Aztec Pearl'
Mexican orange blossom
Needs pruning only to shorten the odd overlong branch that spoils the shape.

7 *Rhododendron* 'Elizabeth'
Rhododendron
Although rhododendrons tolerate even drastic cutting back to renovate, they need no regular pruning.

8 *Magnolia* x *loebneri* 'Leonard Messel'
Magnolia
Be sure to site magnolias where their mature size can be accommodated; it is best to keep pruning to a minimum.

Climbers

Climbers increase height and variety in planting, while taking up little space. Traditionally, climbers are trained on walls, fences, and trellises, or up arbors and freestanding supports. They can also be grown up through other plants, suiting the vigor of the climber to the "host": a rambling rose, for example, climbing up a sturdy tree, or a lighter clematis scrambling through a shrub.

Tying in Ties made of natural fibers rot with time and are unlikely to cause constriction. But check ties regularly on a plant whose stems are expanding rapidly, and loosen them if necessary.

Climbing techniques

Self-clinging climbers such as ivy and *Parthenocissus henryana*, which have tiny roots or suction pads that adhere to the surface, are perfect for surfaces where you cannot attach climbing supports. Others, such as wisteria, are twiners that will wind up ropes, poles or branches, or, like passion flowers (*Passiflora*), cling on with the help of little tendrils; the leafstalks of clematis twine themselves around twigs, string, or wire. Spined plants, such as roses, claw their way up by hooking themselves onto their support. This is effective when they are scrambling up vegetation masses, as would happen in the wild, but they need to be tied in if you want to guide them along walls or posts.

Training climbers

It pays to spend some time during spring and early summer, when climbers are growing rapidly, to guide them along their support. For many plants, particularly roses, terminal buds (the topmost ones on the stems) are the ones producing flowers, while the sideshoots produce only foliage. When branches are trained in a near-horizontal position, all those sideshoots will start growing vertically, and, like the terminal bud, will produce flowers. So, by tying the branches down to an existing framework and training them across, rather than upward, you will ensure a much better crop of flowers, which can be enjoyed at eye level.

Never use plastic or metal ties, as these will cut into the wood as the branches grow and fatten, cutting off the sap stream and creating a weak point. Natural fibers will rot eventually, and will snap and release as the branch expands. By then the plant has usually been tied again at a higher point and will stay in place. It is still advisable to check climbers regularly, loosening tight ties and tying in new shoots. The younger the growth, the more pliable it is and the easier to train.

CLIMBERS THAT NEED PRUNING

■ **Clematis viticella** is a summer-flowering clematis with many cultivars and hybrids that lend themselves well to annual cutting back to 12 in (30 cm). This promotes vigorous new growth that can then be carefully trained to produce flowers at eye level.

■ **Climbing roses** should be pruned annually, removing the old flowering stems, and thinning out some of the older stems to encourage new growth at the base. The flowered stems should be cut back to the main stem, leaving approximately two buds or "eyes"; then tie in the main stems again, as close to horizontal as possible.

■ **Wisteria sinensis** (*below*) needs to be pruned in two stages. In summer, when the main growing season is over, the new shoots are pruned back by about half. In winter these shoots are then further shortened to two buds. This may seem elaborate, but will give much joy when the heavily scented trusses of delicate lilac flowers appear the following spring.

CLIMBERS REQUIRING NO PRUNING

■ **Clematis montana** (*above*) is one of the more vigorous spring-flowering clematis. Its dark green foliage complements the blush pink flowers that cover it in late spring. Although it dislikes being pruned, its vigorous habit occasionally necessitates severe cutting back, which it will withstand. This should take place after flowering.

■ **Hydrangea petiolaris** will happily work itself up a north-facing wall, making it ideal for hiding unsightly garage walls or sheds. Although it will take a few years to establish, its flaky, rust-brown stems will soon charm you, as it produces its fresh green foliage in spring, soon followed by delicately scented white lacecap flowers.

■ **Parthenocissus henryana** is a deciduous, self-clinging climber that has attractive foliage and stunning fall color. Its vigor makes it ideal for covering a facade—or allow it to clamber through a tall pine, where its fall foliage will contrast beautifully.

Roses

Loved by many gardeners, roses are often considered to be the most noble of garden flowers. They can be difficult to grow, and account for a high proportion of pesticides used in nonorganic gardens. With careful selection and good growing conditions, however, roses can be grown successfully organically. Breeders are still searching for the fully disease-resistant rose, but some species and cultivars are known to be less susceptible than others (*see facing page*). Providing good growing conditions will help to keep them healthy.

Fruit for the birds Roses that flower once only in summer, such as *Rosa glauca*, *R. moyesii*, and *R. rubiginosa*, will produce colorful, bird-attracting rose hips in the fall. Although many roses benefit from deadheading, never deadhead roses grown for their fruits.

Choosing which roses to grow

Certain roses are less suited to organic gardening than others. Bush roses, such as the hybrid tea and floribunda (cluster-flowered) types, dislike competition at root level and so are often grown as a monocrop in a rose bed. They require ample spacing, dislike underplanting, and due to the fact they are grown *en masse*, tend to be more susceptible to pest and disease outbreaks.

Species and shrub roses are better suited to the organic garden. They are less sensitive to competition from other plants and are often less susceptible to diseases and pests. Most are of greater value to wildlife and are much less labor-intensive, as they require less pruning and deadheading. Look for roses with rose hips. These are popular with pollinating insects, provide an excellent food source for birds and mammals, and create a colorful seasonal display. The more informal habit of species and shrub roses means that they look more at home in a mixed border. Species roses, such as *Rosa glauca* or *R. moyesii*, can be mixed into a shrub or herbaceous border. Most rugosa roses make a good, thorny hedge, with glossy hips.

How and where to plant roses

Roses will perform at their best in an open, sunny site. Good air circulation and moisture-retentive but well-drained soil will help prevent disease buildup. Avoid planting in sites susceptible to waterlogging, or in very acidic or alkaline conditions. Where possible, grow roses in a mixed border. Low-growing flowering plants can be grown around the outer edge of a bed of bush roses—which dislike competition—to add diversity and encourage natural predators.

Resistant roses

1 'Charles de Mills'
An old-fashioned shrub rose of the gallica type, unusual in having no thorns. Very good grown as a hedge.

2 'Blanche Double de Coubert'
A shrub rose, dense and spreading in habit, with the distinctively wrinkled leaves of the rugosa group. The flowers are sometimes followed by bright hips. 'Roseraie de l'Haÿ', with rich red-purple flowers, is another good rugosa.

3 'Buff Beauty'
Very popular modern shrub rose, flowering very freely in clusters. 'Cerise Bouquet', with cherry red flowers, and 'Fritz Nobis', in warm pink, are other modern shrub roses that rarely suffer disease problems.

4 'Bonica'
A ground-cover rose—a modern shrub rose with a low, spreading habit, often flowering in these tight clusters all along its arching stems.

5 *Rosa filipes* 'Kiftsgate'
A rampant climber, only for those with a substantial garden wall or fence or a robust arbor. 'Maigold', with bronze-yellow flowers, and 'Climbing Cécile Brünner', in light pink, are much more manageable climbers with good disease resistance.

6 'Frühlingsmorgen'
A shrub rose with pretty, hay-scented single flowers—that is, with the central boss of stamens fully visible—the type of rose bees prefer.

7 'Gertrude Jekyll'
One of the "English" roses, old-fashioned in their flower shape but repeat-flowering just like a modern shrub rose. Very fragrant.

8 'Just Joey'
Along with scarlet-flowered 'Remembrance', this is among the most trouble-free traditional bush roses.

Caring for woody plants

There are, as yet, no recognized organic growing standards for ornamental plants. Raising your own is a slow process; you may have to make do with conventionally grown plants, and then plant and care for them following organic principles.

All plants benefit from being planted in a well-prepared site. The better the soil, the quicker they establish. Remove all weeds, particularly perennial ones (*see pp.76–81*). If planting a new border, prepare the whole area, digging and adding soil improvers as necessary, depending on the state of the soil and the type of plants. When planting a mix of species with different requirements, prepare the whole area with a low-fertility material such as leaf mold, then add compost or well-rotted manure to individual planting holes as appropriate.

When to plant
Although container-grown stock can be planted at any time of the year, the ideal planting season for woody plants is between fall and spring. Trees planted in early fall will benefit

PLANTING TREES AND SHRUBS

1 Dig a generous hole around 18 in (45 cm) deep, or twice as deep as the rootball. In heavy soil, gently fork over the base and sides of the hole to allow the roots to penetrate. Soak the rootball of the plant well before planting.

2 As you position the plant in the hole, use a cane as a guide to check that the surface of the plant's rootball will be at or just below soil level. Make sure the plant is upright, and showing its best side.

3 If staking is required (*see facing page, top*), put the stake in now to avoid damaging the roots. Set the plant in the hole and backfill the hole with the removed soil, mixed with a bulky soil improver if necessary.

4 Step down the soil firmly and evenly, water well, and mulch.

STAKING TREES

Trees shorter than 5 ft (1.5 m) do not need a stake, unless planted on a very windy site. Larger trees usually need to be staked when planted, to stop the wind from rocking the plants in the soil. A diagonal stake hammered into the hole outside the rootball (*left*) suits most trees; use a buckle-and-spacer tie (*shown here*) to keep the stake from chafing the bark. A tree planted as a large specimen may need to be staked for 3–5 years, but in most cases the stake can be removed after a year or two. There is no point in using a preservative-treated stake that will last for decades when the tree is only to be staked for a couple of years.

from the still-warm soil, sending out new roots before winter sets in. Spring-planted stock may not get the chance to establish roots before the start of the drier seasons, making them more susceptible to drying out. In mild climates, it is possible to plant throughout winter, as long as the ground is not frozen or waterlogged. To promote rapid establishment, keep young plants moist and free from weeds or grass. Mulch an area of at least 3 ft (1 m) around each plant with a loose mulch or a mulch mat. For really low maintenance, plant through a permeable membrane (*see pp.74–75*), covered with loose mulch or gravel.

Care after planting

Do not be shy about pruning trees and shrubs when planting. Remove any diseased or damaged shoots and, if necessary, shape the plant. Water new plantings during dry periods. Continuing to mulch with an organic soil improver (*see pp.34–35*) during establishment years will help to retain moisture and suppress weeds, which will promote rapid growth.

Planting climbers Put any support system, such as stretched horizontal wires, in place before planting the climber. To avoid siting it in a "rain shadow," plant it a little distance away from a wall or fence, guiding the stems of the plant in with canes.

Pests and diseases

In organic gardening, pest and disease management is all about prevention rather than cure. By choosing the right plant and planting it in the optimum position to ensure strong, balanced growth, the likelihood of its suffering a disease attack is small. Prepare the soil well and provide good aftercare, observing sensible hygiene rules, such as removing and destroying

Where to cut On plants with alternate buds on each side of the stem, prune at an angle (*top*) just above an outward-pointing bud. Shrubs with opposite buds (*above*) should be pruned level, as close to the buds as possible.

Cutting to new growth To thin a crowded shrub or climber, cut back some of the older or flowered stems to the point at which you see a strong young sideshoot emerging.

dead and diseased material and promoting good air circulation. A little tolerance is also to be advised. Plants are part of the natural world, and are inevitably going to be less than perfect; a leaf spot here or a nibbled leaf there is not going to be life-threatening. The A–Z of Plant Problems (*see pp.320–341*) contains more detailed advice on specific problems affecting woody plants; the entries on aphids, black spot, powdery and downy mildew, and rose rust are particularly applicable to roses.

Pruning woody plants

Check plants regularly for any dead, damaged, or diseased wood. Whatever the plant, always cut this out cleanly; it will help to control disease outbreaks. This is often the only pruning that trees ever require; in the case of mature tall trees, it may mean consulting an arborist.

Formative pruning is usually applied to younger plants, correcting the shape where necessary. It may also be applicable where a mature shrub has outgrown its space, or when a neighboring plant has been removed, leaving the remaining ones lopsided. Pruning is also an important part of training many climbers, especially once they have covered their allotted space. Think before you make such pruning cuts, making sure that the cut will enhance the shape. Generally this means cutting just above an outward-pointing bud, whether you are pruning a three-dimensional bush or a flat-trained climber: the aim is always to stop growth from crossing in the middle of the plant.

Annual pruning of shrubs

Many shrubs need very little pruning other than that needed to remove dead, diseased, or damaged growth (see p.165 for some examples); indeed there are some shrubs, such as daphnes, that react very badly to pruning. However, a rejuvenating or renewing trim each year encourages many shrubs to produce strong new shoots, and often improves their flowering performance. Such pruning can range from a light "haircut" with shears, as with lavender, to a drastic cutting-back, almost to ground level, which benefits, for example, *Buddleja davidii*.

You can ask for advice on regular pruning requirements when buying your plants. But generally speaking, it is safe and often beneficial to prune hard those trees and shrubs that put on more than 12 in (30 cm) of growth in a season—this includes the modern bush roses, such as hybrid teas and floribundas, as well as the examples given on page 164. The harder such plants are pruned, the more vigorously they regenerate. Plants that grow slowly, putting on less than 12 in (30 cm) per year, do not take kindly to severe pruning, so avoid it unless absolutely necessary. Any cuts you do make should be gentle, formative trimming, either thinning the growth by cutting some older or flowered wood back to a strong young shoot or, once the plant is older, using loppers to remove an entire main branch at the base.

If you are unsure of the best time to prune a shrub, be guided by its flowering time. Spring-flowering shrubs, such as forsythia, produce flower buds along the stems during the preceding fall. These buds open to flower in the spring. When flowering is over, the shrub will come into growth; this is the time to prune it. Shrubs flowering in late spring and summer, such as weigela, come into growth in early spring, producing new shoots that in turn will have flower buds by early summer. These can be pruned at any stage between autumn leaf-fall through to late winter. If you are concerned about the hardiness of the plant, leave the branches on to protect it over winter, then prune in early spring.

Cutting off a small branch Never attempt to cut large limbs off a tree yourself, or climb a tree to prune it. But if you need to remove a small, low branch, first equip yourself with a garden pruning saw, as shown below. Make an undercut about 1 in (2.5 cm) from the trunk of the tree first (*below left*), to stop the bark from tearing should the branch fall, then cut cleanly down (*center*) to the undercut. Do not cut flush to the trunk: leaving the branch collar intact (*far right*) helps the tree recover from the wound much more quickly.

ROSE SUCKERS

Many modern roses are grafted (*see also* Apples, *p.294*) onto the roots of wild roses, and occasionally strong shoots of the wild rose grow from these roots. If not removed, these suckers will take over the plant. They usually emerge at ground level, and look quite different from the rest of the plant. To remove them, scrape away the soil at the roots of the rose until you can see the sucker's point of origin, then pull it off completely with a sharp tug.

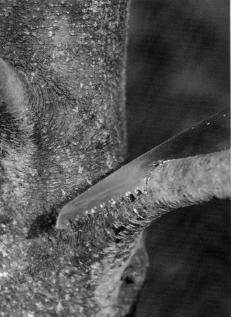

9. Herbaceous Plants

The term "herbaceous" applies, botanically, to any plant that does not form a persistent woody stem. Confusingly, though, "herbaceous" is commonly used as shorthand for "herbaceous perennial," to mean plants such as hostas, delphiniums, and the like, that die down in the winter, and return every spring. These plants may also be referred to simply as "perennials." This chapter, however, covers the whole spectrum of herbaceous plants—annuals, biennials, bulbs, and half-hardy perennials grown as annuals, as well as herbaceous perennials, and including grasses.

Foliage and flowers While trees and shrubs form the permanent structure of most garden plantings, herbaceous plants bring a wealth of seasonal variety.

What is an herbaceous plant?

There is a huge range of plants to choose from in this group, from tiny to gigantic, providing color and interest all year. Plants may be grown for their foliage alone, for their flowers, or for both. The color spectrum is unrivaled, covering all shades imaginable. It is possible to find suitable plants for all garden environments, from dry to wet, sunny to shaded.

The herbaceous year While the herbaceous season begins with the jewellike colors of spring bulbs, fall is a time for subtle, elegant tones, as flowerheads fade.

Herbaceous perennials

Although a few early perennials such as *Doronicum orientale* kick off the spring season, the main flowering performance starts in early summer and lasts into fall, with delights like asters and rudbeckias continuing until the start of winter. Flower stems, seedheads, and foliage can extend the display through to the following spring. Many border perennials, such as helianthus, originate from prairie environments and cope well with hot, dry summers. Others come from woodland habitats, preferring cool shade. Many of these finish flowering before summer, as by then trees leave little moisture for comparatively shallow-rooted perennials. Cranesbills (hardy geraniums), decorative deadnettles (*Lamium*), and tiarellas are reliable shade-loving plants. Other perennials originate from wetland areas, growing along streams and lakes, and require moist soil. Many have large leaves: gunneras, ornamental rhubarb (*Rheum*), and rodgersias are very bold in character, adding drama to a garden scene.

Annuals and biennials

Plants, both hardy and half-hardy, that germinate, flower, set seed, and die within one year, such as marigolds, are known as annuals. Biennials, such as foxgloves, take two years to complete this process. Both can be more labor-intensive than bulbs, perennials, and woody plants, as you have to sow them each year; however, this does allow for an annual change of color scheme.

Tender perennials

Perennials that do not normally survive a cold winter are usually classified, with annuals, as bedding plants, as they too need to be replanted annually. Plants such as pelargoniums or felicia can be overwintered in a frost-free greenhouse or a cool basement, cutting them back and then repotting at the start of spring.

Bulbs

Most bulbs are late winter- and spring-flowering, but some flower in summer and fall. Shade-loving woodland bulbs like cyclamen and snowdrops start to awaken after trees shed their leaves, allowing water and sunlight to penetrate to the woodland floor. They then leaf out, flower, and set seed in early spring. Others, such as tulips, come from areas where summer creates near-desert conditions. They too come to life between fall and late spring. Avoid large, highly hybridized tulips and daffodils, as they can have difficulty building up enough energy to keep producing those huge flowers. Instead, opt for the species, or closely related selections.

Grasses

Strictly speaking, grasses are either herbaceous perennials or annuals, but they deserve to be in a category of their own. Grasses can play an important role in our gardens. The flowering spikes of the taller ones provide great height while remaining translucent, creating a lace curtain effect. Grasses' slender, elegant foliage and feathery flowers add softness to a planting scheme. They bring movement into the garden, creating ripples when planted in larger masses and rustling in the breeze. With their simple elegance and boldness, they look stunning *en masse*. Many dry gracefully to warm tones of yellow and rust that glow in low fall and winter sunlight.

HOW THEY GROW

1 **Annuals** Completing the cycle of seed to seed in one year, annuals (this is the annual poppy 'Danish Flag') can create an intense patch of color over many months.

2 **Biennials** These plants need one year to build up a large, strong plant that will flower, set seed, and die the following year. A few short-lived perennials are often treated as biennials to avoid disease (such as hollyhocks, which are prone to rust as they get older).

3 **Perennials** Faithfully returning year after year, perennials such as columbines provide reliable color, with attractive foliage and seedheads if the right ones are chosen.

4 **Bulbs** Late winter and early spring flowering bulbs such as tulips are ideal among perennials and spring bedding, and planted under deciduous trees and shrubs.

Planting styles

Herbaceous perennials can be planted in beds or borders by themselves, or mixed with bedding plants, shrubs, or roses. They can be placed in bold groups, lingering drifts, or small clumps, depending on the plant, its character, and the desired effect. Many flowers can be cut for flower-arranging, avoiding the high pesticide input and air miles associated with most commercial cut flowers.

Traditional borders

England is renowned for its sumptuous herbaceous borders. They display carefully coordinated color schemes, where plants blend with each other in seasonal succession. They became popular at the start of the 20th century, when they were usually part of larger gardens maintained by small armies of gardeners, and had to be stunning for six or eight weeks of the year only.

Today, many garden owners expect a much longer season of interest from a great deal less space. The mixed border provides an answer, offering a home for shrubs, roses, and all kinds of herbaceous flowers, so that height, structure, and interest can be provided all year. It can include both herbaceous and annual climbers, which look particularly effective scrambling over and through shrubs and trees. Annuals and bedding plants can be used to extend the season, filling gaps where early bulbs and perennials have finished flowering.

Traditional mixed borders, and even more so herbaceous ones, can be hard work to maintain to the immaculate standards needed for them to look stunning. The secret is careful planning and regular attention to keep everything looking its best (*see* Caring for herbaceous

plants, *pp.190–193*). The so-called "Continental" technique of planting (*see overleaf*) is a more naturalistic style that, when successful, can greatly cut down on border chores.

Doing your homework

When faced with the choice of so many cultivars, there are several criteria to assist in making your choice. Hardiness and suitability to soil type and exposure are the starting point. Color also plays an important role. By considering time and length of flowering, you can plan to provide color during months when otherwise little would happen. Flowering height is relevant if you want a plant to attain a particular size to fit in with its neighbors. If height is not important, consider a smaller plant, as it is less likely to require staking.

Disease resistance is another important factor in any garden, let alone an organic one. Certain plants are more susceptible to diseases like mildew or rust. Plant breeders have been working hard to produce cultivars that are more resistant. If in doubt, opt for an old, well-established cultivar that has proved its worthiness. Wildlife value is also important in organic gardens; choose plants providing edible seeds or berries, nesting material, or shelter for garden friends (*see pp.106–117*).

Planting annuals and bedding plants

Some gardeners like to dedicate beds especially to bedding plants, but from an ecological point of view, they are best mixed in with other plants, even in the vegetable garden. Besides adding a colorful note, their flowers attract predatory insects such as hoverflies and lacewings, which control pests. Short-lived plants like forget-me-nots, cornflowers (*Centaurea cyanus*), and California poppies (*Eschscholzia*) are perfect gap-fillers around newly planted perennials, trees, and shrubs.

Consider the environment Moisture-loving plants, such as mimulus, irises, and ferns (*facing page*), must have damp conditions to thrive and look "at home." A sunny border with free-draining soil looks good planted with flowers in warmer hues (*below*); here, North American prairie flowers mingle with crocosmias from the grasslands of South Africa.

The Continental approach

To cut down on the labor and other needs of the traditional herbaceous border, a naturalistic, environmentally sound approach to herbaceous perennial planting was initiated in Germany during the 20th century. Having been further developed in the Netherlands and other European countries, it is broadly referred to as the Continental style. Usually applied to large-scale planting, it is particularly suited to public spaces, but there is no reason why the basic principles cannot be used in any garden.

Creating the look

The principles of the Continental style are easy to understand. Plants are chosen to suit the garden conditions. Depending on whether they originate from woodland, woodland margin, prairie, steppe, rocks, water margin, or water,

they will be used in the corresponding environment in the garden. Unlike traditional borders, where plants are grouped simply for their aesthetic value, the aim is to create plant communities that will require management rather than regular maintenance. These communities are allowed to evolve and develop. Plant species can migrate, increase or decrease as circumstances change, just as they would in a natural setting.

Furthermore, by observing a plant's natural growth habit, it is possible to mimic its normal growing pattern. Certain plants, such as verbascums (or mulleins), scatter themselves

Nature's way In this Continental-style, naturalistic planting, the soil is covered by a matrix of ground-covering plants, out of which arise seasonal highlights. Vegetation is planted in clumps or drifts or scattered through as solitaires, mimicking natural vegetation cover.

Persistent seedheads Bulbs such as *Allium giganteum* (*right, above*, among the oatlike *Stipa gigantea*) can provide years of color with little attention. Their seedheads may persist through the winter when, along with the faded flower spikes of grasses, they give structure (*right, below*) to the winter scene.

by shedding their seeds away from the plant. Others, such as asters, have spreading rootstocks and are best planted in drifts or clumps. By imitating these reproduction processes, a much more natural effect will be obtained than when perennials are planted in the traditional "clumps." For a naturalistic effect it is preferable to work with generous drifts of one or more intermingling species, repeating key plants. Finally, to discourage weeds, the ground is covered (as would be the case in nature) with a permanent mulch such as gravel or crushed stone, or with low-growing ground-cover plants.

Reducing the workload

This naturalistic style of planting does not depend on regular maintenance. Initial ground preparation is important to ensure freedom from perennial weeds. If plants have been chosen correctly to suit the site and soil, there is no need to add soil improvers or fertilizers. Ground-cover means weeding is reduced to a minimum once plants are established. The plants receive no fertilizers or nutrient-rich mulches, nor any additional watering, so they tend to grow squat and sturdy, removing the need for staking. Apart from some selective deadheading, the plants are only cut down once a year, and not until late winter. Many plants have attractive seedheads that provide winter homes for beneficial insects. Frost enhances their architectural outlines.

It is important to monitor the progress of more vigorous plants or those that self-seed in great quantity. Remove as necessary to prevent them from taking over completely.

Perennials for cut flowers

1 *Helianthus* 'Triomphe de Gand'
Sunflower
Children love to grow the single-stemmed, tall annual sunflowers; this is a perennial that will reappear year after year, bearing masses of flower stems.

2 *Dierama pulcherrimum*
Angel's fishing rod
Perfect by a pool or water feature, though it must have sun and well-drained soil. The drooping flower spikes are borne in succession in summer.

3 *Eryngium* x *tripartitum*
Sea holly
All of the sea hollies make striking (if spiky) cut flowers in silver and steely blue shades. They dry very well.

4 *Stipa gigantea*
Giant feather grass
Sometimes called golden oats, this lovely grass bears loose panicles of flowers on stems that may reach 8 ft (2.5 m) in height. They dry well.

5 *Crocosmia* 'Jackanapes'
Crocosmia, montbretia
You may also find this bicolored cultivar on sale as 'Fire King'. It bears plenty of well-branched flower stems.

6 *Aster turbinellus*
Aster
The aster tribe are as welcome for cutting in late summer as they are in the border. Look for species and hybrids that are less prone to mildew.

7 *Aquilegia formosa*
Columbine
Although they lack their powerful fragrance, slender columbines rival hothouse freesias in beauty.

8 *Astilbe* 'Irrlicht'
Astilbe
These border stalwarts make good, if short-lived cut flowers; the feathery flowerheads remain attractive as they dry to shades of brown.

Perennials for winter interest

1 *Helleborus argutifolius*
Hellebore, Christmas rose
Flowering in the darkest days of winter in mild regions, hellebores are ideal for a raised bed, where their drooping flowers can be seen at closer quarters.

2 *Foeniculum vulgare*
Fennel
Whether the plain green species or one of the bronze-leaved forms, fennel will persist through winter to provide an elegant tracery of frosted stems.

3 *Bergenia* 'Ballawley'
Elephants' ears
There are several bergenia cultivars whose glossy leaves color up in winter in deep burgundy and purple shades.

4 *Ajuga reptans* 'Burgundy Glow'
Bugle
Spreading, evergreen ground cover that carpets the ground through winter, its silvery leaves suffused with deep pink.

5 *Stachys byzantina*
Lambs' ears
A hard winter may cut it down, but in most years the silvery leaves are even more effective when dusted with frost.

6 *Iris foetidissima*
Stinking iris
In winter, the seed capsules of this evergreen perennial split to reveal bright orange fruits. The common name refers only to the unpleasant smell of the leaves when crushed.

7 *Hakonechloa macra* 'Aureola'
Hakonechloa
A Japanese grass whose leaves, brilliantly striped in yellow and green through summer, become flushed with pink in fall and winter.

8 *Allium tuberosum*
Chinese chives, garlic chives
Use the leaves for flavoring, but leave the flowers to be transformed into these decorative frosted drumsticks.

Herbaceous plants in containers

While trees, shrubs, fruit trees and bushes, and even vegetables (*see p.222*) can be grown in containers, there is a special case for using herbaceous flowering plants to fill pots and tubs, especially if you live in the city. Wildlife often struggles to find a home, or even a "pit stop," in the urban jungle, and even the smallest courtyard filled with a diversity of flowers is of immense value.

Making an impact A large container crammed with plants is much easier to care for than several small ones. Here, annual climbers—sweet peas and nasturtiums—are grown up a twiggy tepee set in a galvanized bin with holes drilled through the base.

Containers and the organic approach

One of the prime tenets of organic gardening is to create healthy, fertile soil that provides plants with all they need—so growing plants in the restricted environment of a container cannot be considered truly organic. Container-grown tomatoes could not, for example, be legally marketed as an organic crop. But containers do have a valuable role in our gardens—especially in the city—and they can certainly be managed along organic lines, with the appropriate choice of potting mix and without the use of synthetic fertilizers and pesticides.

Urban oases

Avid container gardeners have a tendency to let their enthusiasm spread to cover the tops of walls, posts, windowsills, and even garden seating with a growing collection of plants. Introducing such variety into urban environments, especially with flowering plants, softens the hard landscape and turns the smallest paved courtyard, balcony, or even rooftop garden or terrace into a welcome refuge for wildlife.

Perennials for containers

The best herbaceous perennials for containers are those with a long season of interest—bold foliage plants such as ferns and hostas, for example, or long-flowerers such as the hardy geraniums. In a shady corner, elegant dicentras and astilbes are striking. Some perennial grasses like hot, dry conditions and grow well in containers. Grow blue-gray *Festuca glauca* and *Koeleria glauca* or bronze *Carex comans* in pots of their own, or as a foil for flowering plants. Blue grama grass, *Bouteloua gracilis*, with distinctive purple-brown flowers, makes a more unusual container specimen. Grasses are less demanding of nutrients than many other container plants.

Hardy annuals and biennials

Many hardy annuals will give only a short display; grown in pots, they can easily be replaced. They are among the best plants for attracting bees and beneficial insects into the garden. Try alyssum, *Convolvulus tricolor*, dwarf rudbeckias or calendulas, or even some of the modern dwarf sunflower cultivars. Biennials such as wallflowers, English daisies, and forget-me-nots give valuable early flowers the following spring.

Bulbs and bedding

A selection of bulbs planted in a good-sized pot in early fall can provide a succession of flowers from late winter through to late spring. Choose bulbs that flower at different times and that are planted at different depths. Plant at least two or three of each cultivar. Once the bulbs are over, they can be replaced with colorful summer bedding that will flower all summer long, for the benefit of many predatory insects.

Choosing containers

Plants will grow in anything from terra-cotta pots to an old pail. A container can be new, reclaimed, or recycled, as long as it has drainage holes—essential if plants are not to "drown" in waterlogged soil during wet spells—and is sturdy enough to be filled with potting mix. Where frost is likely, containers should also be frostproof.

Choose the container to suit the site or design style you have in mind. A Versailles box or "aged" stone urn will give a very different feel from florists' buckets or a brightly painted wooden box. You don't have to spend a lot to look sharp. Even the simplest containers can be used to formal effect if several are planted similarly and arranged in a neat row.

(Below, from left) **Planting ideas** Perennial bronze heuchera and fragrant lemon verbena, backed by the eccentric, grasslike *Juncus effusus* 'Spiralis'; hen-and-chicks and campanulas in old kitchenware recycled as cheerful containers; a spring grouping of narcissi, *Iris reticulata*, and primulas.

POTTING MIX OPTIONS

Large garden centers may carry specifically formulated potting mixes designed as a growing medium, for raising seedlings, or for maintaining plants in pots over longer periods.

Don't be tempted to save money by digging up garden soil and putting it in your containers. Even healthy topsoil, once placed in a pot, can become hard and compacted, making it difficult for plant roots to grow.

Cramming them in One of the joys of container gardening is the way that a profusion of plants can be packed into a small space—like a living flower arrangement. In nature, no community of plants could survive for long in such crowded conditions, but by giving plants good-quality potting mix and regular watering and feeding, you can ensure a colorful display all summer long.

Growing mediums for pots

Use an organic, peat-free, multipurpose potting mix—homemade or purchased—to fill pots and containers. Do not stint on quality; your plants will be growing in a restricted environment and need the best. The growing medium should of course suit the plants you are growing. Plants that thrive in dry situations will need a freer-draining, leaner mix than leafy ferns and hostas. A tub of annuals can get by with a general multipurpose mix, while a perennial that is to be in a pot for several years—a spiky phormium, for example—will need a richer mix, preferably one based on loam or soil. These have the advantage of being heavier, and the additional weight can stop pots of tall plants from blowing over. A soilless mix, being lighter, is useful for hanging baskets and on balconies, and where containers need to be moved around.

Peat and the environment

Over the last 50 years, soilless products have almost entirely supplanted loam-based growing media. They are light, easy to handle, and more versatile than their predecessors. The chief reason for their success has been the use of peat: the decayed remains of sphagnum moss or other bog plants. Peat extraction, however, is responsible for the destruction of rare habitats—the unique and fragile ecosystem of a bog—so its use is not appropriate in an organic garden. Nor is it needed. In response to the concerns of organic gardeners, wildlife organizations, and

Pots on display Vintage terra-cotta pots can be as attractive as the plants within them, and many gardeners collect them avidly. Clay pots do, however, dry out quite quickly; to save water, display them somewhere that is shaded during the hottest part of the day.

AVOIDING PEAT

While peat-based growing mix may be used in commercial organic horticulture, no gardener needs them. Alternatives range from the traditional loam-based potting mixes, good for longer-term plantings, to the newer "eco-friendly" products such as those based on composted municipal green waste.

(Below, from top) **Peat-free growing mixes** Loam-based mix; green waste mix; coir-based mix.

environmental groups, "peat-free" products have been developed (*see panel, right*). These are based on a variety of bulky materials, including coir (coconut fiber) and various composted waste products, such as crop residues, bark, and municipal green waste. Using these recycled products rather than disposing of them reduces environmental pollution.

Adding a drainage layer

All containers must have drainage holes in the base, but in addition, to encourage good drainage, fill the bottom of the container with coarse material before adding the growing mixture. To add weight for stability, use large (1¼-in/3-cm) gravel. Broken-up polystyrene packaging is a lightweight alternative and also a good way of recycling material. Aim for a layer 1½ in (4 cm) deep for most containers. If the pot is stone or terra-cotta, and freezing is likely, a drainage layer one-fifth of the total depth of the pot will give it some protection. Standing the pot on bricks or "pot feet" also improves drainage if necessary.

Plants from hot, dry environments often also appreciate a layer of gravel or stone chips over the surface of the soil; it reflects the heat, and ensures that the bases of the stems stay dry and thus less prone to fungal rots. As a bonus, it will also suppress weeds. For a colorful alternative, use rounded glass chips made from recycled glass.

Hanging baskets

Hanging baskets are an excellent way of decorating a wall or post, adding color and interest. They can also increase the growing space in a greenhouse. Ornamentals, herbs, and even tumbling tomatoes can all be grown successfully in baskets.

Use the largest basket you can manage; buy a bracket that will take its weight, and attach it securely. A 16-in (40-cm) basket can be rather heavy to handle, but is easier to care for. A 14-in (35-cm) basket will do for general use, but a 12-in (30-cm) basket is really too small. An open wire framework increases the planting area, which ultimately makes a better show. It needs to be lined, however, and will dry out more quickly than a solid basket.

Linings and potting mixes

Avoid sphagnum moss, the traditional lining material for hanging baskets, as harvesting it can cause environmental damage. Liners made from alternative, often recycled, materials are available, or you can make your own. Winter baskets can be lined with conifer cuttings. An old wool sweater can be cut to fit a basket, or you can use hay twisted into ropes. Hay does tend to grow some interesting surprises during the summer; unwanted additions can be snipped off with scissors.

"Mock moss," made from wool or coir and often dyed green, is the closest alternative to real moss. It is available loose, or in preformed sheets. Wrapping a little of this mock moss around the rim of a basket will prevent it from chafing or cutting through stems.

Given new life Many hanging baskets and the chains sold to suspend them are made from plastic-coated metal, which is very hard to recycle, so try to avoid this material. You may be inspired to create "recycled" baskets, like this old wicker shopping basket, lined with an environmentally friendly material and suspended with natural rope; old kitchen colanders are also popular choices.

A soilless potting mix is best as it reduces the weight of the basket. Improve water retention by adding an organic moisture-retainer, based on coarse seaweed meal. Worm compost (*see pp.46–49*) added to the mix (up to 25% volume) increases the level of plant foods and improves the water-holding capacity.

Basket plants

In late spring, garden centers and other outlets begin to fill up with a huge choice of plants for pots, tubs, and baskets. Remember that many of these are frost-tender—do not be tempted to buy your plants until all danger of frost has passed, or you risk losing them. Baskets look their best with a combination of trailing and upright plants, and plants with a long flowering season are most suitable. Choose a selection of plants to suit the season and location of the hanging basket. Half-hardy plants, both foliage and flowering, are usually used in summer baskets. Bush tomatoes make a novel choice, with the added bonus of a delicious crop. Trailing plants should be planted around the rim and through the mesh of wire baskets. Do not stint on numbers if you want a really good display. With ornamentals, aim for a plant every 2–4 in (5–10 cm), in all directions.

Basket care tips

▧ Avoid siting baskets in windy sites, such as the corner of a building; the basket will dry out more quickly.

▧ To prevent a basket from swinging in the wind, tie the back of it to the bracket behind.

▧ In cool climates, hang a newly planted basket in a greenhouse, or set it on top of a large pail or bucket in a sheltered, sunny spot, for a couple of weeks before hanging it in its final position. The extra warmth will help the plants get off to a good start.

▧ Water baskets daily—even in wet weather. Twice a day may be necessary in hot or dry, windy weather. Once a basket has dried out, it is very difficult to rewet.

▧ Take the opportunity when watering to look for pests and diseases, and snip off any infested foliage.

▧ A weekly dose of high-potash organic liquid fertilizer (*see pp.194–195*) is necessary for flowering plants and tomatoes. For baskets of herb plants, use a general-purpose liquid fertilizer every two weeks. Seaweed extract added to the fertilizer can be beneficial.

▧ If a whole plant is unhealthy, remove it and replace it with another plant.

Environmentally friendly liners
Conifer clippings, 6–8 in (15–20 cm) long, can be used to line a basket (*top*). "Mock" moss (*bottom*) is also a good choice for the organic gardener; to increase water retention in an open-sided basket, add an inner liner of an old plastic bag or, as here, a piece of a discarded growing bag.

Caring for herbaceous plants

While annuals are grown from seed each year (*see pp.196–199*), perennials and bulbs, if well cared for, should give years of enjoyment. To ensure that you get the best performance from your plants, prepare the soil well, and choose the healthiest, most vigorous specimens. You may be able to find organically grown plants and bulbs, but these are not widely available yet.

Planting perennials and grasses

Container-grown plants can be planted at any time, but spring and fall are the traditional and best planting seasons. Soak plants in their pots in a pail of water first, so that their potting soil is wet through. Dig a hole big enough to take the rootball comfortably, loosening the soil at the base to help the roots penetrate to lower levels of soil moisture. Firm plants in after planting, and water in, even if the soil is moist. This will eliminate air pockets, ensuring that the roots make good contact with the soil.

(Below, from left) **Giving them the best start** Firming in the soil around a newly planted perennial; a bark mulch for weed control; twiggy sticks that will support the new growth.

Planting bulbs

Bulbs are normally planted when dormant, as dry bulbs. For spring displays, bulbs must be put in the ground in fall; summer- and fall-flowering bulbs are planted in spring. Only the very small bulbs such as snowdrops and winter aconites are usually planted while in leaf, just after flowering, as they can easily dry out. If you have to plant them as dry bulbs, soak them for 24 hours in lukewarm water prior to planting.

Bulbs prefer well-drained, humus-rich soil. If you fear your soil may be too heavy and wet, incorporate plenty of poultry grit into the soil, or put some grit or coarse sand in the bottom

of the planting hole. As a rule of thumb, plant bulbs at a depth twice the size of the bulb. Avoid planting bulbs at the front of a bed or border. The dying foliage will be unsightly, and it is vital that you allow the leaves to die back naturally for around six weeks after flowering; do not cut the leaves off or tie them in knots.

Watering herbaceous plants

Newly planted plants need regular watering in dry spells, but to cut down the need to water the plants once established, select plants to suit the soil type. Good soil preparation before planting, breaking up compaction to encourage extensive rooting, and incorporating bulky organic soil improvers (*see pp.34–35*) to aid water retention also cuts down the need to water, as does mulching (*see below*). If watering is needed, soak the soil thoroughly rather than giving it a light sprinkling. To reduce evaporation losses, water in the early morning. You can also water in the evening, though this increases the risk of slug damage.

Mulching and feeding

A wide range of mulches can be used on herbaceous plantings to retain moisture, control weeds, and feed the soil (*see also pp.72–75*). Always apply the mulch to moist, weed-free soil. Fertile soil should be mulched with bark, leaf mold or green-waste compost, whereas poorer soil may need a medium- or high-fertility material like garden compost, mushroom compost, or well-rotted manure until fertility builds up. Alternatively, apply a dressing of a general organic fertilizer (*see pp.54–55*) every few years.

There should be no need to feed beds of annuals and biennials. A short-term mulch such as leaf mold or fine bark will help to keep the soil moist. Cocoa shells are also suitable for annual plantings, but may be too rich for fertile soil.

Staking perennials

Taller herbaceous perennials, such as delphiniums, may need support to prevent wind damage, or simply to stop them from flopping over their neighbors. The need for support can be reduced by selecting shorter, stockier varieties or cultivars, or in the case of peonies, those with lighter, single flowers. Excess food and water will also encourage taller and less sturdy growth.

Traditionally, perennials are staked with bushy hazel twigs, put in place as the plants come into growth. They provide a sturdy

BULBS IN THE LAWN

Fall is the ideal time to plant bulbs under sod to create spring flower displays. These will enrich the lawn environment with blooms that are attractive to many insects. Crocus, snowdrops, snake's-head fritillaries (*above*), and dwarf narcissus grow up well through sod to produce a colorful seasonal display. Some can be planted using a bulb planter, taking out a core of soil and sod, dropping in the bulb, then replacing and firming down the plug. Smaller bulbs can be spread out over an area after peeling back the sod just 1 in (2.5 cm) or so deep. Loosen the soil slightly, space out the bulbs, then fold back and water down the sod.

Aim to give the lawn a trim in late fall, or even during winter if conditions allow, so that bulbs grow up through a neat, low green carpet.

After flowering in spring, allow six weeks before cutting down the leaves of the bulbs; either refrain from cutting the grass, or mow around those areas of lawn where the bulbs are sited. The plants need their leaves during this period to produce food for the bulb to ensure a repeat flowering performance the following year.

and unobtrusive support that can be removed at the end of the season and composted. The twigs are placed around the base of the plant, and folded over the center, at two-thirds of the final height, creating a dense network of fine branches that supports the flowering stems as they grow up through the twigs. If available, use your own twiggy yard prunings. Another option is to circle the plant with bamboo canes and then create a network of garden twine between them. For some very tall plants, such as delphiniums, each stalk may need its own cane, supporting the bloom for most of its height.

There are all sorts of commercial supports available. Quick and easy to use are the galvanized metal or plastic circles with a grid, or L-shaped plastic-coated wires that hook into each other. Suitable candidates for this type of staking are clump-forming perennials such as heleniums, phloxes, and chrysanthemums. Large clumps that threaten to fall in one direction can quickly be propped up with hefty supports made from a metal stake, bent to form a semicircular hoop.

Always use natural fibers such as twine and raffia for tying up plants. They are less likely to strangle a plant than plastic or wire, and can safely be composted. To avoid eye injuries, top canes with purchased, or homemade, cane-toppers.

Tidying up Leave dying growth on herbaceous plants over winter as shelter for wildlife. In spring, rake out grasses (*top*) or cut them back along with other perennials (*below*), and take the debris and spent mulch to the compost pile.

Deadheading and cutting back
Regular removal of flowers as they die will strengthen bulbs, and helps keep annuals and biennials looking good; it may extend the flowering period. Do not deadhead plants such as honesty and nigella if you want to retain the attractive seedheads.

Removing flowers from some perennials, such as phlox, will encourage sideshoots to flower, and delphiniums, lupines, and many achilleas may develop a second flush of flowers if cut back. Otherwise, resist the temptation to remove flowerheads as they fade. Be patient, and wait a few weeks to see if the plant produces seedheads that will add a decorative element during winter months, and provide food for birds and small mammals and hiding places for insects. Dead flower stalks and leaves also protect plants against severe cold weather. Some, such as sedums, remain attractive right through winter. Others start rotting at the base, and will succumb to wet and windy weather. Tidy up occasionally, removing unsightly material. What is left at the end of winter can be raked off.

Dividing perennials

While annuals and biennials must be grown from seed (see pp.196–199), perennials can also be propagated by vegetative means—by division, and also by cuttings (see pp.202–203). Division is the simplest option, reinvigorating the plant as well as producing more, identical plants, so it should be done regularly once plants are mature, whether you need to increase your stock or not. Divide herbaceous perennials when plants begin to die back in the center, look congested, or show a reduction in vigor. This can be after two to three years in the case of vigorous plants, while those that are slow to establish may stay undisturbed for 15 years or more.

How to divide

During fall, winter, or early spring, when the ground is not too wet to work and there is no risk of frost, lift plants and divide them. Grasses prefer to be divided in the spring. Most perennials can easily be divided. Dig up a clump and insert two forks, back to back, into the middle. By pushing the two handles toward and away from each other, the roots are gradually teased apart. Repeat this, using your hands as the clumps become smaller, until you have the number of plants you require. Really tough or fleshy rootstocks, such as hostas, may have to be chopped up with a spade or cut apart with a knife.

Once bulbs become overcrowded, they do not flower so freely. Lift bulbs as they are dying back or when they are dormant. The clump can usually be teased apart by hand, and individual healthy bulbs can then be replanted.

Deadheading spring bulbs It is well worth deadheading spring bulbs such as daffodils and tulips. By doing so, you direct all the plant's energy into building up the bulb for next year's flowering performance, rather than expending its resources in the production of seed. You must leave the foliage to die down naturally, as it is the leaves that feed the bulb.

Dividing perennials Cut or break up the plants until you have pieces with rootballs of about fist size. Discard any divisions that seem weak, with aging growth (often those from the center of the parent plant) and replant the remainder just as you would a purchased new plant, firming and watering each one in well.

Container care

Plants in tubs, pots, and other containers can be fed with the same range of composted organic materials and organic fertilizers that are used on plants in open ground. They are applied as a topdressing to the container. In addition, liquid fertilizer appropriate for use in an organic garden can be watered on or applied as a foliar spray. How much and how often container plants need to be fed will depend on the richness of the growing medium used, the volume of the container, the plants being grown ,and the intended life span of the planting.

How often a container plant needs watering depends on the plant type, its size in relation to the container, the type of container (terra-cotta dries out more quickly than plastic), the site (a windy site increases the demand for water), the weather, and the season. Never let containers dry out—plants are much more prone to problems if they are short of water, and dry potting mix is difficult to rewet. In practice, most container plants need daily watering during summer, even after rain, and very little in winter. Always direct water under the foliage rather than splashing the leaves.

Liquid fertilizers

Liquid fertilizers provide plants with nutrients in a readily available form. Although this goes against the organic principle of feeding the soil, not the plant, there are times when a liquid fertilizer can be necessary in an organic garden. Ingredients used to produce commercial organic liquid fertilizers are: manures (not sourced from intensive systems), fish emulsion (a byproduct of the fishing industry), plant and animal wastes, and rock minerals. These are basically the same materials that are used for feeding the soil, but in a different form, and they are subject to the same constraints regarding source of supply.

When buying liquid fertilizers, choose those with an organic symbol of approval if available. They may be formulated as balanced products for general use, or with a high potash

High maintenance A watering "lance" attached to a standard hose makes light work of watering hanging baskets. Alternatively, take the baskets down and set them on top of a pail to water them; the pail will catch any surplus, which can be reused.

Emergency aid If a container plant has dried out to the extent that the plant has started to wilt, the soil may be hard to rewet from above. Stand the plant in a container of water for a few hours so that it can draw up all the water it needs from below.

Deadheading bedding By removing faded flowers from half-hardy annuals and tender perennials grown as bedding, you can prolong flower production, which is a valuable consideration if you are gardening in a small space and want the longest possible displays from your container plantings.

content—the latter being used for tomatoes and other fruiting plants. You may also find that an application of seaweed extract is beneficial to container plants.

Seaweed extract

Seaweed extract is a plant growth stimulant rather than a liquid fertilizer; it contains little in the way of major plant foods. What it does contain is a wide range of trace elements, plus ingredients such as plant hormones and specific carbohydrates that can stimulate plant growth. Seaweed extract can be used in various ways, at various stages of plant growth. It seems to work best if applied to the soil or roots early on in the life of a plant, and as a foliar spray later on. Applied to the soil, it seems to have the added benefit of reducing the possibility of some root diseases; as a foliar spray, it appears to discourage sap-feeding insects and possibly increase resistance to frost.

Plant problems

Keeping plants growing well is the best defense against pests and diseases. Potbound plants in overcrowded pots, watered erratically, will be more prone to pests such as red spider mite and aphids, especially in hot and dry locations such as a sheltered patio. Deal with any problem as it arises; check plants regularly and pick off pests or diseased shoots or leaves as you notice them. Remove sickly and badly infested plants.

Some plants will need protection to survive the winter. Move tender plants under cover, or protect plants with fleece. Wrap up pots, too, so that neither the pot nor the plant roots freeze.

KEEPING PESTS AT BAY

You can avoid many soilborne pests and diseases by using fresh potting mix, but root-eating creatures may still move into a pot, where their effects can be devastating. Vine weevil grubs can soon kill plants in containers and baskets: a biological control agent (*see p.97*) is available that controls both these pests and slugs, the other main enemy of plants in pots. Copper-coated tape around the rims of pots (*below*) has also been shown to deter slugs, but can be expensive if you have lots of containers; consider instead siting a slug trap (*see p.102*) discreetly among the pots. Grow flowers to attract predatory insects (*see p.95*) to keep other pests in check.

Raising your own plants

Economical, environmentally friendly, and intensely rewarding, propagation—raising plants from seed and cuttings—comes as naturally to the organic gardener as composting and mulching. And while woody plants may take years to reach maturity, herbaceous plants—especially annuals—give satisfyingly rapid results.

Moment of truth There is something almost magical in seeing your own seedlings make their way into the light. Even the tiniest seeds, like those of poppies (*top*), contain all the necessary information to form a beautiful plant.

Starting from seed

Starting from seed is a cost-effective way of obtaining large quantities of plants, particularly annual bedding, and you can be sure that the plants are raised organically. Raising your own plants also gives you the chance to try some of the more unusual annuals, such as the blue lace flower (*Trachymene coerulea*) or the green-flowered tobacco plant *Nicotiana langsdorffii*, rather than relying on the same bedding selections year after year.

Herbaceous perennials from seed will take a year or two to reach flowering size. Raising perennials from seed is mostly restricted to true species; seed sown from a plant with a cultivar name is unlikely to produce a plant identical to the parent. Some perennials, such as columbines, will self-seed freely. The flower color may bear no relation to the parent plant, but that is not necessarily a bad thing.

What seeds need

For successful germination, seeds require moisture, air, and an appropriate temperature. Most prefer to germinate in darkness, although some, especially fine seeds, need exposure to light. Success also depends on the vigor of the seed. Fresh seed, or seed that has been stored in good conditions (*see p.201*), will germinate more rapidly and produce more vigorous seedlings than old or poorly stored seed.

Seed can be sown directly into the soil (*see panel, right*), or into a special growing medium, such as a seed-starting or multipurpose potting mix, in a pot or tray (*see overleaf*). An appropriate temperature in the soil or growing medium is essential for germination. Catalogs and seed packets will give advice on the particular requirements of the seed in question.

Sowing annuals direct

Most hardy annuals and many half-hardy annuals, particularly the large-seeded ones such as French marigolds (*Tagetes*) and nasturtiums, are easy and cheap to grow from seed. Most seed packets recommend a suitable sowing period for annuals, but it is worth experimenting with later sowings to fill gaps left by early-flowering perennials or bulbs. A display for late spring or early summer can be achieved from fall sowings of hardy annuals such as love-in-a-mist (*Nigella*) and cornflowers (*Centaurea*).

Where practical, apply a leaf-mold mulch to sowing areas the previous fall. This will improve the structure at the soil surface, where germinating seedlings need it, without adding too many nutrients, which would encourage lush growth at the expense of flowers. Even a covering of fallen leaves will be of benefit; these can be raked off before sowing.

A few weeks before the anticipated sowing date, prepare the soil to suit the plants that are to be sown. Do not work the soil if it is too wet—this will destroy the soil structure and give poor germination and growth rates. If mud sticks to your boots, abandon the work until the soil is drier.

Many hardy annuals, such as calendula (pot marigold), *Phacelia tanacetifolia*, and the poached-egg plant (*Limnanthes douglasii*), will self-seed, reappearing year after year. Self-sown plants tend to be much sturdier, and flower earlier, than those you sow yourself. Unwanted seedlings can simply be hoed off, or transplanted to a more appropriate site.

SOWING DIRECT

Rake the soil to a fine tilth (*see also p.254*) and draw straight or curved drills across the soil (*below, top*). Sowing in rows rather than broadcasting helps you tell your seedlings from weed seedlings; once the plants grow, they will not look regimented. Water along the drills (*center*). Sow the seeds evenly and thinly along the drills (*bottom*); larger seeds such as nasturtium are easy to space out. Rake the soil lightly over the seeds and gently firm with the back of the rake.

SOWING SWEET PEAS

All organic gardeners should grow sweet peas. Not only do they produce a succession of beautifully fragrant flowers, ideal for cutting; being legumes (*see also p.242*), their roots have nodules that "fix" nitrogen in the soil, to the benefit of other plants. A row of sweet peas in the vegetable garden is widely believed to improve pollination of peas and beans, too. Sweet peas can be sown outdoors, but will flower earlier from sowings under cover. Their seeds have a tough covering and germinate better if you rub the seed coat with sandpaper (*top*) or nick it with a sharp knife. Sweet peas dislike having their long roots disturbed, so "root-trainers" (*below*), deeper than normal module trays, are ideal, with one seed sown in each cell.

Sowing seeds in pots

Raising seedlings in pots and trays allows plants to be started earlier than might be possible outdoors, and helps keep them safe from pests. It is particularly appropriate for the more tender plants, but can be useful for hardy plants, too. Seedlings can be growing in their containers while the ground where they are finally to be planted is still occupied by other plants.

Where you raise your plants will depend on what temperature the seeds need to germinate, and the hardiness of the young plants that will emerge. A greenhouse could furnish all the plants a small garden might need, but a windowsill will suffice for a few pots of sweet peas, for example. A heated propagator is a useful investment for seeds that need extra warmth to germinate, but a warm spot near a heat register will be adequate. Once the seedlings emerge, though, you must move them to a light, warm windowsill and turn them every day, or they will become spindly.

What to sow seeds in

You can sow in all sorts of containers, purchased or recycled from household items. The basic requirement is that whatever you use allows adequate drainage, is robust enough for the job, and is free from disease organisms and chemicals poisonous to plants.

■ **Pots** Clay pots are porous, allowing air to reach the roots and moisture to evaporate through the clay, reducing problems caused by overwatering. Plastic pots are easier to clean and plants will need less watering. Biodegradable pots, made of paper, coir, or similar materials, are planted out along with the plants to minimize root disturbance.

■ **Seed trays** Trays are usually 2–3 in (5–7 cm) deep and of variable size. Wooden trays are rare these days. Plastic ones are cheaper and easier to clean.

■ **Modules** Multicelled seed trays—also known as module trays—are available in plastic and polystyrene. The plastic ones are easier to remove plants from, and thus use again. Each seedling grows in its own individual "mini-pot," so its root system is not disturbed on transplanting.

■ **Homemade pots and seed trays** Foil carry-out containers, deli and margarine tubs, polystyrene coffee cups, and yogurt cartons can all be used. Clean them thoroughly and make holes in the bottom. Egg cartons can be used as module trays. Toilet paper rolls and homemade paper tubes can be planted along with the plant and are useful for plants that resent root disturbance.

Sowing the seeds

Use a multipurpose organic potting mix, or one that advertises itself as a "seed mix," which will be lower in nutrients (ideal for germinating seeds), and usually finer in texture. The finer the seeds, the finer the growing medium needs to be. After filling pots or trays with moist potting mix, lightly firm the surface of the soil. Fine seeds can be sown on the surface and covered by gently sifting a little more potting mix over the top. Large seeds can be pushed in individually with a finger, or dropped into holes made with a pencil or dibble, then covered.

Spacing

Give seedlings plenty of space to grow. Densely sown seedlings compete for limited light, water, and space, and diseases thrive in these conditions. Plants that suffer a setback at this stage may never catch up. Using modules is one of the best ways to avoid the problems caused by overcrowding. If you have used pots or seed trays to sow fine seed in, and thus have a plethora of seedlings, you must either ruthlessly thin them, or "prick them out" (*see below*) so that each has more room. Do this when the first pair of true leaves, rather

Covering up Covering pots and trays with clear plastic will help maintain moisture levels during the critical germination stage. Once you see that germination has begun, remove the covering.

than the initial seed leaves, appears. There will be far more seedlings than you need, so retain only the healthiest and most vigorous ones.

Hardening off

All young plants grown under cover must be acclimatized gradually to the cooler and less humid conditions outside. This is known as "hardening off." The best place to do this is in a cold frame, but you can also cover plants with a cloche or fleece and remove it gradually over a few days.

PRICKING OUT

A chopstick or swizzle stick makes an excellent tool for transplanting seedlings. Before transplanting, water the soil well. Pry the seedlings gently out of the growing medium and very carefully hold them by one of the seed leaves as you lower them into a hole poked into the growing medium in the new container. Make sure the seed leaves are well above the soil surface; otherwise, they are likely to rot.

Bountiful harvest Most plants have evolved to produce an abundance of seed as a survival mechanism. Leaving a few plants to flower and set seed will give you many more seeds than you could ever get in a seed packet, for virtually no cost. Surplus seed need never go to waste. Join a local gardening club and swap seed with other members—or grow plants for friends, for schools, for community gardens, or to raise funds for local good causes.

Saving seeds

Seed-saving is something all gardeners can do. You might simply save a few seeds from a favorite flower or vegetable for the next season, or you might take on the more complex task of maintaining a specific variety from a seed library or collection. The techniques you use will depend on the type of plant, and on how important it is that it is kept pure, or true to type. Though it is possible to harvest seed that is borne within fruits and berries, it is far easier to harvest from "dry-seeded" plants, where the seeds remain on the plant in their capsules or pods until they are crisp and dry.

Good reasons for seed-saving

■ Seed-saving adds another dimension to gardening. It's a fascinating process that extends your knowledge of how plants work.
■ It is not possible to buy organically grown seed of every plant. Saving your own in an organic garden helps to ensure a supply of the plants you want.

■ Many old and less commercial cultivars have been dropped from seed catalogs, and may disappear altogether. Some of these may have excellent characteristics, particularly suited to the gardener, or may simply be your particular favorites. By saving seed of threatened cultivars, and sharing them with others, you will be helping to conserve our genetic heritage.

■ It will cost you nothing, and be fresh, too. Home-saved seed often has a high germination rate and produces vigorous seedlings.

Harvesting and storing seeds

Seeds, like any other part of the plant, can harbor unwanted organisms. Having harvested and winnowed your seeds (*see below*), look through them carefully and remove any that are diseased, moldy, or half-eaten. There is no point in storing seed that is already weakened by pest or disease attack.

Some seed can be sown right away, but in most cases you will want to keep your seeds for spring sowing, and it is important to store them carefully over the winter. The drier and cooler the seeds are kept, the better. Seeds stored in breathable envelopes or packets in a cool, dry room will fare much better than in a warm, damp one.

You can improve the viability of the seeds—the number that will germinate when you eventually sow them—by drying them out still further, using silica gel in the form of color-indicating crystals. These are sold by florists and craft suppliers for use when drying flowers. Place the seeds in their envelopes in a rubber-sealed glass jar with an equal weight of dry silica gel. After a week, the gel will have absorbed all the moisture and turned from blue to pink. Remove the packets of seed and store them in another airtight container in the freezer or refrigerator. A few days before you are ready to sow, take the jar out so that the seeds reach ambient temperature and humidity levels. To reuse the silica gel, drive off the moisture, reversing the color change, in a very low oven (200°F/95°C) or in a microwave.

COLLECTING SEEDS FROM DRY-SEEDED PLANTS

Leave the faded flowerheads to mature on the plant until the capsules, pods, or seedheads have matured. When ready to harvest, they should have a crisp feel when squeezed and should not show any sap, moisture, or green pigment when scratched by a fingernail. If you have to harvest when the weather is damp, lay the seedheads out on paper, or enclose them in a paper bag and hang it up, until they are fully dry. They then need to be threshed to free the seeds from all the rest of the dry debris. Some capsules and pods are large enough to pick apart by hand to extract the seeds, or you can crush the seedheads with a heavy rolling pin or board, or put them in a bag and step on them or beat them with a stick. Then, winnow them to remove the debris, or chaff: keep them on the paper or place them in a bowl, and alternately toss them and blow gently on or over them. Because the chaff is usually lighter than the seeds, it will be blown away.

Taking cuttings

Propagation by cuttings basically means growing a whole plant from a part of a plant. It can be used for all leafy herbaceous perennials, but will not work on grasses and bulbs, which grow in a different way. Don't forget that many of the bedding plants we grow as annuals, discarding every year, are in fact tender perennials that can be propagated by cuttings over winter, provided you can give them warmth and shelter.

One advantage of raising plants in this way is that the offspring will be identical to the parent, without the genetic variation that can result when you save seed from a plant. And it is the only way to propagate plants that do not produce viable seed—for example, the lawn chamomile 'Treneague', bred not to flower.

Another excellent reason for taking cuttings is as "insurance" should borderline hardy plants not survive a hard winter in the garden. Taking cuttings during the growing season, and growing them on under cover through the winter, will ensure that you have exactly the same plant ready to replace any that have been lost to the cold.

Easy to root Among the most successful plants for beginners to try are fuchsias, pelargoniums (*below*), and nepeta (catmint).

What cuttings need

While all cuttings root faster with bottom heat, provided by a propagator, most do not need it. But shelter under glass, or on a windowsill, is necessary for cuttings taken from soft growth that would quickly dry up and fail if exposed outside. While these cuttings need a humid atmosphere, it is important that they do not become waterlogged, or the soft tissue will rot, so the growing medium you use must be free-draining. You can buy bagged mixes especially for cuttings, formulated with an open texture, or use a multipurpose potting mix blended with a little coarse sand.

Hormone rooting powders are not a suitable organic input. Most plant species root effectively without any special treatment.

Soft stem-tip cuttings

These are nonflowering shoots taken primarily from hardy perennials and tender bedding plants in spring and early summer while they are producing strong, soft, fleshy growth. Because the shoots are actively growing, you need to provide adequate levels of moisture, light, and warmth to encourage rooting, so the cuttings must be potted and kept under cover (*see panel, facing page*).

PENSTEMON CUTTINGS

1 Choose strong nonflowering shoots 3–4 in (8–10 cm) long, severing them just above a leaf joint. Trim the cutting to just below a leaf joint, and remove the leaves from the bottom half of each cutting.

2 Insert the shoots into a pot of growing medium suitable for cuttings so that the first leaf is just above the level of the soil. Keep this moist, but not sodden.

3 Cover with a plastic bag to maintain high humidity. Use split canes or wire hoops to construct a frame to support the bag so that cuttings do not touch it and rot. Keep it out of direct sunlight.

4 You will know when a cutting is making good root growth when the shoot starts to grow. Once it is growing strongly, plant each cutting into its own individual pot.

Other ways of making more plants

With some perennials, including delphiniums and dahlias, you can take "basal stem cuttings" from the new growth that springs up from ground level in the spring. Pull some of the new shoots carefully from the base, or crown, of the plant when they have four or five leaves, trim the base neatly, and root them in small pots of free-draining growing medium.

When lifting and dividing clumps of bulbs (*see p.193*), the little bulblets, resembling garlic cloves, that form around the larger bulbs can also be snapped off and grown into individual flowering plants if potted and grown on under cover. They may not be big enough to plant out until their second year.

Growing on and planting out

Once your cuttings have rooted, they need more space to grow and should be moved into individual pots. Cuttings taken in spring may be ready to plant out by fall, provided that the weather is still mild; later cuttings are usually kept under cover until the spring. A greenhouse or cold frame is ideal for growing on young plants of hardy perennials, or use a cool and light spare room; do not keep garden plants in a warm, stuffy place. Plants raised under cover need to be gently acclimatized to outdoor conditions; put the young plants outside in their pots during the day and bring them in at night for a week, then leave them out at night for a few days, before planting into their final homes.

10. Growing Vegetables

There exists no stronger connection with the soil and the changing seasons than through eating food you yourself have sown, nurtured, and harvested. Vegetable-growing can be satisfyingly quick: most vegetables can be harvested within a few weeks or months, although some can take longer to begin cropping. Vegetables can be grown virtually anywhere—a "kitchen garden" in the traditional sense is not essential. You can start small, then gradually expand your edible horizons.

Seasonal bounty Fresh salad leaves and the promise of tender young carrots and beans to come, then sweet corn ripened by the summer sun; expectation is part of the pleasure of vegetable-growing.

Why grow organic vegetables?

Growing vegetables organically is positive, empowering, and rewarding, with many health benefits. The shared enthusiasm for growing food cuts through barriers of class, age, race, and culture like no other. Plants of all types can bring people and communities together, but none succeeds quite like those that we eat. However much food you decide to grow, or whatever constraints you have to work with, growing at least some of your own vegetables organically satisfies more than the fundamental human desire to eat healthy, fresh, uncontaminated produce—it is also a way of minimizing our impact on the wider environment.

The bigger picture

Many common fruits and vegetables travel for thousands of miles around the planet before they reach their final destination. Transport is often by air, then road, both of which consume vast amounts of fossil fuels, contributing to atmospheric pollution and ultimately to global warming. The number of so-called "food miles" traveled by supposedly "fresh" produce can be enormous, resulting in much food being eaten a long way from where it was grown. Cultivars created for the rigors of travel and longevity, rather than nutritional value and flavor, are the direct fallout of worldwide monocultures and the move toward increased globalization. These growing systems depend almost exclusively on high, unsustainable inputs of energy, artificial fertilizers, and synthetic chemical pesticides. Concerns over food safety are increasingly frequent, ranging from worries over pesticide

WHY GROW YOUR OWN ORGANIC CROPS?

■ Produce is fresher; food has better flavor and higher nutritional value.

■ You can grow more unusual crops and old or "lost" varieties that you cannot buy (*see* Heirloom vegetables, *overleaf*).

■ It helps educate future generations about where food comes from.

■ It helps build communities.

■ It is kinder to nature, with many environmental benefits.

■ You regain control over what you eat.

■ It's fun!

residues to the many uncertainties surrounding the widespread use of genetically modified food crops (*see panel, right*). By growing your own food, you can regain control over what you and your family eat and free yourself of such anxieties.

Environmental benefits

Growing your own vegetables, and growing them organically, provides not only safe, uncontaminated food but also has significant environmental benefits. Food miles are virtually eliminated, organic waste can be recycled through techniques like composting, and threats to our health are reduced. Increasing attention is being focused on the "localization" of food, where produce grown locally, using environmentally friendly, sustainable, organic techniques, is sold directly to the people of that area. The term "locavore" has even been coined to describe those people who try to eat only locally produced food. Such initiatives reconnect people with where their food actually comes from, but growing your own is still the ultimate in locally grown food.

You can read books, talk to other gardeners, and think about it forever, but the best way to start growing vegetables is simply to give it a try. Your first few successes will give you confidence, and you will soon start to get a feel for which crops grow really well in your conditions.

GENETICALLY MODIFIED ORGANISMS (GMOS)

All organisms contain genes, which pass the blueprint for that particular organism on from one generation to the next. In nature, unrelated species cannot interbreed, so the genes of a fish could never end up in a plant—but this bizarre notion is now a reality. Genetic engineering has made cross-species transfer of genes possible: the characteristics carried by the introduced gene become part of the new organism. Vitamin A–enhanced rice, for example, contains genes from a daffodil.

There are both ethical and safety concerns about GMOs. Although the developers, and others, are happy that the technology is safe for human health and the environment, others disagree. This is why GM plants and animals are not organically acceptable.

GM crops have been introduced rapidly, without extensive testing, on the grounds that they are similar to nonengineered crops. But the process involves creating gene combinations that could not have occurred naturally. Once released into the environment, genes that "escape" from the GM parent plant, via soil bacteria or cross-pollination, will be impossible to retrieve. Once incorporated into wild plants, we can only surmise what the outcome might be.

At the point of writing, no GM crops are yet available to gardeners, but developments on the horizon include peculiar colors, such as blue carnations and roses; grass that does not need mowing; and novel perfumes. This novelty may prove to be more costly than we can possibly imagine.

Heirloom vegetables

Diversity is a keystone of organic growing, and freedom of plant choice is something that all gardeners appreciate. Hundreds of vegetable varieties, with wide genetic diversity, are facing extinction due to commercial pressures that favor durability and uniformity over flavor and character. Many old-fashioned vegetables are now available only through seed exchanges and specialty seed suppliers.

Genetic loss

Most of us buy vegetables from supermarkets, where what counts is a flawless appearance— not a quality that carried much weight with earlier generations. Flavor, continuity of picking, and delicate skins were what mattered to our gardening predecessors. In Victorian England, for example, gardeners grew over 120 different varieties of tall garden peas, providing freshly shelled peas throughout the summer. A century later, frozen peas reign supreme in the UK. The food industry requires dwarf varieties, where all the peas ripen at once. Consequently, only one tall pea variety remains. As a result of developments like these, many small, family seed producers have gone out of business, or have been taken over by multinational corporations that are not interested in traditional varieties.

Seed exchanges

Many gardeners are dismayed to see their favorite vegetable varieties disappearing from cultivation, and some have responded by setting up seed exchanges to preserve threatened cultivars and family treasures handed down through generations. Unlike deep-freeze "gene bank" collections, seed exchanges keep vegetables and flowers in cultivation so plants can continue to evolve and adapt to changing environmental conditions. Members save seed for their own use, and pass it on to others. One of the best-known seed exchanges is Seed Savers

Heritage potatoes 'Highland Burgundy Red' (*left*) and 'Salad Blue' (*right*). Gardeners prepared to search for heirloom seed potatoes have a choice of around 100 varieties.

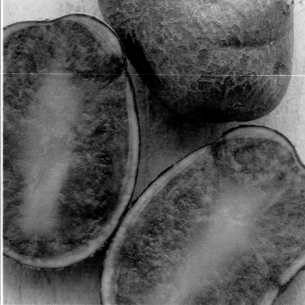

Exchange in Decorah, Iowa, a nonprofit that encourages members to share seed and also sells seed to nonmembers.

Past meets future Seed exchanges and heirloom seed companies are a source of uncommon produce. Clockwise from top left: the climbing string bean 'Cherokee Trail of Tears'; 'Salmon-Flowered' pea; tomato 'Tigerella'; leek 'Babington'.

Why it matters

We cannot know what the future holds for vegetable growing. In a globally warmed world, varieties bred for today's conditions may become unsuitable—and we may have to contend with new types of pests and diseases. So it is vital that we keep as broad a genetic base as possible. Older varieties may contain valuable genes that could prove vital to plant breeders in the future. In addition to this, growing, cooking, and eating vegetables is much more exciting and pleasurable when there are lots of varieties to choose from.

Where to grow vegetables

There are many ways of growing vegetables: in rows, beds, or containers; on their own, or mixed with flowers and shrubs. The ideal place to grow vegetables is often described as fertile, well-drained, and moisture-retentive soil in a flat, sunny, but sheltered position. Most gardeners do not have these "perfect" conditions, but still grow fine vegetables by making the best of what they have.

When selecting a site for your vegetables, consider the following:

■ **Sun and shade** Deep shade will severely limit the growth of vegetables, but some can tolerate light shade, including lettuce, chard, beets, and kohlrabi. In cool climates, position tall vegetables so that they will not cast a shadow on lower-growing ones, but in hotter climates use them to provide welcome shade.

■ **Drainage** Vegetables will not thrive in a waterlogged site, which is better used for something else, such as a pond or bog garden. Improve heavy soil gradually by adding low-fertility organic material; consider growing on raised beds (*see p.214*).

Starting small A small plot is easy to manage and can still produce a good range of vegetables. Being overambitious may result in more crops than you are able to care for successfully, which can lead to disappointment.

■ **Shelter** Protect exposed sites with permanent or temporary windbreaks such as hedges, fences, or netting. Protect individual crops with barriers, cloches, or other covers, especially when young.

■ **Slopes** Use terracing to prevent soil erosion. Position rows or beds across the contours of a site, rather than up and down. Be aware that the bottom of a slope can be a frost pocket.

■ **Space** Select vegetables to suit the space available. Even quite small areas can be very productive, using vertical as well as horizontal growing space. Remember to allow space for making leaf mold and compost.

■ **Children and pets** Depending on what else you use your yard for, you may conclude that growing vegetables is just not compatible with the other demands on it. In this case, consider a community garden.

Preparing the ground

You may already have a clear piece of land suitable for growing vegetables, but if not, there are various organic methods of preparing it. You could dig up part of the lawn, remove existing plants from flower beds, or use a light-excluding mulch to clear a weedy patch (*see* Weeds and Weeding, *p.74.*)

(Above left) **City smart** Framed raised beds packed with plants are ideal in a small urban yard: garden compost and manure can be added to the beds with relatively little mess.

(Above right) **Potted crops** Provided that it is fed regularly, a single zucchini plant (this is the yellow type known as "summer squash") will be happy in a good-sized container.

Before you start growing, find out more about your soil and start to care for it organically. Use organic soil improvers and fertilizers as necessary to build fertility.

Plans and records

Even if you are only growing a few vegetables to start with, it makes sense to draw up a simple plan for a crop rotation (*see pp.230– 233*). Keep an eye on what happens through the season, so you can deal with any problems and adjust growing conditions accordingly.

Keep records. This is helpful for all gardeners, not just beginners. At its simplest, this could simply mean writing the cultivar name and sowing date on a plastic label used to mark a row. Soon you will be able to record information on yields, pests, and diseases, weather conditions, and what grew well where. Don't worry if not everything goes according to plan. Even experienced gardeners will tell you that they still get surprises.

Vegetable beds

Growing vegetables in their own dedicated beds has many advantages. It maximizes output from the growing space, makes cultivation and crop rotation easier, and looks pleasingly neat and organized. Making the beds narrow, separated by paths from which you can tend the crops, makes them simpler to manage and fits in perfectly with organic gardening principles of soil management.

Growing vegetables in narrow beds, divided by access paths, has many advantages over traditional row cropping. On a traditional vegetable plot, soil improvers and fertilizers are applied across the whole area, and then dug in. The soil between the rows is compacted as crops are watered, fed, weeded, and harvested. A bed system breaks with this constant cycle of compaction followed by cultivation.

The most important factor when setting up beds for vegetable growing is that you should be able to reach the center of the bed easily without stretching or having to step on the soil. Although rectangular beds are easy to set out and manage, beds can be of any shape as long as the center is reachable from the path.

Beds can be flat or raised, edged or with no edging, dug, double-dug, or not dug at all. Choose the combination that suits you.

Flat or soil-level beds

A flat bed, without any edging, is the simplest and least labor-intensive to set up. Each corner of the bed is marked with a post, and string is tied between them to define the edge. The height of the bed relative to the paths will increase, however, if the soil is medium to heavy, and it is well dug. Soil improvers will also tend to raise it, while the paths become lower due to compaction. Flat beds are best suited to light soils, which would tend to dry out more quickly if raised up.

Everything in its place When beds are narrow, vegetables can be grown closer together because there is no need to walk between them. With their neat rows of uniform crops, the traditional look (*facing page*) can be very attractive; but there is no reason why the beds themselves should not form an ornamental feature, as in the potager shown below. Grouping vegetables of the same family in different beds (*bottom*) makes crop rotation (*see pp.230–233*) much easier to organize.

Raised and edged beds

Edging provides a neat, defined boundary between bed and path. It contains the soil on the bed, and any mulching material on the path. Edging is to be recommended for medium to heavy soil where the level of the bed tends to rise above the path. Where topsoil is thin, edging allows the bed to be built up with soil and bulky organic matter. Raised beds are especially useful where drainage is poor.

An edge 4–12 in (10–30 cm) high is adequate in most situations. Beds raised to 2 ft (60 cm) are useful where there is difficulty in bending, or if cultivation is done from a wheelchair.

The main drawbacks with raised beds are the initial cost of materials and the labor required to construct them; both obviously increase the higher the bed is raised. Slugs also tend to find the edging an attractive home, and may be more of a problem on some edged beds.

"No-dig" or double-dug?

The soil in a bed is treated in the same way as the soil on an open plot. If the soil is dug, this is done working from wide wooden boards to avoid compaction. Beds are particularly appropriate where a "no-dig" system is used (see p.216). At the opposite extreme is the intensive deep bed—prepared by double-digging to a depth of around 2 ft (60 cm). A low-fertility soil improver such as leaf mold can be incorporated as the bed is dug initially. This deep cultivation is useful where the soil is compacted. It results in a deep, fertile zone with an open, free-draining structure into which roots can easily penetrate. Medium- to high-fertility materials, if required, should only be mixed into the top 6–8 in (15–20 cm). Increases in yield are noticeable and plants cope better in drought. Make the edging at least 6 in (15 cm) high as the soil level will rise considerably.

Planning and design

For most purposes, small square beds or narrow rectangular beds are most practical. A width of 3–4 ft (90–120 cm) allows easy access to the center; the exact width depends on your height and reach. With a maximum bed length of 10 ft (3 m), you will not have to walk too far to reach the other side. Beds can be grouped formally where food production is the main objective, or in patterns for a decorative "potager" effect.

Manageable plots In these small raised and edged beds, soil improvers, fertilizers, water, and the gardener's labor are concentrated on the growing areas, not wasted on paths.

Paths

Paths between beds should be a minimum of 18 in (45 cm) wide, with some up to 2 ft (60 cm) for wheelbarrow access. Bare paths will require hoeing to control weeds. Light-excluding cardboard covered with wood chips or sawdust is effective and clean to walk on. A porous membrane covered with gravel, pine needles, bark, or similar can also be used. More formal paths of slabs or bricks can look more elegant but are more expensive. Grass paths can be effective between vegetable beds, provide an all-weather surface, and look attractive. If grass is used, the paths should be set up to the width of your lawn mower, and brick or other permanent edging should be used to act both as a "mowing edge" and to prevent grasses from invading the beds. The clippings can be used as a mulch. The addition of soil improvers tends to raise the beds, while paths sink as they become compacted.

Siting and orientation

Beds should be in an open, sunny position. Wherever possible, rectangular beds should run north–south to minimize shade from taller crops; these can be grown down the center of the bed, with smaller crops on each side. If your beds have to run east to west, grow tall crops in the bed farthest from the sun, or in blocks with rows running across the bed, to minimize shading.

EDGING MATERIALS FOR RAISED BEDS

Bamboo rolls

Upended bottles

Bricks

Concrete blocks/slabs

Pavers

Logs*

Landscape timbers*

Railroad ties *

Lumber, recycled if possible (for example, old floorboards) *

Synthetic "wood"

Woven willow or hazel (see p.160) **

Edging rolls made from recycled plastic

* Untreated, or treated with environmentally friendly preservative (see pp.132–133).
** Soil along bed edges may dry out rather quickly.

Easy to negotiate These widely spaced high beds can be tended from a wheelchair or a garden stool. They are narrow enough to make the plants accessible even where reach is limited. Fragrant herbs enhance the sensory pleasures of gardening.

"No-dig" vegetable growing

"No-dig" is an organic technique that can be used for growing all types of vegetables. In no-dig, apart from any initial cultivation required, the soil is never turned over. Soil improvers and fertilizers are spread over the soil surface as required but are not incorporated by digging, which in the long term can be detrimental to soil structure; this job is left to earthworms and other organisms. Earthworms improve drainage through their burrowing activities, while their crumbly, aerated casts enhance soil structure. Soil organisms further decompose what the worms drag down, releasing food for the growing plants and forming humus.

Getting started

To get the best results from no-dig, the soil should be in reasonable condition, structurally, at the outset. This may involve digging to improve drainage and relieve any compaction (see The Soil, pp.32–33). On soil that does not have any major problems, the no-dig approach can be adopted right away. If the plot is weedy, or you are converting a patch of lawn, it can be cleared without digging, using a membrane such as black polythene (see p.74), or a sheet mulch (see facing page). Before sowing or planting, spread appropriate bulky soil improvers evenly over the soil, or over individual planting positions for widely spaced crops like pumpkins. Organic fertilizers, if needed, can be raked in before spreading soil improvers.

Sowing and planting

Most crops are grown in the same way as they would be on a dug bed. In an established no-dig

The no-dig approach If your soil is in good condition, you can begin using the no-dig technique right away (*below left*). If there are perennial weeds, a sheet mulch can be used to suppress them, again without any digging; within two years it should be possible to sow seed of crops such as chard (*below right*).

system, the surface soil will be fine, crumbly, and ideal for seed sowing. Young vegetable plants can be set into holes made with a trowel. Scrape back any layer of soil improver before sowing or planting; spread it back as the plants begin to grow.

Weeds and weeding

On a no-dig plot, weeds are drastically reduced as dormant seeds are not brought to the surface by the soil's being turned over. A mulch further reduces weed numbers, but is not essential. Light hoeing is effective on bare soil and gradually depletes the reserve of weed seeds. Loosen any perennial weeds with a fork and lift them out, disturbing the soil as little as possible.

Harvesting

You may be able to simply pull root crops out of the ground. If not, use a fork to loosen them gently, causing minimal disruption to the soil. As when planting, some soil disturbance is inevitable, but this is minimal compared with that caused by digging.

Sheet mulching

Sheet mulching by combining layers of various materials (*see panel, right*) is an easy, highly effective way of clearing ground such as a weedy patch or a lawn. It is particularly useful when establishing a no-dig system. You can grow a crop on the land in the first year, without any digging.

Growing through a sheet mulch

In the first year, potato tubers and young plants of brassicas, zucchini, and pumpkins can be planted through the mulch into the soil, in pockets loosened with a trowel; mix in some compost if available. Initially, plants may need more frost protection than usual, as the mulch cuts off some of the warmth of the sun, making the soil radiate back less heat at night. Cover plants with horticultural fleece; alternatively, plant a little later in the year.

Small seeds and root crops are unsuitable for sheet mulches in the first year, but in the following season the surface of the ground should be crumbly and very suitable for sowing. It is useful to continue to keep the soil mulched to prevent the germination of weed seeds, protect the soil from crusting after heavy rain, and conserve moisture.

Once a sheet mulch has cleared the ground, the area can be maintained using no-dig techniques.

SHEET MULCHING

Always mulch when soil is warm and after heavy rain. Mulching cold soil delays soil warming, slowing plant growth and increasing the risk of slug damage. Make up the sheet mulch with two or three layers.

Base layer
(Biodegradable; excludes light)

Large sheets of cardboard
Cardboard boxes, flattened
Newspapers, full thickness

Middle layer
(Soil improver; anchors base layer)

Garden compost
Grass clippings
Leaf mold or fallen leaves
Well-rotted manure
Mushroom compost (Note: this is
   very alkaline)
Shredded soft prunings
Spent straw or hay

Top layer—optional
(Retains moisture; looks good)

Straw
Hay

A flourish of foliage Leaf size, color, shape, and texture are important considerations when designing ornamental effects with vegetables, as many are not allowed to flower. Here, a ribbon of bold pumpkin leaves runs through flowering plants.

VEGETABLES FOR EDGING BEDS

For summer and fall

Loose-leaved lettuce—frilly, plain, and oak-leaved
Curly endive
Red-leaved plantain
Strips of seedling crops
Dwarf Savoy cabbage

For winter

Lamb's lettuce
Mizuna
Ornamental cabbage and kale
Rosette bok choy
Chinese (garlic) chives
Salad burnet
Red, yellow, or rainbow chard

Edible landscaping

Many vegetables are not just delicious to eat, they are also gorgeous to look at. Edible landscaping takes account of the ornamental aspects of edible plants alongside their practical value. It also means you can grow edible plants in a garden without the need for a separate vegetable area.

An edible landscape can be large or small, formal or relaxed, and include fruit, vegetables, herbs, and flowers. A famous example can be found at Villandry in France, designed to complement the chateau on a grand scale: vegetables provide blocks of color within a formal layout of paths and beds that are edged with immaculately clipped hedges. At the other extreme is a mixed border, where both edible and ornamental plants all tumble together in merry confusion.

Potager gardens

A potager is a garden or bed planted for both ornamental and edible appeal. Maintaining a balance between appearance and yield can be difficult, and careful planning is needed to keep it looking good all year. Planning for either summer or winter is easier, with the garden resting during one of these seasons.

Creative planting

Edible landscaping offers the creative gardener the opportunity to try out all sorts of unusual planting combinations. Vegetables may be chosen for color, leaf shape and texture, and overall form, and as visual statements. They can be trained up screens, trellises, or other plants to provide height, or used to create colorful shapes and patterns at ground level. Allowing some vegetables to go to seed can bring unexpected delights; lettuces, for example, turn into elegant tapering towers up to 4 ft (1.2 m) high. They are no good for eating, but you can save seed from them, and they look delightful. Onions and leeks allowed to flower produce "drumstick" flowerheads on tall stems that are striking, colorful, and attractive to bees.

Beautiful plants are healthy plants

Plants in an edible landscape need to be healthy and flourishing to look their best. Pay careful attention to maintaining the soil in good condition and, just as you would in a traditional vegetable garden, observe the principles of crop rotation (*see pp.230–233*) when planning from one year to the next, to produce best results. Replacement or substitute plants kept in reserve at varying stages of growth will be useful to take the place of any damaged or unhealthy plants, keeping the display looking good.

Eating the landscape

Harvesting inevitably leaves gaps in an edible landscape. Solve this problem by using varieties that can be picked over a long period, such as kale or loose-leaf lettuces. In addition, select crops that still look good after the edible part has been harvested, such as green beans, runner beans, or zucchini.

SOME EDIBLE FLOWERS

Borage (blue or, rarely, white)
Calendula (orange)
Chives (pink or purple)
Cowslip (yellow)
Daisy (pinkish white)
Lavender (purple, white, or pink)
Nasturtium (above; yellow/orange/red)
Rose (pink/red flowers taste best)
Sage (purple/pink)
Viola (purple, rarely white)

Potager style Colorful crops planted in patterns can rival the brightest bedding displays, and are edible too.

Attractive vegetables

Many vegetables have relatives that are grown as ornamental plants—think of bronze fennel, for example, or compare the flowers of a potato with those of the lovely wall shrub *Solanum crispum*. But a glance through any illustrated seed catalog will reveal vegetable plants that are beautiful enough for any border, with the added bonus of being productive, too.

1 **Fine fruits** Squashes come in a variety of sizes, shapes, and colors; their flowers and foliage are impressive, too. They have long been used to disguise compost piles and other garden eyesores. Although usually left to scramble along the ground, they can be trained up sturdy tripods and even over arches, and also look spectacular growing over a formally clipped hedge.

2 **Tall and stately** Globe artichokes add height and drama to any border. It is the flower buds that are eaten, but if you can leave a few to open, you will be rewarded by these enormous purple thistlelike blooms, which are also enjoyed by wildlife.

3 **Brilliant stems** Ruby chard makes a brilliant splash of color, and because you can harvest just a few leaves and leave the rest of the plant to grow, it remains ornamental for quite some time. Rainbow chard, with a mixture of white, yellow, pink, orange, and red stems, has cheerful good looks, too.

4 **Beautiful brassicas** Garden centers are full of ornamental cabbages in fall, but there are edible brassicas with red, purple, and even "black" leaves, some of them frilly, that are just as good-looking.

5 **Charming climbers** A tripod or obelisk covered with climbing beans makes a striking focal point for a border, or can be grown in a large tub. The scarlet flowers of these runner beans open over many weeks if the beans are regularly picked.

6 **Clouds of glory** Many people grow seakale (*Crambe maritima*) without ever realizing that it is edible. Plants may reach 8 ft (2.5 m) tall, and are covered with white flowers in late spring or early summer.

Vegetables in containers

Almost any vegetable can be grown in a container. Zucchini, tomatoes, potatoes, and eggplants do well in large individual containers. Salads, green onions, chard, leaf beet, green beans, beets, carrots, radishes, and Asian brassicas can be grown in a mixed pot or trough, or on their own. Avoid vegetables with deep roots such as parsnips, and those with a long, slow growing season, such as cauliflower, or with high demands for food and water, such as pumpkins.

SOME SOIL MIX REQUIREMENTS

- **Eggplants** 10 quarts (liters) per plant.

- **Green beans** 2.5 quarts (liters) per plant.

- **Beets, kohlrabi** Minimum depth of soil 8 in (20 cm); plants 3–4 in (7.5–10 cm) apart.

- **Leaf beet and chard** 4 quarts (liters) per plant.

- **Zucchini** 30–40 quarts (liters) per plant.

- **Sweet peppers** 5 quarts (liters) per plant.

- **Tomatoes** 15 quarts (liters) per plant.

Both useful and beautiful

Remember that vegetables can look good, too, and an "edible" container can look as striking as one filled with ornamentals. You might also like to add some herbs (*see p.279*) and edible flowers (*see p.219*). In cool climates, pots of fruiting vegetables such as tomatoes and peppers can be started off under cover (*see p.226*) and moved outside to a warm, sunny spot when the weather improves.

Container size and potting mix

Vegetables each have different growing requirements. Baby salad leaves can be grown in potting mix that has already been used once, while heavy feeders such as tomatoes need fresh soil and, once they are established, additional fertilizer. Generally, the larger the container, the better, since vegetables need a good supply of food and a consistent supply of water to do well. Growing several plants in one large container may give better results than using individual pots, and the plants will be much easier to care for.

As containers come in all shapes and sizes, it can be easier to talk volume rather than dimensions (*see panel, left, for some examples*). Measure the approximate volume of a container by filling it with potting mix from a container of known volume. In general, use a container that is at least 8 in (20 cm) deep. Baby salad leaves can go in shallower pots or trays, as long as you keep them watered. Heavy feeders like tomatoes and zucchini need a container at least 10–12 in (25–30 cm) deep. Carrots grow well in containers, and are easily protected from carrot rust fly by draping fleece over the pot. Grow early, short- or round-rooted varieties such as 'Amsterdam Forcing' and 'Early Scarlet Horn', in a container at least 6 in (15 cm) deep. Pull the bigger carrots first, leaving the others to grow.

GROWING TIPS

■ For a quick impact, buy young plants, or raise plants under cover and transplant, rather than sowing direct.

■ Never let pots dry out. Many vegetables are likely to "bolt" (go to seed) or split if the water supply is erratic.

■ Line clay pots with plastic to cut down on water loss.

■ Choose dwarf or miniature cultivars.

■ Feed with a general or potash-rich liquid fertilizer (*see pp.194–195*) as appropriate. Seaweed extract will give plants a boost.

■ Grow annual flowering plants such as calendula (also edible) or *Convolvulus tricolor* to attract predators to improve pest control.

Edible delights In this courtyard, vegetables benefit not only from the shelter of this sunny wall by day, but also from the warmth it radiates back at night. A sheet of wide-gauge wire netting fixed to the wall allows the plants at the back—tall tomatoes and eggplants, and a scrambling cucumber— to be tied in as they grow.

Crops under cover

Not everyone has room for a greenhouse, but if you do, it is well worth the investment. Even the smallest allows you to raise your own young plants for outdoor vegetable beds. And some crops are traditionally grown to harvest under glass—especially the more tender, fruiting vegetables, such as tomatoes, cucumbers, peppers, and eggplants. Hardy crops can also be grown to crop out of season, either earlier or much later than they would outside.

With the help of a greenhouse, the "hungry gap" between late winter and summer, when outdoor crops are scarce, can be filled with midwinter sowings of spinach, spring cabbage, calabrese, potatoes (*see panel, facing page*), and other traditional outdoor crops. Crops may either be sown direct in soil beds, or raised in seed trays with some warmth (either in a propagator, or on an indoor windowsill) and potted up. When frosts are forecast, a layer of woven fleece over the plants will protect them. At the other end of the season, greens for fall

and winter salads and stir fries can be sown, from late summer onward, up to four weeks later than outdoor sowing times. Try salad arugula, French sorrel, giant red mustard, corn salad, endive, land cress, bok choy, Chinese greens, and baby beets. You don't need a lot of room to produce a few meals' worth of fresh vegetables out of season.

Vegetables under cover Watercress (*below left*) and salad leaves (*below right*) can be grown in containers when greenhouse shelves are bare; by high summer, space under glass will be filled with fruiting crops (*facing page*).

Stir-fry leaves and salad mix

Stir-fry leaves and salad mixes can be grown on a bench in a container 6 in (15 cm) deep, filled with an organic multipurpose potting mix. Sow seeds very thinly in rows every eight weeks from early spring until mid-fall. Water the soil without wetting the leaves. Pick individual leaves as required.

Watercress

Watercress is quick and easy to grow. Germinate the seeds in a propagator, in a pot of potting mix standing half-submerged in a tray of water. Prick out seedlings into module trays (*see p.198*), and grow them on, half-submerged in a tray of water.

Seal the small holes in a growing bag with electrical tape. Remove most of the top of the bag by cutting three large square holes. Soak the soil. Plant five plants in each hole. Begin harvesting regularly as soon as the shoots are large enough.

NEW POTATOES FOR CHRISTMAS

Save a few tubers from a crop of early potatoes, such as 'Swift', 'Maris Bard' or 'Rocket'. Leave them in the sun to turn green, then store until late summer. Then plant them in a 3-gallon (12-liter) tub with drainage holes, or a commercial "potato bag." Put a 6-in (15-cm) layer of multipurpose or potting mix into the bottom of the container and place three tubers, buds upward, on top. Cover with 3 in (7.5 cm) of the potting mix, then water in. As the shoots grow, continue to fill the container with potting mix, always leaving the tops of the shoots in the light. You can reuse the contents of used growing bags, or other once-used growing media, to save costs. Protect from frost with a layer of horticultural fleece.

Water regularly, taking care not to allow the compost to dry out. Feeling the weight of the container is a good test for moisture content. The foliage can be supported with four canes (topped with cane caps to protect your eyes) pushed inside the rim of the pot, supporting two horizontal circles of string; or the stems can be allowed to trail from the pot. Stop watering when the leaves and stems die off. Empty out the contents on Christmas morning and harvest the new tubers.

Fruiting crops under glass

Tomatoes are without doubt the most popular crop for a cool greenhouse. Eggplants and peppers can also give excellent results; both need slightly higher temperatures and eggplants need a long growing season. All three belong to the same botanical family (*see pp.248–251*), making crop rotation difficult if you are growing plants directly in the soil (the preferred organic choice). Alternate them with crops from another family—cucumbers, for example—or use pots and growing bags.

Starting off

Young plants may be bought from late spring onward—but for the best choice of cultivars, and organic plants, raise your own on a warm windowsill or in a propagator. You can start tomatoes as early as midwinter if you can keep the young plants frost-free. If not, sow in spring, 8–10 weeks before the last frost.

Tomato cultivars are available specifically for growing under cover, but most outdoor cultivars grow well in an unheated greenhouse. Indeterminate types, which make tall plants with a single vertical stem called cordons, make best use of limited space. Bush and trailing types do well in pots and baskets. Eggplants and peppers make more compact, bushy plants, to 30 in (75 cm) tall.

Germinate seeds in a warm spot, pricking out the seedlings into 3–4-in (7.5–10-cm) pots. Keep them growing in a warm place (54–61°F/12–16°C, depending on the plant). Once the first flowers show, they can be planted in a soil bed or into pots or growing bags.

Soil beds, pots, or growing bags?

To grow in soil beds in a greenhouse, apply a medium-fertility soil improver such as garden compost to the soil or, if available, a light dressing of worm compost. Check that the soil temperature 4 in (10 cm) below the surface is at least 56°F (14°C). If not, move your young plants into a pot one size larger and wait. If plants get leggy, they can be planted in the soil an inch or two deeper than they were in the pot. Spacing will depend on the cultivar. Follow the advice on the seed packet. Never crowd plants; it encourages disease.

To grow in pots, use 8–10-in (21–25-cm) pots filled with a rich organic potting mix. Arrange them at a spacing appropriate to the crop and cultivar. Organic growing bags are available to buy. Two plants per bag are easier to manage and give larger yields than the three usually recommended.

Fine fruits An unheated greenhouse is a perfect environment for growing warmth-loving fruiting crops such as (*above, from left*) tomatoes, peppers, cucumbers, and eggplants.

Supporting stems In addition to the support given by twine, canes, or frames, bottomless pots filled with potting mix around the base of tomato plants will encourage rooting from the stem and hence a more stable plant. It also makes directing water to the roots more efficient.

Watering and fertilizing

Early in the season, take care not to overwater or overfertilize. Once plants are growing well, however, do not let them go short of water. Cropping will be reduced, and tomatoes and peppers may develop a condition known as blossom end rot (*see p.86*). Plants in pots and bags may need watering twice a day in hot weather. Make an inspection hole at one end of growing bags to enable you to test the moisture content of the soil with your finger. Start feeding with an organic liquid fertilizer (*see p.194*) once the first fruit has set. Plants in soil beds will not need so much watering, nor feeding if the soil is in good condition.

Support and training

To support cordon tomatoes, attach a length of twine to the greenhouse frame above each plant, and tie the other end loosely around the stem at the base of the plant. As the plant grows, twist the tip around the string. Alternatively, tie the stem to a tall cane. Pinch out sideshoots as they appear for the best crop, and pinch out the growing tip of the cordon after four or five clusters of fruit have formed (*see also p.251*). Taller eggplants and peppers may also need support with canes and twine.

Keeping plants healthy

Always keep the greenhouse clean and tidy; do not allow it to fill up with old pots and general gardening equipment. Keep the glass clean—it may need to be washed down several times a year—and once a year, find time to give all of the interior a really good scrub with hot, soapy water. As soon as the weather warms up in spring, start opening doors and window vents during the day, but close them again at night.

Inspect plants daily for pests and diseases: problems can build up rapidly in a confined space. Remember to look under leaves, where many glasshouse pests tend to congregate. Pick off or prune out any leaves or shoots that are diseased or badly infested with pests; if a whole plant has succumbed, then take it out of the greenhouse and dispose of it, and check its neighbors carefully. Biological controls (*see p.97*) are ideal for controlling many common glasshouse pests. For more tips, see p.250.

Harvesting

Harvest tomatoes when they are ripe. Peppers may be picked green, which encourages more fruits, or left to ripen. Pick eggplants when the skin is still shiny and taut.

Planning the produce year

Planning ahead can help you get the best results from growing vegetables, make the best use of space if it is limited, and harvest fresh produce all year. Thinking about the whole year ahead also helps to spread the workload. It enables you to set aside time for important jobs such as making compost, collecting fall leaves, incorporating green manures, and applying soil improvers, as well as the more obvious tasks of sowing, planting, and harvesting.

Spread the harvest

In mild regions you can get ahead by planting some vegetables in fall to overwinter, such as fava beans and some onions, but most vegetables are sown or planted in spring, to be ready to harvest between early summer and late fall. A few hardy crops can be harvested in the new year. Crop and cultivar choice, combined with a range of sowing and planting times, makes it possible to avoid summer gluts and spread the harvest over a longer period. A greenhouse can extend the cropping season at both ends.

The hungry gap

In cool climates, the period between late winter and late spring is known traditionally as the "hungry gap," because there is not much to harvest from the garden at this time. To fill this gap, grow vegetables that are hardy enough to stand through mild winters, such as leeks or kale, or that mature very quickly from an early spring sowing, such as radish or seedling lettuces. One of the difficulties in filling the hungry gap with hardy vegetables is that they need to be in their final growing position by

midsummer, when the ground may still be occupied by summer crops. In this case, allocate less space to summer vegetables, or try intercropping smaller summer crops with winter ones (see p.259 for more about intercropping).

Cultivar choice

Some vegetables, such as cabbages, carrots, cauliflowers, leeks, lettuces, onions, and peas, have a range of cultivars for different seasons; some can even be available to harvest all year, depending on the severity of your climate. Cultivars described as "quick" or "early" are especially useful at both the beginning and the end of the growing season, as they produce a crop more quickly than main crops. Others have been bred to tolerate cold conditions.

Successional sowing is another way of spreading the harvest, and it is particularly suitable for fast-maturing crops. What it means is that you sow a small amount of the same crop—your lettuces or radishes, for example—at intervals of two to three weeks, rather than sowing all the seed at the same time—which would mean that all the plants reach maturity simultaneously, giving you a glut. A good rule of thumb for salad crops is to sow the next batch of seeds when the previous ones are just starting to show as seedlings. Suitable vegetables include kohlrabi, lettuce, radish, arugula, spinach, green onions, and turnips.

VEGETABLES THAT FILL THE HUNGRY GAP

Brussels sprouts
Chard
Kale
Leaf beet
Leeks
Radishes and radish pods
Seedling lettuces
Sprouting broccoli
Winter cabbage
Winter cauliflower
Winter spinach

(From far left) **Crops through the year** Fava beans, here in flower, are one of the first major crops of the year. Summer is a time for salad leaves and tender young vegetables, while pumpkins and squash soak up the sun to ripen in fall. Hardy Brussels sprouts are a reliable winter stalwart.

Crop rotation

This is the practice of growing related vegetables in different areas of the garden in consecutive years. If crops from the same family—the lettuce family, the brassica family, and so on (*see pp.234–253*)—are grown in the same place year after year, related soilborne pests and diseases may become established. In small plots, moving vegetables just a few yards may not have much effect on pest and disease control, but it is still worth doing for other benefits.

Why use crop rotation?

■ **Nutrient availability** Vegetables differ in their nutrient requirements, so moving them around the growing area helps to prevent the soil from becoming depleted locally and makes best use of the soil reserves.

■ **Soil treatments** Some crops need soil amendments to do well, others make good use of residual fertility left by a previous crop. Grow crops with similar requirements together, so you can apply the appropriate soil treatments for them. This means that all parts of the vegetable area will receive the same treatment over the period of the rotation.

■ **Weed control** Some vegetables, such as squash and potatoes, produce weed-suppressing foliage and are easy to weed. Others, like onions and carrots, are more difficult to weed and do not have a growth habit that competes well. Alternating vegetables with these two opposing characteristics helps keep weeds under control.

■ **Soil structure** Plant roots occupy different levels of the soil. Alternating deep-rooting with shallow-rooting vegetables has a positive effect on soil structure.

How are the vegetables grouped?

Vegetables from the same botanical family (these families are described on pp.234–253) are susceptible to the same pests and diseases.

Parsnips, for example, belong to the same family—the Apiaceae—as carrots, and are also a favourite of the carrot rust fly.

Some vegetable relationships are easy to see: peas and beans all belong to one family; onions, shallots, and garlic to another. But the parts of the plant eaten—their shape and flavor—are not always a good basis for guesswork. Brussels sprouts, for example, obviously seem to belong with cabbages in the brassica family, which they do—but rutabagas, radishes, and turnips are also related.

Sweet corn does not fit in with any of the other family groups. It makes a useful filler for gaps in your rotation plan. Also exempt are the perennial vegetables, which occupy the same space year after year (*see overleaf*).

How long is a crop rotation?

Three or four years is the usual recommended minimum for a crop rotation, but it can certainly be longer. If you know that your soil has a serious, persistent problem, such as potato cyst nematode, onion white rot, or clubroot, you may need a much longer rotation to grow susceptible crops with any success.

(Right) **A basic four-year rotation** In this illustration, the family groups move around the "plots" clockwise each year. Note that there is more than one family on each plot. This is just one example: devise your own system to suit your cropping needs using the advice on the following pages.

1 Potato family; cucumber family Dig in any green manure. Apply manure or rich compost in spring, then grow potatoes, tomatoes, and zucchini. Follow early potatoes with leeks; the rest with fall onion sets, garlic, and/or a green manure such as phacelia.

2 Onion family; pea and bean family Sow fava beans and peas and plant onion sets in spring, then string beans and runner beans in early summer. Follow harvested garlic and fall onions (see Plot 1) with a late sowing of dwarf string beans. Sow winter vetch as a green manure, liming first if necessary.

3 Cabbage family Dig in winter vetch in the spring, or add compost. Sow and plant summer brassicas; plant overwintering brassicas with lettuce and other intercrops (*see p.259*) between. If you don't want so many brassicas, grow sweet corn. Apply compost to the overwintering plants in late summer; spread leaf mold over the rest of the plot.

4 Carrot family; beet family Grow carrots, parsnips, celery, beets, spinach, and chard on this plot. On poorer ground, add compost to the soil, except where carrots and parsnips are to be sown. Sow winter rye or buckwheat as a green manure over winter.

GROWING PERENNIAL VEGETABLES

Perennial vegetables, which can stay in the same spot for many years, obviously do not fit into the usual crop rotation. Asparagus and rhubarb are best given their own, separate beds. Others, such as globe artichokes and seakale, make beautiful border plants, given sufficient space.

As with all perennial plants, appropriate soil preparation, including removal of all perennial weeds, is essential before planting (*see* The Soil, *pp.34–35*, Weeds and Weeding, *pp.76–79, and also* Herbaceous plants, *pp.190–191*). When replacing perennial vegetable plants, or dividing and replanting (*see p.193*), do not replant on the same site. Check for pests and diseases on perennial crops, especially those such as nine-star broccoli that are related to other vegetables. Pests and diseases that become established on perennial crops can be a source of infection for other plants.

Perennial vegetables include:

■ Asparagus

■ Cardoons

■ Globe artichokes

■ Nine-star broccoli

■ Rhubarb

■ Seakale

(Right, clockwise from top left) **Asparagus; rhubarb; globe artichoke; cardoon**

Planning a crop rotation

Plan your own rotation according to the crops you want to grow, or follow the basic four-year plan given on page 231. This is a plan designed for a cool climate, with robust, hardy crops overwintering in the ground, but if you garden in a very mild area, or have a warm and sheltered garden, you could try the alternative plan given on the facing page. Remember that you do not have to grow the same vegetables every year, although there will probably be some favorites you want to repeat. Make a list of the vegetables you want to grow over a whole season (a seed catalog is handy for this), and in roughly what quantities, then:

■ **Group the vegetables together** according to botanical family (*see pp.234–253*).

■ **Draw a plan** of the growing area. Set aside an area for perennial vegetables, if desired, and divide what remains into equal-sized sections according to how many years the rotation is to last. If you will be using several different areas of the garden for growing vegetables, treat each one separately, changing the crop each year for the period of the rotation. Distribute the vegetables around the sections, keeping

Soil treatments in a rotation

■ **Compost, manure** and other medium- to high-fertility soil improvers: use for heavy feeders such as potatoes, leeks, cabbage family, and squash. Apply in spring before planting.

■ **Lime** Add to cabbage family section to control clubroot, in the fall before planting, but only if necessary to raise pH, not routinely. Do not lime when growing potatoes, as it can encourage scab.

■ **Leaf mold** and other low-fertility soil improvers: these are beneficial preceding root crops. Apply anywhere as a mulch to improve structure, especially over winter.

■ **Green manures** Grow these soil-improving plants (*see pp.50–51*) over winter, sowing in late summer and fall, or as catch crops (*see p.259*) in spring and summer. When following a crop with a green manure, choose one that belongs to the same family. Do not use winter rye before sowing seeds direct, as it inhibits germination when it decomposes. Vetch is excellent before brassica family crops, supplying them with all the nitrogen they need.

families together. If one family does not fill a whole section, try to combine it with another that requires similar soil treatments. Fast-maturing crops, and miscellaneous ones such as sweet corn, can be fitted into gaps.

■ **Be flexible** and prepared to adapt your plans, while sticking to the rotation principles. Unexpected weather and other crop disasters can affect everyone.

■ **Keep records** of what you planned, and what actually happened! This will be useful information if you want to adjust the rotation in following years.

ROTATION FOR A WARMER CLIMATE

Plot 1 Tomatoes, eggplants, and peppers, then to overwinter, garlic, onions, and fava beans.

Plot 2 Sweet corn, intercropped with salads in the early season. Follow with a green manure.

Plot 3 Manure in spring, then grow pumpkins, squash, and zucchini.

Plot 4 The onions, garlic, and fava beans planted the year before (see Plot 1). Grow salads over winter. Add leaf mold in spring.

The cabbage family

Brassicas—the popular term for members of the cabbage family— are grown for their leaves, buds, roots, stems, or shoots. They thrive in cool, moist climates and are very nutritious, being rich in minerals and vitamins.

Many familiar "western" vegetables, such as cauliflower and cabbage, belong to the brassica tribe; it also includes Asian vegetables such as Chinese cabbage and mizuna greens. Some, such as kale and sprouting broccoli, need a long growing season, but they are very hardy and provide useful winter food.

Indeed, some forms of brassica can be picked at almost any time of year. Leafy crops include kale and cabbages for winter, spring, and summer use. The immature flowerheads of broccoli, cauliflowers, and sprouting broccoli are eaten; Brussels sprouts develop their small, cabbagelike edible heads along a tall stem.

Cress, mustard, and radishes are used as sprouted seeds, and many can be eaten as seedling crops. The perennial vegetable seakale is grown for its forced shoots, harvested in mid- to late winter. Kohlrabi produces crisp and juicy swollen stems.

Root crops include rutabagas, turnips, and radishes. Spring and summer radishes tend to have small roots, apart from the long white "mooli" types. Winter radishes are much larger. Radishes can also be grown for the peppery seed pods that follow the flowers.

Asian brassicas, such as bok choy and Asian mustard, are fast-growing, producing tasty,

FAMILY MEMBERS

This family takes its botanical name, Brassicaceae, from the genus—*Brassica*—to which so many of its members belong. This diverse group, which includes annuals, biennials, and perennials, would all, ultimately, produce the same, characteristic flower, with the four petals arranged in a cross (another name for this family is Cruciferae). The same four-petal arrangement can be seen in ornamental members of the brassica family, such as wallflowers.

Edible family members include:

- Arugula (*Eruca vesicaria*)
- Asian mustard (*Brassica juncea*)
- Bok choy (*Brassica rapa* Chinensis Group)
- Broccoli (*Brassica oleracea* Italica Group)
- Brussels sprouts (*Brassica oleracea* Gemmifera Group)
- Cabbage (*Brassica oleracea* Capitata Group)
- Cauliflower (*Brassica oleracea* Botrytis Group)
- Chinese cabbage (*Brassica rapa* Pekinensis Group)
- Cress (*Lepidium sativum*)
- Kale (*Brassica oleracea* Acephala Group)
- Kohlrabi (*Brassica oleracea* Gongylodes Group)
- Mizuna greens (*Brassica rapa* var. *nipposinica*)
- Mustard (*Brassica hirta*)
- Radishes (*Raphanus sativus*)
- Rutabagas (*Brassica napus* Napobrassica Group)
- Seakale (*Crambe maritima*)
- Sprouting broccoli (*Brassica oleracea* Italica Group)
- Turnips (*Brassica rapa* Rapifera Group)
- Upland cress (*Barbarea verna*)

(Clockwise from top left) **Bok choy; curly kale; spring cabbage; summer radishes**

(Clockwise from left) **Bird netting** This needs to be stretched taut, or birds may sit on the cabbages and peck through the mesh. **A brassica collar** This square of material prevents the female cabbage root fly from laying eggs at the base of the stem. **Removing dying leaves** This can help prevent fungal diseases from spreading from the soil up the plant.

nutritious leaves and shoots that are good in salads and stir-fries.

Some brassicas have a typical strong, mustardy flavor, but others, such as kohlrabi and broccoli, are more delicate. Many can be eaten raw, as well as cooked or pickled.

Brassicas may not be an obvious choice for an ornamental garden, but some are very attractive. Red, curly, and "ragged-leaved" kale can look stunning over winter. Kohlrabi, in purple or green, makes an interesting addition, and the glaucous green of many cabbages and cauliflowers makes a perfect foil for brightly colored annuals. Asian mustard greens and some "mini" cabbages could be grown as bed edging.

Soil treatment and crop rotation

Brassicas need firm, moisture-retentive soil; they do not thrive in dry conditions. In a crop rotation, this family best follows on from the nitrogen-fixing pea and bean family (see p.242). A green manure crop of winter vetch or clover provides leafy brassicas with all the nitrogen they need. In the absence of a green manure, a medium-fertility soil improver, such as compost, can be applied to the brassica bed. Acidic soils (pH 6 or less) should be limed (*see p.55*) in fall prior to growing brassicas.

Brassicas are easily raised from seed or by planting ready-grown "starter" plants. Western brassicas are usually sown in spring and summer; many Asian types, which tend to bolt in hot, dry conditions and when day length is increasing, are best sown in the shortening days after midsummer—providing useful fall crops. Fast-growing crops like arugula and radishes, directly sown, will be ready quickly; kohlrabi and broccoli can crop in as little as eight weeks. A succession of sowings will maintain a supply. Many brassicas, however, are slow-growing and take months to reach maturity. Avoid tying up the growing space for this long by sowing in a nursery bed or modules and transplanting when the ground becomes available.

Empty ground between young plants of those winter brassicas that will make large plants is useful for catch- and intercropping (*see pp.258–259*). However, careful choice of cultivar and close spacing can produce smaller, meal-sized heads of vegetables such as cabbage and cauliflower.

Protect the crop

Brassicas may make up a high proportion of the crops you grow, so it is important to have a thorough crop rotation plan to try to avoid clubroot, their most serious disease. Spores can survive in the soil for 20 years in the absence of a host crop. Avoid bringing in the disease on plants and soil.

Cabbage root fly larvae also attack the roots of this family, causing plants to wilt and die. Young plants can be protected with a root fly collar or a crop cover. Fleece can also be used to protect young plants from flea beetle, and netting may be needed against some birds that, when hungry in winter, can completely strip standing mature crops.

From late spring onward, various moths and butterflies, such as the large cabbage white, may lay their eggs on brassica plants. The resulting caterpillars can be picked off by hand, if wasps have not removed them first.

Because some form of brassica crop can be growing at any time of year, cabbage whitefly and mealy aphids can build up in considerable numbers. It pays to remove all members of this crop family once a year—in early spring, for example—to break the cycle.

For more information and advice see the A–Z of Plant Problems (*pp.320–341*).

(Near right) Cabbage root fly
Wilting, followed by general collapse and death of the plant, is a sign that the larvae of the cabbage root fly have eaten through the roots of the plant. By this stage the plants may be lost.

(Far right) Cabbage caterpillars
These hatch from eggs laid in clusters on the underside of leaves by the large cabbage white butterfly. If too numerous to pick off one by one, remove the whole leaf. Wasps love caterpillars, and may remove them all for you.

The onion family

Plants in the onion family or Alliaceae (they all belong to the genus *Allium*) have a pungent flavor. If left to flower, many produce typical "drumstick" flowerheads, like ornamental alliums. Crops include tiny pickling onions, multicolored shallots, slender green onions, pungent garlic, and red, white, and yellow globe onions.

All members of the onion tribe are hardy, cool-climate crops. Green onions, a quick filler crop, are eaten as slim young plants, leaves and all. Onions, shallots, and garlic are usually harvested once they are mature; when dry, they can store well for many months (*see p.271*). Leeks, which do not produce a bulb, are grown for their long white, cylindrical shank. They can be left in the ground to harvest in the winter months.

The herbs chives and garlic chives also belong to this family, as does the perennial Egyptian or tree onion, which produces aerial bulbs in place of flowers; these may sprout and grow in situ. Flowers of leeks and garlic may also produce tiny bulbs in place of seed.

Growing the crop

Members of this family are simple to grow. By choosing a range of types and cultivars, you can have onions available all year, either fresh or from storage. Green onions and leeks are grown from seed; leeks can also be bought as young plants for planting out in early summer. Onions and shallots can be grown from seed or, more easily, from "sets" (immature bulbs), and garlic is always planted as cloves. Garlic must undergo a period of cold to crop well, which is why it is traditionally planted in fall. Shallots may also be planted in fall, and late summer is

Onions for storage Once harvested, bulb onions need to be kept in a warm, dry, airy environment for a week or two to "harden" their skins so that they will store well. In sunny weather you can leave them on the soil surface (*see also p.271*).

Fungal diseases Black, sunken patches on leaves (*far left*) are caused by the fungal disease downy mildew. Pick off infected leaves and dispose of them immediately; next year, be sure to rotate crops. Leek rust (*left*) need not spell disaster for your crops, but in future years, look for leek cultivars that offer some resistance to this fungal infection.

the time to sow or plant "Japanese onion" cultivars for an early crop the following year.

Soil and spacing

Members of this family prefer well-drained, relatively fertile soil. Avoid heavy fertilizing, which encourages disease and cuts down on storage life. Soil that has been fed for a previous crop, such as potatoes or brassicas, should suffice. Leeks can benefit from the addition of medium- to high-fertility soil improver in poorer soil.

Bulb onions and leeks respond well to variations in plant spacing (*see pp.256–259*), which can be used to control the size of the plants. A crop of baby leeks, for example, can be grown as close as 2 in (5 cm) apart.

Protect the crop

Onion white rot is a serious disease that can survive in the soil for 20 years or more. Try to avoid introducing it on plants and in soil, and use crop rotation. If you find the maggots of onion fly tunneling into bulbs, protect crops with fine mesh netting. Various fungi may attack onion foliage. Downy mildew is common in wet seasons, its dark spores turning leaves black. The orange pustules of leek rust may appear in summer. They look alarming (*above*), but plants often grow out of the disease in fall. See the A–Z of Plant Problems (*pp.320–341*) for more details and information.

FAMILY MEMBERS

- Garlic (*Allium sativum*)
- Leek (*Allium porrum*)
- Onion (*Allium cepa*)
- Shallot (*Allium cepa* Aggregatum Group)
- Welsh onion (*Allium fistulosum*)
- Tree onion (*Allium cepa* Proliferum Group)

The cucumber family

Members of the cucumber family, widely known as cucurbits, are typically vigorous plants with big, bold leaves and yellow, trumpet-shaped flowers. They require a lot of space. Trailing cultivars can be trained to scramble over arches or up netting. Bush cultivars are more compact.

This family is grown mainly for its fruits, which may be eaten young or mature. They come in a wonderful array of shapes, colors, and sizes. Flowers and seeds can also be eaten.

All cucurbits are striking in appearance. Pumpkins and squashes show some of the widest variety of form, from the glowing lanternlike spheres of 'Atlantic Giant' to the curious, infolded 'Turk's Cap'. All are tender annuals that need warm conditions to do well.

CUCURBIT FLOWERS

In most cases, cucurbit plants bear flowers of two types, either male or female, and the latter must be pollinated by the former to set fruit. Female flowers have a tiny fruit behind the flower that swells once pollination has taken place. The flowers are normally pollinated by insects, but you can also hand-pollinate zucchini by moving pollen between flowers with a small paintbrush. If you find yourself with too much zucchini, you can slow down the production of fruits by eating the flowers. Pick them, wash and dry them, and deep-fry them in a light batter.

In cool climates, zucchini, marrows, pumpkins, squashes, and cucumbers can crop outdoors if raised in warmth and transplanted into warm soil, after the last frost. In warmer regions they can be sown direct outside. Melons need warm conditions and may have to be grown in a cool greenhouse or cold frame if you live in a region with a short growing season.

Growing the crop

All members of this family benefit from a dressing of medium-fertility soil improver, such as compost, at planting time. Unless you are growing for competition or in a container, no further fertilizing is required. In an outdoor crop rotation, they can be included in potato or brassica beds, or given their own section.

Once planted, most cucurbits need little attention and make good weed-suppressing plants. Melons require more training, watering, and feeding, and are a good choice for the more experienced gardener.

Protect the crop

Cucumber mosaic virus (*pictured on p.89*) can, despite its name, affect all members of this family, and many other plant families, too. There is no cure, but some cultivars show some resistance. Protect young plants from slugs. Powdery mildew may be a sign of dry soil; late in the year it will not affect the crop. Under cover, biological controls can be used to control pests like red spider mite. Crop rotation, good ventilation, and hygiene are the best defense against fungal diseases.

See the A–Z of Plant Problems (*pp.320–341*) for more advice and information.

Harvesting and storage

Cucumbers, zucchini, and summer squashes are eaten young and picked regularly to maintain the supply. They tend to have a mild flavor. Melons are picked when ripe, and pumpkins and winter squashes are left to mature on the plant, to develop a tough skin for storage (*see also p.271*). Some are bland and watery while others develop sweet, rich, densely textured flesh—excellent as a roasted vegetable and for soups and stews.

Preventing rot Marrows are closely related to zucchini and have thinner skins than the winter squashes, so they can succumb to rot spreading up from damp soil. Prop them up on a brick or board to give them some protection.

FAMILY MEMBERS

In addition to the outdoor and greenhouse cucurbits, the cucumber family, or Cucurbitaceae, also includes the luffa vine, whose desiccated fruits are more familiar as the bathroom loofah.

- Zucchini, marrow, summer squash (*Cucurbita pepo*)
- Cucumber (*top left*), gherkin (*Cucumis sativus*)
- Luffa (*Luffa cylindrica*)
- Melon (*top right*) (*Cucumis melo*)
- Gourd, winter squash, pumpkin (*below, left and right*) (*Cucurbita moschata, C. pepo, C.maxima*)
- Watermelon (*Citrullus lanata*)

The pea and bean family

Members of this family, called the Papilionaceae for its butterfly-like flowers (as in *papillon*, French for butterfly), are also referred to as legumes. Legumes characteristically develop root nodules containing bacteria that "fix" gaseous nitrogen from the air. When the nodules decay, this nitrogen is released into the soil, which is why the green manures in this family are so valuable.

Climbing beans "Scarlet runners," with their cheery red flowers, are the most widely recognized climbing bean, but there are others that are equally attractive; this is 'Viola Cornetti', with purple stems, pinky mauve flowers, and deep purple edible pods.

The vegetable crops of this family are grown primarily for their fleshy pods and/or seeds. Peas and fava beans are hardy, cool-season crops, growing best below 60°F (15°C). String beans and runner beans are frost-tender and need warmer conditions (although runner beans cannot stand dry soil). Young fava bean pods and shoot tips can be eaten, but the seeds are the main crop. Traditionally, peas are shelled from their pods, but snow peas and sugarsnap pods are eaten whole.

Peas vary in height from 2 to 10 ft (60 cm–3 m), and most need to be supported with twiggy branches or wide-mesh pea netting. "Leafless" cultivars, with more tendril than leaf, are self-supporting when grown in a block. Dwarf bush beans are ideal for small spaces and containers. Climbing cultivars (known as pole beans) will twine up canes or sticks in a tepee or double row. They do best in warm-to-hot weather and are much more tolerant of dry conditions than runner beans. Runner beans are generally climbers, although dwarf cultivars are available. The edible flowers can be red, white, salmon pink, or bicolored red and white, making an attractive feature trained up a trellis or wigwam. The pods are long and green.

Soil and crop rotation

Legumes thrive in well-drained but moisture-retentive soil that has been fed for a previous crop, such as potatoes. In a rotation they can

Aphids on fava beans The black bean aphid is a common pest of fava beans, congregating on the tender shoot tips to pierce the plant and suck sap. If you nip out the shoot tips, the aphids usually shun the less palatable older growth.

be followed by brassica-family crops, which will make use of the nitrogen provided by the pea and bean nodules, as long as the roots have been left in the ground.

Protect the crop

Fall- and early-spring-sown seed of peas and beans may be eaten by mice because other food is scarce; later sowings may be safer. The pea and bean weevil eats notches out of leaves from early spring. Plants growing well can usually withstand the damage; if necessary, protect young plants with a crop cover such as fleece, put on at sowing time. The black bean aphid first appears on the tips of fava beans. Early sowings are less likely to be attacked. Both early and late sowings of peas may miss the egg-laying period of the pea moth, whose larvae eat peas. Chocolate spot is an early-season disease of fava beans, common in wet soil. Powdery mildew on peas tends to occur on dry soil later in the season. Young string and runner beans are attractive to slugs and snails. In cooler areas, the first crop is best transplanted, rather than directly sown, with individual bottle cloches added for extra protection.

See the A–Z of Plant Problems (*pp.320–341*) for more advice and information.

FAMILY MEMBERS

As well as the crops below, the pea and bean family includes a number of crops grown as sprouted seeds, and also the green manures alfalfa (*Medicago sativa*), clover (*Trifolium*), fenugreek (*Trigonella foenum-graecum*), field bean (*Vicia faba*), lupine (*Lupinus angustifolius*), trefoil (*Medicago lupulina*), and common vetch (*Vicia sativa*). Edible legumes grown in the garden include:

- Asparagus pea (*Lotus tetragonolobus*)
- Fava or broad bean (*Vicia faba*)
- String bean (*Phaseolus vulgaris*)
- Hyacinth bean or lablab (*Dolichos lablab*), for warm areas or greenhouses only (*near right*)
- Pea (*Pisum sativum*) (*far right*)
- Runner bean (*Phaseolus coccineus*)

The beet family

This family includes both leaf and root crops suitable for warm and cool climates. Spinach and red orache are fast-growing, leafy catch crops. Spinach is best sown in the cool temperatures of spring and fall, as it rapidly goes to seed in hot, dry weather. Sow little and often for a good supply.

Concentrated color Rich, dark colors of both roots and leaves are a hallmark of this family. Beet pigments decay when heated, but are used as dyes for cold foods such as ice cream.

Beets

Beets are grown for their substantial, juicy roots, commonly dark red, but gold, white, and bicolored target-patterned types are available. The deep green and magenta leaves are decorative and can also be eaten when young, either raw or lightly cooked. Fast-growing baby beets are eaten when only 1–2 in (2.5–5 cm) across. Larger roots of maincrop cultivars can be stored for winter use. Bolt-resistant cultivars are used for early sowings.

The leafy beets

Leaf beet and chard are known by a confusing range of names. The former has large, mid-green leaves; the latter tends to have a dark green glossy leaf with a wide, prominent

FAMILY MEMBERS

The beet family is botanically named the Chenopodiaceae, or goosefoot family. As well as the crops below, it includes the grain quinoa, and several "edible weeds" such as fat hen, which loves the fertile soil in a vegetable garden.

- Beets (*Beta vulgaris* subsp. *vulgaris*)
- Chard, Swiss chard, seakale beet (*Beta vulgaris* Cicla Group) (*ruby chard shown near right*)
- Good King Henry (*Chenopodium bonus-henricus*)
- Leaf beet, also called perpetual spinach or spinach beet (*Beta vulgaris* Cicla Group)
- Red orache, or mountain spinach (*Atriplex hortensis* 'Rubra')
- Spinach (*Spinacea oleracea*) (*far right*)

midrib, which can be eaten as a separate vegetable. The midrib color ranges from white through yellow, orange, and luminous pink to glowing red. Leaf beet and chard are easy to grow, much less prone to bolting than spinach, can be picked over a period of many months, and are able to withstand low winter temperatures. Two sowings, one in spring and one in fall, should give a year-round supply.

Although a rampant self-seeder if allowed to flower, red orache is a very decorative plant whose leaves make a colorful addition to salads. The little-known perennial Good King Henry is another old-fashioned salad plant. Its leaves can be picked early in the year; the flowering shoots are also eaten. It prefers good rich soil and tolerates some shade.

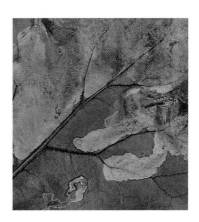

Beet leaf miner
These tunneling pests move between the upper and lower epidermis of the leaf, eating the soft material within. Remove affected leaves, and squash the maggots within the "mines."

Growing the crops
Crops in this family all prefer fertile soil that does not dry out easily. They are often included in the "roots" section of a rotation, in soil that has been improved for a previous crop. They may appreciate a mulch of a medium-fertility soil improver on poorer soils. Spinach beet and chard can be raised in modules (*see p.198*) for transplanting, and beets are suitable for "multi-sowing" (*see p.258*). All can be grown in a cool greenhouse for out-of-season cropping.

Protect the crop
These crops are relatively trouble-free, although some tend to bolt in adverse conditions. Beet leaf miner (*see above and p.323*) has little effect on beets, but it can spoil leaf beet and chard. Downy mildew can be a problem on young spinach when the air is moist.

The lettuce family

Vegetables in this family range from the compact annual lettuce to the towering stems of Jerusalem artichokes, which can grow to 8 ft (2.5 m) tall. Depending on the crop, the leaves, shoots, flower buds, roots, or stem tubers may be eaten.

Lettuce is perhaps the most widely grown member of this family, eaten, along with chicory and endive, as a salad. All three can be very decorative, with leaves in diverse shapes and colors. Some cultivars produce a hearted lettuce; individual leaves can be picked from the "loose leaf" types over several weeks. Chicory and endive are often blanched to reduce their bitterness. Using a selection of cultivars, and winter protection under glass, these crops can provide leafy salads all year. They also do well in an unheated greenhouse, and are useful for intercropping and for growing in containers.

Jerusalem artichokes are simple to grow, producing starchy, edible stem tubers and tall, leafy stems. Some cultivars produce a rather

FAMILY MEMBERS

The lettuce family is correctly called the Asteraceae; it includes asters, dandelions, and ornamental sunflowers, closely related to Jerusalem artichokes.

- Chicory (*Cichorium intybus*)
- Endive (*Cichorium endivia*)
- Lettuce (*Lactuca sativa*) (*near right*)
- Cardoon (*Cynara cardunculus*)
- Globe artichoke (*Cynara scolymus*)
- Jerusalem artichoke (*Helianthus tuberosus*) (*center*)
- Salsify (*Tragopogon porrifolius*) (*in flower, far right*)
- Scorzonera (*Scorzonera hispanica*)

unexpected "sunflower," with the characteristic flower form of this family: many ray florets surrounding a central boss. The stems of cardoons are blanched in fall; the large, immature flower buds of the stately globe artichoke are eaten in early summer. Salsify and scorzonera are little-grown root crops, the former white-skinned, the latter black. They are harvested in fall and winter. The following spring, the shoots can be blanched for eating, or left to produce edible flower buds.

Soils and situations

All prefer well-drained soil. Leafy crops can be fitted into a rotation or put among ornamentals; cardoons and globe artichokes, which need space, look good in an ornamental border. The roots can join other root crops in a crop rotation, while Jerusalem artichokes make a good windbreak. Lettuce and endive do well in containers.

Protect the crop

Lettuce is the most pest- and disease-prone member of the Asteraceae. Common pests include slugs, cutworm, leaf aphids, and root aphids. Under cover, downy mildew and gray mold (botrytis) can be a problem, especially in cool, damp conditions. Cultivars with resistance to aphids, downy mildew, and various physiological disorders are available. For more advice and information, see the A–Z of Plant Problems (*pp.320–341*).

Lettuce alone Young lettuce plants are very tempting to slugs. When they are small, plants can be protected with cut-down plastic beverage bottles, pushed into the soil. When they outgrow these, a ring of poultry grit or crushed eggshells (*as above*) can protect in the short term against slugs, but baited traps are also helpful (*see also pp.100–103*).

The potato family

This family is characterized by producing substances that have dramatic effects on humans and animals: the toxins in deadly nightshade, mandrake, and datura; the nicotine in tobacco plants; and the burning capsaicin in chili peppers. But it also contains cool, juicy sweet tomatoes and bell peppers; eggplants, with their rich, creamy flesh; and the ultimate in comfort food—the potato.

Soil and rotation

All of these crops need sun and do best in fertile soil, rich in organic matter, where manure or rich compost has been applied. They follow on well from a winter rye green manure.

Potatoes, despite being frost-tender, crop well in cool climates. Other members of this family—tomatoes, eggplants, and peppers— need warmer conditions and good light levels for reliable cropping. They are popular crops for a cool greenhouse (*see* Fruiting crops under glass, *pp.226–227*), but tomatoes especially may also be sown under cover then planted outside, in the soil or in pots, when conditions are right.

Potatoes aplenty

Potatoes need quite a lot of space but are easy to grow, giving you a far wider choice of cultivars than is ever seen in supermarkets.

FAMILY MEMBERS

The members of this family—botanically named the Solanaceae, after the nightshade plant—are all valued for their fruits, with the exception of the potato, where it is the tubers that are eaten. Potatoes do bear small, green tomato-like fruits, but these are poisonous, and should never be eaten. The family includes:

- Potato (*Solanum tuberosum*)
- Tomato (*Lycopersicon esculentum*)
- Pepper, sweet (*Capsicum annuum* Grossum Group)
- Pepper, chili (*Capsicum annuum* Longum Group)
- Pepper, hot (*Capsicum frutescens*)
- Eggplant (*Solanum melongena*)

They store well for winter eating. Potatoes are planted as tubers, never as seed. Always use certified disease-free tubers. In the case of some heirloom varieties, "micropropagated" plants may also be available, usually by mail order from specialty suppliers.

Seed potatoes are often allowed to sprout, or chit, before planting to get growth under way (*see p.263*). Spring planting is the norm; you can choose from groups of cultivars known as first earlies, second earlies, and maincrop in order to give a harvest that stretches over many weeks. It is the maincrop cultivars that are stored for eating over winter as "old" potatoes. However, a late summer planting of earlies can, with protection, give a fresh winter crop of new potatoes (*see p.225*).

Growing potatoes
As soon as the soil has warmed up in spring, potatoes are planted either into individual holes or into trenches 6 in (15 cm) deep; or they may be grown on the soil surface under a thick layer of mulch using the "no-dig" technique (*see p.216*). Because they are frost-tender, they need extra covering, with straw or with horticultural fleece, if a late frost is forecast. Thereafter, management consists mainly of ensuring that

(Above left) **Earthing up** As soon as potatoes are 6 in (15 cm) tall, draw soil up around their stems, leaving shoot tips visible. Repeat when the foliage meets between plants.

(Above right) **End of the season** As the stems of maincrop potatoes die down, it is wise, especially if you see any signs of disease on the foliage, to cut the stems back. The tubers can be left in the soil, but all must be lifted before the first frost.

plants have adequate water, and that the new tubers developing on the roots are never exposed to the light (the greening this causes makes them poisonous to eat). This can be achieved either by mulching, or by earthing up as the plants grow (*see above*). Once the plants are well-grown, their leaves shade the root zone.

Flowering (though not all cultivars flower) is an indication that the tubers are large enough to harvest; otherwise, scrape soil away from the roots to check. Maincrop potatoes can be left in the ground and used as required until the foliage dies back. Only store disease-free, undamaged tubers (*see also p.271*).

Tender fruiting crops
Homegrown tomatoes, left to ripen on the plant, surpass anything store-bought for flavor. Again, the diversity available to the gardener is staggering—from compact, manageable, bushy plants to indeterminate or cordon cultivars that

would grow yards tall up their supports if not stopped (*see facing page*); from tiny, cherry-sized fruit to those that make a meal in themselves, in red, yellow, orange, and green. Tomatoes can be grown in pots, baskets, and growing bags. More vigorous cultivars are easier to manage grown directly in the soil.

The taste of peppers can be sweet or hot-to-blistering, the latter as in hot or chili peppers. Sweet peppers can be cropped when green, or left to ripen to red, yellow, orange, or purple. Hot peppers usually produce smaller, longer, more pointed fruit.

Eggplant fruits are now typically a dark, shiny purple, but the originals were a very egglike white. Modern cultivars bearing no more than four or five fruits per plant make cropping more reliable. Both eggplants and peppers grow well in containers or in the soil, doing best under cover in cool climates.

Protect the crop

Using resistant cultivars is a good way to protect potatoes and greenhouse tomatoes in particular against a range of problems. Potato blight, a fungal disease also attacking tomatoes, can be a

Family resemblance Flowers of potato (*left, above*) and eggplant (*below*) clearly demonstrate that these two crops are related.

KEEPING GREENHOUSE CROPS HEALTHY

■ Keep the greenhouse very neat—store pots and other equipment elsewhere.

■ Keep the glass or plastic clean—it may need to be washed down several times a year.

■ Clear out and scrub down the structure at least once a year. Use hot, soapy water and finish off with a powerful jet-rinse from a hose.

■ Prune out dead and diseased parts of plants, and clean the pruners before moving to another plant.

■ Dispose of dead plants, or those badly infected with pests or disease, immediately.

■ Raise your own plants where possible to avoid the risk of bringing in pests and diseases.

■ Check purchased plants and their potting mix. Quarantine them in another area for a week or two before introducing them to the greenhouse.

■ Use crop rotation to prevent the buildup of soilborne pests and diseases.

■ Inspect plants daily for signs of pests or disease. Problems build up rapidly in a closed environment.

■ In summer, mist plants that are susceptible to red spider mite with a fine spray of water.

■ Use yellow sticky traps to monitor pests.

■ Use biological control agents (*see p.97*) to deal with regular pest problems. Remove sticky traps before introducing flying biological control agents.

(Right, top) **Training cordon tomatoes** To support the tall stems, tie them in as they grow to twine tied to the greenhouse roof or to tall canes.

(Right, center) **Restricting growth** Sideshoots growing from the main stem of cordon tomatoes must be pinched out when small, leaving the single main stem to grow tall.

(Right, bottom) **Stopping cordon tomatoes** In cooler climates, plants are usually "stopped" after 4 or 5 clusters of flowers, or trusses, form. Simply pinch off the growing tip of the plant. This stops fruit from developing late in the season that will not ripen, directing energy into the existing, ripening fruit.

major problem in a wet season. Little can be done to prevent it, although there are some resistant potato varieties. Early potato crops may avoid it, and clearing up all potential sources of infection can delay its start.

Under cover, good management and hygiene in the greenhouse is the key to raising healthy plants and ensuring good crops. Biological controls can be used to combat the glasshouse pests whitefly, red spider mite, and aphids.

See the A–Z of Plant Problems (*pp.320–341*) for more advice and information.

The carrot family

This is a diverse group of crops with a range of flavors. The family likeness appears when they flower—tiny individual flowers are produced in creamy white, umbrella-shaped flowerheads, known as umbels, very like those of their relations cow parsley and bronze fennel. They are very attractive to beneficial insects.

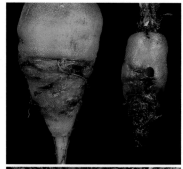

Carrots and parsnips are traditional root crops; Hamburg (turnip-rooted) parsley is less well known. Celery and celeriac leaves and stems have the same distinctive flavor, as does the knobby swollen stem base of celeriac, which is eaten more like a root crop. Florence fennel "bulbs" (in fact stem bases) have a crisp texture when raw, and a mild aniseed flavor. The attractive feathery foliage can be used in place of the herb fennel. Best sown after midsummer, Florence fennel is the fastest of these crops to grow. Most others need a long growing season. Parsley, an herb, is often grown along with these vegetables.

Growing the crop

Carrots and parsnips are direct-sown hardy crops that may be left in the ground for use over winter, or harvested for storage. Early carrots, quicker to crop, are eaten fresh. Both crops prefer

Plant problems Tunneled roots (top) are the work of the carrot rust fly, while forked roots (center) occur when carrots are grown in stony soil. Discolored foliage (bottom, on parsley), is another sign of root damage by carrot rust fly, which is attracted to all family members.

FAMILY MEMBERS

- Carrot (*Daucus carota*)
- Celeriac (*Apium graveolens* var. *rapaceum*)
- Celery (*Apium graveolens*)
- Florence fennel (*Foeniculum vulgare* var. *dulce*)
- Hamburg parsley (*Petroselinum crispum* var. *tuberosum*)
- Parsley (*Petroselinum crispum*)
- Parsnip (*Pastinaca sativa*)

(From left) **Carrot in flower; parsnip; parsley; Florence fennel**

New carrots Carrot seed is extremely fine and hard to sow thinly; to keep thinning to a minimum, as it attracts carrot fly, leave enough carrots growing to harvest a small, early crop of small roots, leaving room for the remainder to expand.

light soil that has been fed for a previous crop, such as brassicas. In stony or heavy soil, consider growing early carrots in a container (*see p.222*). Root crops may fork in stony soil.

Celery and celeriac will bolt if growth is checked. They are best planted out as young plants when the soil has warmed up. The soil should be rich in organic matter, so it never dries out, and dressed with a medium- to high-fertility soil improver.

Although the members of this family have differing soil requirements, they are kept together in a traditional rotation as they are prone to the same problems.

Protect the crop

Larvae of the carrot rust fly will feed on the roots of all members of this family, but it is only a major pest of carrots. Barriers and crop covers (*see pp.100–103*) are the most effective way to prevent damage, although some people swear by alternating rows of onions and carrots, to confuse the pests. Parsnip canker, a disease of parsnips only, is exacerbated by carrot rust fly damage. Good drainage and close spacing can prevent it. See the A–Z of Plant Problems (*pp.320–341*) for more information and advice.

Sowing vegetables

The simplest way to grow the vast majority of vegetables is from seed sown outdoors where the plants are to crop. Although you can raise young plants under cover (*see p.260*) for a head start, sowing directly into the soil is quick, easy and effective, and there are various techniques you can use to make best use of space.

Preparing the ground Seeds germinate most successfully when sown into fine-textured, crumbly soil—what gardeners call a "fine tilth"—which is prepared by gentle raking.

TIPS FOR SUCCESS

■ Different vegetables need different soil temperatures to succeed. Check the advice on timing before you sow.

■ Seed sown too early is more prone to pest and disease attack.

■ Use fresh seed, or seed that has been stored in a cool, dry place.

■ Raise tender plants, such as string beans, tomatoes and sweet corn, indoors or under cover (*see pp.198–199*) to give them a head start, then transplant to their growing positions when outdoor conditions are right.

Choosing seeds

Organic seed is produced to recognized organic standards, without the use of artificial fertilizers or pesticides. "Conventional" seed is produced using artificial fertilizers and pesticides, and its use is acceptable when organic alternatives are unavailable. Where possible, use good-quality organically grown seeds from a reliable source, or save your own. If organic seed is not available, check on the seed packet to make sure that the seed you use has not been treated with pesticide dressings after harvest. Heirloom varieties (*see pp.208–209*) are available from seed exchanges, and increasingly, specialty seed merchants now offer a selection of traditional or "old-fashioned" cultivars. Cultivars developed using genetic modification (GM) techniques (*see p.207*) are not appropriate in an organic garden.

Always keep seed in a cool, dry place. The packet, or the supplier, should give you advice on how long it can be kept.

Seed formats

Most vegetable seeds are sold dry and loose inside a foil or paper packet. Various treatments and formats can make sowing easier and enhance performance.

■ **Coated/pelleted seed** Each seed is coated in clay to make handling and station-sowing easier. Check that no pesticide is present in the coating.

■ **Chitted (pregerminated) seed** Seeds (usually of cucumbers) are shipped with their seedling root already growing.

■ **Primed seed** Seeds are germinated under ideal conditions then "dried back" before being dispatched for immediate sowing or storing at 40°F (5°C). Emergence is rapid, even, and unaffected by fluctuating soil temperatures. Carrots, celery, leeks, parsley, and parsnips are among crops available as primed seed.

■ **Seed tapes** Seeds are embedded in a biodegradable paper tape that is laid in a drill (*see facing page*). Thinning is unnecessary.

Sowing techniques

Most seeds do not need to be buried deeply: a fraction of an inch is quite sufficient. Larger seeds can go in at a depth of twice their diameter. Sow peas at a depth of 1–1½ in (2.5–4 cm) and beans 1½–2 in (4–5 cm). Seed can be sown in rows, in individual positions or "stations," or broadcast over a larger area.

■ **Sowing in drills** Seed is sown in a shallow trench or "drill," created with the corner of a hoe, or a stick. It may be sprinkled along the row, for later thinning, or placed at the final spacing required. Water the bottom of the drill before sowing; rake back the soil to cover the seeds, and firm in gently.

■ **Station sowing** Seed is sown in individual "stations" at the final spacing required. Two or three seeds can be sown at each station if necessary, then thinned to one seedling. Station-sow along a drill, or into individual small holes. Station sowing can cut down on the amount of seed you use, especially for widely spaced plants.

■ **Broadcast sowing** Seed is scattered over the soil and gently raked in. Useful for sowing grass, green manures, and other small to medium-sized seed that has to be evenly distributed over an area. As it is difficult to cover every seed, some protection against birds may be needed. Fleece is particularly effective as it also speeds germination by warming the soil. Water after sowing if rain is not forecast.

Thinning

Unless seeds are sown very thinly or are station-sown or multi-sown (see p.258), some of the seedlings will need to be removed to allow others enough space to develop. Thin in stages, leaving each seedling just clear of the next until the recommended spacing is reached. Water before and after thinning, disturbing the soil as little as possible.

Spacing

Using spacing techniques, combined with suitable cultivars and, where possible, a system of narrow beds (see pp.212–215), will help make the best use of any growing space. Where there is no need to walk between rows, vegetables can be grown using closer-than-traditional spacings. The practice of growing vegetables in long rows, with the soil between them hoed regularly, grew out of changes to agricultural practice during the 18th century. This system still has its merits for field-growing, but in a garden context, better results can often be achieved by block planting, spread out evenly across the bed or growing area, using equidistant or square spacing.

■ **Equidistant spacing** Plants are grown in staggered rows and each plant is an equal distance apart from all the others. The between-plant spacing is an average of the recommended in-row and between-row spacings. For example, plants normally grown 6 in (15 cm) apart in rows 12 in (30 cm) apart, can be grown at 9 in (23 cm) apart each way. Plants receive equal amounts of light, moisture, and nutrients and soon form a canopy over the soil, which helps reduce weeds.

■ **Square spacing** Plants are grown at the same spacing in the row as between the rows, resulting in a square pattern. This is useful where only two or three plants can be fitted

Sowing a row of seeds
1. After raking the soil to a fine tilth, use a line and pegs to create a guide along which to sow. Using a hoe, or even the handle end of a rake, draw out a shallow V-shaped trench or "drill" along this line. Water along the bottom of the drill before sowing. **2.** The seeds being sown here are of beets, and are "multigerm" seeds: each one is in fact several seeds clustered together. They can thus be "station-sown" at regular intervals along the drill. Finer seed is best poured first into your hand, then sprinkled thinly and evenly along the drill. **3.** With the back of a rake, gently cover the seeds with soil; most need only the lightest covering. **4.** Once the seedlings emerge, thin them to the desired spacing, or to that recommended on the seed packet.

across a bed. A planting grid can easily be made by pressing the edge of a plank or other straight edge into the soil to mark out evenly spaced lines at right angles to each other. Sow or plant where the lines cross.

The effect of plant density

The spacing of vegetables such as onions and cabbages affects their final size; the more space you allow them, the larger (up to a point) they will grow. By reversing this and growing them more densely, with less growing space, you will get vegetables of a smaller, often more convenient size. In most cases, overall yield is also increased. There is a lower limit below which closer spacing becomes counter-productive, because plants are simply too close together to be able to develop to a harvestable size. Equidistant spacing (*see p.256*) is generally the most effective way to influence plant size and can be varied to suit different vegetables.

Bulb onions illustrate the influence of spacing on size. For large bulbs, an equidistant spacing of 8 x 8 in (20 x 20 cm) is ideal. By reducing this to 6 in (15 cm) between plants each way, smaller, medium-sized onions are produced. At an equidistant spacing of 2 ft (60 cm), summer cabbage will produce the largest heads possible, but if the spacing is reduced to 1 ft (30 cm) there will be a higher total yield of smaller heads, which are generally more convenient for use in the kitchen.

Multi-sowing

Multi-sowing simply means sowing several seeds in the same place, spacing them at around twice the normal spacing, and allowing all to grow to fruition. You can multi-sow under cover in multicelled module trays, sowing several seeds in each cell, letting them all grow, and planting them out, when ready, as a complete cell unit. Either way, the result is a cluster of smaller roots or bulbs, instead of one large one. Crops suitable for multi-sowing include beets, leeks, and bulb onions (4–5 seeds sown per station), round cultivars of carrot (4 seeds per station) and salad or green onions and chives (10 seeds per station).

Intercropping and undercropping

Intercropping is the sowing (or planting) of fast-growing or small vegetables, in rows or patches, on unused ground between slower-growing main crops.

Many combinations of crop and intercrop can be used, but the guiding rule must always be that the intercrop should not be allowed to thrive at the expense of the main crop and must be harvested before the slower crop needs the space. The space between winter brassicas can be usefully filled with a wide range of crops. Green onions, small lettuces, spinach, bok choy, radishes, arugula, and many other summer and winter salad crops are particularly good intercrops.

Tall plants like sweet corn, which initially cast little shade, can be undercropped with lower-growing plants like dwarf string beans, lettuce, or mizuna, or spreading vegetables such as zucchini and pumpkins, to make maximum use of space. Shade-tolerant vegetables like lettuce and spinach can be sown between rows of climbing beans.

Catch cropping and double cropping

Catch crops are fast-maturing vegetables sown on spare ground between the clearance of one main crop and the planting of another. Leaf lettuce, radishes, arugula, seedling cutting crops, and fast-growing green manures are good examples. With double cropping, seeds of fast-maturing crops are sown between slower-growing station-sown crops such as parsnips, and harvested before the latter need the space.

Successional sowing

By sowing fast-maturing vegetables like lettuce and radishes little and often, at 2–3 week intervals, you can avoid gluts and have a continuous supply over many months. Other suitable crops include corn salad, arugula, and other salad leaves; calabrese, kohlrabi, spinach, string beans, green onions, and turnips.

(Below, from left) **Sowing and spacing techniques** Close-planted lettuces, thinned so that plants are staggered in their rows; multi-sown onions; leeks interplanted with lettuces; radishes sown between parsnips, being harvested just as the emerging parsnips are ready to benefit from the light and space.

Planting vegetables

Many vegetables benefit from being started from seed, under cover, then transplanted into their final growing positions as young plants. Leeks and brassicas may be raised in an outdoor seedbed. Some, such as asparagus and sweet potatoes, are more convenient bought as young plants; onions and shallots are much easier to plant as "sets" rather than seed. And some crops—such as potatoes, planted as tubers, and garlic—are never raised from seed.

Raising your own plants

Vegetable seed packets will tell you whether getting a head start by sowing the seeds under cover is an option for that crop. There are several reasons for doing this. Some plants need a long growing season—for example, tomatoes and eggplants—and to ripen fully by the end of the year, they may need to be started off inside before it becomes warm enough outside for them to be planted out. Where outdoor space is at a premium, seedlings can be grown on in pots until ground is freed up. Or you may simply find you achieve better germination from the seed, and grow stronger and healthier plants, by starting them off in controlled conditions with a little extra warmth. You can raise seedlings in a greenhouse or a cold frame, in a heated propagator or indoors on a windowsill, depending on the temperature the seeds need. They may be sown in pots, trays or, for individual "plug plants," in module or cell trays (*see pp.198–199*).

(Right) **Planting out zucchini**
1. These young mail-order "plug plants" are protected by a rigid plastic case. In this situation they must be planted as soon as possible, or they will start to deteriorate. **2.** Make individual holes in well-prepared soil and plant them with the top of the rootball just below the soil surface. Firm the soil, and water the young plants. **3.** A light mulch applied around each plant will keep the soil moist and warm, encouraging the roots to establish. In cooler areas it is best not to mulch until the plants have started growing strongly. Individual cloches or cut-down plastic bottles can be used to protect the plants against the cold and wind. **4.** Water the young plants regularly until well established.

(Left) **Saving space** Leeks and many brassicas spend a long time taking up space in the vegetable plot. Most are happy to be transplanted, so it makes sense to start these plants off elsewhere, so that you can be using that space for something else as they grow. Brassica and leek plants are easy to raise yourself, sown into a "nursery" bed, then dug up and planted out when large enough. You can also raise them in pots or trays, or buy plants. Note that some brassicas—Chinese cabbage and other Asian greens, calabrese, turnips, radishes, and rutabagas—are not suitable for growing in a nursery bed, as they will not crop well if their roots are disturbed.

Buying in young plants

If you don't have the space, time, or conditions to grow your own young vegetable plants, you can buy them from nurseries and by mail order, although you may find you have a more limited choice of cultivars. Buy organically grown plants wherever possible. Do not be tempted to buy young plants of half-hardy vegetables such as tomatoes, sweet corn, zucchini, string beans, and runner beans before weather conditions have become suitable for planting out—that is, once all danger of frost has passed and the soil has warmed up.

Seed potatoes and onion sets

Potatoes are always grown from tubers. Always buy certified seed potatoes from a reliable source. They usually grow better if chitted before planting (*see panel, opposite*). Bulb onions and shallots can be grown from seed, but most gardeners find it less fiddly to grow them from small "bulblets" known as sets, planted in fall or in early spring. They need to be pushed into the soil with the tips of the sets just showing. Garlic is always grown from cloves, separated from heads that are sold specifically for planting and put in the ground in late fall.

Perennial vegetables

Perennial vegetables such as globe artichokes and rhubarb crop much more quickly if grown from divisions or "offsets" taken from a mature plant (*see also* Herbaceous Plants, *p.193*) rather than seed. Asparagus should not be harvested until plants are in their third year, so one-year-old plants, known as crowns, are usually planted (*see above, far right*). Jerusalem artichokes are grown from tubers, like potatoes, and seakale from sections of fleshy root known as "thongs."

(Above, from far left) **Planting techniques** Plant leeks in 6-in-(15-cm-) deep holes and water into the holes rather than filling them with soil. Tomatoes will have more space for their roots and are easier to water if planted into bottomless pots called "ring pots," fitted into holes in a growing bag and filled with potting mix. Plant sweet corn in blocks, not a single row, for better pollination by the wind. Asparagus plants have a spidery root system, best spread out over a slight mound at the bottom of a trench.

CHITTING POTATOES

Seed potatoes usually appear in nurseries, or are shipped by mail-order suppliers, in late winter to early spring, in order that they may be "chitted" for a few weeks before planting out. Lay out the tubers in shallow trays—egg cartons (*near right*) are ideal. Place the end with the most "eyes" (dormant buds) uppermost. Put them in a light, warm place until they sprout. Once frost has become rare and the soil has warmed up, plant them out (*far right*) with the sprouted end uppermost.

Caring for vegetables

Once established, many crops need little maintenance. Check them over regularly though, and provide any extra care they need to ensure healthy growth. Frequent inspections become increasingly pleasurable as the crop approaches maturity.

Watering
Stress caused by lack of water can cause bolting, make plants more susceptible to pest and disease attack, and reduce yields. Seedlings and transplants should never dry out. Once established, watering thoroughly but infrequently is more effective than little and often. Water that soaks down into the soil encourages deep rooting and helps plants draw on reserves during dry spells.

Feeding
If the soil has been prepared appropriately in advance, most crops should not need extra feeding. Long-term crops may benefit from mulching with a medium- or high-fertility soil improver.

Mulching and weed control
Mulching bare soil reduces water loss through evaporation and prevents germination of weed seeds. If a high- to medium-fertility soil improver is used, this also adds plant nutrients. Apply mulches to warm, moist soil in spring and summer.

Weeds compete with vegetables for food, light, and moisture, so keep beds as weed-free as possible. Sow your seeds in drills or stations so you can distinguish them from annual weeds. Vigorous crops may need only a single weeding before they outgrow competition. See also Using mulches to control weeds (*pp.72–75*).

Minimizing plant problems
Healthy, well-grown plants are more resistant to pest and disease attack. Pest- and disease-resistant cultivars should be used where problems are known to exist. Pests attack vegetables above and below soil. They range from large animal pests such as rabbits, which cause general damage, to microscopic nematodes that

(Clockwise from top left) **Preparation and aftercare**
Bulky soil improvers spread over vegetable beds to condition and feed the soil; applying water correctly at the roots of plants, rather than pouring it over the leaves; the need for hoeing is reduced in these close-planted beds; shallots growing through a mulch membrane for moisture retention and weed control.

WATERING TIPS

■ Some crops benefit from water at particular stages of growth (*see p.63*); concentrate watering at these times.

■ Do not overwater; excessive, unnecessary watering can reduce the flavor of crops such as tomatoes, and wet soil can encourage fungal rots.

■ Apply water at the base of plants in the cool of the evening, when less will evaporate (or if slugs are a problem, early in the morning).

■ Use a can with a fine spray for small seedlings, or a watering lance attached to a garden hose.

■ Crops needing lots of water, such as runner beans, can have pails of water poured around their roots.

■ Consider laying drip or soaker hoses to use water more efficiently.

■ For more tips on water use, *see* Water and Watering, *pp.56–67*.

attack specific crops such as potatoes. Knowledge of pest life cycles aids control, as can timing of sowings to avoid pest-prone periods of the season. Pest control can range from hand-picking slugs and snails to using natural biological controls (*see p.97*). Physical barriers can prevent some pests from laying their eggs near crops. See Organic pest control (*pp.100–103*) for more advice on traps, barriers, and deterrents.

Do everything you can to prevent disease, as it can spread rapidly. Virus diseases are very difficult to control and affected plants should be removed and composted as soon as you notice them. The risk of infection by some fungal diseases can be reduced by raising the pH of the soil with lime (*see p.55*). Crop rotation (*see pp.230–233*) also plays an important role in reducing the severity of other soilborne diseases and some pests.

Certain problems with vegetables are caused by bad cultural practice or mineral deficiencies in the soil. Bolting happens when plants go to seed prematurely and is caused by drying out, sudden fluctuations in temperature, or sowing at the wrong time. Poor fruit or pod set can be caused by lack of pollination, drought, or erratic watering. Planting flowers around vegetables that attract pollinating insects can help improve pollination in some crops, as well as brightening up the vegetable plot (*see also pp.94–95*).

Many specific problems affecting vegetable crops are covered in more detail in the A–Z of Plant Problems (*pp.320–341*).

Plant protection

Half-hardy vegetables planted outside in spring are vulnerable to cold and frost. Very hard late frosts may damage any small seedlings. Plants can be protected individually with cloches or cut-off plastic soda bottles, or covered with horticultural fleece. Sheets of fleece stapled along two edges to wooden battens make convenient covers for vegetable beds that can easily be taken on and off, and rolled up neatly for storage. Protection can also be given to vegetables such as outdoor tomatoes in early fall to help ripen late fruits.

Training and support

Erect supports for peas, climbing beans, and cordon tomatoes before you sow or plant. For climbing beans, make tepees of canes, or double rows of canes tied together at the top, with one plant at the base of each cane. The beans may need to be guided to their supports and tied in, but will then start to spiral up the canes unaided. Peas have tendrils that will cling to twiggy sticks or wide-mesh pea netting.

Tall nonclimbing vegetables, such as taller varieties of Brussels sprouts, sprouting broccoli, and fava beans, may need the support of sturdy stakes—sprouts especially so if they are planted in an exposed, windy spot.

Perennial vegetables

Vegetables that stay in the ground year after year should be cared for just as you would ornamental perennials (see pp.190–193), although to keep them growing well, they benefit from being mulched with a medium-fertility soil improver (see pp.34–35) such as garden compost or hay every year. A layer of straw over the crowns of globe artichokes and rhubarb plants in winter will protect them from frost. Most perennial vegetables benefit from division and replanting every few years, although an asparagus bed is best left undisturbed and, once established, should crop well for anything up to 20 years.

Dividing globe artichokes These large perennials will be reinvigorated by division every three or four years.

(Below, from left) **Plant supports** Broad beans staked with thick garden prunings; squashes scrambling over a support of canes bound together with twine; short, twiggy sticks pushed in the soil for peas; cordon tomatoes need the sturdy support of a thick cane or stake; earthing up the base of sprout stems to reduce wind rock; a young broccoli plant staked with a length of batten.

Harvesting and storing

Some vegetables—peas and sweet corn in particular, but also young and leafy crops—taste best when eaten as soon as possible after picking. However, most keep well for a few days in a cool garage or in the refrigerator. Potatoes, onions, carrots, and other root crops can be stored to feed you over the winter months.

When to harvest

Harvesting requirements vary widely. Leeks and potatoes, and some cultivars of other vegetables, will stay in good condition in the ground for weeks. Others, such as early cabbage and calabrese, need to be picked almost as soon as they are ready. Peas, runner beans, and string beans will stop producing more pods if not picked regularly. Get to know your crops so you can get the very best from them. Whatever you are harvesting, try to eat it as soon as possible. Fresh produce has the best flavor and the highest nutritional value. Sweet corn must be the most extreme example of this, tasting best if cooked within 15 minutes of picking. On the other hand, vegetables such as squashes and onions can be kept in good condition for months (*see overleaf*).

Harvesting crops to store

Best results will be obtained from maincrop cultivars that mature toward the end of the season and are harvested in cool conditions.

■ **Harvest vegetables just as they reach maturity**
Picking too early means they will not have developed their full flavor; leave it too late and they become fibrous and woody.

Sprouts on demand Hardy Brussels sprouts can stay in the ground all winter in mild areas. Pick as needed, working upward from the bottom of the stem.

Clean cuts A small, sharp garden knife is the ideal tool for making clean cuts when harvesting (*from left*) zucchini, globe artichokes, and cabbage.

"CUT-AND-COME-AGAIN" VEGETABLES

"Cut-and-come-again" is an expression you may see used in seed catalogs to describe those lettuce plants where, instead of having to cut the whole head, you simply pick a few leaves as required for salads, leaving the plant to grow more. This continuous supply is also a useful feature of many leafy vegetables, such as spinach, chard, and Asian greens. But there are other vegetables that, once the main crop is taken, can be left in the ground to produce a smaller secondary crop. Calabrese, once the main head is cut, will go on to produce several smaller, usually looser florets, ideal for dishes such as stir-fries (*above, left and right*). And if, after cutting the "bulb" (swollen stem base) of Florence fennel, you leave the stump and root in the ground, it will sprout pretty, feathery young shoots ideal for flavoring and garnishes (*below, left and right*).

■ **Only store top-quality produce**
Anything that is blemished or has pest and disease damage will only deteriorate, and may also spread rots to other, sound fruits and vegetables.

■ **Handle with care** Even quite sturdy crops, such as potatoes, are easily bruised. The damage may not be apparent at first, but it may allow rot to set in once in storage.

Certain vegetables can be stored through the winter, to eat fresh when produce from the garden is scarce. Some very hardy crops, such as parsnips and Jerusalem artichokes, can even be left in the ground over winter if your climate allows, but there are disadvantages to this. It increases the likelihood of pest damage, and any disease present will have an opportunity to spread. In addition, the soil may freeze solid, making harvesting difficult.

Many vegetables can be stored successfully without any special equipment as long as you are able to provide the right conditions. Once your vegetables are in store, they need to be inspected regularly. Adjust conditions if

DRYING VEGETABLES FOR STORAGE

▨ Onions, shallots, and garlic

Harvest garlic when the first 4–6 leaves turn yellow. Leave onions and shallots until all the leaves have fallen over naturally. Lift carefully, and leave in a warm, dry place for a couple of weeks. In dry weather, do this outdoors, lifted off the ground on racks or pallets. Otherwise, bring them under cover to finish drying. Bulbs are ready to store when the skins are papery and rustle when handled. Braid into ropes or hang in net sacks in a place where air circulates freely. Ideal storage temperature is 36–39°F (2–4°C).

▨ Potatoes

Lift and leave exposed to dry for a few hours. Store in thick paper sacks, tied or folded loosely at the neck. Potatoes must be stored in the dark to prevent them from turning green and developing high levels of solanine, a toxic alkaloid. Frost protection is essential. Ideal storage temperature is 41–50°F (5–10°C).

▨ Pumpkins and winter squash

These need a few weeks of sunny weather at the end of the season to develop a tough skin for optimum storage. Harvest before the first frost. Cut with a long stalk, leaving part of the vine attached. As this dries, it hardens and protects the stem, which is otherwise vulnerable to rotting. Store in a dry, airy place, if possible on slatted shelves or in nets for good air circulation. Can last 6–9 months if well-ripened at harvest. Ideal temperature 50–59°F (10–15°C); storage at higher temperatures causes the flesh to become fibrous.

▨ Beans

Choose varieties recommended for producing dry beans, such as these borlotti beans. Leave the pods on the vine until dry and crisp; you may be able to hear the beans rattle inside. Harvest on a dry, bright day; if that is not possible, spread the picked pods out somewhere warm, dry, and airy to dry out thoroughly. Shell the beans and store in an airtight container. Discard any beans that show signs of disease or of having been nibbled or tunneled by small pests.

necessary, and remove anything that shows signs of decay to stop it from spreading.

Where to store vegetables

Ideal storage conditions for vegetables vary according to type. In general, the best place is somewhere cool and dry, with an even temperature, free from mice and other pests. A basement or cellar is ideal, but an unheated shed or garage, or an unheated room in the house is also suitable. Lift storage containers off the floor on boxes or pallets; use old blankets, sacks, or rugs for extra insulation if required.

Storage requirements

Details of preparation and storage conditions for crops that last well through the winter are given here (*see panel, left*). Some other crops can also be stored for shorter periods: for example, carrots, parsnips, beets, rutabagas, and celeriac keep well if packed in moist sand or fine leaf mold in shallow trays or boxes.

Kept in the dark Just as potatoes are earthed up while growing (*see p.249*)—or grown under mulches—to prevent the tubers from being exposed to the light, so they must be protected in storage. Clear plastic bags are the worst form of storage. Always close the sack once you have taken what you need.

11. Growing Herbs

Walk into any herb garden for a sensory experience—the plants it contains will have been selected for their aromatic foliage and flowers. Valued for their many uses, herbs are also attractive plants, and many insects will visit their flowers. Herbs have rich associations with human history. Here are plants that have, over many centuries, helped people sleep, soothed pain, repelled insects, calmed fussy babies, and flavored foods and intoxicating drinks. Herbs are still worth growing today for their useful qualities, as well as for their beauty.

Familiar friends Perhaps because of their long association with humankind, we associate herbs with the "traditional" country garden style—but they can be used strikingly in more modern designs.

Why grow herbs?

Known for their fragrance, flavor, and healing properties, herbs are easy to cultivate organically. Whether edging a vegetable bed, arranged in their own herb garden, or grown in pots or among ornamentals, they enhance any garden.

What is an herb?

Annuals, biennials, perennials, bulbs, shrubs, climbers, and trees can all have herbal value. In many cases, it is the leafy part of the plant that is used as an herb, but different parts, such as roots, fruits, seeds, and flowers, even the bark of some trees, are utilized according to the species.

The broadest definition of an herb is simply that it is a plant that people use or have used for a specific purpose. Nowadays herbs are most commonly known for their culinary, medicinal, aromatic, and decorative qualities. In earlier times, people relied

An herb "wheel" Plant a selection of herbs that reflects your own taste. Choose plants for their fragrance, foliage, culinary use, or simply for their beauty alongside garden ornamentals.

on herbs for an even greater number of uses: some were used in dyeing and cleaning fabrics; others had a role in ritual and ceremony; and many were used in everyday life as flavorings for food and drink, to promote good health, and to cure illness.

Herbs and safety

The majority of herbs are safe to handle and consume, but not all of them. Some herbs can be toxic to humans and animals even in small doses, so they need to be treated with respect. Never use anything that you are not sure is completely safe, and consult a medical herbalist first if you want to use herbs for their medicinal properties.

Growing herbs organically

Herbs are easy plants to grow, beautiful to look at and, in many cases, free from pest and disease problems. Growing them yourself means that you can have fresh supplies available when you need them, and using organic methods means you can be sure they have not been treated with pesticides.

Growing herbs of any kind will increase the diversity of a garden—one of the key principles behind a successful organic system. With such a huge range of herbs to choose from, there is almost certainly one for every situation. Herbs can be selected to climb, creep, tumble, form dense carpets, or be trained up walls. Some will be happy in boggy soil, others on top of walls, in between paving stones, under trees, and in meadows—success depends on matching the right plant to the available conditions. Herbs also vary in size, from the tiny, ground-hugging Corsican mint (*Mentha requienii*) to stately giants such as angelica or lovage, reaching 6 ft (2 m) high. Herbs can be grown for their appearance alone. Some plants have spectacular flowers, some are valued for their foliage, and they all have something to contribute to a garden.

Herbs for wildlife

Many herb plants attract wildlife: birds eat the seeds and berries, butterflies and bees enjoy the nectar and pollen offered by the flowers, while beneficial insects will lay their eggs near sources of aphids and other pests (see panel, right, for some suggestions). Dense plantings of ground-covering herbs such as thymes provide habitats for many beneficial creatures, including beetles, spiders, and even frogs and toads.

Out of the blue Borage flowers are characteristically blue, but more unusual white flowers can sometimes be found.

HERBS TO ATTRACT WILDLIFE

For bees

Borage, chives, lungwort (*Pulmonaria*), sage, thyme, teasel (*Dipsacus fullonum*), mint, marjoram, oregano, lavender

For butterflies and moths

Evening primrose (*Oenothera biennis*), catnip (*Nepeta*), hemp agrimony (*Eupatorium cannabinum*), valerian, lavender, coltsfoot (*Tussilago farfara*)

For birds

Poppy, rose, teasel, elder (*Sambucus*), hawthorn (*Crataegus*)

For hoverflies and other useful pest predators

English marigold (*Calendula officinalis*), fennel, yarrow (*Achillea millefolium*), dandelion, angelica, cilantro, feverfew (*Tanacetum parthenium*), tansy (*Tanacetum vulgare*)

Where to grow herbs

Herbs grow well in all sorts of situations, from a few culinary herbs planted in a windowbox to a rambling wild garden full of teasels, nettles, and brambles. Plant according to your personal taste, and how you intend to use the herbs: a few herbs can be scattered throughout a garden, but if you use lots of herbs in the kitchen, it is worth dedicating a separate area to them.

Creating an herb garden

Formal herb gardens are based on a system of paths and beds, often edged with low-growing hedges. To remain neat, this type of garden requires quite a lot of maintenance, with hedges trimmed two to three times a year and careful attention paid to weed control.

Thorough preparation of beds and paths at the outset is essential to prevent weed problems later on. Close, dense planting not only helps suppress weeds once beds are established, but also enhances the ornamental effect.

An informal herb patch is equally attractive, or herbs can be mixed in among other flowers, shrubs, and even vegetables. Put them in beds and borders, against walls and fences—in fact, anywhere you have space!

Shade-tolerant herbs

Herbs that enjoy dappled shade thrive on the edges of shrubs or by groups of small trees. Add a low-fertility soil improver on an annual basis in order to mimic the leaf litter layer that occurs naturally in woodland areas. Vigorous

HERBS FOR FORMAL EDGING

Boxwood (*Buxus*)
Hedge germander (*Teucrium* x *lucidrys*)
Wall germander (*Teucrium chamaedrys*)
Winter savory
Rosemary (choose *Rosmarinus officinalis* 'Miss Jessop's Upright')
Lavender (especially 'Munstead' and 'Hidcote')
Hyssop

Grand style This large, formal herb garden features geometric beds immaculately edged with boxwood. The bed in the foreground is filled with different types of mint.

ground-cover herbs can become rampant in favorable conditions, so cut them back regularly and remove runners to control their spread, or plant in containers. It is mainly the aromatic and medicinal herbs rather than the culinary types that enjoy shade; they include bugle (*Ajuga*), periwinkle (*Vinca*), sweet violet, woodruff (*Galium odoratum*), foxglove, lungwort (*Pulmonaria*), creeping Jenny (*Lysimachia nummularia*), and lily-of-the-valley.

Drought-tolerant herbs

Drought-tolerant herbs—many of which come from the Mediterranean—look stunning growing together in a sunny spot in well-drained soil. A naturally dry part of the yard is ideal. A gravel mulch around the plants will mimic the stony ground of their native habitat, helping to control weeds and keep the basal area of the plants dry. These herbs also grow well in containers, where you can provide ideal soil conditions for them; you can also move them around the yard to make best use of the sunniest spots.

(Above left) **Informal edging** Good choices for informal, cottage-garden style edging include alpine strawberry, chives, parsley (*pictured*), common thyme, and cotton lavender (santolina).

(Above right) **Drought-tolerant herbs** Rosemary and lavender (*pictured*) are perfect companions in a dry, sunny spot. Other drought-tolerant herbs include sage, thyme, curry plant, cotton lavender (santolina), and artemisia.

Herbs for damp soil

Herbs that like damp soil will grow well in a naturally boggy area, or you can create one by the edge of a pond. Try meadowsweet (*Filipendula*), water mint, valerian, and hemp agrimony (*Eupatorium cannabinum*). In dry summers you will need to keep the water levels in the pond or bog garden topped off. Note that some of these species can become invasive once they are established in the garden.

Herbs for a vegetable garden

Leafy herbs such as parsley, chervil, cilantro, summer savory, and dill all enjoy the slightly richer soil found in a vegetable garden. These types of herbs are best sown direct in the spring once the soil is warm enough.

Herbs for paved areas

Choose low-growing herbs that thrive in dry conditions for planting among paving stones. Fill the cracks with potting mix and sow the seed directly into position in spring. Keep watered, and avoid walking on the herbs until they become established.

Herbs in containers

Many herbs grow well in containers. Use any container with drainage holes and a minimum depth of about 12 in (30 cm). Put a layer of large stones or pot shards at the bottom of the container, then fill it with general-purpose organic potting mix. For drought-tolerant herbs such as rosemary (*see also p.277*), which prefer light soil, mix five parts potting mix with one part gravel or poultry grit to ensure adequate drainage. Tender herbs, such as basil and French tarragon, are often more successful if grown in pots.

Invasive herbs

Be careful where you site vigorous herbs such as horseradish and mint that will take over if left to their own devices. These species are excellent for growing in wild areas, where they will be controlled by equally vigorous neighbors. In other situations, they need to be restricted: bury a large plant pot, a pail with the bottom removed, or a permeable sack with extra drainage holes, and plant invasive herbs within it. Other herbs, such as borage and evening primrose, invade by self-seeding prolifically: if you would rather they didn't, remove flowerheads before seeds form, or hoe off the seedlings in spring.

(Facing page) **Pots of flavor** A strawberry pot planted with a selection of small culinary herb plants is a useful feature to site by the kitchen door.

(Below left) **Pretty in paving** Soften hard landscaping by planting low-growing herbs such as creeping thymes, creeping savory, and Corsican mint between paving slabs.

(Below right) **Space invaders** Rampant herbs include horseradish and Russian tarragon (*pictured*), plus feverfew, tansy, mint, comfrey, borage, evening primrose, coltsfoot, and creeping Jenny.

Culinary herbs

1 Basil
A frost-tender perennial usually grown as an annual in a sunny, sheltered spot or in a greenhouse. It prefers light, free-draining, fertile soil, and grows well in containers. Cultivars vary in leaf size, color, and flavor. Pinch out shoot tips for bushy growth; remove flowers to promote leaf production.

2 Bay
An evergreen shrub or small tree that can grow up to 10–20 ft (3–6 m), though it can be pruned to limit its size and makes a small bush grown in a pot. It can be frost-tender, especially when young; it needs a sheltered, sunny spot and light, free-draining soil.

3 Sage
Evergreen shrubs, up to 36 in (90 cm) tall. There are many types, some with purple or variegated leaves. The flowers attract bees. Sages prefer sun and poor, light, free-draining soil.

4 French tarragon
Herbaceous perennial with a much finer flavor than Russian tarragon, which can be invasive. It needs sun and light, free-draining, low-fertility soil. It cannot tolerate waterlogging. Remove flower spikes to encourage leaf growth. French tarragon cannot be grown from seed.

5 Cilantro
A tall, pretty flowering annual grown for leaves and seeds (called coriander). Special selections for leaf production are available. Needs a sunny spot, in light but fertile soil. Sow direct from spring to fall for a continuous supply of leaves. Goes to seed quickly in hot weather.

6 Lavender
Evergreen, mostly hardy shrubs, 24–40 in (60–100 cm) tall. The flowers are very popular with butterflies and bees. Many forms, including more tender prostrate, dwarf, and pink- and white-flowered varieties, are available. Needs a sunny, sheltered spot with light, free-draining soil. Trim in spring. Remove flower spikes after flowering. Plants may need to be replaced every 3–5 years.

7 Rosemary

Evergreen shrubs, mostly 4–5 ft (1–1.5 m) tall, though there are dwarf and prostrate cultivars. They bear masses of lovely blue, white, or pink flowers in early summer. Give them a sheltered, sunny spot, in free-draining, low-fertility soil; they cannot tolerate waterlogging. Prune in spring; dwarf types can be clipped for hedging. Tender cultivars need winter protection.

8 Parsley

A biennial grown as an annual for leaves with the best flavor. Quite hardy, but needs winter protection in cold regions. There are both curly and flat-leaved varieties. Parsley enjoys partial shade and moist, fertile soil and is good in containers. Sow in spring and summer for summer harvest, and in late summer for a winter crop grown under cover.

9 Fennel

A statuesque, feathery herbaceous perennial, to 6 ft (2 m) tall. Leaves, stems, and seeds are all used. The flowers attract many beneficial insects. The cultivar 'Purpureum' has bronze foliage. Fennel prefers a sunny position and free-draining, fertile soil.

10 Mint

Hardy, spreading perennials, varying in height from ground-hugging to 40 in (1 m) tall. Many types available, including ginger mint, spearmint, and peppermint. Plant in containers to limit spread. Grow in sun or light shade, and moist but not waterlogged soil.

11 Thyme

Low-growing evergreen shrubs; creeping thymes make good ground cover. Many types, including lemon-scented, golden-leaved, and variegated. Choose a dry, sunny spot with poor, free-draining soil. Grows well in gravel, pavement cracks, and rock gardens. Trim after flowering.

12 Chives

A hardy perennial, with purple drumstick flowers attractive to bees. Both leaves and flowers can be used. Prefers sun and moist, fertile soil, but tolerates shade and most soils. Cut back to 2 in (5 cm) after flowering to promote fresh growth. Divide established clumps in spring or fall.

Caring for herb plants

Herbs are often recommended to the novice gardener because most are tough, vigorous, reliable plants that have been passed down in cultivation for centuries; easy to grow, they rarely suffer from pest and disease problems. All of these qualities make herbs ideal candidates for the organic garden.

Soil preparation and planting

Check the preferred soil conditions of your chosen herbs (*see pp.280–281*) before planting. Many thrive in free-draining, low-nutrient soil, so the addition of bulky organic matter may not be necessary. If your soil is heavy, incorporate a low-fertility soil improver to improve drainage. Constructing raised beds will also help. For a short-term solution, add a couple of handfuls of poultry grit or gravel to the bottom of the planting hole. Other herbs that prefer more fertile soil may benefit from a medium-fertility soil improver. Remove weeds, especially perennials such as couch grass, before planting.

Maintenance

Remove flowering stems from shrubby herbs such as lavender and sage after flowering. Prune these herbs in the spring to control the size of the plant and to prevent them from becoming bare and woody at the base.

Always remove flowers if you want to harvest the maximum quantity and quality of leaves. Pinch out growing tips to encourage bushy growth, and cut out any plain shoots on variegated herbs. Established clumps of perennials are best divided (*see p.193*) every two to three years, in spring or fall.

Propagation

Many herbs are easy to raise in the garden. Young herb plants are widely available in garden centers, although specialty herb nurseries offer a more varied and interesting selection. Annuals and biennials such as parsley and basil are grown from seed. Some perennials, such as fennel and chives, are also easy to raise from seed, and may self-sow.

Planting chives Almost every retailer selling plants will have a selection of young culinary herbs, including chives. You can even plant out the pots of living herbs that are sometimes sold in supermarkets. Scoop out a hole in the soil somewhat bigger than the rootball, and firm in. Chives prefer medium-fertility, water-retentive soil but, like their ornamental relatives the alliums, they do look very good surrounded by a loose gravel mulch. Established plants can be divided to increase stocks.

TAKING SOFTWOOD STEM-TIP CUTTINGS

1 Choose strong, nonflowering shoots 3–4 in (8–10 cm) long, severing them cleanly just above a leaf joint.

2 Trim each cutting to just below a leaf joint, and remove the leaves from the bottom half of the stems.

3 Insert the cuttings into a pot containing a free-draining potting mix—for example, a 1:1 mix of sand and coir-based multipurpose mix—so that the first leaf is just above the surface of the mix. Water gently; the soil should be moist but not sodden. Tent the pot with a clear plastic bag supported by wire hoops to maintain an atmosphere of high humidity around the cuttings. Stand the pot somewhere light but out of direct sunlight. When the young plants start to grow, pot them into their own individual small pots and grow on. Before planting out, stand them outside during the day and bring them in at night for a few days, so they get used to the difference in temperature and light levels.

Remember that cultivated varieties do not always come true from seed, or do not produce seed. In this case, vegetative propagation is the only option—by cuttings (*see also pp.202–203*) or division, depending on species.

It can be worth taking cuttings each year from tender shrubby herbs such as some lavenders and variegated sage, which may not survive the winter. Softwood stem-tip cuttings (*see above*) from shrubby herbs such as these and from curry plant, cotton lavender, and rosemary are some of the easiest cuttings to succeed with. Not only do they act as insurance should you lose the parent plant to a harsh winter, but raising your own eliminates the transportation costs of buying new plants.

Trimming lavender Lavender benefits from trimming with shears to keep it bushy, but never cut back into old, bare wood; it will not regrow. Sage, likewise, should never be cut back hard.

Harvesting herbs for drying

Small quantities of herbs can be picked throughout the growing season and used immediately. Harvesting large amounts of herbs for drying, or using them in some other way, requires a different approach. Whichever you do, always harvest thoughtfully, without stripping a plant bare. As a general rule, never harvest more than about one-third of a plant at any one time.

HERBS THAT DRY WELL

Bay
Mint
Rosemary
Sage
Lavender
Tarragon
Thyme (*below*)

Knowing when to harvest

Allow perennial herbs to become established before harvesting them. This will usually be in or after the second year of growth. Never harvest from plants that are struggling to grow.

The majority of leafy herbs reach maximum flavor just before the flowers open. After that point, the texture and flavor of leaves change as the plants put energy into flower and seed production. Remove all flowers to extend the production of tender leaves, unless you are growing the herbs for flowers or seed.

Herbs harvested for drying need to be collected with as little moisture on them as possible. A dry, warm, but not too sunny day provides ideal conditions. The ideal time is after overnight moisture has dissipated but before strong sunlight has caused the volatile oils to evaporate. In most cases this is around mid-morning, depending on the climate and weather conditions.

Preparing herbs for storage

Drying is an excellent way of preserving herbs: many leaves and seeds keep their flavor well and, stored correctly, should last up to a year. Providing the ideal range of temperatures and ventilation for drying individual herbs is not easy in a domestic situation, and if you dry herbs at home you may find that the drying process results in some loss of flavor and color. Some herbs do not retain their flavor well when dried, and are best used fresh, or frozen. Check all the plant material carefully before you dry it and discard any parts that are diseased or damaged.

There are two main methods of drying herbs: either suspended in bunches, or lying flat on racks or trays. For the enthusiast, electric dryers are available. It is best to dry each type separately, as they tend to dry at different rates. Choose a dark, clean, dry, well-ventilated spot, free from dust and insects. Always dry herbs out of direct sunlight, which causes loss of color and flavor.

Once dried, store the herbs in airtight containers to prevent them from reabsorbing moisture from the atmosphere. Glass jars, tins, or screw-top containers are all suitable. Keep them in the dark in a cool, dry place.

Drying in bunches

Keep the bunches of herbs small; a good guideline is to gather up no more than enough stalks to fit comfortably in your hand. Hang the herbs upside down; this helps preserve their appearance if you are planning to use them for decorative purposes. Use rubber bands to tie the bunches, as these will shrink with the herbs. Be aware that the rubber bands will eventually deteriorate and need to be replaced. Tie a large paper bag or sheet of newspaper loosely over the flowerheads if you want to collect the seeds.

Drying on racks or trays

To dry herbs flat, strip the leaves from each stem and arrange them in a single layer on a rack or tray. Inspect the herbs regularly to be sure they are drying properly, and turn any of the larger leaves frequently to ensure that they dry evenly. Look also for anything that shows signs of mold or decay and remove it. The herbs are ready when they are crisp to the touch but not brittle. They should crumble but not shatter when you crush them; leaves should strip easily from the stems.

Bunched herbs Use rubber bands when drying the herbs, then replace these with twine once they are dry.

Seeds and seedheads The seedheads of some plants, such as poppies (*below left*), are dried mainly for decoration, but others contain seeds popularly used as flavorings, such as fennel (*below right*) and cilantro (coriander).

12. Growing Fruit

Blossoms in spring, shade in summer, and abundance at harvest time—fruit is the treasure trove of the garden. Fruit has been part of our diet since we gathered our harvest from the wild forests. Now tamed, improved, and cultivated, fruits offer instant gratification as the original nutritious fast food, straight from the plant. This chapter deals with a range of fruits suitable for temperate climates—tree fruits such as apples, pears, plums, cherries, and peaches; and soft fruits: strawberries, raspberries, blackberries, currants, gooseberries, and blueberries.

All-around attraction Every garden should have an apple tree—not only productive but beautiful in flower, leaf, and fruit, with silvery bark on branches that become ever more gnarled and characterful with age.

Why grow fruit?

All fruits are attractive, and some also deliciously scented, in blossom. Fruit is sufficiently versatile to be restricted and managed to fit even a small garden—trained against a wall or fence, for example. Where there is space, however, the crown of a freestanding apple or pear tree provides dappled shade and much-sought-after medium height to the plant architecture of the garden. Finally, the harvest is both luscious and beautiful. There may be no fruit in some years, but generally there is a surplus to spare for friends—and for wildlife.

Deciding what to grow

You will have personal preferences for fruits, but it is also important to know which fruits will succeed in your garden conditions, and what you have space for. Some fruits may benefit from growing against a wall, especially in colder areas, but most fruit also grows well in the open garden. The free flow of air in this situation helps to reduce disease infections. Many fruits are very attractive to birds, squirrels, and raccoons and will need to be grown inside a netted cage or netted individually.

Choosing the crop A plum tree (*left*) needs no intricate pruning to crop heavily year after year—enough to share with wildlife. Strawberries (*below*) need more nurturing and protection, but will repay your care handsomely.

Your garden microclimate

Although most of the fruits described in this book are hardy, few, if any, will cope with frost when in blossom or in early fruit. It is vital to avoid planting in frost pockets, and to avoid creating new frost pockets by erecting fences or establishing plantings that trap and hold frost, rather than letting it drain away. Frosty air sinks downward to the lowest point. Fruit trees and bushes can, therefore, be planted above the danger level and thus escape damage. It is worth mentioning also that some fruits, such as some strawberry and black currant cultivars, need cold winter temperatures to flower well the next year.

Wind has the obvious effect of damaging branches. Less obvious is the fact that pollinating insects cannot visit blossoms in blustery weather, and this will affect the size of the harvest. Some gardens are naturally sheltered. If not, thought needs to be given to creating shelters against the wind.

Without doubt the greatest contribution to a successful harvest comes from the sun. Sunshine provides energy for plants to grow, ripens wood, and improves the flavor and color of fruits. If your garden receives sun for only part of the day, you will be limited in what tree fruits you can successfully grow—

WHY GROW FRUIT ORGANICALLY?

▪ **Fast food** Fruit can be eaten straight from the plant.

▪ **Produced without pesticides** There is no need to peel or scrub the fruit before eating.

▪ **Connect with the seasons** Summer strawberries, fall apples— harvesting your own fruit makes you more aware of seasonal change.

▪ **Endless choice** The range of fruits and cultivars is amazing; apple cultivars, for example, run into the thousands.

▪ **Fresh and tasty** Homegrown fruit can be harvested and eaten at the peak of natural ripeness and freshness.

▪ **Less work for greater returns** Growing most fruit takes little time in comparison with what you get.

▪ **Local production** Saves on food miles; allows you to taste fruits and cultivars that would never make it into a supermarket.

▪ **Enhance the garden** Fruit trees and bushes can be attractive garden plants in their own right.

▪ **Anyone can do it** Fruit can be fitted into even the smallest of yards.

although sour cherries may be possible—but with the exception of strawberries, the soft fruits in this chapter (red currants especially) all tolerate some shade.

Fitting fruit into the garden

If your yard is small, you may have to adapt your plans for fruit to fit the available space. You may decide that even just two raspberry plants, grown up each side of a freestanding post, are better than none. Even in the smallest garden, however, you can grow plentiful supplies of strawberries along the edge of a border or path, or in containers.

Pollination

A single fruit tree can, when mature, produce a generous crop, but some cultivars of tree fruit need other trees nearby that are compatible "pollinators" in order to set a crop. All flowers need to be pollinated for fruits to form. Many fruits, including the majority of soft fruits, are self-fertile: they do not need pollen from another plant or tree to set fruit. Many cultivars of plum and a few cherries are self-fertile; many apples are to some extent self-fertile, but still benefit greatly from cross-pollination with another apple cultivar. But some fruit varieties must have a pollinating neighbor. A single pear tree of the variety 'Louise Bonne de Jersey' in your garden, for example, is unlikely to set a crop—unless your neighbor has a compatible cultivar. But thanks to the development of dwarfing rootstocks (*see also* Apples, *p.294*) for many fruit trees, and their amenability to training, two or more cultivars grown as cordons, for example, could be fitted into most yards.

Apple blossoms Coordinating the flowering time of cultivars may be crucial to achieving good cross-pollination and thus heavy crops; from top, the apple cultivars 'Kidd's Orange Red', 'King of the Pippins', and 'Red Devil' in flower.

Will it grow in my soil?

Fortunately, most soils are suitable for growing fruit. Some soils, however, do pose problems that are hard to rectify. Shallow soil prevents good rooting, and high-pH soil will cause some fruits to suffer.

Blueberries need very acidic conditions (pH 5.5 or less) and most fruit thrives in slightly acidic soil (*see* Soil chemistry, *pp.30–31*). However, the majority of fruits will tolerate alkaline conditions. Raspberries are an exception and become iron-deficient and weakened in soil with a pH higher than 6.5.

The acidity of the soil is not the only factor. The structure of soil is also important. In good, friable soil, plant roots are able to spread freely and deeply and make good use of the nutrients already present.

It comes as no surprise, perhaps, that fruit prefers deep, rich loam that is free-draining but moisture-retentive. You may not have these conditions at first, but much can be done to improve soil structure, open up heavy soil, and increase the water-holding capacity of light soil (*see* The Soil, *pp.34–35*). If starting with very poor soil, start to improve it a year in advance of planting fruit trees or bushes.

Drainage

Fruits are composed largely of water and so adequate supplies are essential (*see overleaf*). In very wet localities, on the other hand, the main preoccupation will be with improving soil drainage. Roots will rot and fungal pathogens attack where drainage is poor. Perhaps the most dramatic effect can be seen in raspberry plantings, where root rot can rapidly run along waterlogged rows, killing canes as it spreads. Do not attempt to grow fruit where the soil cannot be improved to remedy wet conditions.

Good neighbors If you are eager to plant several cultivars of apples or pears, but have limited space, you could use a wall or fence, or even, as here, a freestanding post and wire support, to grow cordons—narrowly trained trees with a single main stem that can be spaced only 30 in (75 cm) apart.

Caring for fruit

Fruit is a long-term investment. Fruit trees, for example, may crop for anything up to 50 years. You might imagine that maintaining such a crop would need regular inputs of organic fertilizers, manure, and compost. This is not necessarily the case. Giving fruit a good start is, on the other hand, of fundamental importance.

It is much easier to improve soil structure and fertility before rather than after planting, and this is crucial to give trees, bushes, and canes a head start. A plant that establishes well soon develops an extensive root system that can forage for water and nutrients more efficiently than a weak plant. Details of appropriate soil improvement are given under individual fruits. Perennial weeds are awkward to remove from growing fruit, so clear the ground well before planting, too (*see pp.78–81*).

Watering needs

If you have only a small number of fruit trees and bushes, you may be able to supply adequate water by watering can or hand-held hose. Where this is impractical, the best solution is to install permanent irrigation lines of drip or seep hose (*see also p.60*). A mulch (*see below*) applied in late spring will help conserve water. Large, established trees should not need watering.

Feeding and mulching

Specific recommendations for supplementary feeding are given for individual fruits. As a general rule, however, with the exception of strawberries and some others, you will not need to add compost or fertilizers more than once every two or three years. An important addition to this is the use of organic mulches. The most common materials used for mulching fruit are straw and hay, although weathered and part-composted shredded prunings and wood chips are excellent if enough is available.

(Left, from top) **Caring for fruit** Seep hose laid around strawberries; mulching around newly planted fruit trees; pruning to create an open-centered gooseberry bush; a simple beer trap protecting ripening fruits from wasps.

You can use your own shreddings or buy in bagged products. Apply mulches thickly to damp soil in late spring when it has had a chance to warm up. Apply hay and straw up to 4 in (10 cm) deep and shreddings 2 in (5 cm) deep, keeping a clear area of about 6 in (15 cm) diameter around tree trunks and the base of plants.

Plant health

The best approach to maintaining healthy fruit crops is to make regular checks on how plants are growing. In this way, signs of any problems are seen early on, and can be dealt with before they become serious. Incipient infections can often be pinched or pruned out and pest colonies dispatched with a swipe of the thumb.

The A–Z of Plant Problems (see pp.320–341) contains more specific information on many common fruit problems.

Weeds—tolerance or zero tolerance

Control of weeds in fruit is just as important as for vegetables—except where fruit trees are growing on vigorous rootstocks. A full-sized fruit tree surrounded by a wildflower meadow gains many benefits from it, and together this association forms a valuable wildlife habitat. But in the case of small trees and all soft fruits, weeds compete with the crop plants for light, water, and nutrients; if very profuse, they can reduce air flow and increase the likelihood of fungal attack. Do not let weeds get out of hand.

TIPS FOR SUCCESS

Prevention is the key to healthy fruit.

- Plant pest- and disease-resistant cultivars.

- Choose the right site.

- Never plant fruit in soil where similar fruit has been growing.

- Prune plants to create an open growth habit, to allow good airflow between branches.

- Do not overfeed with nitrogen.

- Remove damaged and diseased fruit, shoots, and foliage.

- Pull away old mulches over winter: this will clear away some fungal spores and expose overwintering pests to hungry birds.

- Spraying with dilute seaweed extract (see p.195) is very beneficial, especially in spring and early summer. Both trees and bushes will take up nutrients more effectively, receive a full range of trace elements, and have enhanced hardiness to frost damage if given regular seaweed sprays.

- Protect crops from birds with netting or a fruit cage.

- Encourage creatures that eat pests (see pp.96–99). Most need no more enticement than an unsprayed garden, but in many cases providing appropriate habitats and food plants too will make all the difference (see Gardening for Wildlife, pp.104–125).

Apples

From cultivars that ripen in midsummer through to the late-keeping fruit that can be stored until spring, apples must offer one of the longest periods of fresh supply of any fruit. Many heirloom cultivars are still stocked by specialty nurseries.

Site and soil

Apples grow best n rich, free-draining soil with a pH of 6.5. If your soil is less fertile, you can compensate, not only by your soil treatment, but also by using a more vigorous rootstock or even growing the tree on its own roots. Choose an open site in full sun but protected from the wind. Avoid frost pockets.

Apples can be grown both as freestanding trees and as formal trained shapes against walls and fences or, for improved air flow, on post and wire supports. Walls that face the setting sun are ideal; cooking apples can be grown on a cool wall. Avoid very hot conditions.

Cultivars and rootstocks

Over many centuries apples have been selected and bred to suit a very wide range of situations. There are now cultivars to suit warm and cool climates (Zones 3–9) with rootstocks to match.

Like most fruit trees, apples are not grown on their own roots. Instead, they are grafted onto the roots of compatible trees, usually other apples. Rootstocks help to control the eventual size of the tree. Depending on the rootstock selected, the same cultivar of apple might grow 8 ft (2.5 m) or 30 ft (9 m) tall. Ask the nursery for advice on heights and rootstocks.

Pollination

Flowers must be pollinated for fruit to form (*see also p.290*). Some apples are "self-fertile"— pollination is achieved by bees flying from flower to flower on the same tree. Others cannot set a crop on their own and need to be planted within bee-flying distance of another cultivar that is both compatible and in flower at the same time. Your neighbors' yard is usually close enough. A crab apple can also make an effective pollinator.

Buying plants

The ideal time to buy trees is in late fall or early spring for immediate planting. At this time they are usually sold with bare roots, but container-grown trees can be found at most times of

Newly grafted fruit trees Fruit nurseries graft many hundreds of young trees each year, binding shoots of chosen cultivars onto the roots of other trees that will control height and vigor. The plant tissue fuses naturally at the graft point, or "union."

Choosing cultivars

McIntosh, Gala, Granny Smith—the names of many apple cultivars are familiar to us all. But there is much more to choosing apple trees than liking the name.

■ Season of harvest and use
If you have room, you may wish to extend your season of harvest with cultivars that succeed each other in maturing or fruits that are suitable for storing. There are late-cropping cultivars that do not actually ripen until stored for a while.

■ Disease and/or pest resistance
If you have a particular local problem, such as nectria canker, seek suggestions and advice on resistant or less susceptible varieties.

■ Suitability for your local climate
Cultivars that do well in a warm climate may perform poorly when planted in a garden with a shorter, cooler season and vice versa. Some older cultivars have strong local associations and these are worth seeking out for general robustness and reliability.

■ Flavor
Not all cultivars have good flavor, and personal tastes vary. If you can, try before you buy.

■ Pollination requirements
See facing page: if you are buying a single tree, check with the supplier that it is a self-fertile cultivar; if buying two or more, ensure that they are compatible.

Feast of fruits 1. 'Kidd's Orange Red';
2. 'Arthur Turner'; **3.** 'Orleans Reinette';
4. 'William Crump'; **5.** 'Lord Lambourne';
6. 'Laxton's Fortune'; **7.** 'Egremont Russet'; **8.** 'John Standish'.

Espaliered apple Just as climbers flower better when their shoots are trained horizontally, so apple espaliers can bear fine crops. With a vigorous rootstock, the tree can be trained with as many tiers of branches as space and inclination permit, but three, or perhaps four, is the norm.

year, though cultivar choice is likely to be much reduced. Consider the intended shape of the tree when buying (*see below*). Good fruit nurseries will offer trees that are two, three, four, or even more years old that are already partly trained to the desired shape, and will give you advice on how to encourage and develop the shape correctly, although gardeners who like a challenge can buy much younger trees and train them from scratch.

The shape of the trees

Apples grown primarily for their fruit are usually grown as bush trees, with a short trunk that branches about 30 in (75 cm) from the ground. Standard trees, with a tall clear trunk, make fine ornamental garden trees, but their height makes them difficult to prune and pick. Apples can also be trained into two-

dimensional shapes, which gives them formal, ornamental appeal and takes up less space in a small garden. The cordon and espalier shapes suit their growth habit and pruning needs best. Trees to be trained flat need a strong wall or fence to support them, with wires stretched horizontally across; for freestanding trained forms, custom-made metal supports can be bought, or you can erect a post-and-wire system.

Cordons are usually planted obliquely at an angle of 45–60°; space trees 30 in (75 cm) apart. Espaliers need much more space. They are usually trained with three tiers of branches, at 18-in (45-cm) intervals. For a three-tier espalier, erect a post and wire support structure with wires at 2, 3½, and 5 ft (60, 110, and 150 cm). Planting distances will depend on which rootstock the tree has been grafted on.

Planting apples

Apple trees should be planted as for any tree (*see pp.170–171*) and, if freestanding, will need staking. Unless your soil is naturally very fertile and well-structured, incorporate soil improvers and fertilizers. Add the following to the topsoil you remove from the planting hole: half a bucket each of well-rotted manure and leaf mold, and 4 oz (125 g) each of seaweed meal and bonemeal, or equivalent organic fertilizer (*see pp.54–55*). Mix well, and return to the planting hole when the tree is in place.

Feeding and mulching

It is important to keep weeds under control around all apples during their early years of establishment. They compete for food and, more importantly, water. For trees on dwarfing rootstocks, good weed control under the canopy is essential throughout the life of the tree. Thick straw mulches, 3–4 in (8–10 cm) deep, will help to smother weeds and conserve moisture (*see also p.292*). Lay mulch in late spring, removing it in winter to the compost pile. Grass can be allowed to grow up to the trunk of large, well-established trees.

Feed trees if they show signs of declining growth with a mulch of well-rotted manure or garden compost applied in early spring.

Pruning established trees

Like all fruit trees, apples need to be pruned annually for best results. Once established, all tree forms benefit from winter pruning. Trained forms—cordons, espaliers, and fans—need extra pruning in summer to keep their shape. Pruning aims to achieve a number of objectives:

■ **Removal of dead, diseased and damaged growth**; always cut well back into healthy wood.

■ **Opening up the branch framework** to allow better air circulation and lessen risk of fungal infection.

■ **Pruning out** colonies of pests.

■ **Shaping of trees**, removing shoots that cross so that they do not chafe each other, creating entry points for disease.

■ **Control of vigor** to maintain a balance between older fruiting wood and new, vigorous growth. This can be achieved on most apple cultivars by a system of pruning called spur-pruning. Ask your supplier whether your chosen cultivar is a spur-bearer, or one of the rarer

Pruning apples Winter pruning may involve anything from removing badly placed branches (*below left*) to shortening shoots so that they develop into fruiting spurs (*center*). To remove a larger branch (*right*), follow the advice on p.173.

Natural wastage In many years, apple trees will set more fruits than they can successfully ripen, and so a natural shedding process takes place, usually of poorly formed or stunted fruitlets, around midsummer. It is sometimes referred to as the June drop.

Apple problems Aphids like to colonize tender shoot tips; if they go unnoticed, it may become necessary to prune out badly infested and distorted growth (*near right*). A protective band (*far right*) used to prevent wingless female winter moths from climbing trees to lay their eggs, may also help with aphid problems—by keeping ants, which farm aphids, out of the tree.

tip-bearers; do not spur-prune these. To spur-prune:

■ Cut back the leading shoot of each branch (the one making it longer overall) by one-third to half, and remove any shoots competing with the leader near the tip.

■ Leave all one-year-old laterals (sideshoots) unpruned unless they are strongly upright-growing or badly placed.

■ In the following year, fat fruit buds will form on these unpruned laterals, now in their second year, and sublaterals will grow out from them. Cut back into the two-year-old wood to leave short shoots (spurs) with four to six fruit buds on them.

■ For the next two years, prune back any extension growth on these spurs to keep them stubby. New one-year-old laterals will arise from the main branches during the following years, which you then treat as above to give spurs of varying ages.

■ Once a spur has completed four years, remove it with a sloping cut to encourage a new lateral to restart the process.

Thinning the fruits

It is normal in summer for many fruitlets to drop naturally, but these may not be the ones you would have selected. For the best quality and size of fruit, it is important to thin fruitlets early. Start thinning about six weeks after most petals have dropped.

Remove the "king fruit" at the center of the cluster. This is usually slightly larger and distorted. Thin the remaining fruitlets to leave one per cluster and 4–6 in (10–15 cm) between each fruitlet. Select the best fruitlet (or the best two, if the crop is light), discarding any affected by insects, or damaged or distorted.

Picking and storing apples Gently twist apples nearing ripeness (*above left*): if they come away easily, they are ready for picking. Do not let apples in storage touch each other (*above right*), to reduce the chance of rot spreading between the fruits.

Protect the crop

Select cultivars resistant to mildew, canker, and scab. In late spring, hang up pheromone traps (*see p.102*) for codling moth. Check new foliage for mildew, and prune out diseased shoots and leaves, cutting back into healthy wood. Look out for aphids on young shoots; squash by hand, wash off with a jet of water, or spray with an appropriate insecticide. Sow flowers to attract natural predators (*see p.95*). Grease bands (*see facing page*) can help reduce aphid infestations on free-standing trees. Watch out for colonies of woolly aphids. Scrub them off, or prune out badly infested shoots.

  Pick up fallen fruitlets, as these may house sawfly larvae. Earwigs may be found on fruits, but do not cause significant damage, and should be tolerated as they are excellent apple pest predators. In fall, remove mulches and rake up all fallen leaves, or mow over them so that they are taken down into the soil quickly, as they may harbor scab spores that could reinfect the tree in spring. Apply grease bands to trees and stakes to deter winter moths; keep in place until early spring. After harvest, remove all unpicked fruits from the tree, and hang up fat to attract birds, which eat pests.

  See the A–Z of Plant Problems (*pp.320–341*) for more information and advice.

Harvesting

The first indication of ripeness will be the development of color on the skin and a few windfalls on the ground. Test by gently lifting and twisting individual fruits in the palm of your hand. Fruit of early cultivars can be eaten from the tree; later cultivars need time to develop their flavor after picking.

Storing fruit

Late cultivars will not ripen until they have been in store for a while. The refrigerator is ideal for storing apples, but a frost-free shed, basement, or attic is adequate and more economical. Aim for cool, dark, slightly damp conditions. Only store perfect fruits.

■ **Slatted boxes or shelves** Traditionally, apples were stored in custom-made slatted boxes or drawers. A good substitute is a vegetable crate. Lay apples in a single layer, not touching each other.

■ **Individual wrapping** Wrap each apple in a square of tissue or newspaper, ensuring that each is completely covered. Fruit can then be laid in boxes or vegetable crates in layers.

Pears

The fact that so many old pear cultivars bear French names shows how valued the pear was in France: the long season and warm conditions of the Continent suit them well. Pears are more difficult to store than apples, but cultivars are available to span a season from midsummer through to winter without special storage conditions. Hardy in Zones 4–9, pears are quite long-lived trees, but the quality and size of fruit starts to decline after 30 or 40 years.

Site and soil

Pears enjoy warmth and an early start to the season. Choose a sunny, sheltered spot, or train them against a warm wall. Blossoming occurs several weeks earlier than with apples, which means that the cooler the climate, the more likely it is that flowers will be damaged by frost and the crop will suffer. If you live in a cold area, you will find that your choice of cultivars is much more limited. Pears need the same soil conditions and soil preparation before planting as apples (see pp.296–297).

Buying plants

To produce fruit, pears need to be pollinated by another compatible cultivar—that is, you need to grow two different pears—and their compatibility groupings are quite complex, so seek advice when you buy. A specialty fruit nursery or mail order company can advise you on appropriate combinations of cultivars. Pears are slower to start cropping than apples. It is well worth buying a tree grown for three years in the nursery to shorten the time before you harvest your first crop.

Pruning and training

Pears can be grown as a pyramid-shaped tree with a central trunk or, as apples are, as a low-branching bush tree. They can also be trained into two-dimensional shapes such as cordons and espaliers. Training pears against a wall that faces the midday or setting sun is ideal, using the warmest walls for the more delicate or best-flavored varieties. A three-year-old tree will already be partly trained into the desired shape; a good fruit nursery will give you advice on how to encourage and develop the form.

From the fourth year onward, pears are pruned as for apples (see pp.297–298); all benefit from routine pruning in winter, and wall-trained trees need additional pruning in summer. Spur-pruning will enhance cropping.

Caring for the crop

Follow the advice on feeding, watering, mulching, and fruit-thinning given for apples (see pp.296–297). In fall, remove mulches and rake up all fallen leaves, or mow over them so they are taken into the soil quickly to remove fungal spores.

■ Pears are susceptible to a bacterial disease called fireblight. If this is a problem in your area, train your pears to have multiple trunks; in this way you may be able to remove infected wood and save the rest of the tree.

■ A unique problem in pear trees is the pear psylla, a sapsucking insect that deposits sticky honeydew, which supports the growth of black sooty mold. Spray psylla with insecticidal soap. The next season, spray with horticultural oil in early spring and again when buds show green.

See the A–Z of Plant Problems (*pp.320–341*) for more information and advice.

Harvesting and storing

The earliest cultivars are ready in midsummer and can be eaten straight from the tree. The majority are picked from early to mid-fall and need at least two or three weeks after picking to ripen. Late-storing cultivars will keep well into winter.

Not all pears have strong skin coloring, making the judging of ripeness difficult. When the picking time for a cultivar arrives, start testing individual fruits. Hold the bulbous end of the fruit in the heel of your hand and tilt the fruit gently upward; it will come away easily when ready for picking.

Pears are more difficult than apples to store well. It is better not to wrap them. Bring batches up to room temperature to complete ripening—it may take a further two to three weeks. When ripe, pears are soft at the stalk end and will give when pressed gently.

Pear psylla Tiny insects called pear psylla suck juice from pear trees and release honeydew that supports the growth of black sooty mold.

Harvesting pears Other than early cultivars, pears should not be left to ripen on the tree, as flavor will be poor. If you have room, choose a selection of cultivars for a succession of fruits.

Plums

Cultivated plums can be sweet, melting dessert fruits or tangy, firm cooking fruits, in shades from yellow to blue to nearly black. In all but the most extreme climates, there is a plum tree for every yard. Wild American plums grow in Zones 4–8, European and damson plums thrive in Zones 5–9, and Japanese plums do best in Zones 6–10. Hybrids between American and Japanese plums combine the cold hardiness of the former with the fruit quality of the latter.

Black knot The fungal disease called black knot produces knobby black galls on plum branches.

Site and soil

Plums grow best in sunny conditions, sheltered from frost and high winds. The blossoms open early in spring, so avoid sites where frosty air collects. North-facing slopes are ideal because they warm up later and delay flowering for a few days, reducing the chance of frost damage.

Good drainage is essential, but otherwise plums and their close relatives are not unduly fussy about soil. Japanese and American cultivars prefer sandy or loamy soil, while European cultivars do well in clay soil.

Buying plants

For general advice, see Apples (*p.294*). Most European plums will set some fruit without cross-pollination, but nearly all will yield better when cross-pollinated by another European cultivar. Japanese plums must be cross-pollinated by either a Japanese or American type. American plums also need cross-pollination for best yields. Rootstock choice can further influence your plum trees' success. Ask a specialty fruit nursery for help in selecting a suitable combination of trees on appropriate rootstocks.

Pruning

Plums are nearly always grown as informal, bushy trees. However, they are well-suited to growing as fans on a wall or free-standing support. A good fruit nursery will give you advice on how to develop and maintain the form.

When grown as free-standing trees, plums need only light pruning, to remove badly placed and dead and diseased growth. You can also shorten too-long shoots that unbalance the shape. Japanese plums grow well with open-center training.

Caring for the crop

Follow the advice on feeding, watering and mulching given for apples (*see pp.296–297*). In a good year, some cultivars will set a great deal of fruit; so much so that the weight can break branches. In such years, after the natural fruit drop in early summer, thin the remaining fruitlets with scissors to about 2–5 in (5–10 cm) apart.

■ **Black knot** is a common disease of plum trees. This fungal infection produces swollen, knobby black galls on branches. Prune out affected branches during the winter, then spray lime-sulfur as buds swell in spring and again a week later.

■ **Bacterial leaf spot** causes small, angular black spots on leaves. Leaves may turn yellow and drop early. Spray lime-sulfur every 10–21 days until leaf drop if weather is wet or humid, or if the spots are spreading.
See the A–Z of Plant Problems (*pp.320–341*) for more information and advice.

Harvesting and storing

There is no doubt when a plum is ripe. It will be fully colored (but note that plums come in many colors, including green) and soft. Fruits will pull away easily. Once picked, eat immediately, or keep them cool until you are ready to use them. They do not keep for long but can be frozen or used in preserves.

Sugary treat Wildlife enjoys the sweet flesh and juice of ripe plums as much as we do. Fallen or bird-pecked plums are a magnet for wasps, so watch out when picking.

Cherries

Cherries are normally classed as either sweet or sour. Sweet cherries are eaten straight from the tree and have either white or dark flesh. Skin color also varies from "white," which is actually usually flushed with scarlet, to very dark. Sweet cherries ripen in midsummer, sour cherries ripen slightly later. Sour cherries are grown for culinary use; they are juicy but very tart if eaten raw.

Site and soil
Cherries flower even earlier than plums, so they need a warm spot. In any area subject to late spring frosts, sweet cherries must be trained against a very warm and sunny, sheltered wall. Sour cherries flower a little later than sweet cherries, and though late frosts can still damage blossoms, they usually crop well on a cooler wall or grown as freestanding trees, provided they are not in a cold, exposed site. Soil requirements are as for plums (*see p.302*); prepare the soil before planting as for apples (*see p.297*).

Cherry fan Fan-trained cherries are a great deal easier to net against birds than freestanding trees. Sweet cherries need the shelter of a sunny wall or fence in cool-climate regions.

Buying plants

For general advice, see Plums and Apples (*pp.302 and 294*). Good dwarfing rootstocks for cherries are now becoming more widely available. This is an important development, because tall trees are difficult or impossible to net—and birds love cherries. Wall-trained cherries are easily netted and ideal for the garden. Most sour cherries are self-fertile, as is the popular sweet cherry cultivar 'Stella'. However, most other sweet cherries need another cherry tree to be grown nearby for successful pollination (this could be a sour cherry). The various cultivars have very complicated compatibilities for pollination: seek advice when buying.

Pruning and training

Like plums, cherries may be grown as informal, bushy trees or as fans; however, sour cherries have quite complicated pruning requirements (*see also below*) when grown as a fan. Both may be bought partly trained in the fan form; ask the nursery for advice on how to develop and maintain the shape.

When grown as freestanding trees, sweet cherries are pruned as for plums (*see p.302*); that is, only as necessary. With sour cherries, you will increase your crop if, once the tree shape is formed, you then each year remove a proportion of the three- and four-year old branches, cutting back to a younger side-branch. This is because the sour cherry has a very different fruiting habit from plums and sweet cherries. It fruits on wood produced the previous year, so pruning aims to keep as much of the tree made up of productive young wood as possible (this is also why maintaining a sour cherry fan can be difficult).

Again, as with plums (*see p.302*), always prune sour cherries in the growing season, not when dormant.

Harvesting the fruits Cherries keep better if harvested with their stalks, so pull at the stalk rather than the fruit, or use scissors or pruners.

Caring for the crop

Follow the advice on feeding, watering, and mulching given for apples (*see pp.296–297*). Cherries do not need thinning.

■ **Cherries are susceptible** to splitting if they take up too much water, too fast. Harvest ripe fruit immediately after a heavy rain.

■ **Cherry fruit fly larvae** burrow into fruits; collect and destroy fallen fruit daily.

■ **Net the crop** against birds before it ripens. It may also be necessary to protect flower buds from hungry songbirds in winter. Allow birds access at other times, to eat pests.

See the A–Z of Plant Problems (*pp.320–341*) for more information and advice.

Harvesting and storing

Pick sweet cherries as soon as they are ripe; either eat them immediately, refrigerate for a short time, or freeze. Sour cherries do not pull away easily from the tree and may need to be snipped off. Fruit is ready when very dark in color and soft to the touch. It can be used to make jam or wine, preserved in brandy, or cooked for immediate use or freezing.

Peaches and nectarines

Peaches and nectarines, with their luscious and juicy fruits, are popular home fruit trees in Zones 5 through 9. Most gardeners are familiar with yellow-fleshed freestone peaches, but you might also consider growing white-fleshed peaches, which are deliciously sweet, or golden clingstones with their firm, aromatic flesh and good canning qualities.

Site and soil

Peaches flower very early in spring and the blossoms are not hardy. For this reason, peaches and nectarines are sometimes grown against a warm, sunny wall. This gives the added advantage of being able to protect them easily from the early spring rain that spreads a fungal disease called peach leaf curl. Peaches and nectarines both prefer slightly acidic soil that is deep and fertile.

Perfect peach Peaches and nectarines sold in supermarkets are usually harvested before they are ripe, and transported in cold storage. Grow your own to experience perfect, juicy ripeness.

Plant peach or nectarine trees in early spring or fall. Follow the advice on soil preparation given for apples (*see p.297*).

Buying plants
For general advice, see Apples (*see p.294*). Peaches are nearly all self-fertile but benefit from hand-pollination (*see* Caring for the crop, *below*). Each cultivar needs a specific period of cold weather before it will resume growth and flower in the spring. In Zones 5–6, look for a "high-chill" cultivar that will only open its buds when spring arrives in earnest. Gardeners in Zones 8–9 should buy a "low-chill" cultivar. Different rootstocks will also give better results in different climates. Ask your university extension service for advice on choosing suitable fruit trees for your area.

Pruning
Peaches and nectarines are very similar to sour cherries in that they fruit on young wood, and are pruned in a similar way (*see p.305*). Carry out all pruning between late spring and early fall (*see* Plums, *p.302*).

Caring for the crop
Follow the advice on feeding, watering, and mulching given for apples (*see pp.296–299*). Both fruits must be kept weed-free.

Although most varieties are self-fertile, they benefit from hand-pollination, moving from flower to flower, dusting lightly with a soft paintbrush on a warm, dry day when flowers are fully open. Do this several times over two weeks, as flowers open in sequence.

For the best size and quality of fruit, thinning is essential. Thin in two phases: when fruitlets are the size of grapes, thin to one fruit per cluster; and then later, when they are walnut-sized, thin again to leave one fruit every 6 in (15 cm) approximately.

Peach leaf curl disease infects leaves as they unfold in spring, causing red blistering and distortion of the foliage. A temporary shelter to keep rain off until all the leaves have appeared should reduce infection.

See the A–Z of Plant Problems (*pp.320–341*) for more information and advice.

Harvesting and storing
Fruits are soft to the touch and fully colored when they are ripe. They bruise easily and should not be dropped, and they do not store.

Hand-pollinating peaches A rabbit's foot is a traditional tool for pollinating peaches, but a soft paintbrush or cosmetics brush is just as effective. Lightly dab each open flower in turn, and you should transfer enough pollen from blossom to blossom to ensure that fruits form.

Strawberries

Few tastes match that of the first strawberry of the year. The earliest cultivars start cropping in late spring; the season then extends through summer, with late-season "perpetual" types continuing into fall. In a small garden, however, it is best to grow only one or two varieties, as fewer than 12 plants of each provides a frustratingly small harvest. Plants crop well for about three years.

Fast food Strawberries are at their best harvested when fully colored and eaten as soon as possible—not that you will need much prompting! They do not keep well, nor do they freeze except as a puree, since freezing destroys their texture.

Site and soil

An open site in full sun is best. Strawberries are relatively unfussy about soil, although high fertility is not good: it encourages big, leafy plants at the expense of fruit. Good drainage, however, is extremely important. Strawberries can also be grown in containers, cropping for one year only; use a 6-in (15-cm) pot for one plant, or grow several in a larger pot.

Buying plants

Strawberries reproduce by sending out "runners"—long stems at the end of which young plantlets form and root. Traditional bareroot runners are best planted as soon as they become available in summer. They can be planted as late as fall, but should then be deflowered in their first year so that they will not be weakened by growing a crop while still so young.

In early summer you may be able to buy what are called "cold-stored runners" for immediate planting. These then rush into growth and produce a crop late in the season. The plants will go on to fruit normally in the following years.

Preparation and planting

■ **Plant where** strawberries or raspberries have not been grown for 6 years or more.
■ **Before planting**, dress the soil with a 1-in (2–3-cm) layer of garden compost or leaf mold and lightly work it in.

■ **Space plants** 12–18 in (30–45 cm) apart in the row with 30 in (75 cm) between rows. Don't crowd plants; a damp atmosphere encourages gray mold (botrytis), which rots the fruit.
■ **Scoop out holes** large enough to fit the rootballs.
■ **Set the plants** with the crown above the soil level (do not bury the center of the plants) and firm soil in with your fingers.
■ **Water** the plants in well.

Caring for the crop

In dry weather, keep plants well watered, especially while fruit is swelling. If soil has been well prepared, strawberries will not need additional fertilizer. To keep the fruit clean and dry, lay a 2-in (5-cm) mulch of straw around plants, tucking it under the foliage. Remove all runners that form, unless you need new plants (*see right*); if so, keep no more than three runners per plant.

After all the crop has been picked, trim off all foliage but leave an inch or so of stalk to protect the newly emerging leaves. Take the debris and the straw to the compost pile. Then apply a light dressing of garden compost or similar (2 gallons per square yard, or 10 liters per square meter) to stimulate new growth.

Looking ahead

You should plan to move your strawberry bed somewhere new after three years, and ideally, somewhere new again after the following three years; in small gardens you may have to settle for alternating between two sites. This means you will need to identify at least two plots for strawberries over the long term.

Protect the crop

■ **Plant certified** disease-free plants, or runners from a crop known to be healthy. Look for pest- and disease-resistant cultivars.
■ **Pick off diseased fruit** and foliage as seen. Powdery mildew symptoms on leaves are more likely in dry weather. Use a drip or soaker hose watering system to avoid wetting the foliage.
■ **Net the crop** before the fruits ripen. This will exclude birds, but squirrels and raccoons may also take the fruit. Slugs love ripening strawberries. Encourage natural predators, and put down slug traps, or use a biological control (*see p.97*) if necessary.
■ **Stunted growth** may be caused by viruses or strawberry red stele disease. Remove the plants; do not replant on the same site with strawberries or raspberries.
See the A–Z of Plant Problems (*pp.320–341*) for more advice.

(Top) **Protective mulch** Tucking straw under fruit will keep it clean and dry, reducing the risk of spoilage by rot and mildew.

(Below) **Making more plants** Using a wire staple, you can peg a few runners into pots sunk into the soil to increase your stocks of plants, provided that the parent plant shows no sign of disease. Once the plantlets are well-rooted, sever them from the parent.

Raspberries

Raspberries fruit at just the right time to take over from strawberries. As well as cultivars that produce through the summer, you will also find fall-fruiting types. Summer-fruiting raspberries crop on long, whippy canes that grew the previous year, so you will get your first crop in the second summer after planting. The canes of fall-fruiting types grow and fruit in a single year, and will produce a small crop in the fall after you plant them.

Site and soil

Raspberries are hardy in Zones 3–9 and will fruit in sites that only get sun for half the day. They prefer fertile, free-draining soil with a pH of 6.5 or below. Raspberries are not happy in alkaline soil. Good drainage is vital: raspberries are prone to a root rot that thrives in wet soils.

Summer treat Birds find juicy raspberries as irresistible as we do, but only place netting over the plants once the fruits form: raspberry flowers can be a major nectar source for honeybees.

Buying plants

Raspberries are usually sold as bareroot plants for winter planting. It is essential to buy certified virus-free stock from a reputable supplier. Well-managed, good-quality stock will crop for up to 14 years if grown in acidic soil.

Soil preparation and planting

Do not plant where raspberries or strawberries have grown in the last six years. If planting into well-cultivated, weed-free soil, all you need to do is add garden compost or well-rotted manure. Fall-fruiting raspberries can do without support in less windy areas, but summer-fruiting raspberries need a post-and-wire support. Use sturdy posts, 5 ft (1.5 m) high, 12 ft (3.5 m) apart, with two or three wires stretched between them. A double support system (*see opposite*) gives greater production. Set the plants about 18 in (45 cm) apart in a row under the wires, with the soil level with the original soil mark on the cane stub. You can also grow two or three plants around a single post.

Caring for the crop

In spring, buds break first on the cane stub; new growth will then emerge from below ground. At this point, cut off the original stub. Hoe or cut off new shoots that appear too far away from the row. When the soil has warmed up, mulch heavily with straw or hay. Newspaper

Summer raspberries In this useful double support system, with two rows of posts and wires (seen end-on here), the fruiting canes of summer raspberries are tied in to the wires, while new canes grow up freely in the space between, to be thinned and tied in when the fruited canes are pruned out.

spread out six or seven pages thick under the mulch will smother most weeds and unwanted cane growth. As raspberries root close to the soil surface, this is preferable to hoeing.

■ Tie in new canes of summer-fruiting varieties as they reach the wires. With these varieties, you only want 10–12 strong canes per yard (meter) of row, so cut out the rest at soil level.

■ Fall-fruiting raspberry canes do not need thinning, but restrict them to a band about 12 in (30 cm) wide. If you have given them wire supports, loop canes in loosely with soft twine.

■ Water in dry weather, and keep weed-free.

■ Fertilizing during the season should not be necessary.

Pruning after fruiting

Leave the canes of summer-fruiting raspberries unpruned in their first year; they will bear next season's crop. In the second and following years, once all the fruit has been picked, cut all the fruited canes only down to ground level. Tie in the new canes and thin if necessary as before.

Autumn-fruiting raspberries are simpler to prune: every year, including the first year, cut all the canes to the ground once fruiting is over.

After pruning, remove the old straw mulch. Spread garden compost along the row to help dead stubs rot down. In alternate springs, give plants a boost with an organic fertilizer (*see pp.54–55*) if required.

Protect the crop

■ **Check for aphids** through the season.

■ **Net ripening fruit** against birds.

■ **Small raspberry fruitworms** may be found in ripe fruit. Removing mulch and lightly cultivating the soil in winter helps to control both this pest and the cane borer, which creates wounds that can be an entry point for diseases.

■ **Through the season**, check the canes for signs of raspberry spur blight, cane blight, and cane spot.

See the A–Z of Plant Problems (*pp.320–341*) for more advice and information.

Blackberries and hybrid berries

Blackberries grow wild, but to guarantee sweet, juicy berries (not all wild berries are sweet), grow cultivated varieties. Hybrid berries such as loganberries and tayberries are mostly crosses between raspberries and blackberries. They are mostly earlier-cropping than blackberries but grow in the same way. All bear their fruit on long whippy stems, or canes, that grew the previous year, so you will harvest your first crop in the second summer after planting.

Training and pruning Tie the canes in along the wires as they grow, looping them up and down in a wave pattern to make the best use of space (*below, top*). Prune canes down to ground level once they have fruited (*below, bottom*).

Site and soil

Blackberries grow in Zones 5–10, depending on cultivar. Most blackberries and hybrid berries are vigorous and need plenty of space. The ideal spot is against a wall or fence, but you can use a post-and-wire support similar to that used for raspberries (*see p.310*). It is important to allow space for the long canes to be tied in; the most vigorous cultivars may need as much as 24 ft (7 m) of space, so ask when you buy about the different cultivars available and their vigor. Beds prepared at the base of walls or fences should be at least 3 ft (1 m) wide.

Blackberries are easy to grow and are not fussy about soil. Hybrid berries generally need more warmth and free-draining, slightly acidic soil. Blackberries will grow in partial shade, but hybrid berries perform best in full sun.

Buying plants

Plants are sold as bareroot canes in the same way as raspberries. If you have a small yard, look for less vigorous cultivars, such as 'Marion' or 'Merton Thornless.' Most cultivars are thorny, but a few are thornless. These are much easier to deal with, but some people think they have less flavor.

Preparation and planting

Prepare the soil as for raspberries (*see p.310*). Attach horizontal wires to the wall or fence 9 in (25 cm) apart, starting at about 24 in (60 cm) above soil level and going up to about 5 ft (1.5 m); or stretch the wires between two 5-ft (1.5-m) posts, set 10–12 ft (3–3.5 m) apart. Plant a single plant at the center of the support, or space several plants out according to their vigor. Bury each stool up to the original soil mark on the cane stub and firm it in.

Pruning and training

In spring, buds will break on the stub, then new growth will emerge from below soil level; when this happens, cut off the old stub at soil level. In the first year, only a few canes will grow. Tie them in to one side; if you have several plants, train the canes of neighboring plants toward each other. By midsummer you will need to tie in weekly, as growth is rapid.

In the second year, the canes will flower and fruit, and new canes will grow. Tie the new canes in on the opposite side from the old ones. Keeping old and new canes apart prevents any diseases from spreading from old to new growth. Allow up to 30 new canes per plant, although some cultivars produce many fewer.

After fruiting, cut all the fruited canes to the ground and spread garden compost over the cut stubs to help them rot down. This frees up that side of the plant for the new canes that will grow the next year, while those on the other side are bearing their crop.

Ripening blackberries Blackberries usually crop heavily, but fortunately, their fruits ripen in succession, making the harvest more manageable; they also freeze well, either as individual fruits or as a puree or compote.

Caring for the crop

After a few years, the plants will send up suckers away from the main plant. These can be hand-pulled as they appear.

Blackberries need little fertilizing. If vigor declines, apply garden compost, well-rotted manure, or pelleted chicken manure. Hybrid berries benefit from a topdressing of garden compost every two to three years.

Water well in dry weather. In early summer, mulch to at least 3 ft (1 m) around the plant with straw or hay to help the soil retain moisture. Netting against birds may be needed. Raspberry beetle grubs (*see p.311*) may also be found in the fruits of these berries.

See the A–Z of Plant Problems (*pp.320–341*) for more details.

Black currants

Black currants, rich in flavor and full of vitamin C, are hardy and reliable, although late frost can damage blossoms and reduce the crop. The berries can be eaten raw, cooked, or pressed for their juice; they freeze well, and make excellent preserves. Black currants are always grown as bushes. You will harvest a moderate crop after two years, and a full crop after three or four years.

Currant events Apart from the harvest, the key time in the black currant year is late fall to winter, when established bushes should be pruned, as below, by sawing out a proportion of thick old branches at the base to leave well-spaced younger wood that will crop well in coming years.

Site and soil

As black currants are pruned hard once mature, they need fertile conditions but are otherwise unfussy about soil. They are best grown in Zones 3–6. They grow into broad bushes; a single bush can be quite productive, so you can still grow black currants even if you have a small garden. Choose a spot receiving sun for most of the day. Bushes become spindly if shaded, and sunshine improves the flavor of the berries.

Buying plants

In areas where pine trees are raised commercially, there may be restrictions on buying and planting black currants due to the potential for spreading white pine blister rust, a fungal disease that is passed back and forth between pine trees and some species of currants and gooseberries. Check with your university extension service before buying plants.

Black currants are generally sold as one-year-old plants, grown in containers. Seek out those cultivars that are resistant to some of the pests and diseases of black currants. They are best planted in early winter or, if that is not possible, early in spring.

Preparation and planting

It is important to prepare the ground well.
■ **Mark out** a site large enough to accommodate the number of bushes you plan. Allow a spacing of 5–6 ft (1.5–1.8 m) apart.

■ **Clear the site** of all perennial weeds.

■ **Just before planting**, work in well-rotted manure at the rate of one 2-gallon (10-liter) pail to every 20 sq ft (2 sq m), or garden compost at twice that rate. If organic matter levels are low in the soil, also apply about 1 in (2–3 cm) of leaf mold and lightly fork it in.

■ **Plant about 2 in** (5 cm) deeper than the surface of the soil in the pot. Cut back all the branches, leaving one or two buds above soil level on each.

Pruning

Black currants fruit best on two- and three-year-old branches. The aim of pruning is, therefore, to cut out branches that are older than this to leave a bush made up of as much healthy new growth as possible to fruit the following year.

In the first year, the new plants will produce branches from above and below ground and there will be no crop. No pruning is necessary. In the second year, the existing branches will fruit and grow. New branches will also grow from below ground. By the third year, you should have bushy plants that are fruiting well.

Prune bushes from the third year onward, in fall. Each year, remove up to one-third of the

Berry bounty If well-pruned, a mature black currant can bear fruit along almost every inch of its branches, so it is ideal for smaller gardens. The cultivars 'Ben Lomond' and 'Ben Sarek' are especially compact, and both have the advantage of being resistant to American gooseberry mildew and leaf midge.

oldest branches as close as possible to soil level (*see opposite*). Start with those lying closest to the ground. In some cases a good new shoot can be found near the base of an old branch. Prune back to this if it is well placed: that is, if it will grow outward from the center, rather than inward, across the middle of the bush.

Caring for the crop

Feed bushes with garden compost, well-rotted manure, or organic fertilizers at least every three years, or every other year in poorer soil. Well-managed plants should last over 20 years. Mulch bushes in late spring with straw or hay.

■ **Look out** for aphids on young shoots and leaves from spring onward. Squash these by hand or spray with insecticidal soap. Sow flowers to attract aphid predators (*see p.95*).

■ **Cut out** any mildewed shoots.

Red and white currants

These two fruits are very closely related and are grown in exactly the same way. With its brilliant berries, the red currant is, perhaps, more dramatic, but some prefer the white for its slightly sweeter flavor. Though related to black currants, they have a different growth habit, cropping on short shoots that grow from a permanent framework of branches. They start fruiting as soon as branches are two years old. The crop will increase annually to reach a peak after five years or so. Expect a well-managed bush to last for 15–20 years.

Site and soil

Red and white currants need less fertile conditions than black currants. They perform well in Zones 3 to 6, are unfussy about soil, and will even crop in cool situations where they receive only short spells of direct sunlight.

Buying plants

First check for any restrictions on growing currants in your area (they can harbor a disease fatal to pine trees). Plants are usually sold container-grown as one-, two-, or three-year-old plants; to train them against a wall, start with one-year-old plants. For bushes, look for plants with a good, fibrous root system, a short single stem, and three or more young branches of about pencil-thickness at the base.

Preparation and planting

If container-grown, red currants can be planted at any time, but winter is best. Bushes need to be spaced 4–5 ft (1.2–1.5 m) apart. Clear the ground thoroughly of weeds and dig over if necessary. Just before planting, work in garden compost or any other medium-fertility soil improver (not farmyard manure), at the rate of 2 gallons (10 liters) per square yard (meter).

Jewel colors These berries may not be as sweet as some fruits, but they can be used in refreshing summer desserts. With a high pectin content, they are also useful in making jams and jellies.

Pruning and training

Red currants are pruned to encourage short, stubby fruiting shoots known as spurs. Winter pruning (*see below*) forms and maintains the basic shape and size of the plants, while additional summer pruning restricts the amount of growth on them, by shortening all shoots on the main framework branches. This concentrates the plant's energy into fruit production, and also helps to remove disease and any aphids in the soft growth at the shoot tips.

Winter pruning of bushes

When planting, cut back all the branches by half, cutting to an outward-facing bud. Shorten any sideshoots to two or three buds.

Repeat this process in years two and three until you have formed a bush with 8–10 main branches, each with a "leading shoot"—the one at the tip that will make the whole branch longer—and, lower down, shortened, stubby branches. If the center of the bush is crowded with shoots growing inward across the middle of the bush, prune some of these out.

Once the bush is formed, each winter prune back the leading shoot by one half, and shorten all sideshoots to two or three buds. As the bushes age and clusters of stubby branches get old and crowded, cut some away.

Summer pruning

Begin summer pruning in the second year. First identify the leading shoot of each branch (*see above*); do not prune this. Prune all the sideshoots on the branch to five leaves.

Caring for the crop

Mulch in late spring with hay or straw. This will conserve moisture and suppress weeds. Do not overfertilize red currants. A dressing of garden compost every three years should do. Clear away suckers (shoots growing up from the soil around the base of the plant) to leave a single clear stem by pulling, cutting, or chopping them away, ideally when they are still small.

■ **Birds especially** enjoy these fruits; you will need to net them.
■ **The currant aphid** can colonize the undersides of leaves from bud-burst onward. Encourage aphid predators.
■ **Check from mid-spring** for imported currantworm larvae.
■ **Clear up fallen leaves** in fall.
See the A–Z of Plant Problems (*pp.320–341*) for more advice.

White currants A variant of the red currant sometimes described as the "connoisseur's currant," cultivated white currants are known to date back at least to the 1920s, although some of the newer cultivars, such as 'White Grape' and 'White Pearl', are also the best.

Planting Dig a hole large enough to take the rootball or spread out the roots. Set the plant in the hole, ensuring that the surface of its soil or the soil mark on the stem is level with the top of the hole, and firm it in.

Gooseberries

If you have no interest in gooseberries, there is a good chance that you have never tasted a fine dessert cultivar. Grown as bushes or cordons, they crop in their second summer after planting and, if well-managed, can last 15–20 years.

Cultivar choice Gooseberries may be white, green, yellow, or red, and for either culinary or dessert use. Some cultivars resist mildew well.

Winter pruning Gooseberries are "spur-pruned" as red currants are: sideshoots are cut back to form short fruiting spurs.

Site and soil

Gooseberries and red currants are closely related, and advice on site and soil for red currants (*see p.316*) is equally applicable to gooseberries. Gooseberries are hardy in Zones 3–7 and can be grown with little direct sunlight, except that choice dessert cultivars are better grown where they will receive sunlight for at least half the day. An airy spot is best to help combat mildew.

Preparation and planting

Prepare the soil, buy, and plant following the advice given for red currants (*see p.316*), including checking for local planting restrictions due to the threat of white pine blister rust. Choose cultivars that are resistant to American gooseberry mildew.

Gooseberries can be rather droopy in habit, and it is important to keep the fruit from touching the soil: this can lead to fungal infections spreading up onto the plant by rain-splash, or attacks by slugs and snails. If necessary, push in canes around the bush and loop twine around them to keep the outer branches off the ground. Keep the bushes pruned to an open center.

Caring for the crop

Follow the mulching and fertilizing advice for red currants (*see p.317*). Prune gooseberries as for red currants, too, but in winter, leave the spurs longer: prune them to three or four buds rather than two, to allow more fruits to grow.

■ **The currant aphid** can colonize undersides of leaves from bud-burst onward. Encourage aphid predators.

■ **In spring**, look out for mildew on shoots and leaves, then on developing fruit. Cut out affected growth.

■ **Check from mid-spring** for imported currantworm larvae, which can defoliate a plant.

■ **Clear up fallen leaves** in fall, especially if currant leaf spot has caused early leaf-fall.

See the A–Z of Plant Problems (*pp.320–341*) for more information.

Blueberries

This North American native plant makes a fine garden shrub with lovely fall coloring. A single plant will crop reasonably well; two or more bushes to cross-pollinate each other will fruit much better. Fruiting will start in the second summer after planting, reaching full cropping after five or six years.

Site and soil

Unfortunately, the blueberry only thrives in very acidic soil. Choose a sunny site, although some shade is not a problem. Protection from late frost is important. If you do not have suitable soil conditions (and most of us do not), you can grow blueberries in a large pot or tub.

Preparation and planting

Select a suitable blueberry type for your zone: highbush (Zones 4–7), lowbush (Zones 2–6), midhigh (Zones 3–7), or rabbiteye (Zones 7–9). Buy two- or three-year-old container-grown plants that are not rootbound. You will need to test the pH of your potting mix or any compost you use for soil improvement to be certain that it is not alkaline. Use only rainwater when watering plants. Plant bushes in late fall or early winter, spacing them 5 ft (1.5 m) apart. Mulch with composted bark or pine needles.

Caring for the crop

Top off the mulch annually, and remember not to give plants alkaline tap water. Prune in late winter or early spring. Blueberries fruit on two- and three-year-old branches. The aim of pruning is to keep a good supply of new branches, removing some that are four years old or more each year. In the first two or three years, prune out only any very weak growth or very low branches close to or pointing down to the soil. In subsequent years, do the same, but also prune out wood that has stopped fruiting.

Fussy fruit The blueberry needs damp but not waterlogged soil with high organic matter levels and a soil pH between 4 and 5.5. On the positive side, it can grow well in containers, in "ericaceous" potting mix, and pest and disease problems are rare.

A-Z of Plant Problems

The following reference section, while it cannot be completely comprehensive, covers the majority of plant problems that you may encounter in the garden, and some problems common in plants in the greenhouse. It may also help in diagnosing and dealing with similar problems on houseplants, too.

Entries are arranged by common name. Each entry briefly describes the problem, whether a cultural disorder, a disease, or a pest. Plants susceptible to the problem are then listed; in some cases, these are quite specific, but in others, groups of related plants, or any plant growing under similar conditions, may be affected. The most commonly seen symptoms are described. Measures for prevention and control are then given—if any are necessary. This latter point cannot be overstressed. Above all, never use sprays, even "organic" ones, unless essential.

Best practice for healthy plants

Use the following general measures to encourage healthy, problem-free plant growth and reduce the need to use controls.

■ Provide appropriate food and shelter to encourage natural predators (see Gardening for Wildlife, pp.104–125).
■ Create good soil structure (see The Soil, pp.26–33).
■ Feed the soil with composted organic soil improvers (see also The Soil, pp.34–35).
■ Grow plants that suit the site.
■ Do not sow or plant when temperatures are too low.
■ Practice good hygiene—clear away pest-ridden and diseased foliage and plants, both in the garden and in greenhouses.
■ Encourage good airflow around plants, by thinning out and pruning.
■ Do not overfeed, particularly with nitrogen, which causes lush growth, attractive to pests.

■ Use crop rotation when growing vegetables (see pp.230–233).
■ Pick off pests and diseases as they appear.
■ Grow resistant cultivars where there is a known problem.

Spraying—best practice

Never:
■ Spray if another method is available.
■ Mix different sprays together.
■ Spray on a windy day.

Always:
■ Identify the problem correctly, so the right spray is used.
■ Check that the product is legally approved for the job and is suitable for use in an organic garden. Regulations are frequently updated.
■ Spray at dusk to avoid harming bees.
■ Follow the instructions on the packaging.
■ Wear protective clothing and use a good-quality sprayer.
■ Avoid spraying pest predators.

Other useful references

Some pests, diseases, and disorders, and the techniques and materials listed here for prevention and control, are given fuller descriptions, and often pictured, in the chapter on Plant Health (pp.82–103); including mineral (nutrient) deficiencies, biological controls, traps and barriers, and "organic" fungicides and pesticides. Chapter 2, The Soil, contains more information on soil nutrient content and soil chemistry and pH (pp.30–33).

Anthracnose

Fungal disease affecting many different plants and causing varying symptoms.

Susceptible plants Beans, cucumbers, melons, peppers, tomatoes, dogwoods, maples, sycamores.

Symptoms On leaves, yellow or brown spots darken and expand to cover leaves. On vegetables, small, dark sunken spots in skin grow and develop pinkish spore masses; fruit eventually rots. On trees, young twig tips die off, or brown spots on young leaves are followed by defoliation.

What to do Select resistant cultivars; remove and destroy affected plants and plant in well-drained soil. Avoid touching plants when wet. Prune out dead wood and collect and destroy infected leaves.

Aphids

Small, soft-bodied, sap-feeding insects to $\frac{1}{8}$ in (4–5 mm) in length. Sometimes called greenfly or blackfly, depending on color; they may be winged or wingless, with long legs and antennae, and prominent tubelike structures at the end of the abdomen. Body color may be red, orange, yellow, green, brown, or black. In favorable conditions, females when only a week old give birth to live young, so colonies can build up rapidly.

Susceptible plants Most plants may be attacked by aphids. Many aphid species are plant-specific, such as the lupine aphid, while others, such as the peach potato aphid, will attack hundreds of different types of plants. Aphids may spend the summer on certain plants, moving to a different host species for the winter.

Symptoms Tender young growth is most prone to attack, but aphids will also colonize leaves, stems, and, in some cases, roots. Leaves and shoots become distorted. Heavy infestation can kill a plant. Leaves are often coated with honeydew, a sticky substance produced by aphids. Black sooty molds (q.v.) grow on the honeydew, inhibiting photosynthesis and spoiling appearance. Root aphids can cause plants to wilt. Aphids also transmit viruses.

What to do Tolerate aphid colonies where they are not causing damage. They will act as a "nursery" for aphid predators and parasites to feed and breed on. To control aphids, rub them off or pick off infested shoots. Grow attractant flowers and create suitable habitats for birds, earwigs, lady beetles, hoverflies, spiders, ground beetles, parasitic wasps, lacewings, and other aphid enemies. Allow these predators time to work. Do not overfeed plants with nitrogen; soft, sappy growth is a magnet to aphids. Keep containers adequately fed and watered, and repot plants as necessary. Use crop rotation to avoid buildup of root aphids. Grow resistant cultivars. Biological controls: Lady beetle adults and larvae and lacewing larvae can be purchased for release into the garden from May to August to augment the natural populations. Pesticides: Insecticidal soap; pyrethrum; plant oils and starch-based products. All of these must hit the aphids to work. Once leaf-curling conceals the pests, a spray is unlikely to be effective. *See also* Cabbage aphid; Lettuce root aphid; Woolly aphid.

Apple maggot

Adult apple maggots are $\frac{1}{4}$-in (6-mm) flies with yellow legs and transparent wings with dark crossbands. They lay eggs beneath the skin of the fruit and the larvae tunnel within. Larvae are white, $\frac{1}{4}$-in (6-mm) maggots in fruit.

Susceptible plants Apples, blueberries, plums. A similar pest affects cherries.

Symptoms Maggots tunnel through fruit, which drops prematurely.

What to do Grow late-maturing cultivars. Collect and destroy dropped fruit daily until September, then twice a month starting in the fall. Hang apple maggot traps from mid-June until harvest. Plant white clover as ground cover to attract beetles that prey on the apple maggot pupae.

Apple powdery mildew

Fungal disease that overwinters in buds. Infected buds open later than healthy ones. *See also* Powdery mildews.

Susceptible plants Apple; also pear, quince, peach, *Photinia*, and medlar.

Symptoms A powdery white coating on buds, leaves, and stems. Flowers drop; leaves distort, wither, and fall. Early infections cause weblike russeting on fruit.

What to do Grow resistant cultivars. Mulch under trees to stop soil from drying out. Water trees in dry weather. In winter, cut out infected shoots. In spring, remove infected leaves and shoots. Spray with seaweed extract to promote strong growth. Fungicide spray: Sulfur, although it can harm some apples. Check the label before use.

Apple scab

This fungal disease overwinters in leaf debris, and in severe cases in twig lesions, and is spread to new leaves in spring by wind and rain. Apple scab is worse when the weather is cool, wet, or overcast in spring and early summer, especially at flowering time.

Susceptible plants Apple.

Symptoms Dark brown/green blotches develop on the leaves; these may expand along the veins and run into each other. Leaves may drop prematurely. Dark spots, which develop into corky patches, appear on the fruit skin. Fruit may crack, but does not rot. In severe cases, twigs blister, swell, and burst to produce brown-green pustules in spring.

What to do Grow resistant apples such as 'Ellison's Orange' and 'Court Pendu Plat'. Mow the ground below trees to shred leaves and speed decomposition, or collect leaves and compost them. Cut out and burn diseased twigs. Prune apple trees to maintain good air circulation.

Asparagus beetle

The adult beetles are up to ¼ in (6 mm) long, with distinctive yellow and black wing cases. Larvae are gray-black with a humped back. Adults hibernate under stones, in soil, and in plant debris, emerging in spring to feed on asparagus foliage. Eggs are laid in June. There may be two or three generations in a year.

Susceptible plants Asparagus.

Symptoms Foliage eaten. Growth may be checked.

What to do Pick off larvae and adults. Clear plant debris where beetles may overwinter. Pesticide: Derris.

Bacterial canker

In fall and winter, canker bacteria, spread by rain-splash from the leaves, enter twigs through leaf scars to cause canker lesions. In spring and summer the foliage is attacked, but no new cankers are formed.

Susceptible plants Plum and cherry.

Symptoms Dark brown spots on leaves in the late spring. These drop out leaving a "shot hole" appearance. Cankers usually occur on plum tree trunks and cherry branches. Initially, amber-colored gum exudes from a slight depression. Leaves become yellow and stems die back.

What to do Not an easy disease to control. There are no fully resistant cultivars, but the plums 'Marjorie's Seedling' and 'Warwickshire Drooper' are rarely badly affected, while 'Victoria' and 'Early Laxton' are very susceptible. Try to avoid damaging the tree bark. Make sure trunks will not rub on any supporting stake, and take care when cutting surrounding grass.

Bacterial soft rot

A common disease caused by soil-dwelling bacteria. It does not appear to survive in the soil, but can survive on plant debris. Infection enters through wounds such as those caused by slugs or carrot rust fly.

Susceptible plants Brassicas, especially turnip and rutabaga; also celery, cucurbits, leek, lettuce, onion, parsnip, potato, tomato, and cyclamen.

Symptoms Water-soaked lesions around a wound that rapidly enlarges. The infected stem, leaf base, or storage organ disintegrates into a foul-smelling, slimy, brownish rotting mass. The skin of most storage organs is not affected, although cracks may appear through which the slimy interior may seep.

What to do Ensure that land is well-drained. When growing vegetables, use a strict crop rotation. Control wound-forming pests like wireworms, slugs, and root-damaging larvae. Once rot has started, there is no cure. Dispose of or bury infected plant material.

Beet leaf spot

This fungal disease overwinters in residue from diseased plants or on seed. It is spread by rain-splash, wind, insects, tools, and by hand. High humidity and warm temperatures encourage it.

Susceptible plants Red beet, spinach beet; also sugar beet.

Symptoms Small, more or less circular spots with a pale ashen center and brown-purple margins on leaves.

What to do Clear up crop debris; use fresh seed. Damage is rarely significant.

Black bean aphid

Small, black winged aphids, forming dense colonies. *See also* Aphids.

Susceptible plants Beans, leaf beet and chard, poppy, nasturtium, and other ornamentals. Winter hosts: euonymus (spindle), philadelphus, and viburnum.

Symptoms *See* Aphids.

What to do Earlier sowings of fava beans are less susceptible to attack. Pinch out tips of fava bean plants in May or early June, or when pests are seen. Remove heavily infested plants. *See also* Aphids.

Black knot

This fungal disease appears as a cancerous black or greenish growth on stems. Wild plum and cherry trees can be a source of infection.

Susceptible plants Cherries and plums.

Symptoms Black knot appears as unsightly swellings on twigs and branches. These swellings are usually black, but they may appear velvety green in early spring. Tips of infected branches often die back. Severe infections can kill whole limbs, and the tree may be stunted.

What to do Look for resistant cultivars. In fall or late winter, prune off infected limbs, 6–12 in. (15–30 cm) below the knots; disinfect pruners in between cuts with a 10% bleach solution (1 part bleach to 9 parts water). Destroy the prunings. Remove any wild plum or cherry trees nearby. For persistent infections, apply 2 sprays of lime-sulfur, 7 days apart, before the buds begin to grow in spring.

Black vine weevil

Adults are wingless, dull dark brown-black, about ⅜ in (9 mm) long, covered in small buff-yellow specks. They emerge in May and June, feeding by night. Virtually all are female and each lays hundreds of eggs in soil or potting mix around host plants from late July. The larvae are a characteristic creamy-white "C" shape with a brown head and can be up to ½ in (1 cm) long. They feed on plant roots until the following spring, when they pupate in the soil. Most adults die at the end of the season, but some survive winter. In the warmth of a house or greenhouse, adults may emerge in fall, and eggs will be laid over a longer period. *See also* Weevils.

Susceptible plants A wide range of plants—especially those in pots—in the garden, greenhouse, and house.

Symptoms Adult weevils eat irregular holes around the edges of leaves. This damage is more cosmetic than life-threatening. Larvae are the main problem as they feed on plant roots. If a plant is growing poorly, even with no leaves eaten, or suddenly wilts and dies, check in and around the root ball for larvae.

What to do Inspect plants regularly for adult weevils, especially at night. Inspect new plants for adults and larvae before planting out. Protect pots with sticky tape smeared with nondrying glue. Check regularly that barriers have not been breached. Biological control: Outdoors and under cover, use *Heterorhabditis megidis*, a parasitic nematode; minimum soil temperature 40°F (5°C). Under cover it may be used year-round as long as soil temperatures are adequate. Outside, it is best applied in April/May, and August/early September.

Boxwood psylla

This insect lays its eggs in late summer in slits in leaf axils and twigs. They hatch in mid-spring. Nymphs (the young) feed on growing points and young shoots from late spring onward.

Susceptible plants Boxwood.

Symptoms The leaves at the tip of infected shoots arch inward to form tight cabbagelike clusters. Growth can be checked if infestation is severe. Sticky honeydew and black sooty molds may be present.

What to do Control is only necessary on young plants if they become stunted. Clip regularly, particularly in early spring, to remove infested shoot tips.

Brassica white rust

Fungal disease spread by wind, insects, and rain-splash. It overwinters in the soil.

Susceptible plants Vegetable and ornamental brassicas.

Symptoms Small, smooth white blotches resembling paint spots on leaves and stems later become powdery. Distortion of affected areas or the entire plant follows.

What to do Destroy diseased plants. Use a strict crop rotation.

Brown rot

Airborne fungal disease that infects plants through wounded bark. Caterpillars, birds, chafing stakes, or hailstones can cause the initial damage. It spreads quickly throughout the plant and cankers may develop. The fungus overwinters on infected fruit and cankers.

Susceptible plants Apple, peach, almond, nectarine, cherry, quince, plum, and pear.

Symptoms A very common fungal problem that produces soft, brown patches on fruit. Concentric circles of white fluffy growth also develop on these areas while fruit is on the tree or in storage. Fruit may turn black. Some fruit on the tree will shrivel, become mummified, and remain attached throughout the winter.

What to do Prune out affected branches and remove fruit from the tree. Pick up windfalls. Do not compost any of this material. Take care not to damage fruit that is to be stored. Do not store any diseased fruit. Prune out cankers and diseased spurs.

Cabbage aphid

Adults of this pest are gray-green in color and are covered in a powdery white, mealy wax. Overwintering eggs, laid on stems and leaves of brassicas, hatch in spring. Infestations occur from midsummer onward, reaching a peak in early to mid-fall. *See also* Aphids.

Susceptible plants Brassicas.

Symptoms Dense colonies cause distortion and discoloration of leaves. A severe infestation can deter growth and can kill shoot tips and young plants.

What to do Remove overwintering brassica plants as soon as they have finished cropping. This should be done by mid-spring. Bury plant debris deep in a compost pile, or in a compost trench. Examine young plants regularly from early summer to fall and squash any colonies of eggs or young. Pesticides: Insecticidal soap; pyrethrum; plant oils and starch-based sprays.

Cabbage caterpillars

There are two butterfly caterpillars that are pests of cabbages. The cabbage white or large white butterfly is creamy white, with a broad black tip to the forewing, and appears in April and May. Clusters of bright orange eggs are laid on and under leaves. The distinctive yellow and black caterpillars, often found in large clusters (*see p.237*), grow up to 2 in (5 cm) long, and feed for a month or so. There are two or three generations a year. The spring brood of the small cabbage white butterfly is white, with clouded, black tips on its forewings. The summer brood has darker tips and black markings on the wings. Eggs are laid singly, under leaves. Caterpillars, up to 1½ in (3.5 cm) long, are velvety green, making them hard to spot, especially when lying along the vein of a leaf. They are often found feeding in the heart of a plant. There can be three generations in a year, with the severest attacks in late summer.

Susceptible plants Brassicas; large whites may also attack nasturtiums.

Symptoms Foliage eaten. A plant may be quickly stripped to a skeleton.

What to do Examine plants regularly when the butterflies have been seen. Squash eggs, pick off caterpillars. Wasps are particularly effective at controlling this pest. Grow crops under fine mesh to exclude the butterflies. Biological control: Spray *Bacillus thuringiensis* (Bt) on infested plants (this is only available in large "commercial grower" packs).

Cabbage looper

Adults are gray moths with a silver spot in the middle of each forewing. They emerge from overwintering pupae in May and lay light green, dome-shaped eggs on the undersides of leaves. The larvae are green, 1½-in (4-cm) caterpillars with two white lines down their backs, one along each side. They feed for 2 to 4 weeks, then pupate 10 days in cocoons attached to stems or leaves. There are three to four generations per year.

Susceptible plants Brassicas (cabbage, cauliflower, and broccoli, for example), as well as many other vegetable crops.

Symptoms Larvae chew large holes in leaves and may destroy whole plants.

What to do Hand-pick larvae several times weekly and drop them into soapy water. Till crop residues into the soil before adults emerge in spring. Attract native parasitic wasps by planting pollen- and nectar-rich flowers.

Cabbage root fly

Adults of this flying insect are ¼ in (6 mm) long and resemble small horseflies. They lay eggs in soil near, or occasionally on, host plants. The legless white larvae feed on roots. Damage is usually worse in late spring and early summer, but a second and even third generation may continue to damage plants into fall. Plants raised in pots and cells are also prone to attack.

Susceptible plants Brassicas; related plants such as wallflowers and stocks.

Symptoms Young plants wilt or grow poorly, and are easily pulled out of the ground. Established plants may show no obvious symptoms. Damage to root crops (radish, turnip, rutabaga) may make them inedible. Larvae occasionally found inside Brussels sprouts.

What to do Cover with fleece or fine mesh netting immediately after sowing or planting. Or protect individual plants with a cabbage root fly mat (see p.236). Plant into a slight hollow; in the event of an attack, earth up to encourage new root growth. Intercrop with string beans or dwarf fava beans.

Capsid bugs

Small, active, sap-feeding winged creatures, up to ¼ in (6 mm) long. Nymphs (the young) are similar to adults but without wings. Color varies with species. These creatures are rarely seen as they quickly drop to the ground or fly away when disturbed.

Susceptible plants A wide range, including runner bean, black and red currant, apple, chrysanthemum, dahlia, fuchsia, and rose.

Symptoms Most capsid species feed on plants, causing small ragged holes in leaves, particularly at shoot tips. The damage is distinctive. Leaves develop a tattered appearance as they grow. Buds and shoots may be killed; flowers and fruit deformed. Apple fruits develop raised bumps and scabby patches. Some capsids are useful predators of small pests, particularly on fruit.

What to do Encourage birds to feed around infested shrubs and trees in winter by hanging fat and bags of nuts from branches. If damage is extensive, tidy up under hedges over winter, raking out leaf litter and clearing away any plant debris. Control is not always easy as adults are elusive, but damage is not usually severe.

Carrot rust fly

Small, shiny black flies lay eggs in small clusters near host plants, starting in late spring. The larvae are creamy-white, up to ½ in (1 cm) long. Pupae, and sometimes larvae, overwinter in soil and roots of carrot and parsnip. There are two or three generations per year, the first causing most damage.

Susceptible plants Primarily a severe pest of carrots. Also attacks celery, chervil, parsley, and parsnip.

Symptoms Young seedlings can be killed. The first sign of attack on mature plants is often a reddening of the foliage and stunted growth. The roots have rusty-brown irregular tunnels eaten away just below the skin. Larvae may be visible.

What to do Avoid growing carrots in sheltered sites, favored by these weak flyers. Delay sowing until June to avoid first-generation attack. Harvest crops by late fall. Some carrots such as 'Sytan' and 'Flyaway' are said to be less susceptible; 'Autumn King' types tend to be very susceptible. Sow seed thinly to avoid the need for thinning; the fly can be attracted by the smell of pinched foliage. If thinning is necessary, remove all thinnings immediately and water to consolidate the soil. Grow one row of carrots between four rows of onions to mask the smell of carrots. This is only effective before the onions begin to form bulbs in early to midsummer, and may not be effective on a small scale. Carrots may be grown to maturity under horticultural fleece or fine mesh netting; or, erect a "fence" of fine mesh netting around them, at least 30 in (75 cm) high. Dig over soil in winter where damage has occurred, to expose overwintering larvae.

Caterpillars

Caterpillars are the larvae of butterflies and moths. Their soft bodies are segmented. The first three segments behind the head carry a pair of jointed legs, making up the thorax, while the remaining ten segments make up the abdomen, which may have up to five pairs of fleshy legs. Sawfly larvae, similar in appearance but not related, have at least six pairs of legs on the abdominal segments. *See* Cabbage caterpillars; Codling moth; Cutworm; Winter moths. *See also* Sawflies, for comparison.

Cedar-apple rust

Cedar-apple rust completes its life cycle only where the fungal spores can travel back and forth between cedar and apple trees. Spores from cedar trees send spores to infect apple trees, but infections on the apple tree do not spread within the tree; they can only send the disease back to infect cedar.

Susceptible plants Eastern red cedars and other species of junipers; apples and crab apples.

Symptoms On cedars, hard, brown swellings appear on branch tips. These galls do not seriously damage cedar trees, but they can mar the plants' appearance. Warm, moist weather in spring causes these galls to swell dramatically, and they produce gelatinous horns that release rust-colored spores. The spores then infect apple trees. The symptoms on apples show up in spring as tiny yellow spots, which later expand and turn orange. These spots form on upper leaf surfaces and on fruit. Brown spots may appear on the undersides of leaves.

What to do Rust fungi need moisture, so promote drying through pruning for good air circulation around the branches and by selecting an airy planting site. Prune off and destroy galls on cedar before late winter. Plant apple trees only if cedar trees are at least 4 miles (6.5 km) away; this will reduce the chance of the disease spreading. If you want to grow both cedars and apple trees, choose rust-resistant species and cultivars of these plants. Many fungicides, including sulfur and lime-sulfur, that are effective against other fungal diseases are not very effective against rust diseases.

Chrysanthemum leaf miner

Small inconspicuous dark flies lay up to 100 eggs in small incisions in leaves during summer months, from which larvae hatch and feed within the leaves. In heated greenhouses, breeding continues for most of the year.

Susceptible plants Chrysanthemum, cineraria, calendula, lettuce, groundsel, sow-thistle, and other members of the Asteraceae family, indoors and outside.

Symptoms First symptoms are a white spotting of leaves caused by the feeding of adult females. Narrow white tunnels appear between the upper and lower leaf surface. These later widen and meander toward the leaf midrib. After 2–3 weeks, small dark bumps can be seen on the lower leaf surface.

What to do Examine plants regularly. Pick off and destroy infected leaves. Control weeds, especially groundsel and thistle, as these can support the pest.

Clematis wilt

This fungal disease originates from the soil or other clematis plants. It is thought infection occurs in conditions of high humidity. Infection enters through small wounds caused, for example, by birds, insects, or bruising by plant ties.

Susceptible plants Clematis.

Symptoms Sudden drooping of young growth. Affected leaves next to the stalks blacken, then wither and die. Dark lesions may be seen on the stem at or near ground level. Patchy blackening can occur on otherwise healthy leaves. Large-flowered hybrids are most susceptible, especially those with *Clematis lanuginosa* in their parentage.

What to do Plant clematis 6 in (15 cm) deeper than originally grown. *Clematis viticella* cultivars are said to be much less susceptible. Avoid mechanical damage to stems, e.g., when securing stems with ties. Cut back infected growth to soil level or below. New healthy growth should emerge from below ground. If symptoms recur, remove the soil to a depth of 12 in (30 cm) and destroy the infected plant. Replace with fresh soil and replant.

Clubroot

This soilborne fungal disease can survive in the soil for up to 20 years in the absence of a suitable host. Clubroot thrives in damp, acidic conditions. It is less of a problem in alkaline soils, in hot dry seasons, and in spring-maturing crops. The disease is spread on infected plant material and contaminated soil. It is easily spread on tools, machinery, footwear, and infected transplants, which may not show symptoms.

Susceptible plants Brassicas; wallflower, stocks, and candytuft.

Symptoms Plants wilt on hot sunny days but may recover at night; they may become stunted and develop red leaf tints. Roots develop swollen galls—either a single large gall, known as "clubroot," or several smaller swellings, known as "fingers and toes." Plant growth and yields are severely reduced.

What to do This disease is very difficult to control, so avoidance is very important. Buy plants from a reliable source, or raise your own. Build up good soil structure and improve drainage. Lime acidic soils (*see p.55*). Where clubroot is present, liming to a pH of at least 7 may help. Remove all infected roots from the soil as soon as possible, preferably before the galls disintegrate; do not put on the compost pile. Earth up crops that have been attacked with fresh potting mix to encourage new healthy roots. If clubroot is in your soil, raise plants in pots using disease-free potting mix. Grow brassicas that show resistance, such as rutabaga 'Marian', kale 'Tall Green Curled', Chinese cabbage 'Harmony', calabrese 'Trixie', and others.

Codling moth

The adult moth, 3/8 in (8 mm) long, mottled gray-brown in color, lays its eggs on fruits and leaves in early and midsummer. Single caterpillars tunnel into a fruit, often through the eye, leaving no obvious signs. The caterpillar, pinkish-white with a black or brown head, grows to 3/4 in (2 cm) in length, as it eats its way to the core of the fruit. After a month or so it leaves the fruit, to pupate under loose bark, tree ties, and similar locations. In a hot summer there may be two generations.

Susceptible plants Apple; less frequently, pear and quince.

Symptoms Caterpillars cause extensive tunnels through fruit, spoiling it. Damaged fruit may ripen and drop prematurely. *See also* Apple sawfly.

What to do Hang sticky pheromone traps in trees from mid-May to the end of July, or early September in a hot year. Traps alone may reduce damage on isolated trees—or can be used to monitor the presence of the moth, so a spray can be timed accurately, before the caterpillars move into the safety of the fruit. Earwigs and some birds are predators. Pesticide: Derris may be used; however; spraying is rarely satisfactory because you have to hit the caterpillars directly, during the brief period between hatching and burrowing into the apple. As eggs hatch over a period of time, there is no best time to carry out the spraying.

Colorado potato beetle

Adults are yellowish orange, 3/8-in (8-mm) beetles with 10 lengthwise black stripes on the wing covers and black spots on the thorax. Over-wintering adults emerge from the soil in spring to feed on young plants. After feeding, females lay up to 1,000 eggs during their several-month life span. The eggs are bright yellow ovals, standing on end in clusters on the undersides of leaves. They hatch in 4 to 9 days. The dark orange, humpbacked grubs feed for 2 to 3 weeks, then pupate in the soil. Adults emerge in 5 to 10 days. There are two generations a year in most areas, three generations in southern areas.

Susceptible plants Potatoes, tomatoes, eggplants, and related plants, including petunias.

Symptoms Adults and larvae chew holes in foliage. Their feeding can kill small plants and reduces the yields of mature plants.

What to do When overwintering adults begin to emerge, shake adults from plants onto a dropcloth in the early morning. Dump the beetles into soapy water. Attract native predators and parasites by planting pollen- and nectar-rich flowers. Mulch plants with a deep straw layer. Cover plants with row cover or mesh until midsummer. Release two to five spined soldier bugs per square yard (sq m) of plants. Release *Edovum puttleri* in southern areas to attack second-generation larvae. Apply parasitic nematodes to the soil to attack the larvae as they prepare to pupate. Apply double-strength sprays of *Bacillus thuringiensis* var. *san diego* (B.T.S.D.) on larvae. As a last resort, spray weekly with pyrethrin or neem.

Corn earworm

Adults are tan moths that emerge in early spring, migrating long distances to find food, if necessary. Females lay white, ribbed, and round eggs on leaves or in the tips of corn ears. Eggs hatch in 3 days. The larvae are 1–2 in. (2.5–5 cm) long, light yellow, green, pink, or brown caterpillars, with yellow heads and black legs, and white and dark stripes along their sides. The larvae feed for 2 to 4 weeks, then pupate in the soil. Adults emerge in 10 to 25 days. There are one to four generations per year.

Susceptible plants Corn and tomatoes are the main targets, but the larvae will also feed on a broad range of vegetable crops, fruits, and flowers.

Symptoms On corn, the larvae feed on fresh silks, then move down the ears, eating kernels and leaving trails of excrement as they go. Early and late cultivars are most affected. On tomatoes (where the larvae are called tomato fruitworms), the larvae burrow into ripe fruits, eat buds, and chew large holes in leaves.

What to do Plant corn cultivars with tight husks to prevent larvae from entering, or open the husk ends and dig out any larvae in the tip before they damage the main ear. Squirt mineral oil on the tips of the ears. Attract native parasitic wasps and predatory bugs. After corn silks start to dry, spray *Bacillus thuringiensis* var. *kurstaki* (B.T.K.) into the tips of the ears, or apply granular B.T.K. Spray B.T.K. on leaves and fruit of plants where fruitworms are feeding. Squirt parasitic nematodes into tips of corn ears. Release lacewings or minute pirate bugs. Paint pyrethrin-and-molasses bait (3 parts spray solution to 1 part molasses) around the base of plants to kill adults as they start to emerge.

Cucumber beetles

Spotted cucumber beetles are greenish yellow, 1½-in (6-mm) beetles with 11 black spots on their wing covers. Overwintering adults emerge from under crop residues in spring and lay eggs in the soil close to plants. Their larvae, also known as southern corn rootworms, are white grubs with brown heads and brown patches on the first and last segments. They feed for 2 to 4 weeks, then pupate. There are one or two generations per year in northern areas, three in southern areas. Striped cucumber beetles are a similar size but have black heads and three wide black stripes on their wing covers. They emerge in April to early June, eat weed pollen for 2 weeks, then lay eggs in the soil at the base of plants. The eggs hatch in 10 days. The larvae—slender white maggots—feed on roots for several weeks, then pupate in early August. Adults emerge in 2 weeks to feed on blossoms and fruit. There are one or two generations per year. The larvae and adults of both species can transmit cucumber mosaic virus and bacterial wilt as they feed.

Susceptible plants Squash-family plants, sweet corn, other vegetable crops, and flowers.

Symptoms Southern corn rootworms feed on corn roots, often killing young plants and weakening older ones. Striped cucumber beetle larvae feed on the roots of squash-family plants only, killing or stunting the plants. Adults of both species feed on leaves, stems, flowers, and fruit of squashes and other crops.

What to do Remove and destroy crop residues where adults overwinter. Rotate garden crops with green manures such as alfalfa. Cover seedlings and plants with row cover or mesh, hand-pollinating squash-family plants. Apply parasitic nematodes to the soil weekly to control larvae. As a last resort, spray adults with pyrethrin.

Cucumber mosaic virus

Viral disease spread primarily by aphids; it may also be spread by handling diseased plants, and on tools. Infection usually occurs when plants are about six weeks old. *See also* Viruses.

Susceptible plants Cucumber, melon, zucchini, celery, beans, and peppers. Ornamentals include anemone, dahlia, aquilegia, campanula, lily, and primula.

Symptoms These vary from plant to plant. In cucurbits, the virus causes mottling or mosaic patterns (*see p.89*) and distortion on the leaves. Flowering is reduced; plants are stunted and may die. Fruits will be small, dark, and pitted, and may develop bright yellow blotches.

What to do Grow resistant cultivars. Remove infected plants as soon as symptoms are seen. There is no cure.

Cutworm

Various nocturnal moth caterpillars are called cutworms. Soil-living larvae, they tend to be fat when fully grown, and will curl up in a "C" shape when disturbed. They may be brown, yellow, or green with dark markings. Cutworms feed at night, and can be found at almost any time of year, both outdoors and in the greenhouse.

Susceptible plants Young vegetable plants, especially lettuce and brassicas; also carrot, celery, beet, potato, strawberry, and many ornamentals.

Symptoms Stems of seedlings and young plants eaten through at ground level. Roots, corms, tubers, and leaves may also be damaged.

What to do Cultivate infested soil in winter to expose cutworms to birds, or allow chickens to scratch it over. Keep ground weed-free, as weeds provide sites for egg-laying. On a small scale, locate caterpillars in soil, or feeding on plants at night, and destroy. Protect susceptible transplants with a collar— such as a cardboard or plastic tube, or a tin can with the base removed—pushed down into the soil around the plant.

Cytospora canker

Also known as valsa or leucostoma canker, this fungal disease can be a serious problem on trees.

Susceptible plants A wide range of woody plants are vulnerable. Some of the most susceptible trees include stone fruits (such as peaches and plums), apples, pears, spruces, maples, poplars, and willows.

Symptoms New shoots turn yellow, wilt, and die back. The inner bark on infected twigs may show black or reddish brown discoloration. Gummy cankers form on trunks and branches and increase in size until they girdle and kill the affected part.

What to do Plant resistant cultivars when available. Vigorously growing trees are less susceptible to this disease. Prune out infected branches during dry weather; disinfect your pruners between cuts. Avoid making unnecessary wounds in the bark, which can provide an entry for the fungus. On stone fruits, it is particularly important to avoid winter damage, which can be caused by fertilizing the trees late in the season.

Damping off

A range of troublesome soil-dwelling fungal diseases. Some survive on decaying plant debris, others exist as spores in the soil. They multiply rapidly in cool, wet, poorly ventilated situations.

Susceptible plants Seeds, seedlings, cuttings, roots, and vegetable parts at or below soil level, such as carrot and celery. Will spread rapidly through trays of seedlings, such as bedding plants.

Symptoms Seeds fail to germinate. Seedlings are attacked at soil level or below; stems become water-soaked, blackened, and thin. Seedlings collapse and die. Reddish-brown root lesions form on seedlings and mature plants, initially just below the soil surface. Rootlets of older plants die. Vegetables such as potatoes, cucurbits, and beans may become infected during extended wet periods. This results in a cottony fungal growth, followed by the disintegration of the vegetable interior into a soft watery mass. May also cause brown patches on lawns.

What to do Scrub pots and trays clean before sowing seed or taking cuttings. Use a sterile medium for seed-sowing. Ensure good drainage—waterlogged plants are more prone to attack. Do not overcrowd seedlings, cuttings, or older plants—good ventilation is essential to reduce humidity, which tends to encourage disease. Sow when soil has warmed up well in the spring. This will encourage plants to grow quickly and without setbacks.

Downy mildew

Disease caused by a range of related fungi that attack specific plants, or groups of plants. These fungi survive in the soil, in crop debris, and on infected plants, not all of which show symptoms.

Susceptible plants Many plants, including lettuce, pansy, nicotiana, onion, brassicas, peas, and wallflowers.

Symptoms Yellow patches on upper leaf surfaces, with corresponding patches of mold beneath in damp weather. Large areas of a leaf may be infected and the leaf may die. Onions rot in store. Most common in damp and humid growing situations.

What to do Grow resistant lettuces such as 'Saladin' or 'Avoncrisp'. Remove infected leaves; if it continues, remove and destroy all infected plants. Use a five-year rotation for vegetables and susceptible ornamentals. *See also* Onion downy mildew.

Earwigs

The earwig can be a pest in some situations, but it is also a useful predator, particularly of apple pests such as codling moth and aphids. Earwigs lay eggs in the soil in late winter, which hatch in early spring. There may be a second generation.

Susceptible plants Dahlia, clematis, chrysanthemum, delphinium, and other flowers.

Symptoms Young shoots and flowers are eaten, leaving ragged holes. Earwigs found in cavities in damaged tree fruits have not usually initiated the damage.

What to do Earwigs do not usually travel far, so clearing up debris where they might hide, and trapping, can make a local difference. Trap earwigs in overturned flower pots stuffed with straw and placed on top of a cane, or in lengths of dry fava bean stalk, or in a "lacewing hotel" (*see pp.112–113*). Shake traps into a bucket of soapy water to kill the earwigs, or liberate them on fruit trees.

European corn borer

Adult females are pale yellowish brown moths with darker zigzag patterns across their wings; males are darker-colored. The adults emerge in early June and lay white eggs in late June to mid-July, in masses of 15 to 20 on the undersides of leaves. The eggs hatch after 1 week into beige, brown-spotted caterpillars up to 1 in (2.5 cm) long. They feed for 3 to 4 weeks. At the end of the season, the larvae overwinter in plant residue and pupate in early spring. There are one to three generations per year.

Susceptible plants Any vegetable crops.

Symptoms Young larvae feed on corn leaves and tassels and beneath husks, damaging the ears. Older larvae burrow in corn stalks and ears; damaged stalks may break. Larvae also tunnel in the stems or pods of beans, onions, peppers, potatoes, tomatoes, and other crops.

What to do Plant resistant corn cultivars, and rotate crops. Remove tassels from two-thirds of corn plants before they begin to shed pollen. Pull out and destroy all infested crop residue

immediately after harvest. Attract native parasites by planting flowers between corn rows. Biological controls: Spray *Bacillus thuringiensis* var. *kurstaki* (B.T.K.) on the undersides of leaves and into the tips of the ears, or sprinkle the granular form into ear tips. For severe Infestations, spray pyrethrin when larvae begin feeding.

European red mite

Tiny, sap-sucking creatures, oval in shape. Their tiny, round, red-brown eggs overwinter on host plants in clusters and hatch from April to June. There may be six generations in a season.

Susceptible plants Apple and plum; also cotoneaster, damson, hawthorn, pear, and rowan.

Symptoms Leaves become speckled and dull green, then bronze, and may fall prematurely. Severe attacks in June or July can reduce fruit bud formation.

What to do Encourage natural predators. Do not overfeed plants. Pesticides: Insecticidal soap; plant oils.

Fava bean chocolate spot

This fungal disease thrives in damp and overcrowded conditions. Spores can overwinter on infected plants and plant debris. The disease is more likely to be a problem where soil lacks potassium.

Susceptible plants Fava beans; rarely, peas.

Symptoms Round, chocolate-brown spots on leaves, stems, pods, and seed coats. These may merge until totally blackened parts of the plant die.

What to do Space plants out well. Grow in well-drained soil. Avoid fall sowing if this disease is a regular problem. Spring-sown beans are more likely to recover than plants infected later in the season. Improve potassium levels if low.

Fireblight

Don't confuse this bacterial disease with sooty mold, a relatively harmless, black leaf fungus that rubs off easily. Fireblight bacteria enter the tree at the growing tips. They may travel down toward the roots and kill the whole tree.

Susceptible plants Many plants in the rose family, especially pears, apples, and quinces.

Symptoms Flowers usually show symptoms first, turning brown and then shriveling. Leaves turn brown or black, and the dead leaves cling to the twigs. Symptoms progress from the tips of the shoots toward the roots. Shoot tips turn black, wilt, and curl downward. Fruit on affected shoots turns black and may cling to the tree. As the growing season progresses, firelight bacteria grow within the blighted shoots, down branches, and toward the roots. During fall, the bacteria form a sunken, dark canker in which to overwinter.

What to do Plant resistant cultivars, or choose fruit trees grafted onto blight-resistant rootstocks. Do not prune susceptible woody plants too severely or overfeed them because both of these practices encourage succulent, disease-susceptible growth. To further discourage succulent growth on mature trees, grow grass right up to the trunk; if needed, also allow the grass to grow longer than normal. Prune out infected branches, along with 6–12 in (15–30 cm) of healthy tissue. Disinfect pruners between cuts by dipping them in a 10% bleach solution (1 part bleach to 9 parts water). Spray with Bordeaux mix during dormancy.

Flea beetle

Tiny shiny black beetles that jump when disturbed. They hibernate in mulch and plant debris. Feeding starts in spring. Eggs are laid in soil near susceptible plants in late spring and early summer. There is one generation a year.

Susceptible plants Brassicas, particularly as seedlings. Also ornamentals such as nasturtium, alyssum, anemone, and godetia.

Symptoms During spring and summer, the beetles eat small holes in leaves and stems. A severe attack will check growth and kill young plants. Damage is always worse in dry weather. Larvae feed on plant roots, or in leaf mines.

What to do Encourage quick, vigorous seedling growth. Sow seeds at the right time, prepare the site well, and never let plants go short of water. Sow under fleece or ultra-fine mesh. Some crops can be uncovered once established; Chinese cabbage, radish, and arugula may need to be covered until harvest time.

Froghopper

Also called the "spittlebug," this sap-feeding pest may be yellow to greeny-brown. It grows up to ¼ in (6 mm) long, with a blunt, wedgelike appearance and large eyes. Adults jump when disturbed. Young nymphs on plant stems protect themselves with froth, or "cuckoo spit."

Susceptible plants Many, but especially roses and rosemary.

Symptoms Young shoots may become distorted and wilt. Flowers may be damaged. The white "cuckoo spit" if extensive may be disfiguring.

What to do Damage is rarely a problem. Spittle and nymphs can be hosed off if necessary.

Frost damage

Tender plants are the most susceptible to this disorder. Normally hardy plants can also be damaged if a hard frost follows warm weather that has encouraged new growth, or if a frost occurs in the summer. Plants that receive early morning sun, which melts the frost rapidly, are also vulnerable.

Symptoms Overnight, flowers and buds become discolored, usually brown. Frosted blooms may not produce fruit. Leaves and stems turn brown or black; young growth toward the outside of the plant will be most affected. Apple skins may be russeted, usually at the flowering end of the fruit opposite the stalk. Damage may not be noticed until the fruit has developed.

What to do Protect susceptible plants with fleece, newspaper, or other cover during risk periods. Harden off plants before planting out. Keep tender plants indoors until risk of frost is past. Avoid planting susceptible plants in frost pockets, or where they will receive the early morning sun.

Fungus gnat

Also known as mushroom fly and sciarid fly. Adult flies—dark brown, midgelike, up to ⅛ in (4 mm) long—are found on the surface of moist potting mix, running quickly and vibrating their wings. They fly up when disturbed. Eggs are laid in the potting mix. Transparent white larvae, up to ½ in (1 cm) long with shiny black or brown heads, hatch a week later. They feed on plant roots. The whole life cycle can be completed within four weeks, and breeding can continue year-round, at a temperature of 68°F (20°C).

Susceptible plants Potted plants under cover; also mushrooms. Seedlings, cuttings, and young plants are most at risk.

Symptoms Seedlings and young plants may collapse and die. Mature plants grow poorly where infestation is high. Plants in soilless potting mix are more susceptible.

What to do Always water from below, and keep watering to a minimum without allowing plants to dry out. Pot up plants as necessary, using a loam-based potting mix. Cover the soil surface with a ½-in (1-cm) layer of sand or grit to discourage infestation. Yellow sticky traps and insectivorous plants, such as Mexican butterwort, will trap flying adults. Check new plants for fungus gnat before introducing into the house or greenhouse. Dispose of badly infested plants. Biological controls: Use the predatory mite *Hypoaspis miles* at temperatures above 52°F (11°C). *Steinernema feltiae*, a parasitic nematode, needs moist soil and a lower minimum temperature, 57°F (14°C).

Gray mold

This fungus survives on plant debris and in the soil. Spores are spread by air currents, and rain or water splash. Infection is usually through a wound.

Susceptible plants Most living or dead plant material.

Symptoms Fluffy, grayish-white mold on infected areas (*see p.89*). Where stems are infected, growth above the infection will yellow and wilt. Flowers—for example, of strawberries—may be infected, but symptoms may not show until the fruits start to ripen.

What to do Maintain good general hygiene. Remove dead and dying plants, or plant parts, as soon as infection is noticed. Ensure good ventilation around plants. *See also* Peony blight; Lettuce gray mold; Onion neck rot.

Greenhouse whitefly

These insects will breed all year round on greenhouse plants. They may move out into the garden in the summer, but will not survive winter outdoors. Can transmit viruses. *See also* Whiteflies.

Susceptible plants Tomato, cucumber; other greenhouse and house plants.

Symptoms Leaves may develop yellow spots and other discolorations. The plant may become sticky and stunted. In bright sun, leaves can wither and die.

What to do Hang yellow sticky traps near plants to control small infestations,

and for monitoring the appearance of whitefly where biological control agents are to be used. Remove traps before introducing biological control agents. Dispose of badly infested plants. Clean greenhouses thoroughly in early spring; wash down all surfaces. Biological control: Under cover, use *Encarsia formosa*, a parasitic wasp (works best at 64–77°F/18–25°C; not recommended below 50°F/10°C); or *Delphastus*, a predatory beetle; optimum temperature 70–82°F (21–28°C). Pesticide: Insecticidal soap. Spray directly onto whiteflies in early morning when low temperatures render adults less mobile. Apply once a week for 3–4 weeks.

Holly leaf miner

Adults of this pest are inconspicuous flies, laying eggs from late spring on holly leaf undersides, near the midrib. The larvae hatch and tunnel into leaves, staying there until the following spring.

Susceptible plants Holly.

Symptoms Not a serious pest but the damage can be unsightly. Narrow, light green tunnels burrowed between the upper and lower leaf surface develop into blotches as the larvae continue feeding between leaf layers.

What to do Where infestation is light, pick off and destroy affected leaves.

Iris borer

Adults are moths with dark brown forewings and yellowish hind wings; wingspan is 2 in (5 cm). They emerge in summer and lay eggs. The eggs overwinter on old leaves and hatch in late April or early May. The larvae are fat, pinkish borers up to 2 in (5 cm) long, with brown heads and a light stripe down the back, and rows of black dots up the sides. They enter the leaves, feed for several weeks, then pupate in the soil near rhizomes.

Susceptible plants Irises, especially bearded types.

Symptoms Leaves may show irregular tunnels under the leaf surfaces. The larvae enter a fan of leaves at the top and tunnel down toward the rhizome, where they may eat the whole interior without being noticed. Borers often introduce soft rot bacteria into rhizomes as they feed, causing a wet, slimy, smelly rot.

What to do In fall, remove dead, dry leaves, which often carry borer eggs, and destroy badly infested fans in spring. You can also crush borers in the leaves by pinching toward the base of the telltale ragged-edged leaves or by running your thumb between the leaves and squashing any borers that you find. Check rhizomes when you divide the clumps for this pest. If you find a few borers, try cutting them out; destroy badly infested rhizomes. In spring, dust the base of the plants with pyrethrin to kill emerging larvae.

Iron deficiency

Also known as lime-induced chlorosis, this may be caused by a soil pH that is too high for acid-loving plants, by waterlogging, or by excessive use of phosphate-rich fertilizers.

Susceptible plants Pear, raspberry; acid-lovers such as camellias and azaleas growing on alkaline soils, but any type of plant can be affected.

Symptoms Leaves turn yellow or brown around the edges, then between the veins. Young leaves may be totally yellow or bleached white, with no green showing. Fruit quantity and quality poor.

What to do Choose plants to suit the soil type. Apply well-rotted manure or compost.

Japanese beetles

Adult Japanese beetles are chunky, metallic blue-green, ½-in (1-cm) beetles with bronze wing covers, long legs, and fine hairs covering their bodies. They emerge in midsummer and lay eggs in late summer. These eggs hatch into plump, dirty white, brown-headed grubs that overwinter deep in the soil. They move toward the surface in spring to feed on roots, then pupate in early summer to start the cycle over again.

Susceptible plants Adults eat flowers and skeletonize leaves of a broad range of plants; the plants may be completely defoliated. Larvae feed on roots of lawn grasses and garden plants.

Symptoms Holes in flowers and leaves, or leaves completely skeletonized (with only the leaf veins remaining).

What to do In early morning, shake beetles from plants onto dropcloths, then drop into soapy water to kill them. Cover crop plants with row cover or mesh. Plant pollen- and nectar-rich flowers to attract native species of parasitic wasps and flies.

Leaf miners

Larval pests that tunnel around feeding within leaves, creating characteristic maze patterns. They can be squashed in their "mines" between finger and thumb, or leaves can be picked off. Damage tends to be more unsightly than harmful, except on leafy crops. *See* Chrysanthemum leaf miner; Holly leaf miner; Spinach leaf miner.

Leatherjackets

The larvae of the crane fly; legless, brown to grayish-black, fat, soft-bodied, up to 2 in (5 cm) long, with no distinct head. In late summer, adult flies lay up to 300 eggs in grassland or in soil near plants. Eggs hatch approximately two weeks later. Larvae feed on roots during fall and the following spring and summer. Adults emerge in late summer–early fall.

Susceptible plants Lawns; also brassicas, strawberry, lettuce, and various ornamentals.

Symptoms Yellowing patches on lawns in dry weather. Starlings may probe lawns in search of leatherjackets.

Larvae also feed on roots of young plants in spring. Plants turn yellow, wilt, and may die. Symptoms can be confused with cutworm damage and also root-infecting fungi; confirm the presence of leatherjackets before taking action.

What to do Raise plants in pots to produce a vigorous root system. Do not plant susceptible plants on newly cleared land. Trap leatherjackets on lawns by thoroughly watering yellow areas and covering overnight with a tarp, burlap, or a similar material. Larvae will come to the surface under the covering. Pick off and destroy the following morning. This method can be used on cultivated land, by placing a layer of grass mowings under the cover. Leave for one or two days, then pick off and destroy any leatherjackets that surface. Repeat, then fork the soil lightly to expose larvae that remain. Biological control: Outdoors, use *Steinernema feltiae*, a parasitic nematode. Apply mid-September, to moist soil.

Leek moth

Caterpillars of this moth tunnel into the leaves of leeks. The damage is worse in warm, dry summers. The adult moths spend the winter in plant debris. There can be several generations in a year.

Susceptible plants Leek; also related onion species.

Symptoms Tiny yellow-green caterpillars tunnel into the leaves, and then through into the stems and growing point of the plant. Small dark brown cocoons may be seen on the plant, and secondary rots may develop.

What to do Where this pest is a regular problem, grow leeks under fine mesh netting to keep the moths out. Once plants are infested, there is no control other than hand-picking of caterpillars and cocoons from the leaves, or removing the whole plant. Clear up all plant debris at harvest. Dig over the leek beds. Encourage predators

such as birds, bats, frogs, and beetles that may feed on the moths. Implement a crop rotation plan.

Lettuce root aphid

Small, yellow-white, wingless, waxy pests with dark spots on the abdomen, found among lettuce roots during summer. Overwinters mainly on Lombardy poplar, moving in June to lettuce and sow-thistle. Root colonies can persist into winter, and may survive in the soil until the next season. *See also* Aphids.

Susceptible plants Lettuce.

Symptoms A severe infestation causes plants to wilt suddenly, then die.

What to do Grow resistant lettuces such as 'Avondefiance', 'Musette' and 'Beatrice'. Rotate crops.

Mealy bugs

The adult female of this pest is small, up to $1/8$ in (3 mm) long, and powdery gray. Eggs are laid in batches of 100–150, with a protective covering of woolly wax. Newly hatched mealybugs crawl over plants for a few days, then settle down to feed. Adult males have wings and can appear in large numbers during the breeding season. Populations are usually highest in the fall and early winter. In very cold areas they are restricted to greenhouses, but in warmer areas they spread outdoors. Breeding can be continuous in greenhouses and in the home.

Susceptible plants Sprouting potatoes; cacti, succulents, plus many tender indoor plants; greenhouse plants such as jasmine, asparagus fern, and oleander.

Symptoms Severe infestations on young growing shoots can weaken plants. Wax-covered colonies are often found in leaf axils and on cactus spines. Leaves may be covered in sticky honeydew. This may in turn be covered in black sooty mold.

What to do Cut out and burn severely infested shoots and branches. Wash out inaccessible colonies with a powerful jet of water or remove with a paintbrush as appropriate. Repeat inspection and removal of mealybugs two or three times at twice-weekly intervals. Examine all new plant introductions; ideally, quarantine new plants for a month. The best biological control is the predatory lady beetle *Cryptolaemus montrouzieri*; optimum temperature 68–77°F (20–25°C). Alternatively, spray with insecticidal soap. Disturb the waxy coating covering colonies before spraying.

Mexican bean beetle

Adults are oval, yellowish brown, ¼-in (6 mm) beetles with 16 black spots on the wing covers. They overwinter in leaf litter in nearby fields. In spring, females lay clusters of oval, yellow eggs on the undersides of bean leaves. Eggs hatch in 5 to 14 days, into plump, yellowish orange grubs with long, branching spines. They feed for 2 to 4 weeds, then pupate on leaves. There are one to three generations per year.

Susceptible plants String beans and soybeans.

Symptoms Adults and larvae feed on the undersides of leaves, leaving lacy-looking patches on the leaf surface. Severely defoliated plants may be killed.

What to do Plant early-season bush beans to avoid main beetle generations. Plant soybeans as trap crops, then destroy them when infested with larvae. Handpick larvae and adults daily in small bean patches. Cover plants with row cover or mesh until plants are large enough to withstand damage. Dig in crop residues as soon as plants are harvested. Attract native predators and parasites by leaving flowering weeds between rows or by interplanting dowers and herbs. Release spined soldier bugs (*Podisus maculiventris*) to control the early generation; release

parasitic wasps *Pediobius foveolatus* when the weather warms. As a last resort, spray weekly with pyrethrin or neem.

Mineral deficiencies

It is unwise to treat soil for a deficiency unless you are sure that it really is deficient in that particular element, as this may simply exacerbate the condition. Deficiency symptoms often occur as a result of over-liming, excessive fertilizer use, or poor soil structure—rather than from a true shortage in the soil (see pp.26–31 and 86–87 for more information). Cold weather, drought, and waterlogging can also cause a temporary deficiency. A soil or plant analysis may be necessary to identify a deficiency accurately. *See also* Iron deficiency.

Moles

Adult moles are about 6 in (15 cm) long, with dense, dark brown fur. Females raise a litter of four or so per year. They do not eat plants, but can undermine them, disrupting growth, and their mounds make lawn-mowing difficult.

Symptoms Mounds of loose soil ("mole hills"). Light, well-drained soils are most affected. Damage is usually greatest in late winter and early spring.

What to do Trapping is the only certain way to control this pest. The best time to trap moles is in late winter and early spring when runs can be more easily located. First locate permanent mole runs by careful observation, probing, and excavation. Place a mole trap in the run, choosing a straight length of run within 6–8 in (15–20 cm) of the soil surface. Examine the trap at least once a day; if it fails to catch a mole within four days, move it to another run. It may be possible to make moles move on by using repellents that create strong smells or by using a device to produce a vibration in the run.

Nectria canker

This fungal disease is spread by wind and rain-splash, and enters the plant through cracks in the bark, leaf scars or pruning cuts. Diseased fruit left on trees can also be a source of infection.

Susceptible plants Apple, pear, hawthorn, and poplar. Some apples, such as 'Cox's Orange Pippin', 'Elstar' and 'Gala', are particularly susceptible. More resistant apples include 'Bramley's Seedling', 'Lane's Prince Albert' and 'Newton Wonder'. Canker is a particular problem on wet, poorly drained soil.

Symptoms Tree bark shrinks and cracks, often in concentric rings with the central piece of bark falling away. Deep lesions develop on the branches. Swelling can occur around the canker, and young twigs may die back. Cream-colored pustules may be seen in summer; red spots are more common in fall. Papery bark can result. Canker can ring an entire stem. Fruit skins crack; fruits dry and can remain, mummified, on the tree.

What to do Do not grow trees on wet sites or badly drained clay soil. Improve drainage. If a young tree becomes affected, it may be advisable to remove it. Once a tree is established, sow a grass seed mixture up to the main stem, to reduce the risk of infection by rain-splash. Cut out diseased branches. Do not use poplar or hawthorn as a windbreak near fruit trees.

Nematodes

Microscopic nematode worms, invisible to the naked eye. Some attack plants, while others are beneficial, attacking slugs and larvae of weevils and other pests. *See* Potato cyst eelworm.

Onion downy mildew

Fungal disease that survives in the soil for up to five years, and in crop debris and on infected plants, not all of which will show symptoms. It can overwinter in seemingly healthy, fall-planted onions, to infect the spring-planted crop.

Susceptible plants Onion, shallot.

Symptoms Leaves turn gray, wither, and collapse. Bulbs rot in storage. The disease is worst in cool wet seasons.

What to do Do not grow onions for five years where onion downy mildew has occurred. Do not save seed from infected onions. Break the cycle—give up growing onions altogether for a year or two. Remove infected plants as soon as seen. Remove weeds to encourage good air flow around plants.

Onion fly

Adults of this pest emerge in May from pupae overwintering in the soil. Eggs are laid on young leaves, stems, or soil near plants. White larvae, up to $3/8$ in (8 mm) long, feed in stems and on roots and bulbs for 2–3 weeks before pupating. There may be three or four generations in a single year.

Susceptible plants Onion; also shallot, garlic, and leek.

Symptoms Young plants wilt and die; leaves and stems of older plants become soft and rotten. Larvae bore into onion bulbs, which then rot. Most severe in early to midsummer. May be confused with stem eelworm and onion white rot.

What to do Grow plants under fleece or fine mesh netting, put in place immediately after sowing or planting. Remove infested plants as soon as onion fly is discovered. Rotate crops; cultivate soil in winter to expose pupae to predators.

Onion neck rot

Fungal disease favored by wet, cool summers. The main source is infected seed. The fungus also survives in soil and crop debris for three to four years. Infection does not spread between bulbs in store, but symptoms do not all develop at the same time.

Susceptible plants Onion.

Symptoms Onions appear healthy when growing, but become soft after 8–12 weeks in store. Brown sunken lesions and a fluffy gray mold develop in the neck. The upper part of the bulb is soft when pressed, with brownish-black discoloration under the dry outer leaves. The fungus spreads downward through the bulb, which in severe cases may decay completely.

What to do Buy seed and sets from reputable suppliers. Space widely to allow air movement. Avoid damage before or during harvest, and allow tops to fall over naturally. Dry well in an airy, warm, dry atmosphere until the skins rustle. Do not store damaged bulbs. Store in cool, dry, airy conditions and remove bulbs that develop symptoms as soon as they are seen. Use a crop rotation.

Onion rust

Fungal disease that survives on crop debris and wild *Allium* species. May be worse on nitrogen-rich soil or where potassium levels are low.

Susceptible plants Leek, onions, chives, garlic, and other *Allium* species; ornamental alliums are less susceptible.

Symptoms Dusty reddish-orange pustules on leaves and stems during summer. In a severe attack the leaves may turn yellow and die. Plant size and therefore crop yield may be reduced. Later growth may be disease-free as infection declines in the cooler weather of fall. In mild falls, the disease may continue to develop.

What to do Do not overfeed with nitrogen-rich fertilizers. Use a potassium fertilizer if rust is a regular problem. Improve the drainage of soil if necessary. Use a crop rotation. Grow more resistant leek cultivars such as 'Poristo' and 'Poribleu'. Do not overcrowd seedlings. Clear away and compost any diseased plant debris.

Onion thrips

See Thrips.

Susceptible plants Onion and leek; mainly a pest of plants under cover.

Symptoms *See* Thrips.

What to do Outdoors, crops can withstand a light infestation. Water plants well during dry spells. Remove and destroy crop debris after harvest. Pesticides: Rapeseed oil, derris.

Onion white rot

Highly persistent soil-living fungus that can survive for 15 years in the soil without a host plant. Fall-planted garlic and onions are vulnerable in mid- to late spring when soil temperatures are ideal for the fungus.

Susceptible plants Onion, garlic, leek, green onion, chives, and shallot.

Symptoms Plants suddenly start to die. Older leaves turn yellow; roots become stunted or rotten. Seedlings keel over; larger plants can easily be pulled out of the ground, and garlic stems pull away easily from the bulb. A few plants may be affected at first, then a whole row as the disease spreads. As the rot progresses, a white, cottony-looking fungal growth develops around the base and up the side of bulbs, with tiny black globules, like poppy seeds— the resting bodies of the fungus.

What to do Grow onions from seed, not sets, so the root system will be small when disease activity is at its highest. Grow garlic purchased from a reputable source, and avoid infecting clean ground. Clean tools and boots well after cultivating contaminated soil or after use in another garden. Use strict crop rotation. Space plants widely; when stimulated by nearby plants, white rot can spread sideways through the soil. Clumps of multi-sown onions should be 12 in (30 cm) apart. If the area of infection is small, remove and dispose of affected and adjacent plants and the surrounding soil. In areas known to be infected with white rot, try growing garlic in 4-in- (10-cm-) diameter holes filled with clean soil. Leeks are worth trying, even on badly infected ground.

Parsnip canker

There are three main types of parsnip canker: black, orange-brown, and purple. All damage the root. Wet sites exacerbate them. Black canker is spread by rain-splash from diseased spots on leaves; spores then enter through damage to roots, e.g., carrot fly wounds. Orange-brown canker is possibly caused by soil-dwelling organisms. Purple canker occurs in peaty soil, high in organic matter.

Susceptible plants Parsnip.

Symptoms Black canker produces dark lesions. Orange-brown canker produces a brown coloration on the skin, initially on the shoulder of the root. Purple canker produces a purple lesion with brown water-soaked margins.

What to do Grow in a well-drained site. Grow a resistant variety such as 'Avonresister'. Earth up in summer to stop the spores of black canker from reaching the roots. Use close spacing to produce smaller roots that may be less susceptible to some cankers. Control carrot fly (q.v.). Use a crop rotation.

Pea and bean weevil

Adults, brown-gray and ¼ in (5–6 mm) long, overwinter in plant debris and vegetation, moving on to plants to feed in early spring. Eggs are laid in the soil, and the larvae feed on root nodules for a few weeks, pupating in the soil. Adults emerge in June/July. *See also* Weevils.

Susceptible plants Peas, fava bean; also related plants.

Symptoms Scalloped holes are eaten out of the edges of leaves in spring and summer. Young plants may be severely damaged early in the season when growth is slow. Otherwise healthy plants can usually tolerate the damage.

What to do Avoid using vetch as an overwintering green manure. Prepare ground well before sowing to encourage strong, fast growth. Place a barrier of fleece or fine mesh over the area immediately after sowing.

Peach leaf curl

Spores of this fungal disease are spread by rain. The disease is worse after cold, wet springs and in cool, damp areas.

Susceptible plants Peach; also almond, nectarine, and rarely apricot, both edible and ornamental types.

Symptoms In early spring, new leaves thicken and start to twist and curl, becoming yellow or orange-red. Red blisters appear on leaves in early summer. Infected leaves develop a pale bloom, turn brown, and fall. Regular attacks reduce vigor and croppings, and disfigure the tree.

What to do Do not plant susceptible trees in cool, damp situations. Avoid sites near ponds. Pick off diseased leaves on sight. Keep trees fed and watered to encourage the development of new healthy growth. You can cover wall-grown trees from mid-winter to mid-spring to prevent rain-splash from carrying the disease onto developing buds and young foliage. Construct a lean-to frame of wood and clear plastic sheeting that can be attached to the wall or fence and secured in the ground.

Pear scab

Fungal disease similar to apple scab (q.v.) but infection also often occurs on bud scales. Scab is worse in cool, wet periods in spring and early summer.

Susceptible plants Pear.

Symptoms Dark scabby spots on shoots, leaves, fruit and buds. Fruit spotting can be more severe than on apples, causing fruit to become deformed by deep clefts. Twigs develop conspicuous swellings which later burst.

What to do *See* Apple scab.

Peony blight

Also known as peony wilt, this fungal disease persists in the soil and on plant debris. It thrives in humid conditions.

Susceptible plants Peony, lily-of-the-valley.

Symptoms Stems become dark brown at soil level. Gray mold develops on young buds and flowers. Stems wilt and collapse. Flowers may fail to open.

What to do Space plants widely to promote good air flow. Cut infected plants down to ground level in the fall. Clear away diseased plant debris. Carefully remove a layer of topsoil around infected plants and replace with fresh soil.

Poor/no fruit set

Disorder especially affecting fruit, zucchini, and runner beans.

Symptoms Plants fail to fruit, or fruit poorly. Raspberry and strawberry fruits may be distorted, or have dry areas. Plants are otherwise growing well.

What to do Identify the cause and then remedy if possible. Causes include: frost at flowering time; lack of suitable pollinators in the vicinity (apples and pears); lack of flowers as a result of inappropriate pruning; male flowers not open at same time as female flowers (cucurbits); poor weather at flowering, hindering pollinating insects; dry soil.

Potato blackleg

The bacteria that cause this disease overwinter in potato tubers, plant debris and soil. Tubers are invaded through damaged skin. Poor drainage, potassium deficiency, or excess nitrogen exacerbate the condition.

Susceptible plants Potato.

Symptoms First seen as small water-soaked lesions on stems. Stems turn brown or black 4 in (10 cm) above and below soil level, becoming mushy. Leaves roll, wrinkle, and blister. Lower stem disintegrates and can be foul-smelling. Tubers can also be attacked, resulting in a gray slimy rot. Can affect isolated individual plants and even isolated stems on one plant. It is more likely during prolonged wet conditions.

What to do Plant in well-drained soil. Less susceptible potatoes include 'Wilja', 'Cara' and 'Pentland Crown'. Lift crops during dry weather if possible, to prevent cross-infection of healthy tubers at harvest. Avoid wounding tubers. Never save tubers from infected plants for seed. Maintain storage temperatures at 39°F (4°C) to inhibit new infections.

Potato common scab

A widespread bacterial disease, common in light, sandy, alkaline soil and encouraged by hot, dry weather. Serious attacks can occur on newly cleared grassland. Following initial infection, the scab lesions produce spores that persist in the soil. Scab is usually present in most soils but is only active given the correct conditions.

Susceptible plants Potato.

Symptoms Scabby, angular spots of corky tissue may almost cover the skin of the tuber (see p.89). They may be superficial or form deep pits. Yield is seldom affected but wastage is increased with the extra peeling needed.

What to do Do not apply lime as this will increase scab incidence. Water potato crops in dry weather, especially when in flower. Add organic soil improvers to increase water-holding capacity. Grow resistant potatoes, avoiding susceptible varieties such as 'Desiree', 'Majestic' and 'Maris Piper'.

Potato cyst nematode

The golden and white cyst eelworms feed in the roots of tomatoes and potatoes. They survive in the soil in the form of pinhead-sized cysts, each containing hundreds of eggs. Cysts can remain dormant for ten years or more, hatching in the presence of exudates from the roots of potatoes and related plants. New cysts—which can be white, yellow, or brown—may be seen on roots from late June to August. Common on allotments and plots where vegetables have been grown for many years.

Susceptible plants Potato, tomato.

Symptoms Plants yellow and die back prematurely, sometimes in patches. Crop yields reduced.

What to do Plant certified seed potatoes. Avoid bringing in soil on plants or tools from sites that may harbor the pest. Grow resistant potatoes. Most are only resistant to the golden form, though some, including 'Cromwell', 'Kestrel', and 'Sante', also have some tolerance of the white form. Use as long a crop rotation as possible. Feed the soil with bulky organic soil-improvers to encourage natural predators. On infested land, the no-dig technique (see p.216) may give a better yield. Early potatoes may produce a reasonable crop before the pest attacks.

Potato late blight

This fungal disease overwinters on infected potato tubers, surviving plants, and any plants growing from potatoes left in the ground at harvest time. It spreads rapidly to new crops in warm, damp weather. Spores are washed from leaves down into the soil by rain to infect potato tubers.

Susceptible plants Potato, tomato.

Symptoms A common, serious problem in warm, wet seasons when it spreads rapidly. Less frequent in dry conditions. Potato: dark blotches on leaves, mainly tips and edges, and on stems. White mold develops under leaves in humid conditions. The whole plant may collapse. Tubers develop dark sunken lesions, which become firm and dry. Tubers may decay to a foul-smelling mush as a result of invasion by bacterial soft rots. Tomato: foliage symptoms similar to potato but less severe. Green fruits and stems show dark markings; mature fruit quickly develops a dry, leathery rot. This may only become evident days after harvest. A whitish-gray mold may also develop over the rot.

What to do Plant good-quality seed potatoes from a reputable source. Grow resistant potatoes such as 'Stirling', 'Cara', 'Sarpo Axona', and 'Sarpo Mira'. Avoid highly susceptible ones such as 'Arran Comet', 'King Edward', and 'Ulster Chieftain'. Destroy volunteer plants including self-set tomatoes and potatoes growing on compost piles and similar sites. Earth up or mulch potatoes to reduce the likelihood of spores being washed down onto tubers. Smooth the sides of the ridges to prevent spores from being washed into the soil through cracks. If blight appears on the foliage, remove all affected leaves immediately. Compost only in a hot pile Do not harvest potatoes for at least 3 weeks to avoid infecting tubers during lifting. Harvest all tubers and do not save tubers for seed from blighted potatoes.

Powdery mildew

The distinctive symptoms of powdery mildew can be caused by a range of fungi, each only affecting a specific group of plants. Most common when conditions are warm and dry during the day and cold at night, and on dry soils.

Susceptible plants Almost any.

Symptoms A white to gray powderlike coating on any part of a plant.

What to do Prune out any infected shoots of perennials in spring and late summer. Make sure plants get the correct amounts of water and nutrients at all times. Prepare the ground well before planting. Mulch to retain moisture. Do not overdo nitrogen-rich fertilizers as this can encourage soft growth, more easily infected by the fungus. New cultivars with a degree of resistance to mildew are constantly being developed. Fungicide spray: Sulfur. This may harm young leaves, and some gooseberries and apples. Check the label before use. *See also* Apple powdery mildew.

Psylla

Small, sap-feeding pests that feed on flowers, leaves, young buds, and shoots of plants, causing distorted growth. Plants may be covered in honeydew leading to sooty mold growth (q.v.). It is the young nymphs that cause most damage. They have wide, flattened bodies, with prominent wing buds and eyes. Adults, $1/16$–$1/8$ in (2–3 mm) long, resemble winged aphids; they can jump and fly. *See also* Boxwood sucker.

Rabbits

Rabbits live in tunnels dug into banks and similar situations. They feed at night or during the early morning and late afternoon on a wide range of plants. A rabbit can eat 1 lb (500 g) of vegetation per day, so a large colony can cause huge damage.

Susceptible plants A wide variety of fruits, vegetables, grasses, and flowers.

Symptoms Rabbits graze on young shoots. Plants can be eaten to ground level and bark stripped from trees. Most damage in spring and early summer.

What to do If rabbit numbers are high, erect a rabbit-proof fence around important plants. Use a mesh size of 1–$1¼$ in (2.5–3 cm). The fence should be 3–4 ft (1–1.2 m) high with a further 1 ft (30 cm) buried below ground level and angled outward. It should be well

supported by posts and straining wires; inspect it regularly for holes. If there are only a few rabbits, protect individual plants with netting or tree-protectors, or surround plants with spiky plant clippings. Some plants are less attractive to rabbits.

Raspberry beetle

Yellow-brown larvae, $1/4$–$3/8$ in (6–8 mm) long, found in ripening fruit. The adults, small brown beetles $1/16$–$1/8$ in (3–4 mm) long, overwinter in the soil near host plants. In spring they emerge to feed on flowers of apple, hawthorn, and other members of the Rosaceae family, moving on to raspberry, loganberry, and blackberry flowers as they open. Eggs are laid on flowers in summer; larvae feed for about a month before pupating in the soil. There is only one generation a year.

Susceptible plants Tayberry, raspberry, blackberry, loganberry, related hybrid berries.

Symptoms Larvae feed on developing fruit, causing segments of the berry to become shriveled and hardened.

What to do If larvae have been found in fruit, at the end of the season remove mulches and gently fork over the soil around canes. Remove netting after harvest to allow birds access, or put in chickens. Cut all canes to the ground at the end of the year. This should kill off the pest, although the next year's crop of summer-fruiting types will be lost.

Raspberry cane blight

Soilborne fungal disease, which enters through cracks in bark, or wounds caused by the raspberry midge. It is spread by rain-splash and on tools.

Susceptible plants Raspberry; also blackberry, hybrid berries, strawberry.

Symptoms Leaves shrivel and die. Dark patches and cracked bark develop on canes just above the soil. Within the

patches, masses of pinhead-sized pustules develop. Canes become brittle. 'Lloyd George' and 'Norfolk Giant' are particularly susceptible.

What to do Handle canes with care to avoid damage. If the canes are infected, cut back to below soil level. Burn all infected material. Disinfect tools.

Raspberry cane and leaf spot

From late spring to early summer this fungal disease infects young canes. Spores overwinter on host plants. Fruiting canes develop lesions from infection the previous year.

Susceptible plants Raspberry, blackberry, loganberry, other hybrid berries.

Symptoms Attacks young growth. Purple spots are found on canes, leaves, blossoms, and stalks. Leaves may drop, bark can split, and small cankers form. Fruit yield is reduced. Severe infection will cause distortion and death.

What to do Cut out and burn infected canes.

Raspberry spur blight

Fungal disease spread by rain and wind, especially during a damp spring.

Susceptible plants Raspberry and loganberry.

Symptoms Leaves may develop dark brown lesions in early summer. In late summer, purplish blotches appear on stems around buds, turning brown-black to silver in winter. Diseased canes become dotted with tiny black fungal fruiting bodies. Plants rarely die but fruit yield is reduced. In a dry summer, canes may become dry and shriveled.

What to do Cut out and burn diseased canes. In spring, thin canes to reduce crowding. 'Leo' and 'Malling Admiral' have some resistance.

Red spider mite

"Red" can be misleading as these tiny pests only become red during fall and winter. For most of the year, they are pale green/yellow with two dark spots. They thrive in hot, dry conditions, reproducing in as little as eight days at 80°F (26°C). The mites hibernate in cracks and crevices, leaf litter, and garden canes. In the greenhouse they may breed year-round if temperatures remain above 54°F (12°C).

Susceptible plants A wide range of plants under cover. In a hot dry season, may also attack outdoor plants, especially strawberry, peach, grape vine, cucumber, French and runner beans, eggplant, fuchsia, and busy Lizzy.

Symptoms Leaves initially show a fine speckling. As the attack continues, they take on a bronzed appearance and may wither and die. A fine webbing is produced, strung between parts of the plant or under the leaves. Using a magnifying glass, mites and their tiny eggs can be seen on the undersides of leaves. In an unheated greenhouse the most severe attacks occur in summer.

What to do Spray plants, if appropriate, with a fine mist of water, twice daily. Ensure that plants have the best growing conditions possible. Red spider mite can be severe on plants that are potbound or overcrowded, or growing in hot and dry conditions. Discard badly infested plants. In spring clean out the greenhouse, and scrub down staging. Use a high-pressure hose on cracks and crevices. Biological control: Under cover, and in warm areas outside, use *Phytoseiulus persimilis*, a predatory mite; optimum temperature 64–75°F (18–24°C). Pesticides: Insecticidal soap; rapeseed oil.

Replant disease

Exact causes of this problem, which occur when a new plant is placed in a site once inhabited by a related plant, are not known. Soil-dwelling nematodes and fungi are probably responsible. It is thought that the number of these organisms increases in proportion to the size or age of the plant, and that they can coexist with the strong woody roots of mature plants, but new plants with soft root tissue are overwhelmed by the level of these organisms in the soil.

Susceptible plants Cherry, rose, viola, China aster, apple, peach, pear, plum, and strawberry.

Symptoms In the first year, the new plant grows poorly. Root systems are weak and may become blackened. Plants may fail to establish.

What to do Avoid planting susceptible plants where the same or a related plant has recently been removed. If you must replant in the same spot, try treating the soil with a generous quantity of well-rotted manure or compost and treating the plant's roots with mycorrhizal fungi—known as "friendly fungi"—at planting. Plants grown in large containers, with a large root ball at planting-out time, may have more chance of survival.

Rose black spot

Fungal disease spread by rain-splash, on hands, and on tools. Attacks are worst in warm, moist conditions. Overwinters on stems, fallen leaves and in soil.

Susceptible plants Rose.

Symptoms Small to large black spots on the leaves eventually merge into large irregular patches. Affects both leaf surfaces. Edges of leaf spots may turn yellow. Leaves fall prematurely. Bushes become weak in severe cases.

What to do Clear up fallen leaves. Prune infected stems hard back in spring. Grow resistant roses such as 'Little Rambler', 'Veilchenblau', and 'New Dawn'. Mulch plants with compost or leaf mold before buds burst in spring, to prevent overwintering spores from splashing up from the ground. Use a liquid seaweed foliar spray. Fungicide: Sulfur. This may harm some young leaves. Check the label before use.

Rose rust

Spores of this fungal disease overwinter on fallen leaves and on the soil surface. They germinate in spring, reinfecting bushes through wind and rain-splash.

Susceptible plants Rose.

Symptoms Initially, bright orange pustules on leaf stalks, branches, lower leaf surfaces, especially along veins, and on any hips from the previous year. During summer, yellow-orange pustules develop on lower leaf surfaces away from leaf veins. Later pustules become speckled with black spores that will overwinter. *Rosa pimpinellifolia* is particularly susceptible.

What to do Grow healthy plants, in well-drained soil. Keep well-pruned to encourage good air circulation. Grow resistant cultivars. Clear away any diseased plant leaves and other debris. Prune out stems showing symptoms immediately when they are seen in spring. Cut well back beyond the point of infection.

Sawflies

Adult sawflies are small, inconspicuous, dark-bodied flies up to ½ in (1 cm) long. The larvae, which damage plants, vary in color from cream to green and brown and resemble moth or butterfly caterpillars. They range in size from ½ to 1¼ in (1.5–3 cm) long. (See also Caterpillars, for comparison.) The larvae feed on leaves, stems, and fruit of a wide range of plants. If infestation is severe, the plant is often reduced to a skeleton. See Apple sawfly, Gooseberry sawfly.

Scale insects

Sap-feeding pests that move only when newly hatched, when they crawl around looking for a plant to feed on. They then settle to feed near the leaf veins or stem and develop a waxy shell (scale). Adults resemble tiny limpet shells; young can be mistaken for small brown flecks.

Susceptible plants A wide range of ornamental plants; also fruit trees and bushes. Bay trees and citrus are particularly susceptible.

Symptoms Plants are weakened by the feeding scales and leaves may fall. Scale insects excrete honeydew, which drops onto leaves below. Black sooty molds (q.v.) may grow on this.

What to do Check plants regularly, especially the stems and the undersides of the leaves, for the presence of scale. Where an infestation is light, individual scales can be removed easily with a fingernail or a cotton swab. Pesticides: Insecticidal soap; plant-oil-based products.

Scorch

Disorder affecting soft and hairy-leaved plants caused by strong sunlight. Scorch is made worse by the presence of water droplets on foliage, which concentrate the sun's rays.

Symptoms Bleached-looking or pale brown patches on leaves. Damaged areas may crisp.

What to do Avoid wetting foliage in strong sunlight. Water susceptible plants from below. Provide shading.

Slugs

Soft-bodied, slimy pests, which vary in color and size. Some, like the gray-brown field slug, live and feed mainly above ground; others, such as the keeled slug, a major potato pest, inhabit the soil. In the daytime slugs may be found in cracks and crevices and under any shelter where it is cool and damp. At night, especially when damp, slugs will be found feeding and crawling over plants. Slug eggs are laid in clusters in soil cavities. They are spherical, opaque or translucent, and colorless.

Susceptible plants A huge range, particularly seedlings and young plants, annuals, and herbaceous perennials. Slugs will also attack tubers and fruit.

Symptoms Irregular holes eaten in roots, stems, bulbs, tubers, buds, flowers, fruit, and leaves of a wide range of plants. Seedlings fail to come up or are eaten off. Most damage occurs at night. Telltale slime trails may be seen.

What to do You need to use a range of techniques, especially when plants are young. When sowing seeds, water the bottom of the drill, then cover with dry soil. Encourage quick germination and growth of seedlings and young plants. Plant out sturdy, module-grown plants rather than sowing directly. Water in the morning; damp soil and plants in the evening encourage slugs and snails. Protect individual young plants with plastic bottle cloches; do not mulch them. Hoe regularly to disturb slime trails that may be used by other slugs and snails to locate food. Dig in winter to expose slugs and eggs to weather and predators. Grow potato varieties that are less susceptible to slugs; harvest all potato tubers by early fall. Hand-pick slugs at night and destroy. Use traps baited with beer, milk, or grape juice; ensure that the lip is raised ¾–1¼ in (2–3 cm) above the soil surface to avoid trapping beetles. Surround susceptible plants with bran; remove slugs found in it. Lay a ring of comfrey leaves around any susceptible plants. This will act as a decoy, but is ineffective after midsummer. Provide alternative food such as lettuce leaves (preferably under stones to keep them moist)—when planting into an empty bed. Protect pots and larger plants with copper-coated tape or copper rings. Encourage natural enemies: frogs, toads, beetles, and centipedes. Chickens can help to clear slugs from empty ground, or in a greenhouse. Biological control: Outdoors and under cover, water on *Phasmarhabditis*, a parasitic

nematode; minimum soil temperature 40°F (5°C). Pesticide: Pellets based on ferric phosphate.

Snails

Active from spring to fall, snails usually hide under shrubs and in cool, damp places during the day. They feed at night, especially during damp weather. The garden snail is the most common pest, with a gray-brown shell up to 1¼ in (3 cm) across. Banded snails are not normally a serious pest. Their shells have white, yellow, gray, or pink bands with darker stripes, or are sometimes entirely pale yellow.

Susceptible plants A wide range.

Symptoms Irregular holes eaten in roots, stems, bulbs, tubers, buds, flowers, fruit, and leaves. Seeds fail to come up and seedlings are eaten. Most damage occurs at night.

What to do Some of the methods suggested for slugs (q.v.) may work for snails. Do not grow susceptible plants near locations such as rock gardens, walls, and wood piles, where snails hide.

Sooty molds

These fungi grow on sugary honeydew excreted by sap-feeding insects. They do not directly damage plants but are unsightly and block out light needed for photosynthesis. Leaves may fall; in bad cases the plant may be weakened.

Susceptible plants Camellia, bay laurel, birch, citrus, linden, oak, plum, rose, tomato, vines, willows, and many others, outdoors and under glass.

Symptoms Black or brown sootlike deposits on upper leaf surfaces and other plant parts. Plants may also be infested with sap-feeding pests such as aphids, whiteflies, scale, or mealybugs.

What to do Control the pests that are producing honeydew. Spray or sponge leaves with water. When cleaned of mold, fruit will still be edible.

Sowbugs

Mid- to dark gray, hard-bodied, jointed, terrestrial crustaceans up to ¾ in (2 cm) long. They hide during daylight under seed trays, pots, stones, and other debris, emerging at night to feed.

Susceptible plants Seedlings and young plants.

Symptoms The main source of food for the sowbug is dead or decaying plant matter, not living plants. They can, however, eat off seedlings at soil level.

What to do Action is rarely necessary, except perhaps in greenhouses and cold frames in spring where seed-raising is going on. Destroy large colonies by pouring boiling water over them. Control survivors by setting baits of bran, boiled potato, grated cheese, or sugar under a plank of wood or a box, or in some other dark location. Collect and destroy. Keep greenhouses clear of plant debris. Do not mulch susceptible young plants.

Spinach leaf-miner

The larvae of this fly tunnel within the leaves of spinach, beets, and related crops, creating pale brown blisterlike papery patches and tunnels. The pest overwinters in the soil, emerging in spring to lay eggs on the undersides of the leaves. There can be two or three generations in one year.

Susceptible plants Beets, spinach, chard, lamb's quarters.

Symptoms Small brown patches appear on the leaves; these rapidly extend, and a small white larva can be seen within the patch. On beets, the damage will not harm the crop, unless plants are very young when attacked. Badly mined leaves are inedible.

What to do Pick off individual leaves as soon as the blotches are seen; squash larvae within before putting the leaves on the compost pile. If you are only growing beets, there is no need to take action if the plants are otherwise growing well. Dig the soil over thoroughly in the winter where infected plants have been growing, to expose pupae to birds.

Splitting

Disorder caused by rapid growth, especially when rain or watering follows a very dry period. Wide fluctuations in temperature can also be responsible.

Susceptible plants Cabbage, carrot, cherries, onion, parsnip, plum, potato, rutabaga, and tomato.

Symptoms Fruits, heads, roots, and stems split lengthways. This can allow organisms that cause dieback or rot to enter. Apple fruits may become hollow.

What to do Improve the waterholding capacity of soil. Mulch soil.

Squash bug

Adults are brownish black, flat-backed, ½-in (1-cm) bugs covered with fine, dark hairs. They give off an unpleasant smell in self-defense. Unmated adult insects overwinter in garden litter, vines, or boards, to emerge, mate, and lay shiny, yellow to brown eggs in groups on the undersides of leaves in spring. The nymphs are whitish green or gray, similar in shape to adults, with a darker thorax and abdomen as they mature; they are usually covered with a grainy white powder. Nymphs take all summer to develop, molting five times before maturity.

Susceptible plants All cucurbit crops; winter squash are the most severely affected.

Symptoms Both adults and nymphs suck plant juices, causing leaves and shoots to blacken and die back; attacked plants fail to produce fruit.

What to do Maintain vigorous plant growth. Handpick all stages of this pest from the undersides of leaves. Support vines off the ground on trellises. Attract native parasitic flies with pollen and nectar plants. Cover plants with row cover or mesh (hand-pollinate flowers).

Squash vine borer

Adults are narrow-winged, olive-brown, 1–1½-in (2.5–4-cm) moths, with fringed hind legs, clear hind wings, and a red abdomen with black rings. They emerge in spring and lay eggs on stems and leaf stalks near the base of the plant. The brown-headed, white larvae feed in vine stems for up to 6 weeds, then pupate in the soil.

Susceptible plants Squash, pumpkins, cucumbers, melons, and gourds.

Symptoms Larvae bore into the vines, chewing the inner tissue near the base and causing vines to wilt suddenly. Girdled vines rot and die.

What to do Early in the growing season, cover vines with row cover or mesh; uncover later for pollinators, or hand-pollinate flowers. To save attacked vines, slit infested stems and remove the borers, then heap soil over the vines to induce rooting. If squash vine borers have been a serious problem in previous years, spray the base of susceptible plants with pyrethrin to kill young larvae before they enter vines.

Stink bug

Adults are shield-shaped, green, tan, brown, or gray ½-in (1-cm) bugs. Most species are smooth, but a few are spiny or rough-textured. They overwinter in weeds in waste areas. Females lay 300–500 barrel-shaped eggs each when the weather warms. They hatch in a week into oval-shaped, wingless nymphs that look similar to the adults. Nymphs develop to adults in about 5 weeks.

Susceptible plants Brassicas, beans, peas, sweet corn, tomatoes, and peaches.

Symptoms Adults and nymphs suck plant sap from leaves, flowers, buds, fruit, and seeds. Feeding punctures in fruit cause scarring and dimpling known as cat-facing.

What to do Control weeds in susceptible crops; remove or mow weedy areas adjacent to garden beds. Attract native parasitic wasps and flies by planting small-flowered plants.

Strawberry crown rot

Fungal disease, soilborne and spread by rain-splash onto the fruit. Spores also enter through damaged plant parts.

Susceptible plants Strawberry.

Symptoms Droughtlike effects. Young leaves wilt, older leaves develop a red coloration. Plants die. When cut through, the crown is brown and dead.

What to do Remove infected plants. Apply a good layer of straw or other protection to keep fruit off the soil surface. Plant new crops far from the previous growing site.

Strawberry red stele

Spores of this fungal disease are released into the soil from the decaying roots of infected plants. The spores can lie dormant for at least 12 years. Infection of healthy roots occurs in wet conditions. It is spread on contaminated plants and in soil on tools and boots.

Susceptible plants Strawberry.

Symptoms Leaves develop a brownish-purplish tinge. A reddish band appears around leaf edges; this may color the whole of the central leaf area. Growth can be patchy, individual plants becoming weak and stunted. Roots are stunted and dark brown or black in color. When the root is split open, the classic symptom is a red core running down the center. It is most noticeable in spring and fall.

What to do Always plant certified, healthy planting stock. Make sure the site is well-drained. Grow cultivars with resistance; check with a reputable fruit

nursery for suitable cultivars. Avoid susceptible ones. Burn affected plants or take them to a green waste recycling site, and do not grow strawberries on the same land again.

Thrips

Small, elongated, cylindrical insects, up to $\frac{1}{8}$ in (4 mm) long, sometimes referred to as "thunderflies." They attack many plants, indoors and out. Color ranges from white/yellow to brown/black. Larvae resemble adults but lack wings. They feed in large numbers on the upper side of leaves, and on flowers and buds, causing a characteristic silvery mottling and some distortion. They can reproduce in as little as a month, eggs being laid on plants. Adults and young stages overwinter in soil, leaf litter, and plant debris. *See* Onion thrips; Pea thrips.

Tomato hornworm

Adults are large, gray moths with a 4–5-in (10–13-cm) wingspan. They emerge in June and July from soilborne pupae, then lay eggs on the undersides of leaves. The eggs hatch in one week into green caterpillars up to $4\frac{1}{2}$ in (11 cm) long, with a black horn on the tail and eight diagonal white marks along the sides. They feed for a month, then pupate in the soil until the next summer. The tobacco hornworm, a related species, has a red horn and seven white marks on the sides.

Susceptible plants Nightshade-family plants, including tomatoes and potatoes.

Symptoms Larvae of both species consume leaves, stems, and fruit. Feeding can kill young plants.

What to do Handpick caterpillars from plants, unless they are covered with small, white, rocklike projections, which are actually the cocoons of parasitic wasps. Spray with *Bacillus thuringiensis* var. *kurstaki* (B.T.K.) while caterpillars are still small.

Viruses

Viruses, invisible to the naked eye, exist in living plant material, where they do not necessarily cause symptoms. They are spread by sapsucking insects, such as aphids, by contact (on hands and on tools, especially cutting tools such as pruners), by birds, and by propagation from contaminated plants. Some viruses are plant-specific, while others will infect a number of unrelated plants.

Susceptible plants A huge range.

Symptoms Many and varied, including stunting, mottled and mosaic-patterned leaves, distorted fruits, and even death. Yield of perennial crops will decline.

What to do Control the pest spreading the virus. Grow resistant cultivars. Plant certified virus-free planting material. Use a crop rotation for viruses transmitted by soil-living organisms. Once a plant is infected there is no cure. Dig up and burn. *See also* Cucumber mosaic virus; Zucchini yellow mosaic virus.

Waterlogging

A common disorder of houseplants and other pot-grown plants, in which cases the main cause is overwatering, especially when growth is slow. May also affect plants in the open ground growing in poorly drained soil.

Symptoms Yellowing of leaves, dry angular blotches on leaves, general stunting of growth. Root-rotting diseases may also be encouraged.

What to do Adjust watering according to plant species and time of year; ensure that pots can drain well. Improve drainage of soil; choose plants that thrive in damp conditions.

Weevils

Beetles with a characteristic snout and clubbed antennae. They range in size from $\frac{1}{16}$ in (2 mm) to 1 in (2.5 cm), depending on species. The larvae have a soft white body and obvious head; they are otherwise featureless. *See* Pea and bean weevil; Vine weevil.

Whiteflies

Adults of this pest, $\frac{1}{16}$ in (2 mm) long with white wings, fly up from plants when disturbed. Eggs laid on host plants hatch into "scales"—oval, immobile creatures found on the undersides of leaves. Both scales and adults are sap-feeders and excrete sticky honeydew, which drops onto leaves below. Sooty molds (q.v.) develop on this. A severe infestation may stunt growth. *See* Cabbage whitefly; Greenhouse whitefly.

Wilt diseases

A common and widespread group of diseases with similar symptoms. Damage is usually caused by a blockage of the water-conducting tissues of the stem, starving the leaves of water. Wilts can persist in the soil for several years, entering plants through wounds. Commonly associated with eelworm attack. Some wilts, e.g., of China asters and peas, are host-specific, while others attack a wide range of plants.

Susceptible plants Fruit, vegetables (especially legumes, tomato, cucurbits), ornamentals.

Symptoms Wilting, which often starts on lower leaves, with some recovery at night initially. A dark discoloration can be seen in the middle of the stem when cut open well above soil level.

What to do Earth up infected plants. If infection is severe, remove all infected plants and associated soil. Do not compost any of the plant material. Do not grow susceptible plants on the same site for at least six years. *See also* Clematis wilt, Peony blight.

Wind rock

Disorder that often affects young trees and shrubs and also herbaceous plants that have a lot of foliage compared to the size of the root system. Plants are rocked back and forth, producing a hollow around the base of the stem. This fills with rainwater that may freeze. This damages the base of the stem and may allow disease to enter.

What to do Firm in any wind-rocked plants. Stake plants if appropriate.

Wind scorch

Disorder affecting many plants.

Symptoms Browning of foliage on the side of a plant facing the prevailing wind. Individual leaf margins or tips may be markedly browner than the leaf centers. Apples and other fruit may show a red/brown russeting on the skin surface.

What to do Grow plants suitable for windy positions—usually, plants for coastal areas are suitable, but check their hardiness in inland and northern areas. Grow or erect a windbreak.

Wireworms

The larvae of click beetles: tough-skinned, slender, cylindrical, 1 in (25 mm) in length and golden/yellow to orange/brown in color. They have three pairs of legs at the head end of the body. Eggs are laid in grassland and weedy soil in summer and larvae may feed for up to five years. Because they dislike disturbance, they are usually found on grassland and newly cleared ground.

Susceptible plants Potato, strawberry, brassicas, beans, beets, carrot, lettuce, onion, and tomato; also ornamentals including anemone, carnation, dahlia, gladioli, and primula.

Symptoms The roots, corms, tubers, and stems of many plants are attacked, most severely in spring and fall, but damage can occur through the year. Potatoes show small entry holes and when cut open a network of tunnels runs through the tuber. Later these holes may be enlarged by slugs or millipedes.

What to do Damage is most severe on newly cultivated land. Cultivate the soil during winter to expose larvae to birds and other predators. Lift potatoes in early fall to limit damage. In greenhouses, trap wireworms on spiked pieces of potato or carrot buried in the soil. Remove regularly and destroy. Grow the green manure mustard on the area. It is said to speed up the life cycle. Biological control: The nematode used for vine weevil (q.v.) may have some effect against wireworms.

Woolly aphid

Small brown aphid living in colonies on stems and branches, protected by a white waxy substance that looks like cotton batting. They are most conspicuous in late spring and early summer. Young aphids overwinter in cracks in bark.

Susceptible plants Apple, crab apple, cotoneaster, hawthorn, pyracantha, other related plants.

Symptoms Leaves and fruit disfigured; galls may develop on branches. Canker may enter through cracks in the bark and dieback may result.

What to do Use a stiff brush to remove colonies. Cut out and burn badly infested branches. *See also* Aphids.

Zucchini yellow mosaic virus

Viral disease transmitted by aphids.

Susceptible plants Zucchini and squash.

Symptoms Bright yellow mosaic pattern on leaves. Plants stunted and distorted. Fruits knobby and distorted.

What to do Remove plants as soon as you see symptoms. There is no cure.

Index

Page numbers in *italic* refer to illustrations

A

Achillea 116, 193
acidic soil 30–31, 291
aconites, winter 190
aerating lawns 147
Agapanthus 61
alder 114
alfalfa *50*
algae: on paving *135*
   in ponds 119, 123
alkaline soil 31, 291
Allium giganteum 181
alyssum 185
amphibians 115, 119
angelica 275
angel's fishing rod *182*
animal manures 21, 35, *35*, 52–3
animal welfare 21
annual weeds 70
annuals 176, *177*
   in containers 185, 186
   deadheading 192, *195*
   as living mulch 74
   planting 178, 179
   sowing 197, *197*
ants *298*
aphids 89, *90*, 91, 321
   black bean 243, *243*, 323
   companion planting 95
   container plants 195
   on fruit trees *298*, 299
   leaf 247
   mealy 237, 331
   plum leaf-curling 334
   predators *97*, 98, 99, 115
   root 247
   woolly 341
apple canker *89*, 321–2
apple powdery mildew 322
apple scab 88, 322
apples *287*, 290, *290–1*, 294–9, *294–9*
Aquilegia 177, *182*, 196

archangel, yellow 71
artichokes *see* globe artichokes;
   Jerusalem artichokes
ash trees 158
ashes 54
Asian vegetables 234–6
asparagus *232*, 262, *263*, 267
asparagus beetle 322
asparagus peas 243
asters *117*, 176, 181, *182*
astilbes *182*, 184

B

Bacillus thuringiensis (Bt) 103
bacteria: diseases 88–9, *89*
   in soil 18–20, 29
bacterial canker 322
bacterial soft rot 322–3
bamboo canes 140, *141*
barberry 114, *144*, 165
bark: colored 159, 160
   mulches 22, 72, *73*
   soil improvers 35, *35*
barriers, pest control 100
basal stem cuttings 203
basil 279, *280*, 282
bath water, reusing 67, *67*
bats 113, *113*
bay *280*
beans 242–3
   crop rotation 231
   storing 271
   watering 62
   see also individual types of beans
bedding plants 179, 185, *195*, 202
beds and borders: edging *160*, 214, *215*
   herbaceous plants 178–9
   raised beds *33*, *211*, 214, *214–15*, 215
   shrub borders 163
   vegetable beds 212–15, *212–15*
beebalm *116*
beech 142, *144*
beehive compost bins *40*, *42*
beer traps 102, *102*, *292*
bees: flowers for 115, *116*, 185
   herbs for 275
   mason bees 113, *113*
   nest boxes for 113
beet leaf spot 323

beetles 90, 96, *99*
   asparagus beetle 322
   flea beetles 328
   ground beetles *29*, 96, 99, 107
   pollen beetles *91*, 334
   raspberry beetles 335
   stag beetles *110*
beets 222, 231, *244*, 244–5
beneficial insects *95*, 96, 275
Berberis 114, 143, *144*, 165
bergamot *116*
berries, ornamental trees *157*
biennial weeds 70
biennials 176, *177*, 178, 185, 192
bilberries 114
bindweed *79*, *80*
biodegradable membranes 74–5, *75*
biological pest control 97
bird cherry *157*
birds 15, 108
   bird scarers *21*, *85*, *101*
   feeding 114, 115
   herbs for 275
   nest boxes *96*, 112, *112*
   netting crops against *236*, 237
   as pests 90, *100*
   as pest predators 20, *96*
   water for 118
bishop's weed 78, 79, *80*
bitter pit *87*
bittercress *79*
black bean aphid 243, *243*, 323
black spot 88, 336
blackberries 312–13, *312*, *313*
black currants 289, 314–15, *314*, *315*
blackfly 97, 326
blackleg, potato 334
blanket weed 123, *123*
blight: potato 39, *84*, 93, 250–51, 335
   raspberry cane 335–6
   raspberry spur 336
   tomato 39, 93, 335
blossom end rot 86
blueberries 291, 319, *319*
bog gardens 277
bok choy 234, *235*
bolting 265, 266
bonemeal 54
bonfires 39

borage 279
borax 54
borders *see* beds and borders
boron 54, 132
botrytis *89*, 247
Bouteloua gracilis 184
boxwood hedges 142, *145*
boxwood psylla *323*
brambles *80*
brassica white rust 323
brassicas 234–7
   crop rotation 231, 236–7
   liming soil 31
   ornamental *220*
   pest control 93, 101, 237
bricks 136
broadcast sowing 256
broccoli 234, *267*
broom *60*
brown rot 324
Brussels sprouts 93, *229*, 234, *267*, *267*, *268*
buckeye, red *157*
buddleja *117*, *164*, 170
bugle *183*
bulbils, weeds *71*
bulbs 177, *177*
   in containers 185
   deadheading *193*
   division 193, 203
   in lawns 191
   planting 190–91
   weeds *71*
bumblebees 115
buttercup, creeping *81*
butterflies 115, *116*, 275
buying: fruit trees 294–6
   vegetable plants 262

C
cabbage caterpillars 324
cabbage root fly 90, 95, 101, *236*, 237, *237*, 324
cabbage white butterfly 101, 237
cabbages 234, *235*, 236
   companion planting 95
   harvesting *268*
   ornamental *220*
   spacing 258

calcium 31, 55, *86*, *87*
calendulas 185, 197
camellias 62, 86
campanulas *185*
candytuft 74, *116*
canes, safety 192
canker 92
   apple *89*, 321–2
   bacterial 322
   parsnip 253, *333*
capillary matting 65
capsid bugs 325
cardboard: composting 37, *37*
   as sheet mulch 74–5, *75*
cardoons *232*, 246, 247
Carex comans 184
carrot fly 95, 100–101, *252*, 253, 325
carrots 252–3, *252*, *253*
   companion planting *94*, 95
   in containers 222
   crop rotation 231
Caryopteris 60
Castanea sativa 60
catch cropping 259
caterpillars 83, *90*, *102*, *115*, 325
   on brassicas 237, *237*, 324
   predators 115
cats 91
cauliflowers 234, 236
celeriac 252, 253
celery 252, 253
Centaurea 179, 197
centipedes *29*, *99*
certification programs, virus diseases 89
chamomile 202
charcoal 158
chard *220*, 222, 244–5, *245*
cherries 290, 304–5, *304–5*
cherry, Higan *157*
cherry blackfly 326
chervil 277
chestnut, sweet *60*
chickens, pest control 102
chicken manure 52, 53, *53*, 54–5
chickweed 70, *79*
chicory 246
chili peppers 248, *248*, 250
chitted seeds 254
chitting potatoes 262, *263*

chives 238, *281*, 282, *282*
   Chinese *183*
   garlic *183*
chlorine, in tap water 66
chlorosis 87
chocolate spot, fava bean 243, 324
Christmas roses *183*
chrysanthemum leaf miner 326
chrysanthemums 192
cilantro *117*, 277, *280*
cinquefoil *165*
Cistus 60
clay soil 26–7, 28, *28*, 155
cleanliness 92–3, 250
clearing ground 78–9
clematis 167
clematis wilt 326
climate 289
climbers 166–7
   planting *169*
   supports 160, *160*
   training 170
   for wildlife 108, *109*
climbing beans 267
cloches *21*, 266
clover 50, *50*, 95, 150, *150*
clubroot 31, 39, 88, 92, 237, 326
coastal gardens 142
coated seeds 254
cob walls 140–41
cocoa shell mulches 72
codling moths 299, 326–7
coir 187
cold frames 199, 203
color: fall *156*
   bark 159, 160
columbines *182*
comfrey 103
companion planting 94, *94*
compost 17, *34*, 35, 36–49
   activators 37
   bins *23*, 36, *40*, 41, *42–3*, 111
   hygiene *92*
   trench composting *43*
   using 43
   vegetables in containers 222
   what to compost 37–9
   worm compost 46–9
conservation 21
containers: care of 194–5

herbaceous plants 184–9
herbs in 277, *278*, 279
potting mix 186–7, *187*
sowing seeds in 198
vegetables in 222–3, *223*
watering 62, *62*, 65
Continental planting style 179, 180–81, *180*
Convolvulus tricolor 185
copper, slug barrier 101
coppicing *153*, 158–9, *158*
cordons 290, *291*, 296
cornel *156*
cornelian cherry *144*
cornflowers 179, 197
Cornus 159
    C. alba 153, 162
    C. mas 143
    C. stolonifera 158, 162
Cotinus 164
Cotoneaster 165
    C. salicifolius 109
cotton lavender 60
couch grass 78, *79*, 81
cow parsley *91*
crab apples *157*
crab spiders *107*
cranesbills 176
Crataegus laevigata 'Paul's Scarlet' *109*
Crocosmia 182
crocuses 191
crop rotation 93, 211, 230–33
crown rot, strawberry 338–9
"cuckoo spit" 91, 328
cucumber mosaic virus *89*, 240–41, 327
cucumbers *227*, 231, 240–41
cucurbits 240–41
cut flowers 14, *182*
"cut-and-come again" vegetables 269, *269*
cutting back herbaceous plants *192*, 193
cuttings 202–3, *203*, 283, *283*
cutworms 247, 327
cyclamen 177
Cytisus 60

D
daddy longlegs *98*
daffodils 177, *193*
dahlias 203
daisies 185
damp soil, herbs in 277
damping off 327–8
dandelions 78, *79*, 81
Daphne 114, *165*, 170
deadheading: bulbs *193*
    herbaceous plants 192–3, *195*
deadnettles 176
deciduous hedges *144*
decking *136*, 137
deficiency problems 30, 54, 84, *84*, 87, *87*
delphiniums 91, 191, 192, 193, 203
derris 103
desert gardens *58*
Dianthus 61
dicentras 184
digging 33
    clearing ground 78
    green manures 51
    raised beds 214
    in winter 93
dill 277
diseases 85, 88–9
    cleanliness 92–3
    in compost piles 39
    container plants 195
    fruit 293
    in greenhouses 227
    herbaceous plants 179
    resistance to 93
    and soil pH 31
    vegetables 265–6
    woody plants 169–70
division, perennials 193, *193*
docks 78, *79*, *80*
dogwood *156*, *157*, 159, 162
dolomitic limestone 55
Doronicum orientale 176
double cropping 259
downy mildew 88, 239, *239*, 245, 247, 328, 332
dragonflies *107*
drainage: containers 185, 187
    fruit 291
    vegetable gardens 210

drills, sowing in 256
drought-resistant plants 58, *58*, 60–61, 62, 277, *277*
drying: herbs 284–5
    vegetables 271
ducks, pest control 102
dwarfing rootstocks 290

E
earth walls 141
earthing up potatoes 249, *249*
earthworms 29, *29*, 31, 46
earwigs 90, *90*, 91, 112, 299, 328
Echium 116
ecosystems 84
edgings: beds *160*, 214, *215*
    herbs as *276*, 277
edible landscaping 218–20, *218–21*
eggplants 222, 226, 227, *227*, 248, *248*, 250, *250*
elder *109*, 114
elephants' ears *183*
Encarsia formosa 97
enchytraid worms *47*
endive 246, 247
Epsom salts 54
Eryngium 61, *182*
Eschscholzia 179
espaliers 296, *296*
eucalyptus 60
euonymus 162
Euphorbia 61
European red mite 328–9
evening primrose 279
evergreen hedges 142, *145*

F
fall color *156*
Fallopia baldschuanica 71
fan training *304*, 305
farmyard manures 21, 35, *35*, 52–3
fava bean chocolate spot 243, 324
fava beans *228*, 242, *243*, 266
feather grass, giant *182*
fedges 160
felicia 176
fences 138, 139–40, *139–41*, 160–61

fennel (herb) *281*, 282, *285*
fennel (herbaceous plant) *183*
fennel, Florence 252, *253*, 269
ferns 184
fertilizers 17, 18
  crop rotation 233
  fruit 292
  hanging baskets 189
  herbaceous plants 191
  lawns 147
  liquid fertilizers 194–5
  organic fertilizers 54–5
  pollution 16
  vegetables 265
  see also individual plants
Festuca glauca 184
flea beetles 237, 328
fleece, horticultural *21*, 100, 266
flowers: cut flowers *182*
  deadheading 192–3, *193*, *195*
  edible 219
  flower-feeding pests *90*
  ornamental trees *157*
  for wildlife 115, *116–17*
foliage: drought-resistant plants 58
  mineral deficiencies 87, *87*
  pests *90*
  scorching 63, 86, *337*
  yellowing *84*
food chain 20
food miles 206, 207
forget-me-nots 179, 185
forks, clearing ground 78, *78*
forsythia 143, *144*, 171
foxgloves 176
fritillary, snake's-head 191, *191*
froghoppers 91, 328
frogs *98*, 112, 115, 122
frost 86, 328
  container plants 195
  fruit 289
  vegetables 266
fruit 286–319
  cages 100
  fertilizers 292
  frost damage 289
  mulches 292–3, *292*
  pests and diseases *90*, 101, 293
  pollination 289, 290

poor/no fruit set 334
  soil 31
  splitting 338
  watering 291, 292
  wind damage 289
  see also individual types of fruit
fuchsias *144*, *164*
fungal diseases 88, *89*, 266
fungicides 88, 103
fungus gnat 337

G
gaillardias *91*
galls *90*
garlic 238, 262, 271
garlic chives 238
garlic oil 103
genetic modification (GM) 17, 207
geotextiles 75
Geranium 184
germination 197
glass chip mulches 72
globe artichokes *220*, *233*, 246, 247, 262, 267, *267*, *268*
Good King Henry 244, 245
gooseberries *292*, 318, *318*
gourds 241
granulosis virus 103
grass: clearing ground 79
  mowings 37, *73*, 149
  paths 215
  see also lawns
grasses 177, *181*
  in containers 184
  division 193
  "matrix" planting 107, 180–81
  weeding *76*
gravel: mulches 72, 181, 187, 277
  paths 136–7
gray mold *89*, 247, 329, 331
gray water 67, *67*
green manures 50–51, *50–51*, 74, 233
green onions 238
green waste compost 35, *35*
greenback 86
greenfly 20, 97
greenhouses: hygiene 250
  vegetables 224–7, *224–7*
  watering 65

greenhouse whitefly 97, 251, 329
griselinia 143, *145*
ground beetles *29*, 96, 99, 107
ground cover: Continental-style planting *180*, 181
  herbs 277
  as mulches 74, *74*
  shrubs as 163
groundsel *79*
growing problems 86–7
guelder rose *109*, *162*
gunneras 176
gypsum 55

H
hail damage 86
hakonechloa *183*
Hamamelis 165
Hamburg parsley 252
hand-weeding *76*, 77
hanging baskets 65, 188–9, *188*, *194*
hard landscaping 128, 130–31, 134–7, *134–7*
hardening off 199
harvesting: herbs 284–5
  seeds 201, *201*
  vegetables 268–71
  see also individual types of fruit and vegetable
hawthorn *144*
hay mulches 72
hazel twigs, supporting perennials 191–2
heathers 31
Hebe 117
Hedera helix f. *poetarum 109*
hedge bindweed *80*
hedges 142–5, *142–5*
  clipping 143
  composting clippings 39
  planting *142*
  plants for 142–3, *144–5*
  for wildlife 108, *108*, *109*, 110
heirloom vegetables 208–9, 254
heleniums 192
helianthus 176
hellebores *183*
hen-and-chicks *185*
herb gardens 276, *276*

herbaceous plants 174–203
  care of 190–95
  in containers 184–9
  planting styles 178–81
  propagation 196–203
herbicides 23
herbs 272–85
heuchera *185*
high-fiber composting technique 37, *37*
hoeing *69*, 77, *77*, *264*
hoggin 137
holly 142, *145*, *157*
holly leaf miner 329–30
hollyhocks *177*
honesty *117*, 192
honeysuckle *109*, *116*
hormone rooting powders 202
hornbeam 142, *144*
horse manure 52
horseradish 279, *279*
horsetail 79, *80*
horticultural fleece *21*, 100, 266
hoses 64
hostas 91, 184, 193
hoverflies 96, *98*, 275
humus 29
hungry gap 224, 228–9
hyacinth beans 243, *243*
hybrid berries 312–13
hydrangeas *31*, 162, *164*, 167
hygiene 92–3, 250

I
iceplant *117*
insect barrier glue 101
insect mesh 100
insecticides 103
insects: beneficial *95*, 96, 275
  feeding 115
  pollination 289
  shelter for 112–13
  see also pests
intercropping 95, 259
irises *183*, *185*
iron deficiency 54, *87*, 330
ironwood, Persian *156*
irrigation systems 59, 64, *64*, 65, 292, *292*
ivy 166

J
Jerusalem artichokes 246–7, *247*, 262
Juncus effusus 'Spiralis' *185*
juneberry 114

K
kale 234, *235*, 236
Kniphofia 61
Koeleria glauca 184
kohlrabi 222, 234, 236

L
lablab beans 243, *243*
lacewings 96, 97, *99*, 112–13, *113*
lady beetles *19*, 20, 96, *97*, *98*, 112, 113, *113*
lambs' ears *61*, *183*
Lamium 71, 176
landscape fabrics 75, *75*
larvae 90
laurel, spotted *145*
laurustinus *145*
lavender *60*, *277*, 280, 282, 283, *283*
lawns 146–51
  bulbs in 191
  clippings 37, *73*, 149
  drought-tolerance 59
  fertilizers 147
  meadows 124–5
  moss 151, *151*
  mowing 148–9
  topdressing 147–8
  weeds in *59*, 150–51
  for wildlife 110, 146
leaf aphids 247
leaf beet 222, 244–5
leaf-feeding pests *90*
leaf miners 330
  beet 245, *245*, 323
  chrysanthemum 326
  holly 329–30
leaf mold 17, 110
  crop rotation 233
  improving soil *34*, 35
  making 44–5, *44*, *45*
  mulches 72, *73* leaf spot *89*, 323
leafhoppers 89
leatherjackets 29, 31, 330

leaves *see* foliage
leek moths 330–31
leek rust 239, 331
leeks *209*, 238, 239, *259*, *260*, *262*
legal issues, pesticides 103
legumes 242–3
lemon verbena *185*
lettuce gray mold 331
lettuce root aphid 331
lettuces 95, 246–7, *246–7*, *258–9*
leylandii 143
lime-induced chlorosis *87*
limestone 55
liming soil 31, 55, *55*
  crop rotation 233
  lawns 151
Limnanthes 74, *91*, 197
liners, hanging baskets 188, *189*
liquid fertilizers 189, 194–5
liquid seaweed extract 85, 195
living mulches 74, *74*
lizards *99*
loam 28
loganberries 312
lovage 275
love-in-a-mist 192, 197
luffa vine 241
lupines 193

M
magnesium 30, 54, 55
magnolias *165*
manganese *87*
manures: animal 21, 35, *35*, 52–3
  green 50–51, *50–51*
maples *156*
marigolds 94–5, *94*, 176, 197
marjoram *117*
mason bees 113, *113*
"matrix" planting 107, 180–81
meadows *105*, 124–5, *124–5*
mealy aphids 237, 331
mechanical cultivators 78–9
mechanical damage 86
melons 240, 241
membranes, mulching 74–5, *75*, 79
metal fences 140
Mexican orange blossom *165*
mice 341

Michaelmas daisies *117, 182*
microclimates 289
microorganisms, in soil 18–20, 29
midges *99, 301*
mildew: apple powdery 322
   downy 88, 239, *239*, 245, 247, 328, 332
   powdery 88, 95, 241, 243, 335
millipedes 29
mineral deficiencies 30, 54, 84, *84*, 87, *87*, 331
mint 275, 279, *281*
mites 90, *99*, 323
mixed planting 94–5, *94*
mock moss 188, *189*
mock orange *164*
module trays 198, 199
moles 331–2
montbretia *182*
mortar 134, *135*
moss, in lawns 151, *151*
moths 275
   codling 299, 326–7
   leek 330–31
   pea 243, 333
   pheromone traps 102, *102*
mowers 149
mowing lawns 148–9
mulches *22, 33, 59*
   animal manures *53*
   clearing ground 79
   in containers 187
   Continental-style planting 181
   fruit 292–3, *292*
   herbaceous plants 191
   leaf mold 45
   no-dig system 217, *217*
   soil improvers 35
   vegetables 265
   weed control 72–5, *73–5*
   for wildlife 111
   see also individual plants
mulleins *61*
multi-sowing 258
mushroom compost *34*, 35

N

narcissus *185*, 191
nasturtiums *184*, 197

neck rot, onion 332
nectarines 306–7
neem 103
nematodes 90, *98*, 328, 334
nest boxes 96, *96*, 112, *112*
netting, pest control 100, *236*, 237
nettles *81*
newspaper, as mulch membrane 74
Nigella 192, 197
nitrates 16–17
nitrogen 30, 34, 50–51, 149, 150
no-dig system 51, 214, 216–17
nutrients 30, 54–5, 230

O

oak, scarlet *156*
oak apples *90*
onion downy mildew 332
onion fly 239, 332
onion neck rot 332
onion thrips 332
onion white rot 239, 332
onions 238–9, *238*
   companion planting *94*, 95
   crop rotation 231
   planting 262
   spacing 239, 258, *258*
   storage 271
orache 244, 245
oregano *117*
organic fertilizers 54–5
organic matter 29, 30
oxalis *80*
oxygenating plants 122, 123

P

paper: composting 37, *37*
   as mulch membrane 75
parasites 96, 97
parsley 252, *253*, 277, *281*, 282
parsnip canker 253, 333
parsnips 252–3, *253, 259*
Parthenocissus henryana 166, 167
passion flowers 166
paths *32, 33*, 77, 215
patios, weeding 77
paving 134–6, *135*, 279, *279*
pea and bean weevils 243, 333

peach leaf curl *89*, 333
peaches 306–7, *306, 307*
pear canker 321–2
pear midges *301*
pear scab 333
pears 290, 300–301, *301*
peas 208, *209*, 242–3, *243*
   crop rotation 231, 242
   problems *84*, 243
   supports *266, 267*
   watering 62
peat 186–7
pelargoniums 176
pelleted seeds 254
pelleted chicken manure 53, 54–5
penstemons *203*
peonies 191
peony blight 333–4
peppers 222, 248, 250
   in greenhouses 226–7, *227*
perennial vegetables 232, 262, 267
perennial weeds 70, *80–81*
perennials: cuttings 202–3
   deadheading 193
   division 193, *193*
   drought-resistant *61*
   herbaceous 176, *177*
   matrix planting 107, 180–81
   planting 190, *190*
   sowing 196
   tender perennials 176
periwinkle 71
Perovskia 116
pesticides 14, 16, 23, 96, 103
pests 85, 90–91, 320–41
   biological control 97
   container plants 195
   fruit 293
   in greenhouses 227
   organic control 100–103
   predators 20, 96–9
   vegetables 265–6
   woody plants 169–70
   see also individual pests
pH values, soil 30–31, *31*, 55
pheromone traps 102, *102*, 299
phlox 192, 193
phosphorus 30, *87*
pinks *61*
pisé walls 141

pitcher irrigation *64*, 65
planning 126–51
  hard surfaces 134–7
  hedges 142–5
  landscaping and materials 130–31
  lawns 146–51
  lumber 132–33
  vegetables 228–9, 232–3
  walls, fences and screens 138–41
plant-based fertilizers 54
plant health 82–103
planting: annuals 179
  bulbs 190–91
  climbers *169*
  hedges *142*
  perennials 190, *190*
  through mulch membranes 75, 217
  vegetables 260–63, *260–63*
  woody plants 168–9
  see also individual plants
plastics 130
plums *288*, 290, 302–3, *303*
poached egg plant *91*, 197
pole beans 242
pollarding 158, 159, *159*
pollination 266, 289, 290, 294
pollution 16–17
polythene mulches 75
ponds 96, 118–23, *118*, *120–23*, 277
poppies *177*, 179, *196*, *285*
potagers *213*, 218, *219*
potash 54, 55
potassium 30, *87*
potassium bicarbonate 88
potato blackleg 334
potato blight 39, *84*, 93, 250–51, 335
potato cyst nematode 334
potato scab 31, *89*, 334
potatoes *208*, 248–9, *248*, *250*
  chitting 262, *263*
  crop rotation 231
  disease-resistance *92*
  in greenhouses 225
  problems *87*, 89
  seed potatoes 262
  storing 271, *271*
Potentilla 145, *165*
pots *see* containers
potting mix: containers 186–7, *187*
  for cuttings 202

hanging baskets 189
  sowing seeds 199
poultry manure 52, 53, *53*, 54–5
powdery mildew 88, 95, 241, 243, 322, 335
predators of pests 96–9
preservatives, wood 132–3
pricking out *199*
primed seeds 254
primulas *185*
privet 114, 142, *145*
propagation: herbaceous plants 196–203
  herbs 282–3
  see also cuttings; division; seeds; sowing
propagators 198, 202
pruning: climbers 167
  hedges 143
  shrubs *164–5*
  woody plants 170–71, *170*
  see also individual types of fruit
prunings: composting 39
  as mulches 72
Prunus 'Otto Luyken' *109*
psylla *171*, 339
pumpkins *229*, 240, 241, 271
pyracantha *143*
pyrethrum 103

Q
quassia 103

R
rabbits 100, 335
radishes 234, *235*, *259*
railroad ties 133
rain barrels 22, 66–7, *66*
rainwater 66–7
raised beds *33*, *211*, 214, *214–15*, 215
rakes *148*
rapeseed oil 103
raspberries 290, 291, 310–11, *310*, *311*
raspberry beetles 335
raspberry cane and leaf spot 336
raspberry cane blight 335–6
raspberry spur blight 336
reclaimed materials 136

records, of cropping 211, 233
recycling 21, 34
red currants 290, 316–17, *316*, *317*
red-hot pokers *61*
red spider mite *90*, *99*, 195, 251, 328–9
red wiggler worms 46–9, *48*
replant disease 336
resistance, to pests and diseases 93
Rheum 176
rhizomes, weeds 70, *71*
rhododendrons 31, 162, *165*
rhubarb *233*, 262, 267
  ornamental 176
rock features *134*
rock phosphate 54, 55
rock rose *60*
rocks, weathering 28
rodgersias 176
root aphids 247, 331
roots: root feeding pests *90*
  trees 155
  weeds 70, *71*, *79*
rootstocks, fruit trees 290, 294
rose black spot 336
rose rust 336–7
rose of Sharon *164*
rosemary *277*, *279*, *281*, 283
roses 168
  climbing 166, 167
  disease-resistance *93*, *169*
  dog roses *109*, *116*
  as ground cover 163
  hedges *144*
  hips 168
  pests 91
  pruning 170–71
  suckers *171*
rotation of crops 93, 211, 230–33
rototillers 78–9
rots: bacterial soft rot 322–3
  brown rot 324
  onion neck rot 332
  onion white rot 332
  strawberry crown rot 338–9
rove beetles *99*
rowan, Vilmorin's *157*
Rubus 164
ruby chard *220*, *245*
rudbeckias 176, 185

runner beans *220*, 242, *242*, 243
runners, weeds *71*
Russian vine 71
rust: fava bean 324
    leek *239*, 331
    rose 336–7
rutabagas 234
rye, winter 50, *50*, 74

S

safety: canes 192
    herbs 275
sage *280*, 282, 283
    Russian *116*
St. John's wort *164*
salad leaves 222, *224*, 225, *228*
salsify 246, 247, *247*
sandy soils 27, 28, *28*
Santolina 60
sapsucking pests *90*
savory, summer 277
sawflies *90*, *102*, 337
    apple 299, 322
    gooseberry *84*, 329
scab: apple 88, 322
    pear 333
    potato 31, *89*, 334
scabious *117*
scale insects 337
scarifying lawns 147
scorching foliage 63, 86, *337*
scorzonera 246, 247
scree gardens *137*
sea holly *182*
seakale *220*, 234, 262
seakale beet 244
seaside gardens 142
seaweed 54, *54*, 55, 85, 195
sedums *61*, *117*, 193
seed trays 198
seedheads *181*, *200–201*, 285
seedlings: in containers 198
    pricking out *199*
    spacing 199
    thinning 256
    vegetables 260–63, *260–63*
seeds: germination 197
    herbaceous plants 196–201
    saving 200–201

seed tapes 254
    vegetables 208, 229, 254–9, *255*, *257*
    viability 201
    weeds *71*
shade: fruit in 289–90
    herbs in 276–7
    vegetable gardens 210
shallots 238–9, 262, *264*, 271
sheds 110
sheet mulches 217, *217*
shield bugs *107*
shredders 39
shrubs 162–3, *164–5*
    coppicing *153*
    drought-resistant *60*
    as ground cover 74, 163
    planting *168*
    pruning 170–71, *170*
    watering 65
    for wildlife *109*, 110, 114
silica gel 201
silt soil 29
sloping sites 211
slugs 29, 90, 91, 337–8
    barriers 101
    container plants 195
    predators 20
    traps 102, *102*, 103
    watering and 63
smokebush *164*
snails 20, 90, 91, 338
snakes 111
snow peas 242
snowdrops 177, 190, 191
soaker hose irrigation 64, *64*, 65, 292, *292*
soap, insecticidal 103
softwood cuttings 283, *283*
soil 24–55
    animal manures 52–3
    clearing ground 78–9
    compaction *32*, 33
    compost 36–49
    crop rotation 230
    digging *33*, 214
    fertilizers 18
    fruit 291
    green manures 50–51, *50–51*
    greenhouse beds 226

    leaf mold 44–5
    liming 55, *55*
    microorganisms 18–20, 29
    mulches *33*, 35, 59
    no-dig system 214, 216–17
    nutrients 30
    organic fertilizers 54–5
    organic management 32–3
    organic matter 29, 30
    pH values 30–31, *31*, 55
    and plant health 92
    raised beds 214
    reducing water consumption 58–9
    soil improvers 34–5
    structure 26–7
    types 28–9, *28*
    waterlogging 86, 340
    see also individual fruits and vegetables
solar power *128*
sooty molds 338
sow-thistles *81*
sowing: herbaceous plants 196–201, *197*
    meadows *124*
    vegetables 229, 254–9, *255*, *257*
sowbugs *29*, 85, 341
spacing vegetables 256–8
sphagnum moss 186, 188
spiders *99*, *107*
spinach 244
spinach, mountain 244
spinach beet 244, 245
spinach leaf miner 245, *245*, 323
spindle trees 114, *157*
spittle bugs 91, 328
splitting 338
sprinklers 64
spurges *61*
"square plants," sowing vegetables 256–8
squashes *220*, *229*, 240, 241, *266*, 271
Stachys 61
stag beetles *110*
stakes *see* supports
station sowing 256
stem cuttings 202, 283, *283*
stepping stones *136*, 137
Stewartia 156
sticky traps, pest control 102

stinging nettles *81*
Stipa gigantea 181, 182
stolons, weeds 70, *71*
stone *134*, 135, 139
stone chips 136, *137*
storage: seeds 201
   vegetables 268–71
   see also individual types of fruit and vegetable
straw 52, 53, 72, *73*
strawberries *288–9*, 289, 290, 308–9, *308–9*
strawberry crown rot 338–9
string beans *87*, 95, *209*, 222, 242, 243
successional sowing 229, 259
sugarsnap peas 242
sulfur 88, 103
sun damage 86
sunflowers *182*, 185
supports: climbers 160, *160*
   herbaceous perennials 191–2
   staking trees *169*
   tomatoes 227
   vegetables *266–7*, 267
sweet corn *74*, *263*
sweet peas *184*, *198*
Swiss chard 244

T
tachinid flies *98*
Tagetes 94–5, *94*, 197
tamarisk *60*
tap water 66
tarragon: French 279, *280*
   Russian *279*
tayberries 312
tender perennials 176
tetanus 53
thatch, in lawns 147
thermal weeding 77
thinning: apples 298
   seedlings 256
thistles, Canada *78*, *79*, 81
thrips 90, 332, 333, 339
thyme *74*, 275, *281*
tiarellas 176
ties: for climbers 166, *166*
   herbaceous perennials 192
   staking trees *169*

toads 20, *98*, 115
tomato blight 335
tomatoes *209*, 248
   in containers 189, 222
   in greenhouses 226–7, *226*
   problems 86, *86*, *87*, 249–50
   ring pots *262*
   stopping 251
   supports 251, *267*
topdressing lawns 147–8
trace elements 30, 195
training: climbers 166, 170
   cordons and espaliers 296
   vegetables 267
traps, pest control 102, *102*, 299
trees 154–9
   drought-resistant *60*
   fall color *156*
   flowers and fruits *157*
   planting 168–9, *168*
   pollarding and coppicing 158–9, *158–9*
   pruning 170, *171*
   siting 155
   staking *169*
   watering 65
   wildlife in 85
trefoil *74*
trellis *139*, 140, *140*, 160
trench composting *43*
tulips 177, *177*
tupelo, Chinese *156*
turnips 234

U
undercropping 259

V
vegetables 204–71
   beds 212–15, *212–15*
   bolting 265, 266
   caring for 265–7
   in containers 222–3, *223*
   crop rotation 93, 211, 230–33
   edible landscaping 218–20, *218–21*
   in greenhouses 224–7, *224–7*
   harvesting and storing 268–71
   heirloom vegetables 208–9, 254

   intercropping 95, 259
   no-dig system 214, 216–17
   perennial vegetables 232, 262, 267
   planting 260–63, *260–63*
   seeds 208
   soil 31
   sowing 229, 254–9, *255*, *257*
   spacing 256–8
   splitting 338
   successional sowing 229, 259
   undercropping 259
   watering 62, 63, 64
   where to grow 210–11
   see also individual types of vegetable
Verbascum 61
verbena *116*
viburnums 143, 162, *162–3*
Vinca major 71
vine weevils 90, 91, *98*, 195, 339
viper's bugloss *116*
virus diseases 89, 92, 266, 339

W
wallflowers 185
walls 138, *138*, 139, 140–41
wasps 90, *99*, *292*
   parasitic 96, 97, *98*
water and watering 56–67
   container plants 194, *194*
   fruit 291, 292
   greenhouses 227
   hanging baskets 189
   herbaceous plants 191
   pollution 16–17
   reducing consumption 58–9
   shortages 86
   types of 66–7
   vegetables *264*, 265
   watering 62–5
   waterlogged soil 86, 340
   for wildlife 118–23
water plants 122, *122*
watercress *224*, 225
watermelon 241
wattle and daub 141
weather 289
weeds and weeding *20*, 21, 68–81
   annual weeds 70
   clearing ground 78–9

composting 37–9
crop rotation 230
digging and 33
fruit gardens 293
in lawns 59, 150–51
mulches to control 72–5, 73–5
no-dig system 217
in paving 134
perennial weeds 70, 80–81
vegetable gardens 265
weeding 76–9
weevils 340
pea and bean 243, 333
vine 90, 91, 98, 195, 339
wheelchairs 214, 215
white currants 316–17, 317
white rot 39, 332
whiteflies 90, 340
biological control 97
cabbage 237, 324–5
companion planting and 94–5
greenhouse 97, 251, 329
virus transmission 89
wildflowers 124–5, 124–5
wildlife 15, 104–25
feeding 114–17
and herbaceous plants 179
herbs and 275
lawns 110, 146
meadows and wild flowers 124–5, 124–5
pest control 20
shelters for 112–13, 112–13
water 118–23
willow 164
fences 141, 141, 143, 160–61, 161
coppicing 159, 159
wigwams 160
wilt diseases 326, 333–4, 340
wilting 86
wind damage 86, 289, 340
windbreaks 211
winter, herbaceous plants for 183
wireworms 31, 90, 341
wisteria 89, 166, 167
witch hazel 165
wood 132–3, 133
coppicing 159–60
fences 139–40
paving 136, 137
wood chip mulches 72
woody waste 39
wood ash 54
woodland plants 176, 177
woody plants 152–73
woolly aphids 341
worm compost 35, 46–9
worm liquid 49
worms 29, 29, 31, 46

Y

yarrow 116
yellowing foliage 84
yew 142, 145

Z

zucchini 211, 222, 240, 241, 241, 261, 268
zucchini yellow mosaic virus 341

Acknowledgments

Garden Organic would like to thank:

Lawrence D. Hills, who founded Garden Organic (then known as HDRA) 50 years ago. One of the pioneers of the organic movement, he would be thrilled to see where, half a century later, his foresight, knowledge, and enthusiasm has taken us.

The original text contributors to the *HDRA Encyclopedia of Organic Gardening*: Pauline Pears, Alan Gear, Jackie Gear, Dr. Isabelle Van Groeningen, Colin Shaw, Owen Smith, Dr. Martin Warnes, Kathleen Askew, Adam Pasco, Sally Cunningham, Bernard Salt, Bob Sherman, Anna Corbett, John Walker, Patsy Dyer, Janet Walker, Rebecca Potts, Maggi Brown, and Andrew Miller.

Proofreader
Sarah Tomley

Index
Hilary Bird

Picture Credits

The publisher would like to thank the following for their kind permission to reproduce their photographs:

(Key: a-above; b-below/bottom; c-center; l-left; r-right; t-top)

Airedale Publishing: 102br, 225tl; Sarah Cuttle 62bl, 67br, 215bl, 257bl, 257br, 257tl, 257tr, 261bl, 261br, 261tl, 261tr, 262tr, 264bl; Alamy Images: Brian Hoffman 40tr; RF Company 122l; Peter Anderson: 58; Leigh Clapp: 176; Charlotte De La Bedoyere: 14bl, 16bl, 37tr, 40br, 42b, 42c, 42t, 42tr, 64br, 65bl, 67bl, 207bl, 235br, 237br, 241c, 245br, 252br, 258bl, 258br, 259bl; DK Images: Sarah Cuttle 223; Jacqui Hurst 137br; Amanda Jensen 205; Dave King 254tr; David Murphy 264tr; FLPA: Nigel Cattlin 29cr, 71c, 84bl, 84cl, 84cr, 86, 87bl, 87br, 87c, 87cl, 87cr, 90cl, 98bc, 98br, 98ca, 98cb, 98tc, 99bc, 99bl, 99ca, 99cla, 99clb, 99tl, 107bc, 107br, 227r, 237l; Rosie Mayer 98cra; Phil McLean 119t; Gordon Roberts 53b;

Peter Wilson 98crb, 119b; GAP Photos: Jonathan Buckley 208br, 253bl; Leigh Clapp 154r; FhF Greenmedia 253tr; Geoff Kidd 76bl; Zara Napier 263tl; Friedrich Strauss 255; Garden Picture Library: Philippe Bonduel 89cr; Chris Burrows 208bl; Sunniva Harte 107bl; Garden World Images: 133t; The Garden Collection: Liz Eddison 211tr; Marie O'Hara 49tr; Stephen Josland: 106, 181b; Andrew Lawson: 19tl, 184l; Joy Michaud/Sea Spring Photos: 99cb, 99tc, 227l; OSF: D. G. Fox 115l; David Fox 98tr; Terry Heathcote 113br; Gordon Maclean 92r; John McCammon 210b; Photos Horticultural: 80ca, 80tc, 80tr, 119c, 227c; Arends Nursery, Germany 187tl; S & O Mathews Photography: 43l; Jo Whitworth: 267br

Jacket image: Front: The Garden Collection: Derek St Romaine

All other images © Dorling Kindersley For further information see: www. dkimages.com